Parables as a Mode of Agrarian-Resistance

Biblical Hermeneutics Rediscovered

The Series as the name suggests will focus on Biblical Hermeneutics, i.e., literary works concerned with methods of interpreting the Old and New Testaments of Bible via different stream of topics like Literature & Poetry, Indigenous Philosophizing, Ethical response towards Ecology, Health & Healing, Science & Technology, Feminist Theology, Sociological approach towards Human Rights, Law & Politics, Arts, History of Ideas, Ancient Civilizations, Cultural Contiguity, Religious Cosmologies & Mysticism, Appraisal of various Theologians, World Peace & Harmony, Global Capitalism, Network Marketing, Cybertheology, Population & Demographics, Epigraphic Studies, Contextualized Education, and many others. We welcome a Mss. on any topic/s mentioned, whether they are original works, scholarly monographs, collections of conference papers, revised dissertations, or translations of historical documents. Through the Series we, the Publishers, are striving to put forward published works that may help Institutions, Academic Bodies, Researchers, Scholars and the World at large in furthering their respective knowledge and understanding on the concerned subject. We welcome your comments on our efforts and further suggestions on how we can enshrine new ray of analysing & explaining the written Texts through our upcoming books.

Biblical Hermeneutics Rediscovered - 39

Parables as a Mode of Agrarian-Resistance

Dynamics of God's Reign and the Subalterns in Mark's Gospel

L. H. RAWSEA

Christian World Imprints

First Published in 2021 by

Christian World Imprints
Christian Publishing & Books from India
C-3, Wazirpur Industrial Area
Delhi-110052
cwidelhi2017@gmail.com
www.ChristianWorldImprints.com
Phone: +91 11 41526079

ISBN: 978-93-5148-515-5 (HB)
ISBN: 978-93-5148-516-2 (PB)

Printed in India.

Dedicated in the loving memory of my late parents
Ngurchhuana
&
Biakthangi

That the book in its original form is the thesis submitted to the Senate of Serampore College towards the Doctor of Theology degree and is published with written permission. The candidate is responsible for the title, contents, and opinions expressed in it.

Contents

L. H. Rawsea is a fine student and has produced an excellent work in the study of the parables of Jesus as narrated in the Gospel of Mark. His research asserts that each parable in Mark reflects an agrarian protest and he has ably demonstrated it by using insights from contemporary scholars in parable studies. He has also shown that the agrarian resistance according to Mark is theocentric in nature as there has always been a link between God and the subaltern uprising in the Markan narration.

Rev. Dr. Joseph G. Muthuraj
Former Professor of Biblical Studies
The United Theological College
Bangalore

Foreword

The literature on parable studies is extensive. Within it, one can observe two broad approaches: the first emphasizes the *Sitz im Laben* of the parables of Jesus that often leads to separation of the parables from the larger context of the Gospels. Such a school of thought probably best represented by historical critics, such as: A. Schweitzer and his critics, in particular C. H. Dodd, A. T. Cadoux, J. Jeremias, and others. The second stream covers an even larger body of literature concerned with literary aspects of the parables with largely isolating the parables from historical Jesus. Such a host of American literary critics, such as: A. Wilder, D. O. Via, J. D. Crossan and others. What these two bodies of work reveal—as touched upon in the introductory chapter of this book—is an innocuous politics that has tended to typecast the agrarian-resistance motifs embedded in the parables of Jesus. Yet, William Herzog II's *Parables as Subversive Speech* (1994) has now shown the nature of the parables is inherently subversive, an angle that this book aims to build upon here.

Deviating from those previous apolitical readers who read the parables as merely premiers of ethics and theology, L. H. Rawsea relocates the parables within the context of first century Roman-Galilee where the agrarian masses including Jesus and his trusted disciples who were subjugated, powerless, and minority in the face of Roman imperial regime. For, the parables of Jesus are the effective mode of agrarian-resistance to the Roman imperial rule and its collaborate. In doing so, Rawsea demonstrates how parables of Jesus can be effective vehicle of resistance to the power by the agrarian masses in Galilee. On the whole, Rawsea's argument that the parables of Jesus are effective instruments of resistance to domination cannot be easily turned down as he employed a theoretical framework devised by James C. Scott, who is widely accepted agrarian political scientist.

With much confidence, I suggest that there is much to be gained from Rawsea's research by taking an interactive and constructive standpoint. From his work agrarian-resistance has as much to do with how the hill people in North-east India hermeneutically define their ongoing varied protest and resistance movements. This study offers many insights to enhance the tribal hermeneutics in the context of North-east India.

Even though, this impressive piece of work is an individual effort by the author, yet, I consider it as the contribution of the Aizawl Theological College to the wider theological research. For the author has been engaged for a number of years as active Faculty member of the College. Indeed, we find the academic interests of our senior Faculty members, for instances Rev. Dr. H. Vanlalauva (Doctrine of God), Rev. Dr. Vanlalchhuanawma (Christianity and Subaltern Culture), Rev. Dr. R. Chhuanliana (Lord God Most high My Saviour), Dr. Lalrindiki Ralte (Socio-economic issues faced by the agrarian folks), *et at*. have been rhythmically intersected together in this book. Greater academic deeds are yet to come from the author of this volume.

Rev. Dr. Vanlalnghaka Ralte
Principal & Professor of New Testament Studies
Aizawl Theological College, Mizoram

Preface

This book is an outcome of my doctoral dissertation. The completion of my dissertation has been made possible through the invaluable help of many individuals and institutions. I express my heartfelt thanks and gratitude to all those who have contributed towards the completion of this work. It is almost impossible to list out all the names that deserve mention here, yet I will not do justice if I do not mention at least a few individuals and institutions from whom I have received inestimable help and support during my research.

With profound admiration and respect, I acknowledge my indebtedness to my esteemed supervisor Rev. Dr. Joseph G. Muthuraj, Professor of Biblical Studies at The United Theological College, Bangalore, who has lovingly supervised my research work. I record my appreciation towards his academic proficiency, openness to new concerns, keen intellect in terms of grasping my thoughts and his skills in terms of offering comments. Throughout the period of my study, his constant encouragement and active support have been a great source of strength for me.

I am grateful to the Mizoram Presbyterian Church Synod, for granting me the required permission for study leave and for financing the entire research project. I thank my colleagues, students and friends of the Aizawl Theological College who have remained supportive in terms of their prayers and words of encouragement. I am particularly thankful to Rev. Dr. H. Vanlalauva and Rev. Dr. Roger Gaikwad, both former Principals of the college and Rev. Dr. Vanlalchhuanawma, the then Principal of the college for helping me in the process of admission towards the present research.

I also convey sincere thanks to the Principal, Dean of Doctoral Division, Faculty and Staff of the United Theological College, Bangalore for their encouragement and support. Rev. Lalawmpuia Hauhnar, the then Registrar had been helpful towards the submission of the dissertation. The staff at the library had helped me to utilize and gain full access to the library facilities. I express gratitude to the United Theological College, Bangalore for facilitating my research at The Lutheran Theological Seminary at Philadelphia, USA for academic exposure.

My gratitude is also rendered to The Lutheran Theological Seminary at Philadelphia for accepting me as their Ph.D. exchange student and bearing all my expenses during my stay during the Spring Semester, 2013. I am thankful to my temporary mentor, Dr. Erik M. Heen, John H. P. Reumann Chair in Biblical Studies, for his expert guidance. He is the first Biblical scholar to use the theory of James C. Scott for the interpretation of Biblical texts, and I have tremendously gained from the deliberations and discussions that I had with him. I thank Rev. Dr. J. Jayakiran Sebastian, Dean and H. George Anderson Professor of Mission and Cultures, and his family for their hospitality, friendship and help. I will ever cherish the experience throughout my life. I had the opportunity to audit their Ph.D. seminars and engage with students and the faculty, during my stay. This aspect was conducive towards my own academic research. I am ever thankful to the staff of Krauth Memorial Library where I had full access to their academic resources.

I owe many personal debts to my sister-in-law, Margaret L. Pachuau, Professor, Department of English, Mizoram University, for helping me in terms of proof-reading, correcting, and improving the syntax of the dissertation. Because of her creativity and hard work, the dissertation has come out in this final form.

I express especial thanks to the Pastor, Ministers, Committee Members of the Bangalore Mizo Church (PCI) for their prayer support, care and concern. The members of the Church were cheerful and encouraging throughout my studies. This infant, which gave me the pain and joy of resistance, had been a great source of spiritual strength throughout my studies.

I am indebted to my parents, brothers and sisters for their constant support and prayers. Special mention must be made of my mother-in-law, Mrs. Liannghinglovi of Zarkawt for taking care especially of David Lalbiaktluanga, my older son, during the entire period of my study, as well as my family at a later point of time, during the latter half of my completion of the work. The dissertation would have not been accomplished were it not for the constant support and encouragement of Julie, my faithful partner in life's journey. Not once did she complain about the many burdens which my studies placed on her and our family. I am equally thankful for the patience of my two sons David Lalbiaktluanga and Matthew Lalruatkima, who adapted their lives unflinchingly, even as I labored to complete this project. They share with me the joy, the pain, and the agony of this work.

Last but not the least, I am inherently grateful to the farmers in the villages of Mizoram who inspired me to pursue the "agrarian-resistance motifs" contained in the parables. This research is as much their accomplishment as well as mine, and because of this, I dedicate this dissertation to them. Glory be to God of the harvest!

L. H. Rawsea
Durtlang Leitan
November 14, 2020

List of Abbreviations

AAAG	*Annals of the Association of American Geographers*
AB	The Anchor Bible
AHR	*American Historical Review*
AJT	*Asia Journal of Theology*
Ant	Jewish Antiquities
ATC	Asia Trading Corporation
ATJ	*American Journal of Theology*
ATLA	American Theological Library Association
BAR	*The Biblical Archeologist Review*
BBR	*Bulletin for Biblical Research*
BBT	*Studies in Biblical Theology*
BTB	*Biblical Theology Bulletin*
BTF	*Bangalore Theological Forum*
CBQ	*Catholic Biblical Quarterly*
CE, BCE	Common Era, Before Common Era
cf. (*Confer*)	Compare
C.P. Jud.	V. A.Tcherikover and A. Fuks, eds., *Corpus Papyrorum Judaicarum* Vol. I (Cambridge, Massachusetts: Harvard University Press, 1957)
DJG	Dictionary of Jesus and the Gospels
ed., eds.	Edited by, editor, editors, edition, editions
e.g. (*exempli gratia*)	for example
et. al. (*et alii*)	and others
etc. (*et cetera*)	and others of the same class
ExpTim	*Expository Times*
f, ff.	following, followings
Gk	Greek
Har.resp	*De Haruspicum response* (Cicero)
ICC	The International Critical Commentary
IDB	The Interpreter's Dictionary of the Bible

i.e. *(id est*)	that is to say
ISPCK	Indian Society for Promoting Christian Knowledge
JAC	Journal of Agrarian Change
JBL	Journal of Biblical Literature
JJS	Journal of Jewish Studies
JPS	Journal of Peasant Studies
JTS	Journal of Theological Studies
JSNT	Journal for the Study of the New Testament
JSNTSup	Journal for the Study of the New Testament Supplementary
JSOT	*Journal for the Study of the Old Testament*
LCL	Loed Classical Library
lit.	literal, literally
Lk	Luke
LNTS	Library of New Testament Studies
Macc	Maccabees
Mat	Matthew
Mk	Mark
NIV	New International Version
NTS	New Testament Studies
NRSV	New Revised Standard Version
NovT	*Novum Testamentum*
NovTSup	Novum Testamentum Supplement
PEQ	*Palestine Exploration Quarterly*
ResQ	*Restoration Quarterly*
rev.	revised, revision
SBEC	Studies in the Bible and Early Christianity
SBL	Society of Biblical Literature
[sic]	thus
SSH	*Social Science History*
TDNT	G. Kittel, ed., *Theological Dictionary of the New Testament* 10 Vols. Trans. G. W. Bromiley (Grand Rapids, Michigan: Eerdmans, 1964-1976)
trans.	translated by, translation
v., vv.	verse, verses
viz. (*videlicet*)	namely
vol., vols.	volume, volumes
War	Jewish War
WBC	Word Biblical Commentary

Glossary

Agrarian:	An adjective related to the land, especially farms, and its ownership or describes a place or a people that is dependent on farming rather than industry.
Chhinlung (Mizo):	A big hole of the earth. Some Mizo tribes believe that their ancestors emerged out of the bowel of the earth.
Lal hlau lo ṭhi (Mizo):	Unimpressive ornament rendered to the chief.
Mautám (Mizo):	A disastrous famine in Mizoram. The cause of the famine was attributed to flowering of bamboos which resulted in the rat population.
Modein Resistance:	Resistance movement that had been started from a village called Modein. It occurred in Judean countryside between 167-169 BCE against the Seleucid empire. It is popularly known as Maccabean Revolt. Because of its inclusivity to non-Maccabean peasants, Modein Resistance is preferred in this research.
Morung (Ao):	Bachelors' dormitory.
Ni leh thla inkara leng kan ni (Mizo):	Literally it means "We are between the Sun and the Moon." An expression of sovereignty of the self-governed tribal chiefs by the Mizo. It connotes there are no intermediaries, except the celestial bodies.
Pasalṭha (Mizo):	Hero, Warrior. A title for men who were experts in activities such as hunting and trapping wild of wild animals and birds. It is also used as a designate for the head-hunter, and the heroes in inter-village wars.
Pum (Mizo):	Blacksmith inn.
Sobaliba (Ao):	Moral code of the Aos of Nagaland.

Tlawmgaihna (Mizo): Moral code of the Mizo, which included chivalry and sacrifices to the well-being of others without seeking any reward.

Tuikhur (Mizo): Cistern or water point. It used to be a site predominately for women folk as there was water scarcity in the hills. It provides a sequestered site for women to exchange their views and ideas.

Ukepenopfii (Angami): An ancestress of all humans according to Angami legend.

Vai lal (Mizo): King of a non-tribal or the valley empire. The villain in a Mizo romantic tale.

Zawlbûk (Mizo): A traditional bachelors' dormitory of the Mizo.

Zu hmun (Mizo): Tavern.

Chapter 1

Problems of Method in the Study of Parables

The resistance—in various forms—by the agrarian communities living in Galilee and Judea during the Greco-Roman imperial rule has not found a central place in the New Testament studies. Questions concerning resistance to colonial rule and administration have been raised in recent times.[1] Among those, with a direct bearing upon a reading of the parables of Jesus, are merely the nature and character of the various movements of resistance by the powerful elites. Even though the rural farmers left no literary remains except their influence on the Gospel traditions, yet many of Jesus' parables, as recorded in the Gospels, seem to convey the general impression that Jesus' campaign in Galilee and the regions beyond can be viewed as a resistance to imperialism.

This research is an attempt to explore whether and how an impact was made by the agrarian communities and to focus on resistance movement that arose from rural habitats.[2] How much impact did the agrarian-resistance in rural areas have on Mark's composition of the Gospel? The research will thus

1 S. G. F. Bandon, *Jesus and Zealots* (New York: Scribner's, 1967); G. R. Edwards, *Jesus and the Politics of Violence* (New York: Harper & Row, 1972); J. H. Yoder, *The Politics of Jesus* (Grand Rapids, Michigan: Eerdmans, 1972); J. Bowker, *Jesus and the Pharisees* (Cambridge: University Press, 1973); D. M. Rhoads, *Israel in Revolution, 6-74 C.E.* (Philadelphia: Fortress Press, 1976); R. A. Horsley & J. R. Hanson, *Bandits, Prophets, and Messiahs: Popular Movements in the Time of Jesus* (San Francisco: Harper & Row, 1985): R. A. Horsley, *Jesus and the Violence: Popular Jewish Resistance in Roman Palestine* (Minneapolis: Fortress, 1993). These innovative attempts, however, have demonstrated great diversity in their methodologies and assumptions regarding the sociopolitical nature of resistance.

2 Following J. C. Scott's research, it is observed that there is a great gulf between the politics of rural elites and the rural communities. See, *Decoding Subaltern Politics: Ideology, Disguise, and Resistance in Agrarian Politics* (London/New York: Routledge, 2013), especially 7-34.

focus mainly on the all parables in Mark and investigate whether these parables reflected the agrarian-resistance. To what extent did the rural life under foreign rules affect the thinking of Mark in his presentation of Jesus' parables? Our cursory reading has shown that, for Mark, God remains at the centre of the present struggle for freedom and justice. Hence, this investigation is designed to examine the notion of God in relation to the subalterns in the parables of Jesus in Mark with the aim of studying how the dynamics of God's reign was set in favour of the marginalised subalterns of the first-century C.E.

1. Elaboration of the Problem

In many ways, our point of departure is this: parables are often more intricate than they are generally made out to be, and less obvious than commonly understood. The intricacy has been the source of both curiosity and apathy for ancient and modern interpreters respectively. While the ancient allegorical interpreters were faithfully engaging with almost all elements in the parables, the modern historical interpreters would see a single point in the parables. In both the cases, as we shall observe, neither the reason for the intricacy nor their political role has been the central focus. When a seminal work on the parables, *The Parables of the Kingdom* was published in 1935, its author C. H. Dodd presents the parables of Jesus as simple, vivid, clear, precise and straightforward to the hearers.[3] In a similar thought, J. Jeremias also expresses the simplicity and clarity of the parables saying: "everything is so simple and clear that [even] a child can understand."[4] Both these pioneer parable scholars, find the parables entirely free from "problematic elements."[5] The only difficulty they claim to confront with the parables, however, is "the recovery of their original meaning."[6]

In contrast to this assumption, the parables of Jesus as found in the Gospels are not straightforward and simple in their meaning, purpose and character.[7] Mark tells us at a time that the disciples of Jesus who also were part of the first audience could not understand the parable and asked for its meaning (Mk 4:10). While answering them, Jesus sternly rebuked the disciples, exclaiming: "Do you not understand this parable?" (v.13). Mark also gives us the impression that Jesus' purpose in using parables is to conceal rather than to reveal (vv.11-12, 33-24). Mark denotes in the Parable Discourse the presence

3 C. H. Dodd, *The Parables of the Kingdom*, rev. ed. (New York: Charles Scribner's Sons, 1961), 5-9.

4 J. Jeremias, *The Parables of Jesus*, rev. ed. (London: SCM Press, 1963), 12.

5 Jeremias, *The Parables of Jesus*, 12.

6 Jeremias, *The Parables of Jesus*, 12.

7 I agree here with R. F. Capon who thinks "a good percentage of them [parables] produce more confusion than understanding." See, *The Parables of the Kingdom* (Grand Rapids, Michigan: Eerdmans, 1985), 1.

of certain "problematic elements" which even the disciples of Jesus could not understand.[8] The possible reason behind the intricacy of the parables must be identified for critical analysis.

1.1. The Intricate Nature of the Parables

Our aim here is to direct our attention to those intricate features that are basic to the parables and raise certain questions concerning their political role in the context of the agrarian politics of Roman Galilee and Judea. Among the many striking features of the parables in Mark, five in particular stand out.

1.1.1. The Word παραβολή in Mark

We notice that Mark embarks a wide variety of materials that are similar to what J. C. Scott devices as "arts of political disguise"[9] in his political discourses. The disguise motif comes into light when we read the usage of the term παραβολή in the Gospel. Mark uses the term παραβολή in five different contexts (3:23 ff.; 4:1-34; 7:17; 12:1-12; 13:28).[10] First of all, the word παραβολή is found in Mark 3:23. Here, Jesus gives a series of parabolic sayings in response to the public reactions of his campaign. Even though Mark 2:18-22 certainly captures metaphor and parabolic sayings, yet Mark does not specifically use the term παραβολή until he records this longer saying,

> [23]And he called them to him, and spoke to them in parables [Gr. ἐν παραβολαῖς], 'How can Satan cast out Satan? [24]If a kingdom is divided against itself, that kingdom cannot stand. [25]And if a house is divided itself, that house will not be able to stand. [26]And if Satan has risen up against himself and is divided, he cannot stand, but his end has come. [27]But no one can enter a strong man's house and plunder his property without first tying up the strong man; then indeed the house can be plundered' (Mk 3:23-27).[11]

Obviously, Mark situates the term and the sayings in a context featured by gossip (v. 21) and rumor about spirit possession (vv. 22, 30). It is mentioned that not only the delegates from Jerusalem, but Jesus' own kindred came to his sabotage. Jesus is said here to have "gone out of his mind" (v. 21) by the people of his own village and Jesus is also accused of casting out demons

---

8 J. D. Crossan, *The Power of Parable: How Fiction by Jesus Became Fiction About Jesus* (New York: HarperCollins Publishers, 2012), 20-21.

9 Scott, *Domination and the Arts of Resistance*, 136-182.

10 Mark uses the Greek term παραβολή thirteen times in his Gospel. Behind every occurrence of the word stand parables. There are also some parables which are not tagged with the word "parable." See, W. Baur, "παραβολή," *A Greek-English Lexicon Testament and Other Early Christian Literature*, trans. W. F. Arndt & F. W. Gingrich (Chicago and London: The University of Chicago Press, 1979), 612.

11 Insertion of the Greek words is mine.

because "He has Beelzebul" by the Jewish leaders (vv. 21-22).[12] The word in Greek takes dative preceded by preposition (*i.e.* ἐν παραβολαῖς). This urges us to determine whether or not Jesus employed these parables as the instrument to respond to the rumor spread by Jesus' critics.

Attention must also be given to the genre of the sayings that follows the term. Commentators like R. M. Wilson, E. Schweizer, R. A. Guelich and others have seen that the word here is not in the sense of what the Greek παραβολή would mean but the Hebrew משל.[13] Guelich comments, "For Mark these sayings or 'riddles' represent a form of judgment directed at the opponents rather than an exchange of viewpoints."[14] If the scholars cited above are correct, then we can safely state that right from the first occurrence of the word, we encounter an ambiguous realm of public political disguise with this term.[15]

Second, Mark uses the word παραβολή in the Parable Discourse (Mk 4:1-34). Mark reveals that the parables of Jesus are here meant to be public but they badly needed further instructions in private. The Parable Discourse consists of a wider range of genre than in 3:23, such as: short narratives (vv. 3-8; 14-20; 26-29; 30-32), a riddle (v. 21), and proverbial sayings (vv. 9, 23; 24, 25).[16] The usage of the term "parables" assumes plurality of parables in numerical terms but it is always not their genre. Mark indicates that Jesus delivered the parable to "a very large crowd" (v. 1b), indeed, "the whole crowd" (v.1c) in public (v.1c) and explained the meaning of the parable to his disciples in private (vv. 10b, 34b). We must be watchful to see if this signifies that the teachings of Jesus in public had been carried out by means of parable. Not only the "similitude" (vv. 3-8; 26-29; 30-32), but "metaphor" and "figurative sayings" in vv. 21-25 are also kept under the framework of Mark's parable. Above all, Mark highlights the tendency of the parable discourse, already mentioned in 3:23-29, in order to depict Jesus' teaching as in some way disguising. Mark's construction of the parable discourse reveals how he conceives of Jesus' secretiveness in the prior episodes. As such, chapter

---

12 Crossan, *The Power of Parable*, 22; H. C. Waetjen, *A Reordering of Power: A Sociopolitical Reading of Mark's Gospel* (Minneapolis: Fortress Press, 1989), 103-104.

13 R. M. Wilson, *Mark*, Peake's Commentary on the Bible (London and Edinburgh: Thomas Nelson and Sons, 1962), 803; E. Schweizer, *The Good News According to Mark,* trans. D. H. Madvig (Richmond, Virginia: John Knox Press, 1970), 85-86; R. A. Guelich, *Mark 1-8: 26*, WBC 34A (Dallas, Texas: Word Books, 1989), 175; B. B. Scott, *Hear Then the Parable: A Commentary on the Parables of Jesus* (Minneapolis: Fortress Press), 8-19.

14 Guelich, "Mark 1-8: 26," 175.

15 C. Myers discusses Mark 3: 20-25 as Jesus' declaration of ideological war. See, *Binding the Strong Man*: *A Political Reading of Mark's Story of Jesus* (New York: Orbis Books, 1988).

16 For the types of parables, see I. M. Boucher, *The Parables* (Wilmington, Delaware: Michael Glazeir, 1983), 19-23.

4 serves as an interpretive index for the other sections of the Gospel. Aside from the fact that the parables addressed a very large crowd gathered by the lake-side, we have least information about the context. We must scrutinize this passage to ensure whether or not Jesus wanted to show the varied responses to his proclamation of the kingdom of God.

Third, Mark uses the word παραβολή in a context where Jesus forwarded parables to certain individuals in public. For instance, Mark records a saying of Jesus, "There is nothing outside a person that by going in can defile, but the things that come out are not what defile," which is directed to the Pharisees and Scribes from Jerusalem (Mk 7: 1-2, 15-17).[17] It is Jesus' disciples who designated this saying as a parable (Mk 7: 17). Unlike the Parable of Seeds Sown on Various Landscapes (Mk 4: 3-9), this parable addresses individuals; but like the previous one, the parabolic saying needs explanation in private (Mk 7: 17-22). Can we assume that the spatial setting of the term (*i.e.*, the private hour of Jesus with his disciples) signifies that this parable has a quality of exhortation?[18]

Fourth, Mark has the word παραβολή in the context is the Parable of Tenants in Vineyard (Mk 12: 1-9). Mark tags the word "parable" to this short story of the vineyard (v.1). There is a certain point that makes this parable unique from the previous parables. That is, Mark situates the parable in the context of Jesus' open opposition to the powers in Jerusalem. Indeed, this parable comes along with a series of five conflicts that Jesus had openly with religious officials in Jerusalem. Jesus perhaps narrated the Parable of Tenants in the Vineyard to expose the religious leaders' plot against him and to indict them under God's judgment (v. 12). Mark might have intended to enlighten his readers to recognize that the parable is about the abuse of power by the Jerusalem Priestly aristocrats. Could it be that Jesus tells this parable in order that they should understand it and become more indignant against him? Unlike other parables, it is observed that everything is straightforward here. Mark denotes that the powerful elites in Jerusalem could notice that the parable is directed to them (Mk 12: 12). This direct confrontation seems to mobilize the oppositional emotion underneath the oppositional ideology into expansive momentum. Thus, it demands a deeper academic investigation.

Finally, there is another context in which Mark refers to παραβολή. In the final part of the long speech of Jesus, called Apocalyptic Discourse, Mark has the word in genitive case, τὴν παραβολήν (13: 28). This deviates from the

---

17 Almost similar to this parabolic saying occurs in Mk 10: 25, "It is easier for a camel to go through the eye of a needle than someone who is rich to enter the kingdom of God." This parable is said in reference to a certain man with "many possessions" (Mk 10: 17, 22).

18 Guelich, *Mark: 1-8: 26*, 377.

previous usage for "it is an object lesson."[19] One must realize that a pair of parables given in this context is not parables for public revelation as generally observed, but revealed only to a few in private. As we have the impression that the parables attached to the term have a sense of didactic, this study must look into this matter by situating them into power relations. As a whole, we have tentatively supposed that Mark uses the designation παραβολή for a variety of wide ranges of the sayings of Jesus. Such materials include: riddles, proverbs, metaphors, enigmatic sayings, and other figures of speech. This study will be sensitive to the question why Mark situates the word in various contexts of confrontation, gossip, rumor, public-private dichotomy, obscurity, exhortation, *etc*. This is imperative as each of the contexts is either directly or indirectly related to the public performance of Jesus.

1.1.2. The Purpose of the Parables

Mark's understanding of the parables of Jesus is prominently featured by a dichotomy between the public and private. Upon this dichotomy, Mark evidently structures Jesus' story including his parables.[20] It is evident that Mark presents Jesus as moving back and forth between the public and private during his entire campaign in the villages of Galilee and beyond. The dichotomy is between the two poles: "public" and "private."[21] This dichotomy is best exemplified in the Parable Discourse (Mk 4: 1-34) in which Mark fits the "public" and "private" discourses in closest proximity, saying:

When he was alone, those who were around him along with the twelve asked him about the parables. And he said to them, 'To you has been given the secret of the kingdom of God, but for those outside, everything comes in parables; in order that

> "they may indeed look, but not
> perceive,
> and may indeed listen, but not
> understand;
> so that they may not turn again and
> be forgiven" (vv. 10-12).

According to this passage, Jesus addressed the crowd with the parables in public; but when he was in private, Jesus gave "the secret of the kingdom

19 Scott, *Hear Then the Parable*, 22.

20 B. M. F. van Iersel, recognizes the Parable Discourse (Mk. 4: 1-43) as key to the division of Mark's Gospel. See, *Mark: A Reader-Response Commentary*, trans. W. H. Bisscheroux, JSNTSup 164 (Sheffield: Sheffield Academic Press, 1998), 110-113.

21 Jesus' journey from Galilee towards Jerusalem is not negated here. As the Earth revolves on its axis while orbiting the Sun, Jesus also moves towards Jerusalem while swinging back and forth between public and private.

of God" to his trusted disciples (vv. 10-11).[22] Again, at the end of the parable discourse, Mark essentially recapitulates the theme, "... he [Jesus] did not speak to them [the crowd in public] except in parables, but he explained everything in private to his disciples" (Mk 4: 34).[23] This is the manner in which Mark pictures Jesus' movement in highly dichotomized terms.

There have been a lot of scholarly works on this subject. One can observe two broad approaches within it. First, there are scholars who emphasize the didactic role and revelatory nature of the parables. This group usually maintains that the parables are designed to make Jesus' message explicit and easier to understand by means of concrete illustrations drawn from familiar field. Dodd—who argues that Jesus used concrete illustrations drawn from everyday life to make the kingdom of God most vivid and explicit—best represents this scholarship.[24] Most possibly, this group draws the meaning of the word παραβολή from its Greco-English and envisaged Jesus as a moral teacher who drew illustrations from the daily life of the Galileans. Hence, the purpose of Jesus is to illustrate the moral or spiritual truths entailed in his preaching without considering what the context would have offered. Even though there have been strong voices that suggests that parables do not always put things clearest and most vivid way in other context (*i.e.* Dodd), yet scholars like J. W. Bowker insist that the expression ἐν παραβολαῖς in 4: 11 is "not in the sense of 'enigmatically,' but 'in clearest possible illustration,'" in order to leave "no possible illusion about those who have failed to receive or come inside the kingdom of God."[25]

Second, there is another group of scholars that concerns itself with the hidden nature of the parables. In Mark 4: 10-12, this stream finds the evidence that the parables are a means of concealing.[26] For them, the passage seems to say that "Jesus withheld his message from those outside not only in order that they would fail to understand in order that they would be unable to repent and

---

22 G. Steele, "The Theology of Hiddenness in the Gospel of Mark: An Exploration of the Messianic Secret and Corollaries," *ResQ* 54/3 (2012): 169-185. (*ATLA Religion Database with ATLASerials*, EBSCO*host,* February 15, 2013).

23 I acknowledge that, but in contrast to the summary statement of the Parable Discourse, Mark records parables given to the disciples in private. In the discourse known as "Apocalyptic Discourse" (Mk 13: 3-36), Mark presents two parables, *viz.* the Parable of Fig Tree (v. 28.) and the Parable of Doorkeeper (v. 34), to his few disciples in private (Mk 13: 3).

24 Dodd, *The Parables of the Kingdom*, 20-22.

25 See, J. W. Bowker, "Mystery and Parable: Mark IV: 1-20," *JTS* 25 (1974): 313, 315.

26 H. N. Roskam, *The Purpose of Mark in its Historical and Social Context* (Leiden/Boston: Brill, 2004), 29.

be forgiven."[27] This strand of thought is believed to be as old as W. Wrede's *The Messianic Secret* (1901) because scholars after him usually referred to the various passages of the secrecy motifs in Mark under the umbrella of messianic secret.[28] One of the most comprehensive works that establishes obscurity as the purpose of parables is Jeremias. For him Mark 4:10-12 belongs to the historical Jesus, but not necessarily in the context of parables.[29] In his 1956 article, T. A. Burkill argues that "the parables of Jesus are not meant to make plain the essential context of the message of salvation, but to obscure it, they are a means of guarding the mystery or secret of the kingdom of God."[30] Most recently, scholars like H. Räisänen, J. R. Donahue, G. Steele have shown their interests in the theology of hiddenness in Markan parables.[31] To those who proposed a didactic purpose for Jesus in using the parable, this passage becomes a stumbling block; hence they regarded this passage as a tendentious invention of Mark. For instance, D. W. Riddle blames Mark for any idea that the parables conceal.[32] They also suggest that Mark, or his tradition, attempts to project the purpose of these verses as an explanation as to why the Jews did not believe. This tradition has been widely popularized during the twentieth-century with a great impact.[33] D. O. Via goes further arguing, "Mark is really saying that parables in themselves are useless."[34]

Besides, there are a few scholars who sympathized with Mark to shoulder all the responsibilities. Dodd thinks that Mark 4: 10-12 owes not to Mark himself, but to the post-Easter Christians which were facing with the issue of explaining the unbelief of a majority of the Jews.[35] Those who argued for the purpose of parables in terms of didactic are struggling to render a satisfactory explanation of Mark 4: 10-12 where Jesus explicitly tells his disciples that he conceals things.[36] What these two camps reveal is: Mark's

27 See, R. H. Stein, *An Introduction to the Parables of Jesus* (Philadelphia: Westminster, 1981), 34.

28 W. Wrede, *The Messianic Secret*, trans. J.C.G. Greiig (Cambridge: J. Clarke, 1971, German original 1901); also see Scott, *Hear Then the Parable*, 346.

29 Jeremias, *Parables of Jesus*, 14-15.

30 T. A. Burkill, "The Cryptology of Parables in St. Mark's Gospel," *NovT* 1/4 (1956): 246.

31 H. Räisänen, *The "Messianic Secret" in Mark* (Edinburgh: T&T Clark, 1990), 132; J. R. Donahue, *The Gospel of Mark* (Collegeville, MN: Liturgical Press, 2002), 140; Steele, "Theology of Hiddeness," 172.

32 D. W. Riddle, "Mark 4:1-34: The Evolution of a Gospel Source," *JBL* 56 (1937): 83.

33 See, K. Snodgrass, *Stories with Intent: A Comprehensive Guide to the Parables of Jesus* (Grand Rapids, Michigan/Cambridge: Eerdmans, 2008), 158, 637.

34 D. O. Via, *The Parables: Their Literary and Existential Dimension* (Philadelphia: Fortress Press, 1967), 8.

35 Dodd, *Parables of the Kingdom*, I4-I5.

36 Burkill, "The Cryptology of Parables," 257.

portrayal of dichotomous typology that has a tendency to typecast purpose of the parables in two different in opposite ways. Thus, our concern: "to reveal" and "to obscure" is not only prominent but also intrinsic to the nature of the parables.[37] One must be critical in assessing their role and place in Mark's Parable Discourse. Is both or any one of these, the ultimate purpose of Jesus?

It is no doubt that Jesus' statement concerning his purpose in using parables (Mk 4: 10-12) has always been a serious concern to parable scholars. It entails a cluster of difficult exegetical and theological problems which the previous scholarship could not handle properly. The confusion over the purpose of the parable among the scholars is seemingly due to the fact that there is no adequate treatment of the dichotomy between "public" and "private" discourses as is the case in Mark 4: 10-12. The modern parable studies in the past failed to appreciate the political role of the dichotomy of public and private discourses, as they failed to discuss this issue in the context of subaltern politics. Rather, the dichotomy has simply been interpreted in terms of "insider-outsider binarism"[38] without taking the possible political discourse involving in this passage. This confusion arises over the purpose of the parables accounts for serious methodological consideration.

1.1.3. The Conflict and Confrontation

Another key feature which is basic to the parables is conflict. Unlike G. A. Buttrick's assertion that the parables "were spoken mostly to common people who heard them gladly,"[39] Mark presents all the parables of Jesus in an oppositional mood. Crossan puts it, "For Mark, from 3: 23-27 through 4: 11-13 and 7: 17 into 12: 1, 12, Jesus tells 'parables' in the midst of rejection by hearers as his own counterrejection of those hearers."[40] The Parable of the Bridegroom's Guests (2: 19) counters the failure of the disciples in terms of practicing fasting, the Parable of Strong Man Bound (3: 22) stands against the scribes from Jerusalem who alleged that Jesus had cast out demons by the power of Beelzebul, the Parables of Sower (4: 4-8, 26-29 & 30-32) could

37 Recent writers reflecting on the Jesus' statement in Mark 4: 10-12 depict that parables contain revelation and hidden nature. This is the viewpoint that the present study aims to build upon.

38 This expression is adopted from T. B. Liew who finds the insider-outsider binary throughout Mark's Gospel. See, "The Gospel of Mark" in *A Postcolonial Commentary on the New Testament Writings*, edited F. F. Segovia and R. S. Sugirtharajah (New York: T&T Clark, 2007), 115-116.

39 G. A. Buttrik, *The Parables of Jesus* (New York/London: Harper & Brothers, 1928), xxiv-xxv.

40 Crossan, *The Power of Parable*, 24.

be observed as standing against the "outsiders."[41] Likewise, the Parable of Defilement (7: 15), the Parable of Camel and Needle's Eye (10: 25) and the Parable of Tenants in Vineyard (12:1-9) are all given in the context of conflict and confrontation.

Our reading of Mark's Gospel reveals that the confrontation is not between Jesus and the disciples or the Jews and the Gentiles; but it is between Jesus and the Jerusalem high priestly aristocrats.[42] If that is the case, we need to further raise certain questions concerning the domination that these urban powerful elites inflicted upon Jesus and the disciple who hailed from rural Galilee. Did Jesus resist their religious authority alone, or others encompassing social, political and economic too? A reading of the parables within the context of agrarian realities would address better the fundamental issue: who resists what, and more importantly, how?

Cadoux and Jeremias long ago have noticed that the parables are situated in an ethos of confrontation and conflict, attack and resistance.[43] But they do not make this insight a parameter for their understanding of the parables. We must go into deeper to ascertain how far Mark's presentation of conflict motif reflects what had historically happened to Jesus-in-movement. It is envisaged that Mark's arrangement of the parables within the context of opposition and resistance has great prospect for further investigation.

1.1.4. Rurality of the Parables

There has been a growing tendency among Markan scholars to situate the Gospel in the rural or small town of Galilee and its environs.[44] Even though

41 R. S. Sugirtharajah, a noted postcolonial thinker, identifies "outsiders" as a crowd led by both the Romans and its client Judean and Galilean rulers. See, *Asian Biblical Hermeneutics and Postcolonialism: Contesting the Interpretations* (Sheffield Academic Press, 1999), 21.

42 J. D. Kingsbury, *Conflict in Mark: Jesus, Authorities, Disciples* (Minneapolis: Fortress Press, 1989), 63. S. P. Mathew argues that poverty and economic exploitation by the temple-state as the main reason behind the conflict. See, *Temple-Criticism in Mark's Gospel* (Delhi: ISPCK, 1999), xx-xxi.

43 Modern scholars have also constantly reminded us that the parables in the Gospels are placed in the context of conflict and confrontation.

44 G. Theissen, *Gospels in Context: Social and Political History in the Synoptic Tradition* (Minneapolis: Fortress Press, 1991), 238; H. C. Kee, *Community of the New Age: Studies in Mark's Gospel* (Macon, Ga.: Mercer University Press, 1983), 105; H. C. Waetjen, *A Reordering of Power: A Socio-Political Reading of Mark's Gospel* (Minneapolis: Fortress, 1989), 13; R. L. Rohrbaugh, "The Social Location of Mark's Audience," *BTB* 13 (1993): 114; P.J.J. Botha, "Mark's Story of Jesus and the Search for Virtue," in *The Rhetorical Analysis of Scripture: Essays from the 1995 London Conference*, edited by S. E. Porter and T. H. Olbricht, JSNTSup 146 (Sheffield: Sheffield Academic Press, 1997), 164-165, 178; B. J. Incigneri, *The Gospel to the Romans: The Setting and Rhetoric of Mark's Gospel* (Leiden/Boston: Brill, 2003), 70-78.

Mark has relatively less parables in comparison with the other Gospels, yet, the evangelist places them very well within the agrarian rural setting of Galilee. That is to say, Matthew and Luke present a greater number of agricultural parables, and they appear to be reflecting more upon urban settings and are thus far removed from the rural milieu.[45] A broad agricultural experience is attested to in the parabolic stories and proverbs of Mark's Gospel. With regard to the parables in Mark, we are struck by: first of all, the presence of overwhelming agrarian pictures, such as that of the sower, seed, sowing, growing, harvesting, soil, rock, amongst other images (Mk 4: 3-8; 26-29; 30-32; 12: 1-12); second, the scenario of the village household, such as unshrunk cloth, wineskins (Mk 2: 21-22), lamp, bushel basket, bed, lampstand, and measures (Mk 4: 21-22; 24); and third, images that were drawn from nature: birds, trees (Mk 4: 4; 13: 28).[46]

As indicated above, there are certain evidences to depict that Mark seemingly arranges the parables in such a way that they originated within the context of opposition and resistance. The parables should be appropriately discussed in the context of agrarian-resistance. Rarely have the parables been read from the viewpoint of resistance. Scholars usually take the agrarian colour in the parables as confirmation that the Gospel was composed or redacted in a rural area.[47] Voices of resistance are hardly heard from the agrarian parables in Mark's Gospel.[48]

1.1.5. God Factor

The prominence of God is inescapable in Mark. Right from the very beginning, Mark introduces his Gospel as the "Good news of Jesus Christ, the Son of God" (Mk. 1: 1). The good news which Jesus proclaimed, according to Mark, is the "good news of God" in which "the kingdom of God" is at the center of the proclamation (Mk. 1: 14-15). Jesus' parables proclaim the kingdom of God as the main theological thrust. Interestingly enough, Mark mentions no parable when Jesus began to proclaim the good news of God. Mark tells us that Jesus' fame spread quickly throughout Galilee, crowds of increasing sizes gathered around and soon expanded into "a great multitude" and "great numbers" from Judea, Idumea, Tyre and Sidon (Mk 1: 27-28; 32-33, 33-39, 45; 2: 1-2; 13, 3: 7-10, 20, etc.). Here, Jesus begins to use parables. We must think seriously

45 Incigneri, *The Gospel to the Romans,* 70; V. J. John, *The Ecological Vision of Jesus: Nature in the Parables of Mark* (Thiruvala: SSS-BTTBPSA, 2002), xiv.

46 For details, see Funk, *A Credible Jesus*, 79-85.

47 Incigneri, *The Gospel to the Romans,* 70.

48 Sugirtharajah obverses that even if clear a voice of resistance or opposition is heard from the Parable of the Tenants (Mk 12: 1-12), commentators would often "invest this parable with allegorical meanings or look for allusions to the Hebrew Bible." See, *Asian Biblical Hermeneutics and Postcolonialism,* 21.

about how Mark presents Jesus' continuing proclamation of the kingdom of God and the manifestation God's power in exorcisms and healings in village assemblies and houses. To what extent does this imply that the people living in the nearby villages of Jesus were in no need of the explanation of what Jesus meant by the phrase "kingdom of God"? How does Mark denote Jesus' campaign beyond the confines of the nearby villages?

Strictly speaking, two parables are introduced by the phrase that unambiguously identifies their ultimate referent as the kingdom of God, such as: the Parable of the Seeding Growing Secretly (Mk 4: 26-29) and the Parable of the Mustard Seed (Mk 4: 30-32). Presumably, the parables of Jesus represent the notion of God as understood by the subjugated agrarian community in the villages of Roman Galilee. In both cases, the kingdom of God is represented as sprouting, growing, and yielding good results. What is equally important, along with the seeds and the sower, is the soil or land. Does it mean that Jesus was more concerned about when the kingdom of God came (*i.e.* already or not yet) and where (*i.e.* space) it comes? We must attempt to rediscover the notion of God and God's kingdom as enshrined in the parables.

1.2. Anachronistic Assumptions in the Previous Research

Parable studies—at least at an earlier part of the twentieth-century singly handled by the western scholars—have been integral to the quest for historical Jesus.[49] Hence, the parable scholarship becomes a discipline of highly specialized historical-critical analysis. One way of analysis that has been prominently and consistently followed by the historical-critics is the separation of the parables from their Gospel contexts. Obviously, one major reason for the separation is that the parables are considered as less historical sources.[50] Most parable scholars removed the parables from their Gospel literary frameworks and created new contexts within which they will be understood.[51] In this process, anachronistic assumption is involved in the previous investigations. This prevents the previous scholars from analyzing those features in the context of subaltern politics. We must be watchful enough to see how the basic features of parables identified above have been approached and treated.

Ever since the publication of A. Schweitzer's *The Quest for Historical Jesus* in 1901, it becomes somewhat standard to appreciate Jesus' sayings and deeds in the context of the historical Jesus. This book can be regarded

49 W. R. Herzog II, *Parables as Subversive Speech: Jesus as Pedagogue of the Oppressed* (Louisville, Kentucky: Westminster/John Knox Press, 1994), 40.

50 R. A. Horsley, *Jesus and the Powers: Conflict, Covenant, and the Hope of the Poor* (Minneapolis: Fortress Press, 2011), 3-4.

51 Herzog, *Parables as Subversive Speech*, 40.

as the first scholarly work to suggest the historical context for parables aside from their Gospel frameworks. Schweitzer looks into the parables for clues in his *Consequente Eschatologie* (thoroughgoing eschatological) reading of Jesus.[52] He finds apocalyptic eschatology to be the context of Jesus' parables. Schweitzer's work has far-reaching impact upon the parable research largely because it has relevance. More and more scholars after him were trying to re-contextualize the parables in contexts which they assume to be the context of the historical Jesus.

It must be pointed here that much of the eschatological hopes and beliefs current among the Jews during the time of Jesus were the products of their experiences of subjugation and indignities during the second-century B.C.E. Considering the political motives lying behind the historical origins and theological concerns of the Jewish apocalyptic movements, Schweizer has many things to offer in the understanding of the parables in their political and economic context. But, the scholar himself seems to be far off from realizing this aspect, because his interest is confined narrowly within the eschatological debate of his time. Still then, he paves the way for future scholars to see the parables of Jesus in the context of resistance to the powerful elites.

Cadoux's *The Parables of Jesus: Their Art and Use* is another considerable attempt to situate the parables in their historical context. Cadoux brings in the aspect of the polemical and the apologetic to the parable interpretation. Cadoux's major contention is that Jesus rendered his parables in the context of conflict and controversy. His theological inclination is central to the Jewish apocalyptic thought. Cadoux understands parables as more than works of art when he asserts, "In its most characteristic use of the parables is a weapon of controversy."[53] In Cadoux's thought, we can see the conflict motifs surfacing out adequately, yet the conflict has a religious colour as he depicts conflict to occur between Jews and the early Christian. For him, Jesus' mission was to win over Israel as a nation for the service of the kingdom of God; but the Jews rejected and killed him. Cadoux interprets a number of parables in order to substantiate this thesis.[54] Understanding the parables of Jesus within faith relations does not help much to explain some basic features of the parables.

The emergence of Dodd's *The Parables of the Kingdom* in 1935 brings a better way of viewing the parables.[55] Like Schweitzer and Cadoux,

---

52 A. Schweitzer, *The Quest of the Historical Jesus: A Critical Study of Its Progress from Reimarus to Wrede*, trans. W. Montgomery, and J. M. Robinson (New York: Macmillan, 1968), 351-397.

53 A. T. Cadoux, *The Parables of Jesus: Their Art and Use* (London: James Clarke, 1930), 13.

54 Cadoux, *The Parables of Jesus*, 80-115.

55 C. H. Dodd, *The Parables of the Kingdom*, rev. ed. (New York: Charles Scribner's Sons, 1961).

Dodd, perhaps even more than both of them, relates the parables as public performance of Jesus. Dodd sharpens the trend which has been initiated at least since Schweitzer by viewing the public proclamation with a particular theme.[56] The theme, for Dodd, is the kingdom of God and he establishes the perspective of viewing the parables as "the parables of the kingdom." More importantly, Dodd enriches our understanding of the parables in relation to the public performance of Jesus. But Dodd does not reveal that he maintains the balance between these public and private aspects upon which Mark evidently structures the parables. While Mark tells us that three out of four contexts Jesus' parables are given private, Dodd makes no distinction when he groups all of them into two clusters: first, the "parables of crisis"[57] which exhorts their hearers to watchfulness;[58] and second, the "parables of growth"[59] which declare the arrival of the kingdom as a small and insignificant.[60]

Dodd can be commended as situating the parables into the "setting in life" of Jesus' ministry. Time and again, he has been praised for managing to discover their relationship to his proclamation of the reign of God by skillfully removing ecclesial accretions and reconstructing the earliest form of the parable. Yet, Dodd fails to re-contextualize the parables in Jesus' proclamation of the kingdom of God marked by the public-private dichotomy. For Dodd the dichotomy has nothing to do with the subaltern politics in Galilee and Judea; rather it simply reflects two different religious assumptions of Judaism and Hellenistic religions. He believes that Jesus' interpretation of the parables to his trusted disciples in private (Mk 4: 14-20) could have originated only in a non-Jewish environment.[61] When it comes to the issue of Mark 4: 10-12, Dodd has nothing else except to blame the early Christian community. Since his understanding of the parables is not grounded well upon the subaltern politics, Dodd's insight on the kingdom of God becomes politically non-essential. This necessitates Dodd to take "special account of the Gospel parables, particularly those which deal with the theme of the Kingdom of God."[62] Dodd argues that

---

56 This is a clear sign that Dodd follows the hermeneutical insight of Jülicher who suggests a "single point of each parable" in Jesus' parable.

57 Parables of crisis consist of the parables of the Faithful and Unfaithful Servants, the Waiting Servants, the Thief at Night, and the Ten Virgins. For Dodd, these parables are intended to be referred directly to the expected second advent of Christ, and to inculcate preparedness for that approaching crisis.

58 Dodd, *The Parables of the Kingdom*, 122-138.

59 Parables of Growth are a group of parables distinguished by the idea of growth: those of the Sower, the Tares, the Seed Growing Secretly and the Mustard Seed.

60 Dodd, *The Parables of the Kingdom*, 140-156.

61 Dodd, *The Parables of the Kingdom*, 2-5.

62 Dodd, *The Parables of the Kingdom of God*, vii.

the kingdom of God had actually occurred in Jesus' public ministry and the eschatology of Jesus was a "realised eschatology."

We have this line of thought having escalated in the work of Jeremias. Jeremias expands and nuances the "setting in life" established by his predecessors. Jeremias seems to be influenced by Cadoux who has argued that Jesus used the parables as weapons of controversy. Jeremias reiterates that parables can be fully understood and only their polemics were set within the context of the debates of Jesus' day.[63] Jeremias also relates the parables to the public performance of Jesus. While Dodd situates himself within the proclamation of a single point (*i.e.* kingdom of God) Jeremias proposes nine distinct theological themes. As W. R. Herzog II observes, Jeremias might have learnt from Dodd that "the meaning of the parable need not be confined to the moral reading as proposed by Jülicher; rather, it could grow out of the theological themes associated with Jesus' ministry."[64]

Like Dodd, Jeremias reveals the centrality of God's reign in the parables of Jesus. Jeremias' beautiful remark—"the parables are weapons of warfare"[65]—touches upon the resistance motifs, though not necessarily the agrarian ones. He locates the parables in a situation of conflict, and thus he can comment that the parables "correct, reprove, attack."[66] In the same way, Jeremias' insight into "the hortatory use of parables by the Church"[67] helps us to reflect upon how the parables have been removed from their polemical context in Jesus' ministry and reset them in the Gospels. Jeremias undoubtedly acknowledges that "the pictorial element of the parables is drawn from the daily life of Palestine."[68] He devotes the substantial portion of his book, *Parables of Jesus* to situate the parables in their original context. His second chapter, "*The Return to the Jesus from the Primitive Church*"[69] contains a number of factors that have to be taken into consideration in search for the meaning of the parables in their original sense. Jeremias' attempt to bring back the parables that have moved from a rural Galilee to an urban Hellenistic setting to their original rural context challenges us to go more deeply into the agrarian-resistance motifs that were embedded in the parables.

63 Jeremias, *The Parables of Jesus*, 115-229.

64 Herzog, *Parables as Subversive Speech*, 10.

65 Jeremias, *The Parables of Jesus*, 21.

66 Jeremias, *The Parables of Jesus*, 21.

67 Jeremias, *The Parables of Jesus*, 42-48.

68 Jeremias, *The Parables of Jesus*, 11.

69 Jeremias, *The Parables of Jesus*, 23-112. J. G. Muthuraj thinks that Jeremias' understanding of the parables of Jesus reflects "oriental ways of speaking." See his article, "New Testament and Methodology – An Overview," *AJT* 10/2 (October 1996): 267.

Since the perspectives of Dodd and Jeremias are conditioned by the theoretical framework of their successors, the primary goal of their study cannot be expected to freely flow in the way the parables themselves were intended to generate. The scene embedded in the parables is understood not as a social scene in their way of reading the parables. While views current in his time had connected the reign of God to, "the seed," "the whole process of growth," and "the harvest" in explaining the parables of growth, Dodd holds "a present crisis" as the key to understanding these parables.[70] Dodd and Jeremias seem to investigate the details of the parable only to the degree necessary to establish theological and ethical concerns. Consequently, the subaltern realties possibly in the parables remain non-essential in their opinion.

These four scholars are representative of the diverse ways in which the parables have been interpreted with reference to Jesus' larger public work. Their analyses are important and very influential in taking care of the complexities of the task faced by the historical-critical theory. However, they have also invited responses which see them and their approach as too deeply implicated in the context of historical Jesus. Radical exponents of existentialist theory such, as R. Bultmann and G. Bornkamm had sought to dismantle and set aside the historical quest for the parables. Bultmann's *Jesus and the Word* (1926; ET. 1934) and Bornkamm's *Jesus of Nazareth* (1956; ET. 1960) have brought forward the existentialist philosophy in order to "supply the hermeneutical key that was needed to unlock the meaning of the apocalyptic materials in Jesus' preaching."[71] Bultmann's Jesus can be observed as proclaiming an existential gospel. He argues in favour of the reign of God that had arrived, and the hour of decision present. Against the view of Wrede and Schweitzer, Bultmann argues that the kingdom of God was contained in apocalyptic speculation.

In Bultmann's existential understanding of Jesus' proclamation, we still have the element of 'on-stage' in Jesus ministry, but essentially not in the context of power relations. Therefore, Bultmann's understanding of the kingdom is no ideal social order. He asserts that "subversive ideas and revolutionary utterances are lacking in Jesus."[72] Bultmann's assertion must be challenged by interpreting the parables as resistive. Bultmann's Jesus moves into the world of Europe of the 1920s, rather than moving among the agrarian villages in Jesus' Galilee. At this point, Bultmann fails to realize the presence of resistance motifs in the teaching of Jesus.

One of his pupils, Bornkamm also believes that Jesus' movement was "not directed against the political rulers, neither against Rome, nor against

70 Dodd, *The Parables of the Kingdom*, 141-143.

71 Herzog, *Parables as Subversive Speech*, 42.

72 Bultmann, *Jesus and the Word*, 103.

Herod,"[73] and that his teaching touched marginally upon political issues.[74] Unlike H. C. Waetjen who sees Jesus' entry into Jerusalem as "negation of the temple institution" and "confrontation with the ruling elite,"[75] Bornkamm argues that Jesus came to Jerusalem "to deliver the message of the coming kingdom of God ... to summon them at the eleventh hour to make their decision."[76] Bornkamm's Jesus is apolitical and unreligious. He was, "a first century existentialist in the Bultmannian tradition whose message was so obscure it could have offended no one."[77] Bornkamm's view must be counter checked by the parables of Jesus themselves which were delivered in Jerusalem, to ascertain whether Bornkamm's view is acceptable or not for the readers who are guided subaltern theories.

The already discussed Bultmannian thought later developed into a powerful movement called "the New Hermeneutic"[78] which helps us to see the "parables as language event." The social scenario still was not attractive to these scholars. Along with the historical-critics, this tradition of scholarship established the parameter within which the debate over the meaning of parables has come down to us. The debate, in the words of Herzog, is between the two: "Are the parables stories of the kingdom (eschatological) or fables of human existence (existential)?"[79] The debate on this issue evidently encouraged scholars to use literary-critical methods to interpret the parables. American literary critics, such as – A. Wilder,[80] Via,[81] Crossan,[82] and others cast their influence on the parable studies. Even after the emergence of a variety of literary-critical approaches, the focus remained on theology and morals by any

73 G. Bornkamm, *Jesus of Nazareth*, trans. I. McLuskey, F. McLuskey, and J. M. Robinson (New York: Harper & Row, [1956] 1960), 153.

74 Bornkamm, *Jesus of Nazareth*, 120-124.

75 Waetjen, *A Reordering of Power,* 179-196.

76 Bornkamm, *Jesus of Nazareth*, 154-155.

77 Herzog, *Parables as Subversive Speech*, 37.

78 A considerable literature has been published on the subject of the New Hermeneutic during 1960s. J. Cobb and J. Robinson, eds., *The New Hermeneutic* (New York: Harper & Row, 1964); P. Achteimeier, *An Introduction to the New Hermeneutic* (Philadelphia: Westminster Press, 1969); E. Fuchs, *Studies of the Historical Jesus,* SBT 42 (London: SCM Press, 1964); E. Linnemann, *Jesus of the Parables* (New York: Harper & Row and London: SPCK, 1966).

79 Herzog, *Parables as Subversive Speech,* 42-43.

80 A. Wilder, *Early Christian Rhetoric: The Language of the Gospel* (New York: Harper & Row, 1964; rev. ed., Cambridge, Mass.: Harvard University Press, 1971).

81 D. O. Via, *The Parables: Their Literary and Existential Dimension* (Philadelphia: Fortress Press, 1967). Since his work is continuing, and since he is a major member of the SBL Parable Seminar, we are only concerned for the time being with the above cited book.

82 J. D. Crossan, *In Parables: The Challenge of the Historical Jesus* (New York: Harper & Row, 1973).

other name, whether "advent" "reversal" and "action" or "literary-existential" remained the same.[83]

At this juncture, the work of Herzog—who uses the work of Paulo Freire—the twentieth-century Brazilian "pedagogue of the oppressed" as a key to understand Jesus of Nazareth, has much to contribute to the parable studies. Herzog believes that Jesus used "parables to present situations familiar to the rural poor, to encode the system of oppression that controlled their lives and held them in bondage."[84] The parables are not a means of communicating theology or ethics, but of stimulating social analysis. Herzog, thus, opens way inculcate parable studies in a more balanced way. Herzog must be praised for using the methodologies of social scientists and applying them to a sampling of two groups of parables in the Gospels, those bearing the world of oppression as well as those describing challenges to that world. However, Herzog should be read with a certain amount of carefulness. He is simply squeezing down Jesus to the level of Freire as he projects Jesus as "Pedagogy of the oppressed."[85] One of his major assumptions that "the parables were meant to be discussion-starters" finds no strong support either in the Gospels.

Herzog urges us to be more critical while discussing the kingdom of God in the parables. In fact, Herzog finds the parables as not focusing upon the glory of the reign of God. He argues that the focus of the parables is on the gory details of how oppression served the interests of the ruling class.[86] Herzog's work emerged upon the platform of parable studies after the Dodd-Jeremias tradition and the literary-critical tradition. For him, both produced mere "idealist readings of the parables."[87] Regrettably enough, in the parable studies prior to Herzog, the socio-economic, cultural and political scenes represented in the parables were valued only for their theological, ethical or metaphorical value.

In his *Parables Unplugged: Reading the Lukan Parables in Their Rhetorical Context* published in 2014, Lauri Thurén offers a new and impressive approach to understand the parables of Jesus in Luke's Gospel by focusing their persuasive features.[88] In spite of providing a comprehensive, unplugged analysis of the parables of Jesus and illuminating their function as

83 Herzog, *Parables as Subversive Speech,* 42-44.

84 Herzog, *Parables as Subversive Speech,* 27.

85 Herzog, *Parables as Subversive Speech,* 25-28.

86 Herzog, *Parables as Subversive Speech*, 7 (see, back over also).

87 By this Herzog seems to denote that the previous studies have interpreted the parables without much regard for the importance of the social scenes from the vantage point of the subalterns. Herzog, *Parables as Subversive Speech*, 13.

88 L. Thurén, *Parables Unplugged: Reading the Lukan Parables in Their Rhetorical Context* (Minneapolis: Fortress Press, 2014).

persuasive writings, Thurén's work does not help much to unplug the agrarian-resistance motifs implanted in the parables.

Among those previous parable studies, Herzog's work throws light upon agrarian-resistance motifs in the parables which have been overshadowed by various themes, namely: moral generalization (Jülicher) a single theological theme (*i.e.* God's kingdom, Dodd), a variety of theological themes (Jeremias), existential theme (Via), philosophical language, perception (Crossan, Funk) and persuasion (Thurén). However, Herzog's replacement of the coming glorious reign of God with the "reigning systems of oppression that dominated Palestine"[89] as the main referent of the parables remains serious enough to distort the message of parables. This is a serious issue that requires further scholarly investigation. It is very clear that the parable research has never been an independent study. Right from the beginning, it has been "an integral of the quest for historical Jesus."[90] Scholars of the historical Jesus generally consider the Gospels much less as historical sources. The parables are treated as "historical data" for analysis so that scholars could draw conclusions of their own.[91] We also notice that the parable studies suffer from what may be called "methodological reductionism."

Many parable scholars, be it historical critics like Schweitzer, Cadoux, Dodd, Jeremias, and others or the new hermeneutic groups and literary critics, all read the parables of Jesus as simply religious narratives separated from politics and economics.[92] Jesus is largely considered merely as a religious figure and he is not rendered as politically significant. Given the increasing marginalization of religion in the West, this is a serious concern that one must take into consideration. T. Asad—in his discussion on the religion in the modern West—reveals that religion in contemporary Western societies has minimum contact with economic production and political order.[93] In contrast, religion in traditional Jewish agrarian societies was intrinsic to the entire societal structure in which fertility, economic production and political-economic order evolved.

Moreover, fuelled by powerful individualism, religion has been further reduced to individual faith or belief.[94] From this point of view, "Jesus was

---

89 Herzog, *Parables as Subversive Speech,* 7.

90 Herzog, *Parables as Subversive Speech,* 40.

91 Horsley, *Jesus and the Powers*, 1-2.

92 On the relationship between religion and politics in the first-century Roman world, I take side with W. Carter who assumes "no one pretended religion and politics were separate." See, Carter, *The Roman Empire and the New Testament: An Essential Guide* (Nashville: Abingdon Press, 2006), 1.

93 T. Asad, *Genealogies of Religion: Discipline and Reasons of Power in Christianity and Islam* (Baltimore: Johns Hopkins University Press, 1993), 45-46.

94 What is referred to here is the general presupposition that "religion is personal, individual, private." Carter, *The Roman Empire and the New Testament*, 1.

primarily an individual teacher of individuals about individual religious ethics or lifestyles."[95] For most of the scholars under review, God is associated primarily with religion, which is separate from politics and economics. The parable interpreters have also argued that that "the kingdom of God" the very center of Jesus' teaching, was an individual, personal spiritual reality, an unmediated relationship with God. The God of marginalised modern theology thus has drastically reduced jurisdiction compared with the God of Israel, consistently portrayed in the Old Testament as comprehensively and directly concerned with political and economic affairs inseparable from religious loyalty.

Similarly in an understanding of the parables, the kingdom of God refers to the comprehensive sovereignty of God. Moreover, there was the interpretation of Jesus as part of New Testament studies, which is a sub-division of Christian theology as a new, supposedly more universal religion from the older, and supposedly more particularistic religion of Judaism. In this frame of thought, Jesus was the revealer, teacher, and healer of individual followers. Only after and as a result of the resurrection faith did a community or movement of his followers form. Jesus himself did not catalyze a movement. So theologically oriented interpreters focus mainly on the features of Jesus' "ministry" compatible with and developed by "early Christianity" as it spread primarily among the "Gentiles" in the Hellenistic world. They see little or no reason to attend to the particular concerns and political conflicts in Galilee and Judea.

1.3. The Research Question in the Context of Agrarian Politics

Rethinking parables in the context of agrarian politics of the first-century Roman Galilee and Judea is inevitable because of two reasons. First, as indicated before, the modern parable scholars have imposed modern western assumptions and worldviews onto the parables. The basic features of the parables in the Gospels have been rarely cropped up in the previous interpretations. Second, the nature and purpose of the parables of Jesus contain some elements that are intrinsic to agrarian-resistance. In seeking to understand the parables in their historical context, however, it makes sense to attempt to understand the worldview, assumptions, and pattern of politics of the first-century Roman Galilee and Judea. This will be a difficult task to carry out, yet, we can at least appreciate the ancient cultures and politics in the interpretation of the parables while being sensitive towards the western culture and worldview; particularly of the assumptions and approaches which have been imposed by the parable scholars in the past.

It is envisaged that to understand the rich accounts of resistance motifs embedded in the parables of Jesus, it will help to appreciate the effect of

---

95 Horsley, *Jesus and Powers*, 4.

coercive power on agrarian masses and the creative alternative forms of political resistance that they can muster. There are certain questions that we intend to answer in this research:

a) Mark's portrayal of Jesus swings back and forth between the public and the private throughout the Gospel and it assumes political significance. To what extent does the performance of Jesus in public and private supposedly recount what had happened to the subjugated agrarian masses in Galilee and Judea during the Roman imperial regime?
b) From Mark's presentation of Jesus' on stage performance, it seems clear that Jesus interacted with the crowd and powerful individuals and used parables in the manner of obscuring his message. Did Mark consider various genres of the parables as basic elementary forms of political disguise and anonymity? If so, what insight can we draw from the parables with regard to the purpose of Jesus' parables when read in the context of subaltern politics?
c) Our survey suggests that out of four contexts of the usage of παραβολή, three times Jesus privately instructs his disciples as they are obscured in public (3:23ff; 4:1-34; 13:28). Did Mark try to impress upon his readers that a generation of the empowerment of the disciples came from the private space where Jesus rendered an articulated and disciplined form to the ideas and emotions in interaction with the people? What is the theological significance of Mark's spatial site of Jesus' off-stage interaction in terms of exposing the true meaning of the parables?
d) Did Mark give us any clue to see God as active in the history of the subaltern politics? Whose experiences and hopes are reflected in Jesus' proclamation of the kingdom of God – people who dominated or people who were dominated? In what manner, did Jesus, by using the parables, interpret the new brand βασιλεία that has been brought about by the divine-genitive, *i.e.* τοῦ θεοῦ?
e) Mark's presentation of the parables is featured by the agrarian imageries. It is, however, doubtful that the parables embraced the agrarian and rural elements only because the parables are meant for the village communities. Mark denotes that more than half of Jesus' parables address the powerful urban elites. What then are the agrarian parables, if many of them addressed the powerful urban elites rather than agrarian villagers? Can we have better insight if the parables are assumed to be the means of speaking truth to the powers?

2. Importance of the Problem

The above research problem has been proposed for a number of reasons. First, in most of the modern interpretations of the parables, the focus was mainly upon theology, ethics, literary value and social aspects. The present research, by giving due consideration to the sociopolitical realities in the parables of Jesus in the Synoptic Gospels, while at the same time denoting equal favour to aspect of God, has the prospect to contribute to a deeper understanding of the parables. Second, the exploration of the agrarian-resistance motifs in the parables of Jesus helps to locate the ministry of Jesus in the context of various movements of resistance in Galilee. However, we are confronted with a further question that challenges us to ascertain what type of resistance it was in terms of the Jesus' movement: was it violent or non-violent? Third, the present research brings out the correlation between God's reign and subalternity in Jesus' ministry as recorded in Mark, and thereby throws some light on the correlation between Jesus' message and the subaltern realities and *vice versa.* It is envisaged that this research would elucidate upon the agrarian-resistance motifs as central to the understanding of the parables of Jesus. It is further hoped that the research will provide significant insight in terms of enhancing the tribal hermeneutics in North-east India.

3. Limitations

The proposed research is limited to the agrarian resistance motifs assumed to be permeating upon the parables of Jesus as recorded in the Synoptic Gospels. P. M. Meagher is right in observing that Markan sources are centered on Jesus who was steeped in rural and peasant images and metaphors.[96] The parables in Mark thus seem to have a clear bearing on the agrarian concerns than any other canonical Gospels, as the entirety of the parable stories have been drawn from an agriculture setting. The Greek word παραβολή and its Hebrew counterpart לשמ have a much broader meaning in the Gospels than the English word "parable." Both can be used of a proverb, a riddle, a comparison, a contrast as well as simple stories and complex stories.[97] Accordingly, the proverbial sayings as well as parable stories found in Mark will be the main focus of the research.

4. Methodology

In methodological terms, this study will dwell upon the traditional historical, literary and socio-scientific critical based reading strategies as well as the emerging approach of postcolonial criticism, which stages the biblical texts

96 P. M. Meagher, "The Liturgical Year," *Vidyajyothi* 64/6 (2000): 458.

97 K. R. Snodgrass, "Parable," *DJG*, ed. J. B. Green and S. McKnight (Downers Grove, Illinois: Intervarsity Press, 1992), 593.

within power relations. The primary shift involved in this methodological move is the exposing of the agrarian-resistance embedded in the parables. Since, Jesus' parables are developed within the discourse of the rural agrarian community's faith, the parables are a foremost theological reality, expressed in terms of its relationship to God, exploring the agrarian-resistance motifs that must be the starting point and ongoing reference point for our hermeneutical endeavours including enquiries into the *Sitz im Leben* of the parables.

Since the nature of relationship between the agrarian communities living in the first-century Roman Galilee—who could be described as subalterns considering their low status with respect power—and the rulers in Jerusalem who were the powerful elites is not immediately evident, the mapping of the political functions of the parables of Jesus in the context of first-century represents a methodological challenge. Many tools, however, lie close at hand on the workbenches of the social sciences—particularly those of political anthropology—that have been tried often enough in recent New Testament study to make a focused analysis of the correlation between the religion and political structures of the agrarian subjugated masses in Galilee. Our investigation of the agrarian-resistance motifs in the parables is grounded in the distinction between the public and private discourses. While this distinction is simple, its application to Jesus' materials points to the central concern of this research, *i.e.* the nature of the relationship between the subaltern classes in rural Galilee and the ruling elites in Jerusalem.

4.1. The Public-Private Problem

Insofar as the parables are considered as social or public interaction between the powerful elites and the subalterns of the agrarian communities, one needs to notice the significance of interplay between the public and the private sphere which is not all a new invention. Mark clearly exhibits the interplay of the public and private discourses in Jesus' campaign in Galilee and beyond. It is a fact that the distinction of public and private discourses generates a lot of debates and discussions among the modern Markan scholars. The debate can be resolved, at least to a great extent, if we apply Scott's analysis of public-private dichotomy. For Scott sees and analyses the dichotomy within the power relations of power elites and the subalterns.

In *Domination and the Arts of Resistance: Hidden Transcripts* (1990), Scott articulates his understanding of the difference between public and private discourses. In this present monograph, Scott moves beyond his earlier investigations of "little" and "great" traditions in specific agrarian peasant societies in order to identify the nature of the relationship between the elites and the subalterns. Scott's interest, according to E. M. Heen, is neither to establish a "self-contained elite culture" nor a separate non-elite culture" as there are no such enmities.[98] In his article, "Prestige as the Public Discourse of Domination" (1989), Scott begins his investigation with an analysis of the public interaction of the elites and the subalterns which seriously address the issue of distinction between history seen "from below" or history approached "from below."[99]

4.1.1. The Public Transcript of the Powerful Elites

In his *Domination and the Arts of Resistance*, Scott devises the unusual concept of "public transcript" to deal with the interactions of the elites and the subalterns in the public life with an aim to deduce the obvious aspects of domination. Scott defines the term, thus:

> I shall use the term public transcript as a shorthand way of describing the open interaction between subordinates and those who dominate. Public here refers to action that is openly avowed to the other party in the power relationship, and transcript is used almost in its juridical sense (*procès verbal*) of a complete record of what was said. This complete record, however, would also include nonspeech acts such as gestures and expressions.[100]

Scott's purpose in developing this shorthand analytical description is ostensibly to reveal the public performance is "highly partisan" and controlled by the powerful. Scott says:

> The public transcript is, to put it crudely, the self-portrait of dominant elites as they would have themselves seen. Given the usual power dominant elites to compel performances from others, the discourse of the public transcript is a decidedly lopsided discussion. While it is unlikely to be merely a skein of lies and misrepresentations, it is, on the other, a highly partisan and partial narrative. It is designed to be impressive, to affirm and naturalize the power of dominant elites, and to conceal or euphemize the dirty linen of their rule.[101]

The public transcript is, thus, the public interaction of the powerful elites and the subalterns on record by the powerful elites to their advantage. If this being Scott's purpose of the public transcript, what is the content of the record of the social interactions? Scott suggests that the public transcript

---

98 E. M. Heen, "Satunalicius Princeps: The Enthronement of Jesus in Early Christian Discourse (Ph. D. Dissertation, Columbia University, 1997), 10.

99 J. C. Scott, "Prestige as the Public Discourse of Domination," *Cultural Critique* 12 (1989): 145-166.

100 Scott, *Domination and the Arts of Resistance*, 2, see also footnote no. 1. Heen comments that the concept *public transcript* is "heuristic device" used by Scott but "no such abstract entity exits in any society." See Heen, "*Satunalicius Princeps*," 11 (footnote 29).

101 Scott, *Domination and the Arts of Resistance*, 18.

consists of the mechanism of "public mastery and subordination" and "ideological justification for inequalities" in order to manage the "material appropriation" which is "largely the purpose of domination."[102] Whereas other scholars' analyses of material domination usually privilege the appropriation of surplus values as the social site of exploitation and resistance, Scott's analysis privileges "the social experience of indignities, control, submission, humiliation, forced deference, and punishment."[103] This inspires Scott to take seriously other aspects, *viz*. status and ideological. Status domination, for Scott, is the result social indignity and indignation of the powerless by the elites; whereas ideological domination comes from justification of their own deeds by the powers.[104] This is one of the major thrusts of Scott's theory as it gives space to reflect upon other aspects of domination—status and ideological—in relation to the material aspect of domination.

4.1.2. The Hidden Transcript of the Subalterns

In his earlier work—*Weapons of the Weak* (1985) that led towards the insights of *Domination and the Arts of Resistance: Hidden Transcripts* (1990)—Scott has already opened our eyes to see the remarkable range of "hidden forms of resistance" as far more prevalent, more widespread, and more effective over the long haul than open revolt, given the repressive power of the dominant. Scott's earlier research and reflection come to a climax of sorts in *Domination and the Arts of Resistance: Hidden Transcripts* (1990). In this book, Scott develops the fuller range of subversive popular politics that standard political science and other fields had been unaware of previously. Scott offers a critical theory of that previously unnoticed fuller range of political involved in domination and resistance that results from the interaction between the "public transcript" controlled by the dominant and the "hidden transcript" of the subalterns that is cultivated off-stage, beyond the control of the dominant. By the term "hidden transcript" what Scott intends, is thus:

> I shall use the term hidden transcript to characterize discourse that takes place "offstage," beyond direct observation by powerholders. The hidden transcript is thus derivative in the sense that it consists of those offstage speeches, gestures, and practices that conform, contradict, or inflect what appears in the public transcript.[105]

Since Scott labels public transcript to the "open interaction between subordinates and those who dominate,"[106] the hidden transcript tells only

102 Scott, *Domination and the Arts of Resistance*, 111.

103 Scott, *Domination and the Arts of Resistance*, 111.

104 Scott, *Domination and the Arts of Resistance*, 198.

105 Scott, *Domination and the Arts of Resistance,* 4-5.

106 Scott, *Domination and the Arts of Resistance,* 2.

part of the story of such power relations. For, Scott says, "every subordinate group creates, out of its ordeal, a 'hidden transcript' that represents a critique of power spoken behind the back of the dominant," usually in sequestered sites.[107] Furthermore, Scott utters behind a few anti-elite action lies "a far more elaborate hidden transcript, an entire discourse, linked to ... culture, religion, and the experience of colonial rule."[108] Scott helps us to study "power relations when the powerless are often obliged to adopt a strategic pose in the presence of the power and when the powerful may have an interest in overdramatizing their reputation and mastery."[109] It is this hidden transcript, as Scott suggests, that provides the seedbed of more extensive and organized popular resistance, such as: the widespread Judean and Galilean revolts in 4 B.C.E. and C.E. 66-70, the popular prophetic movements in mid-first century Judea and Samaria, Jesus' campaign in Galilee and beyond.

4.2. Varieties of Popular Politics Rooted in Hidden Transcript

4.2.1. Off-stage Performance

If the public transcript involves performance by the dominant elite, then it requires performance by the subalterns even more. What appears to be acceptable of the dominant order may be only a mask of acquiescence. Neither the slave nor the serf nor the sharecropper dare "speak truth to power." Living constantly under the repressive power and sometimes the regular surveillance of the dominant, the subalterns learn to wear a mask of obedience. Unable to say what they are really thinking or to act upon their emotions, they learn rather to act the part they are given in life while on the public stage.

When they are "offstage," however, the subordinate do say what they think and feel to each other. "The practices of domination and exploitation typically generate the insults and slights to human dignity that in turn foster a hidden transcript of indignation."[110] Subaltern classes have always "a shared interest in jointly creating a discourse of dignity, of negation, and of justice."[111] In addition to its continuing cultivation as a shared discourse, Scott understands the hidden transcript to encompass a whole range of practices such as: poaching, pilfering, and clandestine tax-evasion.[112] But it definitely has an ideological dimension. "Inasmuch as the major historical forms of domination have presented themselves in the form of metaphysics, a religion, a worldview, they have provoked the development of more or less equally

107 Scott, *Domination and the Arts of Resistance,* xii.

108 Scott, *Domination and the Arts of Resistance,* 15.

109 Scott, *Domination and the Arts of Resistance,* xii.

110 Scott, *Domination and the Arts of Resistance*, 7.

111 Scott, *Domination and the Arts of Resistance*, 114.

112 Scott, *Domination and the Arts of Resistance*, 14.

elaborate replies in the hidden transcript."[113] Since subaltern groups "confront elaborate ideologies that justify inequality, bondage, monarchy, caste, and so on ... resistance to ideological domination requires counter-ideology (*i.e.* a negation) that will effectively provide general normative form to host of resistant practices invented in self-defense by any subordinate group."[114]

4.2.2. Articulation of Indigenous Discourse of Dignity

R. A. Horsley articulates that one of the most important potential gains in recognizing the reality of the hidden transcript for the New Testament studies is Scott's enlargement of the field of vision to include the emotional-cultural dimension of subaltern people's lives.[115] It is true that Scott sees material domination such as extraction of labour or grain from a subordinate population as a generic quality that shapes the socio-culture of subjugated people. To quote,

> We know relatively little about a Malay villager if we know only that he is poor and landless. We know far more about the cultural meaning of his poverty once we know that he is particularly in despair because he cannot afford to feed quests on the feast of Ramadan ... that he cannot bury his parents property ... To know the cultural meaning of his poverty in this way is to learn the shape of his indignity and hence, to gauge the content of his anger ... It is these experienced indignities that for the bridge between his condition and his consciousness.[116]

Awareness of such indignities enables the interpreter to understand what motivates a popular movement and to explain and interpret its origins and politics. In explaining how a hidden transcript develops and works, Scott makes two interrelated moves that have potential importance for the parable studies, a field dominated by methodological individualism. Scott points out that the articulation of anger requires language—an unarticulated feeling of anger—and that resistance is social. The articulation of indignation and indigenous discourse of dignity requires social space for their cultivation. The expression of anger in language moreover "will impose a disciplined form to it."[117] As "raw" anger becomes "cooked" indignation, the most resonant expressions rise to the sub-cultural surface.[118] If a particular expression of indignation and

---

113 Scott, *Domination and the Arts of Resistance*, 115.

114 Scott, *Domination and the Arts of Resistance*, 118.

115 R. A. Horsley, "Introduction: Jesus, Paul, and the 'Arts of Resistance': Leaves from the Notebook of James C. Scott," in *Hidden Transcripts and the Arts of Resistance: Applying the Work of James C. Scott to Jesus and Paul*, edited by R. A. Horsley (Atlanta: SBL, 2004), 9.

116 Scott, *Domination and the Arts of Resistance*, 113.

117 Scott, *Domination and the Arts of Resistance*, 119.

118 Scott, *Domination and the Arts of Resistance*, 119.

dignity "is to become the social property of a whole category of subordinates it must carry effective meaning for them and reflect the cultural meanings and distribution of power among them."[119] Furthermore—in contrast to the previous treatment of Jesus' sayings—"the hidden transcript has not reality as pure thought; it exists only to the extent it is practiced, articulated, enacted, and disseminated."[120]

4.2.3. Social Space for Dissident Sub-culture

Scott also suggests that two requirements are necessary for the cultivation of a hidden transcript. One is a "social space insulated from control, surveillance, and repression above."[121] It is especially difficult for slaves to create and defend such sequestered spaces. Many peasantries already have relatively autonomous social spaces in village communities with which the dominant do not interfere except to collect taxes or to further humiliate and subordinate those who fail to pay up. Elites, of course, may deploy retainers to keep the sites of the hidden transcript under surveillance, and subordinate groups may have to defend their sites which are often won only through resistant struggles.[122]

The second, particularly if subject people's indignity is to be transformed from "raw" to "cooked," is the role of active human agents who cultivate and disseminate the discourse.[123] Such carriers of the hidden transcript are often people who have become displaced and marginalized, which has perhaps made them usually sensitive to fluctuations in the fortunes of the subordinated and less vulnerable to the power that the dominant still wield over ordinary peasants or slaves. If the hidden transcript is to give birth to a movement beyond local venting of indignation, moreover, a third component emerges in the discipline and infrapolitics that would develop between leaders and participants. The sequestered sites in which the hidden transcript becomes more "cooked" are little centers of localized power in their own right; they "serve to discipline as well as to formulate patterns of resistance."[124] Thus "the hidden transcript is a social product and hence a result of power relations among subordinates" as they struggle to win and defend a relative autonomy "in the teeth of power."[125]

4.3. The Politics of Disguise and Anonymity

Scott believes that the subalterns do not confine the struggle within the sequestered site. He argues on occasion that the subalterns continue against

119 Scott, *Domination and Arts of Resistance*, 119.

120 Scott, *Domination and the Arts of Resistance*,119.

121 Scott, *Domination and the Arts of Resistance*, 120-123.

122 Scott, *Domination and the Arts of Resistance*, 124-133.

123 Scott, *Domination and the Arts of Resistance*, 123-124.

124 Scott, *Domination and the Arts of Resistance*, 118-119.

125 Scott, *Domination and the Arts of Resistance*, 119.

domination beyond the confines of their sequestered sites. What then happens when the hidden transcript moves beyond the sequestered sites? G. C. Spivak poses a serious question: Can the Subaltern Speak?[126] Scott, almost in similar tone, but quite different in its implication, says truth is hardly spoken to the powers. Scott devises how the subalterns communicate their struggles against domination by devising a politics of disguise and anonymity. This is a politics of disguise and anonymity that takes place in public view but is designed to have double meaning or to shield the identity of the actors. Rumor, gossip, folktales, songs, rituals, codes, and euphemisms – a good part of the folk culture of subordinate groups – fit this description. As a case in point, one must consider the Brer Rabbit stories of slaves, and trickster tales more generally.[127] At one level these are nothing but innocent stories about animals; at another level they appear to celebrate the cunning wiles and vengeful spirit of the weak as they triumph over the strong. We argue that a partly sanitized, ambiguous, and coded version of the hidden transcript is always present in the public discourse of subordinate groups. Interpreting these texts which, after all, are designed to be evasive is not a straightforward matter. Ignoring them, however, reduces us to an understanding of historical subordination that rests either on those rare moments of open rebellion or on the hidden transcript itself, which is not just evasive but often altogether inaccessible.[128]

Given that the nature of historical sources generally prelude access to the private discourse of subordinate groups, it is to this third realm, somehow between public and private, that one is forced to attend in order to bring out a fuller picture of how subaltern groups viewed their relationship to those who dominated them.[129] In addition to rumor, gossip, folklores, jokes, and the slave and trickster tales which Scott lists as medium through which the private discourse of subject peoples emerge into public realm, it should be noted that the religion of subordinate groups provides one important context for rituals, songs, and codes of private discourse, however, veiled and sanitized, to emerge into public space. Also to note Scott's caution that the reconstruction of such covert meanings is not a "straightforward" affair. One of the principal modes of the politics of anonymity is rumor. Rumor travels in a process of elaboration in which it is adapted to the hopes and fears of those who hear it and retell it.[130] Mark clearly mentions that Jesus and the movement around him moved the continuing struggle against domination, beyond the confines of their own

126 G. C. Spivak, "Can the Subaltern Speak?" in *Marxism and the Interpretation of Culture*, edited by C. Nelson and L. Grossberg (Urbana: University of Illinois Press, 1988).

127 Scott, *Domination and the Arts of Resistance*, 163.

128 Scott, *Domination and the Arts of Resistance*, 18-19.

129 Heen, "*Satunalicius Princeps*," 26.

130 Scott, *Domination and the Arts of Resistance*, 145.

villages. Mark's portrayal of Jesus' mission in Galilee and beyond resembles other peasant movements that were spread through rumor.

4.4. Public Declaration of Hidden Transcript in the Face of Power

There is another important dimension in Scott's explanation of the popular politics of resistance, *i.e.,* the public declaration of the hidden transcript in the face of power. Scott says, "Finally, the most explosive realm of politics is the rupture of the political *cordon sanitaire* between the hidden and the public transcript."[131] He continues to denote that some brave subordinates who "can't take it anymore," speak truth to power." Such "moments of challenge and open defiance typically provoke either a swift stroke of repression or, it unanswered, often lead to further word and acts of daring." Scott speaks of the spokesperson or the catalyst of the subjugated people who will speak for the subjugated people. Scott also insists that there are key factors often ignored by social scientists – "the emotional dynamics" of domination. We should take special note that the breakthrough act of defiance must be public in order to have any impact.[132] Scott makes a distinction between "raw" and relatively "cooked" declarations of defiance. He explains,

> Cooked declarations are more likely to be nuanced and elaborate because they arise under circumstances in which there is a good deal of offstage freedom among subordinate groups, allowing them to share a rich and deep hidden transcript. In a sense ... [it] already has a quasi-public existence.[133]

In a usually favourable conjunction of circumstances they may also lead to a wider popular movement, even one that might pursue a revolutionary vision of ending domination and establishing a just social order. Scott thus opens up for New Testament interpreters a whole range of popular political dynamics that often lie hidden between passive acquiesce and active revolt.

5. Summary

The parable scholars generally have reached an impasse on Jesus' purpose in using the parables, partly because they do not consider the political role that the dichotomy of public and private discourses could have played in the first-century subaltern politics; and partly because they read the parables in the relatively narrow term of public affairs on the public stage. Scott's work can help us transcend this discerning from an ordinarily unrecognized area of political activity and forms of agrarian-resistance to powers present in the parables within the Gospel of Mark.

---

131 Scott, *Domination and the Arts of Resistance*, 19.

132 Scott, *Domination and the Arts of Resistance*, 214-215.

133 Scott, *Domination and the Arts of Resistance*, 216.

Chapter 2

The Protest and Resistance in Judea and Galilee during the Roman-Herodian Period (63 B.C.E.–C.E. 70)

For generations, both before and after the ministry of Jesus, the Galileans and Judeans had gone through Roman imperial rule. The Roman imperial empire, according to Daniel 7:7, was the "terrifying and dreadful exceedingly strong" fourth beast. Even though they were the subjects of the destructive and devouring imperial empire, Judeans and Galileans were still commendable to be a people who were determined in reasserting their independence, defending their traditional way of life, and persisting in their resistance.[1] It is not surprising to see at least four widespread revolts and many lesser protests by groups and individuals over a period of nearly two centuries that featured the many repeated revolts during the Roman regime. Our concern in this chapter is not only to find out the reasons for their persistence, but also to investigate into how the subjugated Jews 'speak truth to powers' in the course of their resistance.

Larger focus shall be given to the Roman-Herodian period as it was the immediate context of Jesus' ministry. However, we must note that any discussion on Roman imperialism cannot be done in isolation from the previous regimes. We shall begin with the Hellenistic period, but this will be done as background studies of the Roman period. The resistance movement that was successfully launched from a Judean village of Modein will be the point of our departure. Since such a great revolt must have been generated by many factors, we shall concentrate on possible factors that were responsible

1 R. A. Horsley, *Jesus and Empire: The Kingdom of God and the New World Disorder* (Minneapolis: Fortress Press, 2003), 35. He makes this statement when he compares the contemporary revolts against Rome in Spain, Gaul and North Africa.

for the revolt and the situation at the aftermath of the revolt. It is hoped that this covers well the most significant events that have bearing upon the Roman period. Above all, the discussion will be carried out from the perspective of the agrarian communities who were at the same time regarded to be the people of the bottom line.

1. The Historical Background: Causes and Effects of Modein Resistance[2]

Factors that gave rise to the Jewish Revolt at the village called Modein have been variously interpreted by modern scholars. Scholar like V. Tcherikover, M. Hengel, and others have considered the conflict between Judaism and Hellenism as the major reason that led to the great revolt against the Seleucid domination.[3] Whereas, H. Koester—who views Christianity as universal religion—proposes that the universalism was inherent of Hellenism.[4] So, the revolt was supposedly a conservative reaction to the spirit of Hellenism.[5] R. A. Horsley considers that these interpretations cannot explain how and why a Hellenistic emperor, even the notorious Antiochus IV Epiphanes, would have mounted such a programme against the Jews.[6] The situation of the Jews under the Hellenistic empires was more complicated than these modern interpretations have allowed. Following Horsley's suggestions in his book, *Jesus and the Powers* (2011), we shall focus on three major factors, such as: escalation of violence and economic exploitation, new opportunities offered to the elite of subjected people, and backing of the local elites by the imperial rulers.[7]

1.1. The Causes of Modein Revolt

1.1.1. Violence and Exploitation under Hellenistic Regimes

The death of Alexander the Great (323 B.C.E.); shortly after he conquered West Asia, led to a long struggle between rival successor regime—the Ptolemies

2 The phrase "Modein Revolt" is used in instead of "Maccabean Revolt" throughout this research. In addition to the benefit of inclusivity of non-Maccabean participation, the phrase conveys the dynamic sense of rural resistance. In some places, the phrase "Maccabean Revolt" is refrained simply because it is so familiar.

3 V. A. Tcherikover, *Hellenistic Civilization and the Jews.* trans. S. Applebaum (New York: Atheneum, 1959, ET. 1975); M. Hengel, *Judaism and Hellenism: Studies in their Encounter in Palestine during the Early Hellenistic Period*, trans. J. Bowden (Philadelphia: Fortress Press, 1974).

4 H. Koester, *History, Culture, and Religion of the Hellenistic Age*, Vol. 1 (Philadelphia: Fortress Press, 1982).

5 Koester, *History, Culture, and Religion of the Hellenistic Age*, 41.

6 Horsley, *Jesus and the Powers*, 66.

7 Horsley, *Jesus and the Powers*, 64.

and the Seleucids—for the control of the Jewish territories.[8] Hengel terms the situation of the Jewish state under the two great powers as "a theatre of war."[9] This clearly indicates how the establishment of the Hellenistic empires in the Jewish agrarian territories brought an escalation of violence and economic exploitation. Judea, which had been ruled over for two centuries in a relatively stable manner by the Persian Empire, found herself lying in the contested frontier area between the Ptolemies and the Seleucids.[10] There were five major wars fought between the two rival Hellenistic rival empires for the control of the contested area during the third century B.C.E. In the course of these prolonged wars, imperial armies moved back and forth through the area, with the resultant destruction of crops, towns and people in their wake. Daniel 11: 5-9 may attest to "a scribal memory of the uncertainty" over which empire would prevail in the third Syrian war (246-241 B.C.E).[11] In the fourth war (221-217 B.C.E.), the Seleucid emperor Antiochus did take control of some areas of Western Syria for a few years.[12] The reference in Daniel 11:10-12 indicates that Judean scribes were still thinking about this conflict over two generations later.[13] In the fifth war (201-200 B.C.E.), Antiochus III finally gained control of the area and, thus brought Judea to be under Seleucid rule over the next half a century (201-142 B.C.E.). Those who suffered most from successive wars were the agrarian peoples whose crops were taxed, whose fields and houses were devastated, and whose families were killed and enslaved. Obviously, the impact of these prolonged wars on the life on people in Judea was compounded by periodic war conflicts between rivals for the throne within each empire, as well as regular rebellions of subject peoples, especially against the Seleucid regime.

As the Seleucids took control over Judea, the Romans began intervening more actively in the inter-imperial politics of the eastern Mediterranean.[14] The historical sources reveal that Antiochus III had skillful or lenient policies to

8 Hengel describes Palestine as "a Bone of Contention between Ptolemies and Seleucids." See, *Judaism and Hellenism*, 6-12. The Jewish territory is always referred to as "Coele Syria." For more details, S. Zeitlin, *The Second Book of Maccabees*, trans. S. Tedesche (New York: Harper & Brothers, 1954) 7-9; Koester, *History, Culture, and Religion of the Hellenistic Age*, 1-31.

9 Hengel, *Judaism and Hellenism*, 11.

10 Koester, *History, Culture, and Religion of the Hellenistic Age*, 208-210.

11 Hengel, *Judaism and Hellenism*, 7.

12 H. Jagersma believes that Palestine suffered a great deal from action during the fourth war. See, *A History of Israel from Alexander the Great to Bar Kochba*, trans. J. Bowden (London: SCM Press, 1985), 33.

13 Hengel opines that Daniel 11 reflects the historical situation of various Syrian wars. See, *Judaism and Hellenism*, 18.

14 Koester, *History, Culture, and Religion of the Hellenistic Age*, 281-293.

protect the temple community.[15] However, the defeat that Antiochus III suffered from the Roman troops at Magnesia in 190 B.C.E. turned things unpleasant not only for the Jews, but for the Seleucid empire itself. Hence, the situation turned out to be the beginning of new and bitter conflicts for Judea, Samaria, and Galilee. The Seleucid king had to pay a huge amount of indemnity to Rome. As Hengel rightly observes, the defeat was "the catastrophe of Magnesia."[16] Antiochus had no other choice but to make peace with Rome which was very damaging to him. M. Noth observes that this was the beginning of the decline of Seleucid power.[17] In the course of this decline, the Seleucid king Antiochus IV Epiphanes was largely responsible. Because of his provocative actions, there existed a great conflict which initiated a new phase in the history of Judaea and Galilee. It was during the high priesthood of Onias III (*ca.* 190-174 B.C.E.) that the temple administration was open to heavy attacks from the Tobiad and from the Seleucids. It is evident that the Seleucid kings were in need of money for the annual payment of indemnity to Rome. Antiochus III's lenient policy of taxation that was introduced favouring the Judeans and Galileans would not have lasted long.[18] Antiochus III was now to raise the annual payment by plundering temple treasures. According to 2 Maccabees 3-4, an attempt was made to seize the temple treasure in Jerusalem during the time of Seleucus IV.

---

15 Our historical sources suggest that the Seleucid administration, was very liberal and lenient towards the agrarian community at least at the initial stage of it rule. For instance, *the Letter of Antiochus III to Ptolemy*, *stratēgos* of Coele Syria—as found in *Ant* 12: 138-144—states that the Seleucid king exempted the priests and the rest of the temple personnel from paying taxes and mentioned the government of Judea was to be in accordance with the ancestral laws. The extracts from a *Royal Edict* (*Ant* 12: 145-146)––a decree of Antiochus about the ritual purity of the temple—denote that no foreigners were allowed to enter the sanctuary in Jerusalem and keeping unclean animals in the city were prohibited. The *Hefzibah Inscription* preserves regulations of Antiochus III that aimed at protecting the inhabitants of villages from the excesses of Seleucid occupying forces. Seleucid soldiers were forbidden to have quarters in these villages or to drive the inhabitants out of their houses. It is even said that very strict penalties were imposed on those who break these regulations. (See, Y. H. Landau, "A Greek Inscription found near Hefziba" *Israel Exploration Journal* 16 (1966): 54-70.). Perhaps, Antiochus III was not just concerned to secure the sympathy of the leading groups in Jerusalem, but he also tried to win the favour of the rural agrarian in Galilee. See, Jagersma, *A History of Israel from Alexander the Great to Bar Kochba*, 39.

16 Hengel, *Jews, Greeks and Barbarians*, 46. As Antiochus III was not content with his victory over the Ptolemies and the conquest of Syria and Phoenicia, he was still eager to extend the Seleucid empire to the north and west. At the time when the Seleucid king had such high political aspirations, Rome had appeared as a new political power in the west. The Romans landed in Asia Minor, where in 190 B.C.E. they inflicted a major defeat on the troops of Antiochus III at Magnesia as reflected in Daniel 11: 18.

17 Noth, *History of Israel*, 351.

18 Hengel, *Judaism and Hellenism* I, 10f, 102f.

Defeat at the hands of Rome had shaken the Seleucid regime and encouraged national independence movements in the provinces ruled by the Seleucids. In what became a central factor in the crisis in Judea, the chronic warfare and extortion by the Romans left the imperial regimes, particularly the Seleucids, desperate for funds. Above all, under the rivalry of these two Greek empires, the imperial arrangement in Judea remained the same and the temple-state in Jerusalem continued to exist.[19]

1.1.2. Cultural and Economic Opportunities for the Elite Subalterns

The Ptolemaic rule was established in Judaea and Galilee during the reign of Ptolemy I Soter (323-283 B.C.E.) and Ptolemy II Philadelphus (283-246 B.C.E.).[20] It was successful largely because it involved the systematic management of land, founding of new *polis*,[21] and the introduction of systematic taxation.[22] It is evident that these brought opportunities for power, position and wealth for some 'to be rural elites.'[23] We must examine how the emerging rural elites were assimilated into the Hellenistic imperial political culture and economic opportunities. Based on archeological findings, Tcherikover argues that the Ptolemies divided the whole land into two categories: βασιλικήγη (royal land) and βασιλικοί γεωργοί ἐν ἀφεσει (land in relinquishment).[24] The "royal land" covered the largest part of the land; it was owned by the king and worked by free tenants, the royal cultivators under the strict supervision of royal officials.[25] Tcherikover suggests the latter one was further divided into γηκληρυχίαι (military occupied land), γηἐνδωρέα (land in gift), and γηἰδιοκτητος (private land).[26] Koester thinks that "the estates owned by the

---

19 F. L. Berquist, "Resistance and Accommodation in the Persian Empire" in *In the Shadow of Empire, Reclaiming the Bible as a History of Faithful Resistance*, ed. R. A. Horsley (Louisville/London: Westminster John Knox Press, 2008), 57.

20 Koester attributes the foundations for the reorganization of Egypt to Ptolemy I who established a Greek administration which took over the existing Egyptian native administrative system. Koester, *History, Culture and Religion of the Hellenistic Age*, 23.

21 J. S. Jeffers uses this word "*polis*" while maintaining the difference between polis established by the Greeks/Romans and Jews. He assumes the latter had resisted cultural inroads by the Greeks and Romans. See, *The Greco-Roman World of the New Testament Era: Exploring the Background of Early Christianity* (Downers Grove, Illinois: InterVarsity Press, 1999), 48-70. D. E. Gowan thinks that the "distinctiveness of Greek life" was to be found in the *polis*. See, *Bridge between the Testaments: A Reappraisal of Judaism from the Exile to the Birth of Christianity* (Pittsburgh: The Pickwick Press, 1976), 70-72.

22 Koester, *History, Culture, and Religion of the Hellenistic Age,* 53.

23 Horsley, *Jesus and the Spiral of Violence*, 9.

24 Tcherikover, *Mizraim IV-V*, ed. N. T. Reich (New York: G.E. Stechert, 1937), 42, 47.

25 Hengel, *Judaism and Hellenism*, 19.

26 Tcherikover, *Mizraim*, 47.

king were managed by royal officials who were directly responsible to the king."[27] The emperor was the sovereign power throughout the land. Behind the king were the Dioikētēs who were very instrumental in the establishment of the Ptolemaic rule. They were given the power to execute the entire possessions and financial matters of the king.[28] The royal officials were responsible for him and not to the people. He had at his command an army which gave him transcendent material power. We can envisage a very fine hierarchical structure in the governance of the Ptolemies, the village being the smallest unit. Between the smallest unit and the royal office were the military *stratēgos* which, as Hengel assumes, functioned as "the *oikonomos* for administration of finance and commerce."[29] As a whole, the Ptolemies took control of administration, while others exclusively took part in the lower ranks of the administration.[30]

How far had the Ptolemies attempted to introduce this system and succeeded in doing so to the subjugated Jewish people? Even though we have fewer details concerning Ptolemaic rule in Judea and Galilee, yet it appears that a similar system, less inflexibly applied, was in operation.[31] It is most likely that Judea and Galilee—along with Syria being conquered land—were the king's "direct possession and was worked by free tenants, the royal tenants under the strict supervision of the royal officials" as in Egypt.[32] S. Freyne believes that the Ptolemies demanded a rigid control by a centralised government.[33] The land was leased to tenants, to the highest bidder, and the crops to be grown were specified. By using this system, the Ptolemies could penetrate the Galilean hinterland which even Alexander the Great did not achieve.[34]

Tcherikover could count as many as thirty Greek cities established in the Jewish territories during the Hellenistic period.[35] Evidently, the Ptolemies adapted to local circumstances when they established their power in these areas. They used these new cities as military bases and the local "sheikhs"

27 Koester, *History, Culture and Religion of the Hellenistic Age*, 209.

28 Hengel, *Judaism and Hellenism*, 19.

29 Hengel, *Judaism and Hellenism*, 19.

30 Hengel, *Judaism and Hellenism*, 19.

31 Gowan, *Bridge between the Testaments*, 80.

32 Hengel, *Judaism and Hellenism*, 19. Koester argues that Syria and Palestine had not been fully subject to the strictly centralized administration of the Ptolemies. See. Koester, *History, Culture and Religion of the Hellenistic Age*, 209.

33 Freyne, *Galilee from Alexander the Great to Hadrian*, 28.

34 Cf. Freyne, *Galilee from Alexander the Great to Hadrian*, 30.

35 Tcherikover, *Hellenistic Civilization and the Jews*, 90-105.

as administrators to control upland areas.[36] The Greek cities were not merely ancient commercial relations by which the Hellenistic culture was spread into the world of the Jews, and they were also the basic instruments in the establishment of the Hellenistic political culture in the areas. The Ptolemaic establishment offered opportunities for power, position and wealth that soon assimilated into the dominant imperial culture. Toubias—a local sheikh in Amnon across the Jordan River—is the best illustration in this regard.[37] In Judea where such new cities were not yet established, the Hellenistic pattern of administration was still found in action. Josephus' report discloses that the collection of taxes was privatized, possibly to get the maximum revenues. This privatisation of the imperial tax collection probably had offered opportunities for the local elites to gain power and position. That is to say, the Ptolemies authorized the highest bidder to collect whatever that bidder required from the Jews, so long as the bidder remitted the required amount to the imperial treasury. Josephus advocates that the highest bidder for the area that included Judea was Joseph the Tobiad.[38]

The emergence of this new elite powerful class from the non-Jerusalem priestly aristocracy created conflict broadly at two levels: conflict between two rival aristocratic fractions on the one hand, and conflict between the urban elites and the subaltern masses on the other. We shall take up the first level in the second section. Much of the history of Hellenistic establishment in the Jewish territories could have been written in terms of conflict between these groups. Cries of the rural masses at what had happened due to the process of the hellenization could be a larger part of the Jewish history. The Zenon Papyri—our basic information of the earlier history of Ptolemaic regimes in Judea and Galilee[39]—are mostly official correspondences. Thus, hidden transcripts of the

---

36 Some scholars believe that Tobiah was the latest family that had intermarried with the high priestly family in Persian family times (Neh. 2: 10; 19; 6: 1-9; 13: 4-5).

37 Toubias is the principal personality among the Jews in Zenon Papyri. His name appears six times on various occasions. See, *C.P. Jud*, 115-118. See, Berquist, "Resistance and Accommodation in the Persian Empire," 57.

38 According to Josephus, Tobiad family flourished during the third quarter of the third-century B.C.E. Joseph—son of Tobiah by a sister of the high priest Onias—had become a key player in Jerusalem politics. Josephus denotes that Joseph outbid all the chief men and magistrates of the cities of Syria and Phoenicia for the tax-farming rights by offering to double the revenue (*Ant* 12: 154-236).

39 The Zenon Papyri mentions a certain Zeno—who was private secretary of Apollonios the *dioikētēs*, an important advisor to Ptolemy II who was in-charge of the treasury and overseeing significant parcels of land—made a tour of inspection to Palestine at about 261-258 B.C.E. (See, *Corpus Papyrorum Judaicarum* Vol. I, ed. V. A. Tcherikover and A. Fuks (Cambridge, Massachusetts: Harvard University Press, 1957), 115-116. M. Noth believes that "Apollonius owned all kinds of estates, some in Palestine and also in the area of the Jordan, which he had probably received in fief from his king Ptolemy II

powers were being discovered and these represented the imperial viewpoint. Besides, there are few references that are relevant to the analysis of Judea and Galilee.

1.1.3. The Imperial Regime's Practice of Backing Local Elites

We have seen the local elites and how they ruled cities so as to dominate and exploit economically the agrarian masses in the surrounding areas. We shall now consider how the empire backed these local elites for power. The Hellenistic regimes (*i.e.*, both Ptolemies and Seleucids) were dependent on the local aristocracies and urban elites for the maintenance of local and regional order and revenues.[40] For this purpose, the Ptolemies allowed the high priestly aristocracy in Jerusalem—that consolidated its power in Judea under the Persian Empire—to continue under their empire. To rule over the larger area of Phoenicia and Western Syria, the Ptolemies appointed a military governor. However, in the case of Judea, they did not continue the practice of Persia assigning the governor to supervise the political affairs. The high priesthood ran affairs in Judea. There is no historical evidence that the Ptolemies formally appointed or approved the high priesthood as the head of the temple-state to rule the territory. This, as Horsley denotes, perhaps makes the position of the high priesthood vulnerable and shaky before the local magnates.[41]

This emergence of the Toubias' family may have restricted the power of the high priestly aristocrats. They lost certain amount of their power and political significance. When Joseph the son of Toubias was granted the tax-farming rights to all Syria, the high priest in Jerusalem was ousted as the representative of Judea to the Ptolemies with regard to the imperial revenues. Joseph used his wealth to consolidate his power in Judea and beyond. He continued with his gifts to the imperial court. Joseph equipped all his sons with the knowledge of Greek language and culture by hiring the best teachers of his day. At the same time, it caused another aristocrat rising to power. Tax-farming by Joseph—no longer by the high priesthood—could have competed with the temple's and priesthood demands for tithes and offerings. The emergence of rival aristocratic fractions had far reaching impact that destined the future of Judea. Joseph, having the connection with the Hellenistic court, could have widely opened up the Hellenistic process at least in Judea.[42] Besides, we can

---

Philadelphus." Noth also assumes that "these estates were crown lands, which may well already have long been in royal possession." See Noth, *History of Israel*, 348.

40 Koester asserts that the Ptolemies and the Seleucids were not interfered with in the internal cultural and religious affairs of Jerusalem. See, *History, Culture and Religion of the Hellenistic Age*, 209.

41 Horsley, *Revolt of the Scribes*, 23.

42 Koester, *History, Culture and Religion of the Hellenistic Age*, 209-210.

expect the high priesthood to choose their traditional way of life.[43] In facing the challenge to their power from the emerging aristocratic power, they resorted to the teaching of the Law. Thus, they cultivated the "great tradition" in accordance with the elite practice. Previous scholars who interpreted the "Tobiad romance" have greeted Joseph as a paradigm of the young enterprising force who endeavoured to break through the constraints of their native land. For example, Hengel considered him as a powerful Judean who was "able to protect his countrymen from excessive exploitation." By contrast, Josephus portrays him as callously oppressive and cruelly fierce.

The Seleucid regime, which was in need of funds, backed the local elites who controlled the agrarian masses. The imperial regimes sent their military forces to suppress local insurrection as and when it arose. We can also expect that the presence of the military could have bolstered the local power holders.[44] Therefore, throughout the Hellenistic regimes, overt resistance of various forms; be it public demonstration or insurrection, were dangerous and frequently lethal. As opposition escalated to the transformation of Jerusalem into the Hellenistic city of Antioch, the Seleucid king sent his troops to suppress resistance.[45] When insurrection spread, Antiochus Epiphanes attacked the city again and left a garrison of troops to enforce the transformation of the city by the reforming aristocratic faction. He deplored imperial armies, a seemingly overwhelming force including war elephants, to suppress the revolt.

1.2. The Modein Resistance

As long as the Hellenistic reformation in Jerusalem was confined to the city, the rural masses had not paid serious attention. But when its impact was felt on them or the spread of reformation touched their feet, the agrarian communities could not be expected to remain silent. Some incidents of local resistance recorded in the Zenon Papyri seem to merit attention. Too much scholarly labour has been expended on the participants of peasant rebellion and too little on the shared values and goals which find expression through rebellion. We must focus more on why the peasants rebelled rather than learn from statistics of taxes, harvests, and hunger. In the context of the emerging elites as power and creating their own sub-culture in the new Hellenistic environment, we can safely say that the peasantry inherited a different way of understanding tradition of the Law and remained faithful to the same. Thus, they cultivated the "little tradition" that established the practices, beliefs and customs, while perhaps resisting that of rural elites. Biblical and classical scholars that do not

43 Koester, *History, Culture and Religion of the Hellenistic Age*, 210.

44 Horsley, *Jesus and the Powers*, 68.

45 Jerusalem was named "Antioch" after its sponsor Antiochus Epiphanes.

regard this subaltern political dimension into account are likely to misconstrue the meaning of peasant passivity.

In Zenon Papyri, we come across a certain Jeddous, a land owner in a Jewish village who was forcibly ejected from the village by Zeno's agent and the representative of the Ptolemaic administration, who were trying to collect a debt. The Letter from Alexandros to Oryas goes thus:

> [Alexan]dros to Oryas, greeting. I have received your letter, to which you added a copy of the letter written by Zenon to Jeddous saying that unless he gave the money to Straton, Zenon's man, we were to hand over his pledge to him (Straton). I happened to be unwell as a result of taking some medicine, so I sent a lad, a servant of mine, with Straton, and wrote a letter to Jeddous. When they returned they said that he had taken no notice of my letter, but had attacked them and thrown them out of the village. So I am writing to you [for your information].[46]

This aspect affirms that the tax farmers were entrusted with the collection of taxes in Jeddous' village. Since the tax farmers were usually "members of their population of the city or region where the taxes were raised,"[47] the tax famers ejected here were possibly from that village. It is also evident that the position of "tax farmer" was held by the most well-to-do. It is also apparent that a great deal of money was needed for it. A large amount of money was often given to the king as 'presents' and above all to officials to exclude rivals. Since, the income from the taxes did not benefit the concerned village, but the central authority in Alexandria (*Ant* 12:169), it could be that the villagers took that resistance measure.

The workers in Apollonius' great estate at *Bet 'Anat* protested against undue taxes and appealed to the minister. Moreover, we also read in Zenon Papyri that when two slaves were sold to Zeno by Idumaean *sheikhs* ran away, they refused to hand them back and asked for a further payment. All these rudimentary collection of information help us to see the agrarian anxiety and the rural resistance to the Ptolemaic economic policy imposed upon the Judeans and the Galileans alike. The resistance and interaction denoted here was taking a transnational character as Judeans, Galileans and Idumeans were found interacting. Though the people were heavily taxed by the imperial administration, it was the high priest in Jerusalem who handed over taxes to the Ptolemies. It was not clear whether the high priest served as a kind of tax

46 Quoted from *C.P. Jud.* I, 130 (PCZ 59018). The main personage is Jeddous, most possibly a Jews. Straton was a messenger of Zenon. A youth sent by Alexandro appeared before Jeddous in order to induce him to pay loan. But Jeddous paid no attention either to the letter of Alexandro or to the threat to seize his goods, and drove the officials out of the village. The place is not mentioned anywhere. What we do know with certainty is that the incident took place in a village.

47 Jagersma, *A History of Israel from Alexander the Great to Bar Kochba*, 25.

farmer nor not. The taxes earlier paid to the Persian rulers had now been shifted to the Ptolemies. Hengel supposes that the Ptolemaic rulers appointed a Judean temple official alongside the high priest to be responsible for financial matters in Judea and in the temple.[48] The existence of such officials and of tax farmers did a good deal to further collaboration with the Ptolemies in higher circles. At the same time, this produced much greater alienation between the priestly aristocrats and the rest of the population. Zenon Papyri mentions that Toubias sent gifts of rare animals, young slaves, and a eunuch to the Ptolemaic king.[49] Toubias knew how to play the Hellenistic game, including the importance of knowing Greek language and culture. This is a clear pointer that the Ptolemaic administration used the services of ambitious local power-holders to draw maximum revenues from its subject peoples.

Our sources are not strong enough to decide whether there were missionaries who lobbied for the Hellenistic reformation in the villages.[50] If there were, as Scott assumes, they would "find themselves in a poignant dilemma when they attempt to carry the message to the peasantry."[51] Any history of Jewish resistance that focused only on uprisings always concluded that the Ptolemaic regime was regarded to be a time of peace and quiet in Judea and Galilee. One must look into what Scott calls "modes of dissimulation" to see the resistance as it occurred in everyday life.

1.2.1. Modein Village: A Social Space for Dissident Sub-culture

Antiochus Epiphanes' violent repression of the Jewish resistance to the Hellenizing reform provoked more intensified forces of resistance. Most possibly, the rural agrarian communities in Judea were unable to organize an open revolt or armed resistance against such a powerful Seleucid empire. Yet, we still have seen well-directed and firm actions against invading Seleucid armies at the village of Modein. This suggests that there was a kind of resistance that was developed a long time back in Judean villages.[52] By using Scott's theory of "dissident sub-culture," we shall examine what occurred in the villages during Antiochus' violent repression.

The author of 1 Maccabees denotes Antiochus' fierce insistence of giving up one's own faith for the sake of the ideal, of oneness or unity, of his

48 Hengel, *Judaism and Hellenism*, 24.

49 A letter from Toubias to Apollonios reveals that on the request of Apollonios, Toubias sends the king some animals, probably rare ones. See *C.P. Jud.*, 128 (PCZ 59075).

50 For example, Zeno was the finance minister of Apollonious who made a tour on behalf of the Ptolemaic administration to Judea and Galilee in about 261-258 B.C.E.

51 Scott, *Decoding Subaltern Politics*, 7.

52 K. Jesurathnam opines that the Modein Revolt was not accidental, rather a reaction of long confrontation of the Hellenistic imperialism by various Jewish groups. See, "Maccabean Revolt and Dalit Revolution: Can They Intersect," *BTF* 41/1 (June 2009): 141.

whole kingdom: "Then the king wrote to his whole kingdom that all should give up their particular customs" (1 Macc 1:41).[53] This is an official decree of Antiochus. The author also mentions that "many even from Israel gladly adopted his religion" (1 Macc 1: 43).[54] H. M. Orlinsky suggests those who adopted Antiochus religion were the Judean upper class as they had gained and to continue to do so from the collaboration.[55] "Many people stood firm and resolved in their hearts not to eat unclean food they choose to die rather than to be defiled by food or to profane the holy covenant; and they did die" (1 Macc 1: 62; cf. 2 Macc 6: 18–7: 42).[56] This text assumes that the subaltern classes—most of them farmers, craftsmen, menial workers, petty merchants, and the like—having little or nothing to gain from the imperial regime stood firmly against them. Mattathias and his family were the best example in this regard. They mourned for Jerusalem by renting their garments and left the city for Modein (1 Macc 2: 14). The Jewish resistance had originated from material appropriation, but took shape in the context of religious humiliation that was motivated by material exploitation. Thus, we can safely say that the religious indignities were the seed bed of the anger, indignation, frustration that nurtured the resistance.

Violent suppression to their ancestral law created crisis for the Jews elsewhere. The temple ceased to be a place of religious centre. At this juncture, the villages in Galilee and Judea were sequestered sites that were off surveillance from the powerful and imperial powers. Modein—a village in Judea[57]—is illustrative of how a village could have provided the subjugated Jews with secure social space where they could freely exchange and elaborate their criticism. Modein had played a decisive role for the Jews in maintaining their

---

53 S. Zeitlin takes this verse as a command to "follow the Hellenistic way of life." See, *The Second Book of Maccabees,* trans. S. Tedesche (New York: Harper & Brothers, 1954), 75. W.O.E. Oesterley comments oneness in terms of religious practice. See, *The First Book of Maccabees* (Oxford: Clarendon Press, 1971), 70.

54 According to J. R. Bartlett's discussion, the motive of the action seems clear that the Hellenizing Jews wanted to remove Jewish exclusivism. See, *The First and Second Books of the Maccabees* (Cambridge: Cambridge University Press, 1973), 29.

55 Orlinsky, "Maccabees, Maccabean Revolt," 199; also Jesurathnam, "Maccabean Revolt and Dalit Revolution," 139.

56 This text implies the observation of ritual cleanliness was becoming very difficult. Bartlett, *The First and Second Books of the Maccabees*, 33; J. A. Goldstein, *I Maccabees: A New Translation with Introduction and Commentary*, AB 41 (New York: Doubleday, 1976), 227.

57 1Mac. 2:15 calls Modein a "town" whereas Josephus reads "village of Modai" (Gr. Μωδαῒν κώμην, see *Ant* 12: 268), following Josephus this research uses "village" to refer Modein. See also, Zeitlin, *The First Book of Maccabees*, 79; Goldstein, *I Maccabees*, 231.

religio-cultural identity and dignity.[58] Evidences suggest that people continued live according to their ancestral laws even under the Hellenistic reform attempt was at height in Jerusalem. Under such circumstances, practice of circumcision (1 Macc 1: 60-61), resolution "not eat unclean food," not to "profane the holy covenants" (1 Macc 1: 62),[59] strict observation Sabbath (1 Macc 2: 32-38), *etc.* are perhaps not simply ceremonial or ritualistic performance; rather they seem to become the hidden transcripts of the subjugated Jews. Our task is to sketch out the dynamics of the link between the hidden transcript and the experience of domination. This includes the unfolding of how coercive performance engenders resistance and the basic form that resistance takes.

1.2.2. Apocalypticism and Resistance

It is unlikely that the people of Modein were the learned and literate who were capable of resisting the Seleucid regime. It was a home of agrarian populace. Even though scribal tradition was of oriental origin, yet it mainly operated in *polis*.[60] Their hope in God could be the major source of inspiration of the people of Modein village to resist the forces of oppression. Apocalypticism might have played a decisive role in the Modein resistance.[61] The regular experiences of domination of the people in Modein village had determined the peasants to preserve their ancestral laws as the laws resisted the worst effect of domination and insisted on justice and dignity. They hoped for God's intervention in their political struggle to overcome the oppressive imperial or indigenous rulers.[62]

It is in this context that we re-consider Hengel's observation "... apocalyptic tendencies were recruited ... predominantly from the growing middle class of the city."[63] Modein became the location in which the "unspoken riposte, stifled anger, and bitten tongues created by the Seleucid domination found a vehement, full-throated expression."[64] When Jerusalem

58 On religio-cultural and political accents of the revolt, see Jesurathnam, "Maccabean Revolt and Dalit Revolution," 142-144.

59 For details on the translation of this verse, see Goldstein, *I Maccabees:* 227.

60 Hengel, *Judaism and Hellenism*, 19.

61 Koester discusses the origins of apocalyptic movement in Israel by highlighting the decisive role played by God. However, he fails to relate the movement with the experiences of the Jews as subjugated people. See, Koester, See, *History, Culture and Religion of the Hellenistic Age*, 230-234. Jagersma is convinced that the period from c. 165 B.C.E. was the "heyday of apocalyptic" writings. See, *A History of Israel from Alexander the Great to Bar Kochba*, 53.

62 R. A. Horsley, "Kingdom of God and the Renewal of Israel: Synoptic Gospels, Jesus Movements and Apocalypticism," in *The Origins of Apocalypticism in Judaism and Christianity*, ed. by J. J. Collins (New York, NY: Continuum, 1999), 305.

63 Hengel, *Judaism and Hellenism*, 53-54.

64 Scott, *Domination and the Arts of Resistance*, 120.

was established as a military colony and the sacred precincts of the temple and other areas in the city were profaned by the religious practices of the Syrian armies, villages in Judea like Modein had provided social sites for the faithful Jews to critique the oppressive powers beyond their reach. In fact, Modein became a social space for the development of a counter-ideology to the Seleucid elites.[65] Being the sequestered site for the Jews where the control, surveillance, and repression of Antiochus IV were least able to reach, the closed confidant groups shared similar experiences of domination that found expressions in folktales, dress, language, song, and religious expression. The Modein village—with the arrival of Seleucid officers to enforce the king's decree—was then under strict surveillance, and was considered the privileged site for the hidden transcript of the Jews. It was the site where protected speech, singing, religious enthusiasm, dreams of deliverance, schemes for escapes, plot of rebellion, *etc.* could be discussed in relative safety.[66] Biblical scholars termed this political discourse of the subaltern groups under surveillance as "apocalypticism."[67]

Recent Biblical scholars are of the opinion that one response to this crisis was an upsurge of the apocalypticism. Some of them have even proposed that Jewish literatures that were believed to be written during this period such as the Assumption of Moses, 1 Enoch 85-90, 92-105 and the Book of Daniel have been considered as resistance to the Seleucid persecution. Desperate to understand their seemingly impossible situation, some faithful Jews sought divine "revelation"—Gr. *apokalypsis*, hence the term "apocalyptic"—to explain their present reality and the plan that God might have to deliver them. There is nothing to doubt that this Seleucid imperial and suppressive rule had rendered an upsurge of apocalyptic literature.[68] However, one must go ahead with this assumption to ascertain where, who and under what circumstances apocalyptic literature came into existence.

However, the only sources we have are the literary products of the scribal class and not of the agrarian non-elites. The apocalyptic literature gives us clues to trace people who were knowledgeable in the ancestral traditions and who became involved in the resistance.[69] Socially, this group consisting of sages, teachers, scribes, *etc.* belonged to the middle class in the Jewish structure under the Seleucid empire, perhaps finding their place between the

65 Horsley, "Kingdom of God and the Renewal of Israel," 307.

66 These are similar to the prominent characteristics of apocalyptic literature proposed by Jagersma. See, *A History of Israel from Alexander the Great to Bar Kochba*, 53-56.

67 This study reads the apocalyptic texts as having stemmed from these groups of resistance to the Hellenistic empires.

68 Here, I do not negate Koester's insistence that the origins of apocalyptic thought predate the Hellenistic period. See, See, *History, Culture and Religion of the Hellenistic Age*, 231.

69 Horsley and Hanson, *Bandits, Prophets, and Messiahs*, 18.

priestly aristocracy and the peasantry. Nevertheless, the wider horizon of the context of the scribal middle class and its cultural and political productions are hardly noted. Central to our investigation is that the resistance of this middle class had taken shape, not in isolation but in close relation, to and on the back of the lower classes at practical and ideological levels.

1.2.3. Testing the Limits

The significance of Modein as social space for a dissident subculture is attested to by the strenuous efforts made by the Seleucid empire to abolish and penetrate the site; and the corresponding efforts by the people in Modein to defend it. The king's appointment of "inspectors over all the people and commanded the town of Judah to offer sacrifice, town to town" (1 Macc 1: 51) is the evidence for the vital importance of Modein as a social site generating the hidden transcript of non-elite Jews.[70] As the king's officers were enforcing the king's order, many of the people forsook the law, the faithful ones, however, were "drove into hiding in every place of refuge they had" (1 Macc 1: 52). It is in this context that the author of 1 Maccabees discusses the pagan worship that was refused by the people of Modein (1 Macc 2: 15-26).[71] 1 Maccabees assumes that the family of Mattathias was driven out from Jerusalem and found Modein as their refuge (2: 1-4). At the time when "the king's officers" arrived in Modein, they acknowledged Mattathias as a leader honoured by the people (1 Macc 2: 17). They tried to persuade Mattathias to be the first to do what the king commanded. He, and his sons had been offered royal status, *i.e.* "friends of king" and material blessings, *i.e.*, "silver and gold and many gifts" (1 Macc 2: 18) if they complied with the king's command.

The corresponding efforts by the people in Modein—which have been displayed in the speeches and actions of Mattathias and the faith practices of a "company of Hasideans"—are equally important for us to acknowledge. The voice of the Modein community, as represented in the speech of Mattathias declares:

> Even if all the nations that live under the rule of the king obey him, and have chosen to obey his commandments, everyone of them abandoning the religion of their ancestors, I and my sons and my brothers will continue to live by the covenant of our ancestors. Far be it from us to desert the law and the ordinances. We will not obey the king's words by turning aside from our religion to the right hand or to the left (1 Macc 2: 19-20).

---

70 The inspectors included the Athenian (2 Macc 6: 1). For Bartlett, people were asked to offer sacrifice "as a sign of their loyalty." See, *The First and Second Books of Maccabees*, 30.

71 It is unlikely that the people of Modein were a representation of the standpoint of the orthodox against that of the liberal Hellenizing manner in which scholars (e.g., Bartlett, *The First and Second Books of Maccabees*, 31) often tend to interpret this text.

Mattathias vehemently turned down the words of the king in this manner. His love for the ancestral laws and desire to live by them could not weigh down the royal status and material offers that had been provided by the king's officers. There was a dramatic moment when an unidentified Jew came forward to offer the sacrifice on the alter. This provoked Mattathias and killed him at the alter as well as the king's officer who was coercing them to sacrifice. Afterwards, Mattathias declared war against the Seleucid government and fled with his sons to the hills to fight the battle. Many people soon joined them in their hiding place (1 Macc 2: 23-26, 27).[72] We are not informed what exactly was the decisive factor that forced Mattathias and his sons to stage an open revolt against the Seleucids. However, we can assume that a dissident sub-culture had already been developed in Modein which could be one of the strongest reasons for the open revolt. Besides, the apocalyptic ideas could have been the factor that emboldened the priest family to settle in Modein.

1.2.4. The Modein Resistance as Peasant war

There are a few scholars who are concerned over the participation of the subaltern class in the Modein Resistance. For instances, E. Bickerman's book, *The God of the Maccabees* published in 1974 understands the revolt as peasant war.[73] K. Jesurathnam's "Maccabean Revolt and Dalit Revolution" (2009) is an academic investigation for intersection between the Modein Revolt and Dalit Revolt, the latter being the subaltern class in Indian society.[74] In pursuance of the trend set by these previous researchers, we shall look into the role and participation of the agrarian masses that lived in the village of Modein.

We must note that the Maccabean priestly family was not the first to resist the Seleucid aggression. The hidden transcript of the non-elites masses in Modein or elsewhere had been at work at ideological and practical levels to negate the Seleucid order. In this sense, the agrarian people in the villages were the first to resist the Seleucid domination, though their resistance might have taken covert form of resistance. In 1 Maccabees 2: 29-38, we come across a group of people "who were seeking righteousness and justice" and their response to Mattathias' appeal. They encamped themselves opposite to the camp of Seleucid military troops and prepared for battle against them.[75] As they refused to take action on the Sabbath day, the group died.[76] We cannot say

72 The Author of 1 Maccabees identifies their hideout as "hills" (v. 29). Bartlett suggests the "hills" to be those descending towards the Dead Sea. See, *The First and Second Books of the Maccabees*, 38.

73 E. Bickerman, *The God of the Maccabees* (Leiden: Brill, 1974), 90-91.

74 Jesurathnam, "Maccabean Revolt and Dalit Revolution," 135-154.

75 Bartlett, *The First and Second Books of the Maccabees*, 39.

76 It is said that many escaped and joined Mattathias to fight even on the Sabbath day. *Ant* 12: 6.

with certainty who these people were. E. R. Bevan proposes the presence of "roving bands" when he says, "If they did not flee and join the roving bands, wither conformed, which was probably the most common, or underwent martyrdom."[77] Though, Bevan does not explain who the 'roving bands' were, but it can be assumed that there existed already some un-organised groups, amongst the agrarian population, who were without clear principles of actions or leadership. When one such band, namely the Hasidim, had been overtaken on the Sabbath by a party from Jerusalem, they allowed themselves to be defeated without resistance.[78] It was when the Maccabean or Hasmonean family came forward that all had changed, thus the covert resistance burst out into that overt resistance. Bevan assumes, "they made a nucleus round which the scattered bands drew together, and they were strengthened by the adhesion of the Hasidim."[79] The first book of Maccabees mentions "a company of Hasideans" and refers to them as "might warriors of Israel, all who offered themselves willingly for the law" (2: 42).[80] This group of Hasideans joined Mattathias shortly after the beginning of the revolt and wanted to collaborate with the newly nominated high priest Alcimus (1 Macc. 7: 13; 2 Macc 14:6).[81]

Although the struggle is popularly known as Maccabean Revolt, after its leader, Judas "the Hammer (Maccabeus), the Maccabees or the Hasmonean family, were not its instigators or root causes, but only its actors.[82] Thus, in this study, we refer to the struggle as "Modein Revolt" after the name of the village where the resistance was launched. Moreover, the Maccabees or Hasmoneans were not the only group which played the greater part in the struggle, but the Hasideans are also a group which played a significant role during the struggle, even though it occurred later.[83] This fact also urges us to sort out alternate or inclusive terms to designate the struggle. Both in 1 Maccabees and Josephus, we are given the account of the manner in which more organised resistance groups came into operation. Mattathias resisted in the Modein village, the decree of Seleucid king to offer sacrifices in accordance with the

77 E. R. Bevan, *The House of Seleucus*, Vol. II (New York: Barnes & Noble, 1966), 174.

78 Bevan, *The House of Seleucus* II, 175.

79 Bevan, *The House of Seleucus* II, 175-176.

80 Bartlett opines that the Hasideans belonged to "the scribal class, the interpreters of the law." See, *The First and Second Books of the Maccabees*, 40.

81 Author of 2 Maccabees explicitly tells us that the Hasideans were "the warmongers and revolutionaries." See, Zeitlin, *The Second Book of Maccabees,* 229. For more details on Hasideans, Osterley, "The First Book of Maccabees," 73.

82 According to 1 Macc 2: 4, Simon was nick-named Μακκαβαῖος, i.e., "the hammer" or perhaps "hammer-like man." This nick-name, which was intended to mark him out as a dreaded and ready warrior, was given to Simon because of his military achievements. For details, North, *History of Israel*, 368.

83 Tcherikover, *Hellenistic civilization and the Jews*, 204-205.

royal command. When the other "people of Judah and those that are left in Jerusalem" (1 Macc 2: 18) had obeyed, the people in the Modein village had the courage to resist the powerful Hellenization. The struggle began not in Jerusalem but in the village of Modein. Jagersma rightly observes that the old conflict between the rich class in Jerusalem and the rural agrarian population had broken out fiercely.[84] As discussed earlier, people like Joseph the Tobiad—great landlords in rural areas—preferred to comfortably settle in Jerusalem. The cost of their rich life-style, as H. Kippenberg observes, was passed on to the rural agrarian population.[85] It is not surprising to see the peasants of Modein village whose leaders belonged to the lower priestly class to take the decisive role in the uprising. Obviously, the priests in rural areas were closer to the ordinary peasants, while the powerful priestly families in Jerusalem had allied themselves to the rich aristocracy there.[86]

1.3. The Post Modein Resistance Era

The Jewish history of the post Modein resistance era is largely characterised by the emergence of groups or parties. Interestingly, two groups *viz*. the Essenes and the Pharisees had developed as opposing groups to the Hasmonean powerful elites. There is a growing tendency among the recent scholars to assert that the missing "religious aspect" in the restoration of the new Judea is fundamental to the emergence of groups. Koester claims that the goal of the Hasmonean regime is political rather than religious. He asserts: "to enlarge the power of the Jewish state, and to make all inhabitants of the country Jewish subjects."[87] In a more specific manner, Horsley and Hanson argue, "What had begun as a Judean peasant revolt, guerrilla warfare against Seleucid armies, ended not in the final establishment of the reign of God, but simply in the establishment of new dynasty of high priests."[88]

However, when we realize that the Modein Resistance was a combined effort of various groups, we can expect these various groups to emerge divergently. 1 Maccabees 2: 42 reads, "Then there united with them a company of Hasideans, mighty warriors of Israel, all who offered themselves willingly for the law." The book of Jubilee, which in its context clearly refers to the Modein Resistance, also denotes this, thus:

> And they shall strive one with another, the young with the old … the poor with the rich, the lowly with the great, and the beggar with the prince, on account of the law and the covenant … And they shall stand

84 Jagersma, *A History of Israel from Alexander the Great to Bar Kochba*, 58.

85 As cited in Jagersma, *A History of Israel from Alexander the Great to Bar Kochba*, 58.

86 Jagersma, *A History of Israel from Alexander the Great to Bar Kochba*, 58.

87 Koester, *History, Culture and Religion of the Hellenistic Age,* 218.

88 Horsley & Hanson, *Bandits, Prophets, and Messiahs*, 22.

> (with bows and) swords and war to turn them back in the way; but they shall not return until much blood has been shed on the earth, one by another (Jub 23: 19ff.).

It must be recalled that those who participated in the Modein Resistance were the priestly family, Mattathias with his five sons, the Hasideans, and probably the "wise" who recently migrated to Modein for refuge, and the agrarian masses who made Modein their home for many generations. Even though these groups came together in a national movement or revolution, yet they had their own causes, interests, and understandings.[89] One cannot understand the meaning of Modein Resistance and the aftermath history without considering the differences within the fighting groups. We shall discuss some of the significant events that had taken place after the revolt as it would give better insight to understand the realities of the peoples.

1.3.1. Establishment of Hasmonean Dynasty

For Simon, the priest and his sons, the goal of the revolt was "to liberate the temple, the city of Jerusalem and land from imperial abominations" which was a possible divergent from that of the villagers.[90] The goal of the revolt was accomplished when Judas defeated the three Seleucid generals sent against him at Emmaus. Peace was restored and the Jews regained complete freedom of worship, and the temple was rededicated in 165 B.C.E. The victory was a combined effort of the priestly family of Mattathias, who were also called the Hasmoneans, the Hasideans – the religious pious, and the peasant community in Modein. Our sources do tell us as to what extent the latter groups were actively involved or not at all in the aftermath struggle. But for sure, the Maccabees did not cease to fight as they found that some Jews were maltreated in some places and Syrian troops were still housed in the fortified citadel in Jerusalem. Above all, Mattathias and his family were of Jerusalem origins, and had migrated to Modein for refuge. They would have committed themselves to strive for the complete independence of the temple state, and not only strive for religious freedom of worship. Thus, the Maccabees continued to struggle under the leadership of Judas who died in 161 B.C.E. and his brother Jonathan mainly by attacking the Syrian armies and resisting the spread of Hellenization.[91] As time passed by, the Seleucid rule in Antioch in Syria was also weakening. It could not afford to support the pro-Seleucid high priests in Jerusalem against popular disapproval. This increased the prestige of the

---

89 My point of reference here is Scott, *Decoding Subaltern Politics*, 4.

90 Koester, See, *History, Culture and Religion of the Hellenistic Age*, 218.

91 Koester alleges Jonathan to "take advantage of the continuing dynastic wars in Syria and the shift of power on the international scene from the Greek kingdoms to Rome." See, *History, Culture and Religion of the Hellenistic Age*, 215.

Hasmonean family and their adherents. The Hasmonean dynasty can be said to have had its beginnings when Jonathan allowed himself to be appointed high priest of Jerusalem. When Jonathan was captured in 143 B.C.E. by a Syrian pretender, he was succeeded by his brother Simon Maccabeus as a captain and high priest. Simon continued with the fortifications which Jonathan had started in Jerusalem. For the final victory, Simon had to overcome the Syrian citadel in Jerusalem and to demand for Jewish freedom (1 Macc 13: 33-52). In 141 B.C.E., Simon was given the title of governor and the right of hereditary succession by his own people (1 Macc 14: 41-49).

1.3.2. Emergence of Various Parties

Even though the Hasmonean rulers could politically establish their kingdom to the extent of the Jewish culture territory, they still had many miles to go in search of a new community. Modern postcolonial theorists like Davidson and E.W. Said have seriously debated about secondary resistance after the period of primary resistance to make possible the establishment of new and independent states.[92] This supposition, to a great extent, finds relevance when the Hasmonean dynasty was established. After the period of Modein resistance—literally fighting against imperial religious-cultural intrusion—there came the secondary period largely in terms of ideological resistance when the pious Jews made efforts to restore the Jewish community that was shattered by the Hellenistic forces. In the post Modein Resistance era, some of the pious Jews might have longed for the utopian community which had been conceived in the Torah. Intellectuals, prophets, leaders and historians of the resistance could have a great role to play in such an endeavour. Some of them might have offered apocalyptic promises—for example, rejecting the temple state and any contract with the others—but all of them responded to the humiliations of Seleucid-Hellenism and resorted to the basic teachings of the Law in order to find an ideological basis for the community that they aimed for.[93] It is evident that as the Hasmonean regime consolidated its rule, the dominant priestly family had moved away from the original goal of the Modein resistance.

Modern scholars have questioned whether the term "Hasideans" or "Hasidim" used in some of our sources refer generally to those who remained actively devoted to the law, or more precisely to a primarily scribal or priestly group or party, who provided leadership in the Modein struggle and

92 B. Davidson, *Africa in Modern History: The Search for a New Society* (London: Allen Lane, 1978), 155; E.W. Said, *Culture and Imperialism* (New York: A.A. Koft, 1993).

93 I am indebted to the insight of Said, see "Resistance, Opposition and Representation," 95. On the fulfillment of the apocalyptic hopes and sectarian groups, see Koester, See, *History, Culture and Religion of the Hellenistic Age*, 234.

produced apocalyptic literature.[94] Decidedly, the Hasideans took part in the Modein resistance while aiming to preserve the Torah for the basis of their living. The author of I Maccabees pointed out that their reputation spread as 'mighty warriors of Israel' (I Macc 2: 42). As they could have not gained this coveted title overnight, it is possible that they were in existence even before the rise of the Modein Resistance and that they would already have existed as a party. I Maccabees 7:12-13 may suggest the inclusion of "a group of scribes" amongst the Hasideans. These groups were brought together during the Modein Resistance. We must, however, note their distinctiveness within them. Josephus mentions three groups emerging in the period of secondary resistance, such as: the Sadducees, the Essenes and the Pharisees. We shall analyze them as products of as well as responses to the crisis caused by political subjugation.[95]

1.3.2.1. The Sadducees

Considering their economic well-being and less or possibly non-interest in the Law, the origins of the Sadducees must be traced back apart from the Hasideans. The Hasmonean conquests of previously non-Jewish Palestine had furnished the opportunity for the enrichment of new leaders from powerful families. The military commanders collected booty and plunder which made them economically powerful. For the landowners, there was a lot of opportunity to expand their holdings. Indeed, new families found places in the temple-state hierarchy. Around Hyrcanus and his successors there emerged a new aristocracy of wealth and affluence, comprising of the new higher priestly families, high military officers, and large landowners.[96] Thus, within a generation or two of the Modein resistance against aristocratically-led Hellenization, there emerged the same class distinctions between the wealthy aristocracy and the agrarian masses and the former dominated the latter.

1.3.2.2. The Essene in Qumran

It now becomes clear that the group known in the ancient sources as the Essenes was the same community living in Qumran.[97] Their writings—the

---

94 J. J. Collins, *The Apocalyptic Vision of the Book of Daniel*, HSM 16 (Missoula: Scholars, 1977), 201-205; G.W.E. Nickelsburg, "Social Aspects of Palestinian Jewish Apocalypticism" in *Apocalypticism in the Mediterranean World and the Near East*, ed. D. Hellholm (Tubingen: Mohr, 1983), 61-54.

95 Horsley, *Jesus and the Spiral of Violence*, 16.

96 Koester, See, *History, Culture and Religion of the Hellenistic Age*, 228-229.

97 The Essenes are known through the reports of Philo (*Quod omn. prob. lib.* 75-91), Josephus (*War*. 2: 119-161, etc.) and the Hippolytus (*Refutatio* 9: 18-28, as well as through passing remarks in Plinny and Dio Chrysostom.

Dead Sea Scrolls—were discovered at Qumran. Perhaps the most common and satisfactory reconstruction of the origins of the Qumran community is that, in direct reaction to the illegitimate assumption of the high priesthood by the Hasmoneans, the Hasideans withdrew in large numbers into the wilderness by the Dead Sea to continue their disciplined preparation for the advent of the kingdom of God.[98] As discussed earlier, the Hasideans not only fought the guerrilla warfare against the Seleucid armies during the Modein Revolt, they were part and parcel of the dissident sub-culture which was developed in the village of Modein. Ideologically, they wanted to regain the Jewish freedom from the Seleucid domination. In the conviction that the theocracy and their sacred traditions were to be restored, they fought guerrilla warfare. As we have discussed earlier, many of them lost the lives at the hands of the Seleucid armies as they refused to fight on the Sabbath day in keeping with their sacred traditions. The priesthood had always been occupied by the Zadokite. This legitimate succession had been broken during the Hellenistic reform in Jerusalem. The Hasmoneans were a priestly family, but not Zadokites.[99] Thus, when Jonathan accepted the appointment to the high priesthood, and when Simon had himself been proclaimed to be the high priest by a national assembly, many among the Hasideans would have been disillusioned. Compounding their illegitimate concept of the high priesthood, the despotic rule of the Hasmoneans must have appeared to be a mere return to the problematic past rather than the advent of the true kingdom of God that many may have been anticipating from the apocalyptic visions. It is likely that the castigations of the "Wicket Priest" in Qumran literature are directed against the Hasmonean Jonathan or Simon.

The Hasideans, especially those who had hoped for the establishment of the kingdom of God under Zadokite priesthood, lost their hopes. They separated themselves from the rest of Judean society. They organized an ideal priestly theocracy in exile, a "true Israel" headed by the only "legitimate" priesthood. Led by their "Righteous Teacher," they abandoned Jerusalem and established a utopian, ascetic community beside the Dead Sea. With their apocalyptic convictions intensified by new revelations to the Righteous Teacher, they believed that they were called by God, in the words of the ancient prophecy of Isaiah: "In the wilderness prepare the way of the Lord" (40:3). The Essenes in Qumran passed the message that the idea of the ancient, Jewish resistance was not merely a reaction to powers, but rather it was an alternative way of conceiving human history in God's way.

---

98 Koester, *History, Culture and Religion of the Hellenistic Age*, 235.

99 Scholars like E. P. Sanders argue that their successful revolt against the Seleucids made the Hasmoneans rise to power. See, *The Historical Figure of Jesus* (London: The Penguin Press, 1993), 25.

1.3.2.3. The Pharisees

It is almost impossible to reach any conclusion with regard to the origin of Pharisaism from the standpoint of the historical sources available to us. Judging from Josephus' personal account of an event (*Ant* 13: 288-296), the Pharisees were already in existence at least as a trend or party under John Hyrcanus I (135-104 B.C.) along with the Sadducees.[100] Josephus portrays them as "one of the Jewish schools" (*Ant* 13: 288), without explaining what school it was. At any rate, the historical existence of the Pharisees can be linked to the consolidation of political and religious power by the Hasmoneans. Positively, we see the Pharisees unlike the Essence, pulled away from the separatist nationalism towards a more integrative view of human community. They organised themselves into a religio-political group and operated within the structure of post Modein Revolt Jewish society. The sentence in Josephus' report—"so great is their influence with the masses that even when they speak against a king or high priest, they immediately gain credence" (*Ant* 13: 288b)—is suggestive of the fact that the Pharisees were a resisting group which gained acceptance among the masses, regularly engaged in defying the powers which included the Hasmonean elites (*Ant* 13: 288). Why, and for what they spoke against the Hasmonean powers needs to be spelt out.

It is evident that the Hasideans continued to struggle to live the Law in the post Modein resistance socio-political scenario. Most possibly, their main aim could have been that of bringing the Law more effectively to realization in Judean society. Even if their hope for the kingdom of God was as not intense as those of the Essenes in Qumran, the Pharisaic hope focused upon the imminence of the final realization of the kingdom of God. While the Essenes sought a radical and absolutely rigorous realization of the law of God in an utopian community constituted by only a remnant of Israel, the Pharisees sought to have the Torah rule in the life of society at large. Unlike the Zadokites of Qumran and their followers, the Pharisaic party was less dominated by priestly elements. They were fully committed to the Mosaic Law as the rule for the people of Israel. In order to achieve such a goal, the Law had to be interpreted and applied to the socio-economic, and religious life of the people. According to Josephus, they practised the highest ideals both in their way of living and in their discourse (*Ant* 18: 15). Thus, the Pharisees did the work of the scribes.

As they struggled for justice and peace based on the idea of applying the Law in everyday life, the Pharisees also advocated a strong concern for the legitimacy of the priesthood. They seem to have viewed the religious policy of the Hasmoneans with ever-growing reservations. When Hyrcanus I begged the Pharisees to correct him if he went wrong or strayed way from the Law, all the Pharisees testified him virtuous except one by the name Eleazar who

100 H. F. Weiss, "φαρισαῖσος" *TDNT* 9 (1974): 13.

frankly told him that he was an illegitimate high priest. Eleazar, as Josephus quoted him, says, "If you wish to be righteous, give up the high-priesthood and be content with governing the people" (*Ant* 13: 291). Eleazar told Hyrcanus I that his hierocratic leadership was not legitimate as his mother was "a captive in the reign of Antiochus Epiphanes" (*Ant* 13: 291-292). Even if this allegation was baseless, as Josephus argues (*Ant* 13: 292), from the side of the Pharisees, the hierocratic leadership is illegitimate; thus, the Law was not fulfilled. The Pharisees wanted to limit the power of Hyrcanus within the political sphere and to give up the high priesthood. The Pharisees accepted the Hasmoneans as political leaders who were to rule over Judea. Their proposal cut the Pharisees off from the Hasmoneans. In this way, the trend developed into a resistance movement within the structure of the Jerusalem temple-state as early as the reign of Hyrcanus who came to power in 134 B.C.E.[101] Their goal was to replace the illegitimate Hasmonean dynasty with an Aaronite or Zadokite high-priestly family.

It is evident that Hyrcanus I was able to secure his government against all resisting groups. Hyrcanus I turned to the old state-supporting party of the Sadducees, the wealthy priestly nobility.[102] Instead of relinquishing the office of the high priest, Hyrcanus broke alliance with the Pharisees. Hyrcanus invalidated the regulations which they had established for the society and he allied himself with the newly formed aristocratic party of Sadducees. This does not mean that Hyrcanus replaced the Jewish law with the Hellenistic legal and political forms. Rather, the Pharisaic interpretation of the law was made invalid. This did not serve as the solution because the Pharisees did not cease in their demand for a legitimate priest as the supreme expression of fulfillment of the Law.[103] Rather, this reversal in internal policy under Hyrcanus I had ushered in a new situation. On the one hand, the break between the Hasmoneans and the Pharisees gave rise to a new aristocracy in Jerusalem. On the hand, it had generated a social situation for resistance. This same event may also have given rise to the formation of the Sadducees as an association that was opposed to the Pharisees. Instead, the Sadducees established the Law alone as the basis of the societal life. The Torah, without the elaborate interpretation and application, was accepted. The Pharisees turned to the people for support since the daily life of the peasantry and urban commoners was based on the Law as interpreted, and the interpretation had been in the hands of the Pharisees. The Sadducees continued in favour and power with the Hasmoneans through the reign of Alexander Jannaeus (104-76 B.C.E.). Open conflict came during the reign of Alexander Jannaeus, who became the high priest after the short rule of

101 Weiss, "φαρισαῖος," 23.

102 Schäfer, "The Hellenistic and Maccabean Periods," 598.

103 Weiss, "φαρισαῖος," 23.

his brother Aristobulus I (104 B.C.E.). He continued the imperialistic policies of his father until 78 B.C.E. Josephus reports that the people threw lemons at the king while he was officiating as high priest during the feast of tabernacles. Under the second successor of Hyrcanus I, Alexander Jonathan-Jannal (103-76) B.C.E, there was civil war for 6 years (93-88 BCE) and the Pharisees became the declared enemies.

1.3.3. Galilee Came Back Under Jerusalem Rule

One of the major contributions of the establishment of Hasmonean and its territorial policy which is extremely significant to the Gospel study is the inclusion of Galilee under Jerusalem jurisdiction.[104] John Hyrcanus and his sons extended Hasmonean rule over the Samaritans to the north, the Idumeans to the south, and finally, in 104 B.C.E., over the Galileans. As the Hasmonean dynasty was established in Judea, their rulers still strived for the extension of the power towards south, east and north of Judea. Among the Hasmonean rulers, John Hyrcanus I (135/34–104 B.C.E.) and his second successor, Alexander Jannaeus (104-76 B.C.E.) were the prominent ones in the pursuance of the territorial expansion policy. Hyrcanus I invaded Transjordan and conquered an important city; Medeba on the Via Regis.[105] Josephus reports that Hyrcanus conquered Idumea with its district capital Marisa (*Ant* 13: 255-258). Here, Hyrcanus I compelled the Idumeans to be circumcised and to observe Jewish laws. More decisively, Hyrcanus subjugated the Samaritans and destroyed their temple on Mount Gerizim (*Ant* 13: 255-258).[106] Consequently, the Hasmonean kingdom was extended to the former boundaries of the Davidic kingdom.

Hyrcanus I was succeeded by Aristobulus I who was regarded as a friend of the Hellenists (*Ant* 13: 318).[107] During his short reign that lasted only for a couple of years (*i.e.* 104-103 B.C.E.), Aristobulus I conquered the greater part of Iturea which included the northern part of Galilee. It is possible that the descendants of the old population of Israel would still have been living there.

---

104 Freyne, *Galilee*, 42.

105 G. Horowitz, "Concerning the Conquest of John Hyrcanus in Moab and the Identity of Samaga," *Eretz-Israel* 15 (1981): 353-355. Medeba is well known and often mentioned in the Old Testament (e.g. Num. 21: 30; Josh. 13: 9). G. Fuks denotes that Scythopolis was possibly occupied in the time of Hyrcanus. See his article, "The Jews of Hellenistic and Roman Scythopolis," *JJS* 33 (1982): 407ff.

106 It is generally supposed that the destruction of the temple of Mount Gerizim by John Hycanus I, (ca. 128 B.C.E.) was an expression of Jewish hostility to the Samaritans, perhaps even the cause of the Jewish-Samaritan "schism." Recently, S. Schwartz argues that there is no evidence for any deterioration in Judean-Samaritan relations until the first century C.E. See, S. Schwartz, "John Hyrcanus I's Destruction of the Gerizim Temple and Judaean-Samaritan Relations" *Jewish History* 7/1 (1993).

107 Aristobulus I was the eldest son and successor of Hyrcanus. He was the first Hasmonean to officially assume the title of king (*Ant* 13: 301; *War* 1: 70).

Subjection of the Galileans and others to the Jerusalem temple-state and the "great tradition" of the Judeans did not mean that they were integrated to the Judean *ethnos*. Even though Greek writers and Roman officials most often refer to the territories under the Hasmonean rule simply as Judea, Josephus, a Judean history, never mixes up the territories. Horsley puts it, "Josephus makes clear distinctions between the Galileans and Idumeans and Judeans as separate *ethnoi* or peoples."[108] Since many of the Galileans were the descendants of Israelites, they would have many things in common. They worshipped the same God and shared the early Israelite traditions. However, in terms of a separation of the northern kingdom and southern kingdom as well as political differences, Galileans would have found the "great tradition" of the Judeans significantly different from their own "little traditions." Horsley highlights the possible differences between the two traditions, thus:

> The "laws of the Judeans" articulated the interests of the temple-state, including demands for tithes, offerings, and other dues to sustain the central institutions of Temple and priesthood. Galilean customs and traditions expressed and guided the life of village communities, with emphasis on local reciprocity and the preservation of all families on their ancestral inheritance of land that formed the basis of their subsistence and place in the village community.[109]

1.3.4. The Jews under Roman Domination

The Roman domination of Judaea and Galilee began with violent conquest followed by a prolonged period of devastating power struggles. Control of the regions was fought for by forces in the Hasmonean fractions, the Parthian empire to the east, and rival factions in the Roman civil war then raging in the Eastern Mediterranean as well as in Italy. As far as the history of Judea and Galilee is concerned, Pompey's conquest of the territories in 63 B.C.E. is decisive. Since then the territories were continuously under Roman regime.[110] The Judeans and Galileans suffered the highly oppressive rule of Herod and his sons, as well as the direct rule by governors of the colonial empire. For the agrarian communities in rural Judaea and Galilee, Roman colonialism meant unusually heavy taxation. Indeed, it was a serious threat to their very existence as many were alienated from their land. With regard to resistance

---

108 R. A. Horsley, *Archeology, History and Society in Galilee: The Social Context of Jesus and the Rabbis* (Valley Forge, Pennsylvania: Trinity Press International, 1996), 27.

109 Horsley, *Archeology, History and Society in Galilee*, 28.

110 R. M. Kallet-Marx discusses how Roman warlords took the decisive decision to expand and consolidate their power in the Eastern Mediterranean in the early to mid-first century (*i.e.* 148-62 B.C.E.). See, *Hegemony to Empire: The Development of the Roman Imperium in the East from 148-62 B.C.* (Berkeley: University of California Press, 1995), 291-344.

or protest movements, the period is framed by large-scale agrarian uprisings: the outburst following the death of Herod in 4 B.C.E. and the massive revolt against Rome in 66-74 C.E. Between these two uprisings, there were a number of protests and resistances.

1.4. Summary

The above discussion indicates that the Jewish society, inclusive of former Israelites, was very complex and highly stratified. The composition of the society included priestly aristocrats, Sadducees, and Pharisees, Essenes, and peasant masses. These distinctive groups cannot in any sense be expected to have a similar degree of resistance or even acceptance to the domination. Each social movement has a location in the social structure and the revolutionary potential of certain classes must be examined historically. Any research on resistance must identify the sociopolitical location of the actions under discussion. Modern Biblical scholarship has focused mainly upon the structure and policies of the imperialists and the role played by the dominant priestly aristocracy and the educated middle class in resisting or restoring the imperial domination. Hence, the initiatives on the part of the rural peasantry in resisting the Hellenistic and Roman powers as well as their local allies have been noticed by very few scholars only.

The author of I Maccabees (2: 15ff) portrays the picture that Mattathias' refusal to obey the king's command and the killing of another Judean who was prepared to do so marked the beginning of the Modein Resistance (cf. *Ant*. 12: 268ff). The same author denotes that Judas "the Hammer," the third of five sons eventually emerged as the leader of the resisting forces. However, we must take into consideration the dissident sub-culture which villagers in Modein had developed as already initiated into a kind of resistance below the radar. Perhaps, the priest family was part of the dissident sub-culture. I and II Maccabees—whose final redaction took place in c.100 B.C.E.—have a polemical character that aims to justify the high priesthood of the Hasmonean. The portrayal of the villagers and their priestly leaders as choosing to fight and even to die rather than to abandon their tradition must also be understood within power differential. Whose tradition it was, became debatable, was it the "great tradition" cultivated by the urban priests or the little "tradition" cultivated by the rural folk? Another group who fought the battle was the Hasideans. The group suffered massacre on a Sabbath because its members refused to offer any resistance on that day (1 Macc 2: 33-38; *Ant* 12: 274).[111] Thousands of resisters were organized into a fighting force in which Mattathias and his sons took significant part. The history of the ancient Jews had been deeply rooted

111 As a result of this, the Modein forces decided from then on to fight on the Sabbath, if they were attacked (1 Macc. 2: 41; *Ant*. 12: 276). It is likely that the surviving Hasidaeans took side of the Modein force in the revolt to further boost the movement.

in protest and resistance. Beginning in 168-167 B.C.E. from a village called Modein, the Judeans had successfully rebelled against the Hellenistic empire of the Seleucid regime in Syria and against their own rulers. This seems to pose confusion over the question of who carried over the original tradition of resistance amongst the ancient authors and their modern interpreters. Our aim here is to analyse afresh the protests and revolts during the Roman-Herodian period by distinguishing the "great tradition" and the "little tradition" proposed by Scott. This helps us to appreciate the agrarian elements embedded in our historical sources and read the protests and revolts during the Roman-Herodian period from the viewpoint of rural communities. It helps us to perceive how the "little tradition" stands against the "great tradition" in the history of the Jewish resistance movement.

Peasants of various space and time, as D. K. Singha Roy (2004) observes, have always "borne the brunt of extreme forms of subordination and oppression in society first by being members of the lower strata of the social and economic hierarchy."[112] Peasants are always portrayed as occupying a lower position in the political structure of the society. In the Jewish context, as the Gospels denote, peasantry represents a vast body of the socially deprived peoples, such as: landless agriculture labourers, sharecroppers, tenants, poor artisans and small and marginal cultivators (*e.g.* Mat 20: 1-16; 21: 28-32; Mk1-12; Lk 19: 11-27, *etc.*). In spite of the fact that the peasant societies in Judea and Galilee had undergone rapid transformation under Hellenistic and Roman rule, their social and economic oppression and domination by the powers assumingly continued unabated in one form or the other. Moreover, modern Biblical historiography confuses the agrarian resistance as a mere by-product of the initiative of the dominant social groups, such as: Pharisees, Sadducees, Essenes, in the course of the anti-imperialist struggles. Notably, the struggles of the Jewish peasantry of Hellenistic-Roman period had a history prior to the advent of the initiatives of the dominant social groups. Ostensibly, they had continued to move in a parallel direction throughout the Hellenistic and Roman regime, and at times as a part of a stream of a national movement which flowed especially under the leadership of Hasmonean priests. It is these movements which provided the Jewish peasantries a social and political identity. Agrarian movements in the Jewish history were, however, not episodic. They underwent a process of transformation along with the broad social, economic and political transformation of the whole society. It is important that we propose, against this agrarian and complex context, a conceptual framework for approaching the agrarian resistance.

---

112 Singha Roy, *Peasant Movements in Post-colonial*, 1.

2. The Domination and Resistance in the Herodian-Roman Period

We have discussed the socio-political, economic and religious backgrounds of Judea and Galilee during the Roman regime. We shall now deliberate upon the repeated protests and resistance that the Jews had mounted against the Romans and their client-rulers, *i.e.*, the Herodian kings and Jerusalem high priests. As it has been indicated earlier, Rome was the "terrifying and dreadful exceedingly strong" beast as foreseen by Daniel. Given the socio-political, economic and religious milieu of Judea and Galilee under Roman rule, the resistance movements might have happened in response to the domination of various forms by the powers mentioned earlier. That is to say, the domination and resistance are nuanced products of the contexts in which they evolved. Therefore, we shall consider and analyze them as relational and not separable into distinct categories or levels.[113] This is important because most of the previous studies on the Jewish resistance, including the most recent ones, have been carried out without taking the prevailing domination seriously as the scholars have usually examined resistance as a separate entity having its own category. Some scholars have even discussed the resistance movements and the actors or agencies simply by categorizing them into violent and non-violent resistance.[114] These approaches are likely to ignore the theological significance of our supposition that domination and resistance are relational.

This study stresses upon the premise that protests and resistance in Judea and Galilee were possibly the measures to various forms of domination taken by the people. Actors or agents in the movements of resistance will be analyzed according to the domination they assumed to encounter. Given that there is plurality within the actors or agents conditioned by the socio-political milieu, it is necessary to re-examine the resistance movements in the light of the forms of domination which they resisted. Among the bandits, some of them might have presumably taken material and status domination as their main targets while the others might have engaged with ideology. Such is the likely case in

113 Turner and Caouette, "Shifting Fields of Rural Resistance in Southeast Asia," 9.

114 For instance, scholars like Horsley (1987) and Crossan (1991) have divided aspects according to the typology of violence. Crossan divides the agents or actors accordingly to the source of violence. For Crossan, there are three types of people: those who acted without human violence (*e.g.* protesters and magicians), those who avoided human effort and depended on divine violence (*e.g.* millennial prophets) and those who combined both human and divine, e.g. Bandits and Messiahs. See, Crossan, *The Historical Jesus*, 124-136, 137-167, 168-204. In their illustrious discourse on popular movements at the time of Jesus, Horsley and Hanson (1985) have proposed three types of popular movements led by bandits, prophets, and messiahs. This work can also be categorized as a study of actors or agents resistance in its entity. Horsley convincingly divides the first-century trajectories of peasant unrest into two: protest and resistance and open revolt. They were products of institutionalized injustice and repression respectively. See, *Jesus and the Spiral of Violence,* 28-58.

the movements that was led by the prophets and messiahs. Therefore, we must attempt to understand what those actors or agents of resistance movements had done in the light of the nature of the domination that had been inflicted by the Romans and their client rulers.

Assuming domination and resistance as a single entity provides us more issues to address. As far as the history of Judea and Galilee during the Herodian-Roman rule is concerned, the domination and resistance is variedly characterized by plurality of levels and forms. This plurality urges us to fairly handle and deal with each of the resistance movements as a measure to a particular form of domination inflicted upon the Jewish agrarian communities by the imperial powers. For this task, Scott has provided us with an alternative framework in order to consider the domination at three levels: status domination, material domination and ideological domination.[115] Besides, the vital question—who dominates as well as resists what?—must be the centre of our discussion. Again, we must also sincerely look into the issue of sociopolitical divisions based on classes and regions as to how far they were responsible for domination and resistance. The chief divisions in Judea and Galilee during the Roman-Herodian period were perhaps between the imperial powers and their client-rulers (*i.e.* Romans, Herodians, and Priestly aristocrats) on the one hand, and the ordinary people (*i.e.* peasants and populace in city and towns) on the other hand.[116] The regional differences between Jerusalem and Galilee must also be maintained as responsible factors creating sites for domination and resistance.[117] It is hoped that the insight about the sociopolitical divisions sheds enough light to advance towards a deeper understanding of the domination and resistance in Judea and Galilee regarding the Roman-Herodian period and that it will better equip us to decipher as to how the people of lower status speak truth to power.

2.1. Resistance to Status Domination

Much of Jewish history regarding the protests and resistance movements during the Herodian-Roman period involved status domination. Indeed, they were aimed at resisting humiliation, insults or assaults on the religious dignity that they enjoyed as the covenantal people of God. We must note that status domination in the context of the first century C.E. Judea and Galilee should not be taken at individual terms but rather it is more collective. The collective aspect must be taken into consideration and should be discussed within the arena of their religious reality. K. Marx's statement that argues "*religious* distress is at the same time the *expression* of real distresses and the *protest*

115 Scott, *Domination and the Arts of Resistance*, 198.

116 Horsley, *Jesus and Empire*, 59-61.

117 On geopolitical conflicts, see Myers, *Binding the Strong Man*, 53-54.

against real distress"[118] is illustrative of how significant religion is for the Jews in their struggle for justice. Religious tenets, such as: the scriptures, temple and festivals, *etc*. were far more than what we think of today as "religious."[119] The Torah contains their fundamental rights and history as a nation. The Passover is not simply a celebration of the annual event; rather it is the celebration of a principal event by which God had given them freedom from oppression. Likewise, the Temple in a Jerusalem can be seen as not only as a worship centre, but also as their parliament house. It is, therefore, not so surprising to see tensions caused by the imperial presence occurring around these religious tenets. This may help us to better understand the embarrassing reports about insults and assaults on the dignity of the Jews within the religious arenas in our historical sources. Key to our investigation is that the Jewish protest and resistance struggles targeted took shape in the context of status domination of the various forms that were not in isolation but in close relation to religious symbols, beliefs and practices.

2.1.1 Open Desecration of the Roman Status Symbols

Against any forces that put down their status, subaltern classes used to make an "assertion of worth" in public by various ways and means. One form of public assertion that appeared time and again in the history of the Jews during the Roman imperial period is the open desecration of the Roman symbols that were erected in public places.

2.1.1.1. The Insurrection on Roman Golden Eagle

One of the most notable incidents that occurred during the life time of Herod is the tearing down of Herod's Golden Eagle that was erected over a portal of the Temple (*War* 1: 648-655; *Ant* 17: 149-167).[120] Josephus calls this incident "an insurrection of the populace" (*War* 1: 648). Given that the erection of Golden Eagle at the gate of the temple entails an imperial hegemonic agenda, this incident requires a deeper investigation within a broader context of Herod's building projects as a whole. Herod's building projects could be seen as a massive display of hierarchy and power. The projects could be seen as "public transcripts" of the ruling groups. Rebuilding of the Temple recounts Herod's public interactions with the people creatively designed to justify his regime. Recognition of this aspect is highly significant towards our chief historical source, *i.e*., Josephus, is biased while favouring the Roman regime over the

---

118 Quoted from *Marx and Engels on Religion*, introduced by R. Nieburh (New York: Schocken Books, 1964), 41.

119 Horsley, *Jesus and the Spiral of Violence*, 34.

120 Myers rightly observes that confrontations between Roman power and Jewish popular resistance always take the form of 'symbolic' actions. Myers, *Binding the Strong Man*, 57.

claims of resistant groups.[121] Furthermore, Herod did not confine his projects within the Jewish areas. He had numerous constructions even in the non-Jewish cities. Josephus denotes that Herod's building projects in the non-Jewish cities were mostly in honour of the Roman emperor (*Ant* 15: 280ff). The king also donated temples and public buildings in Athens, Sparta, Rhodes, and other Greek cities. The case of the Temple in Jerusalem is quite different. It was not possible for Herod to dedicate the Temple to Caesar or any other Roman powerful elites. However, Herod used symbols and architectural designs to depict the superiority of Rome. Thus, the architectural designs of Herod's theatre and Amphitheatre in Jerusalem are said to have been aliened to Jewish customs (*Ant* 15: 267-268). Josephus criticizes the king for "departing from the native customs and through foreign practices gradually corrupted the ancient way of life" (*Ant* 15: 267). Most obviously, the building projects were an embodiment of the hegemony and power of the Romans. We are not certain whether Herod erected the Golden Eagle in the other buildings as well, but the temple did have the Golden Eagle at the main entrance which signified the hegemonic symbol.

In the course of justifying his principle of political injustice through which he came to power, Herod made himself vulnerable to criticism perhaps at least to the pious Jews. Inasmuch as Herod claimed that his massive building projects performed valuable social, cultural and religious functions of the powerful elites, the subaltern classes in the Jewish communities opened themselves to attack the failure to perform the functions adequately. For the Torah forbade setting up of any images or making of dedications in the likeness of any creature. Josephus links the erection of the Golden Eagle as a violation of the Jewish sacred tradition. He explicitly states that Herod's action was done "in defiance of their law" (*War* 2: 650). Josephus adds, "For the king had erected over the great gate of the Temple, as a votive offering and at a great cost, a great golden eagle" (*Ant* 17: 151). The public exhibition of the object (*i.e.* the Golden Eagle) at the temple's main gate was a constant visible reminder for the Jews that they were a subjugated people.[122] As Josephus' report seemingly indicates, the concern about Herod's violation of the Torah's provisions clearly is not new. The Jews had already approached Herod on this matter. The report of the king's declining health, however, provided the occasion for a bolder expression of the same concern. "This was the fitting moment to avenge God's honour and to pull down those structures which had been erected in defiance

121 This view is well supported by recent scholars. For instance, R. Fenn, *The Death of Herod: An Essay in the Sociology of Religion* (Cambridge: Cambridge University Press, 1992), 59.

122 Horsley seems to consider the eagle as symbol of Jewish subjugation to Rome. See, *Jesus and the Spiral of Violence*, 76; *Jesus and the Powers*, 73-74.

of their ancestral law" (*War* 1: 649). Thus, the "insurrection of the populace" was launched and received strong support from the masses.

The protest was initiated by δύο σοφισταὶ ("two sages/doctors") of the Jewish law and their students (*War* 1: 648a). The two teachers—Judas, son of Sapphoraeus and Matthias, son of Margalus—are described by Josephus as "two doctors with a reputation as profound experts in the laws of their country, who consequently enjoyed the highest esteem of the whole nation" (*War* 1: 649b). One must assume that the most learned and recognized interpreters of the Law were no other than the Pharisees.[123] Josephus suggests that these two experts were working with, and for the masses. "Their lectures on the laws were attended by a large youthful audience, and day after day they drew together quite an army of men in their prime" (*War* 1: 649). So, the teachers exhorted their disciples to cut down the Golden Eagle from the Temple.[124]

The experts and their students appear to have undertaken the protest out of a dual motivation. They acted primarily in resistance against domination in order to maintain their ancestral law (*Ant* 17: 152; *War* 1: 650). Such a bold act and commitment could be expected only from those who loved and followed their ancestral law. It could also be observed that the actors could be the victimised people of the domination whose status had been sidelined under the power of money and hierarchy. Josephus reports that there was a demonstration at the time of the funeral of Herod, wherein the above mentioned martyrs were mourned as victims of Herod's oppressive and violent rule. Josephus' narrative reads:

> Towards evening, however, a large number of those who were bent on revolution assembled on the same spot, and, now that the public mourning for the king was ended, began a lamentation on their own account, bewailing the fate of those whom Herod had punished for cutting down the golden eagle from the gate of the Temple (*War* 2:6).

Like the earlier martyrs (Dan 12; 2 Macc 7), these two scholars and their students had acted out the bold action in the confidence that God would vindicate them.[125] This demonstration expanded into a small rebellion against Archelaus, but the king put down the rebellion with certain difficult measures (*War* 2: 3ff).

123 Horsley, *Jesus and Spiral of Violence*, 71.

124 Horsley advocates that their action reverberated with wide 'demonstration value' in Jerusalem into the chaotic period of Herod's death and its aftermath." See, *Jesus and the Powers*, 73.

125 Horsley, *Jesus and Powers*, 74.

2.1.1.2. Pilate's Iconic Standards in Jerusalem

A more provocative incident occurred when Pontius Pilate was sent by Tiberius as procurator to Judea.[126] Normally, the previous Roman governors appeared to have taken into consideration the special sensitivities of the Jews about their sociopolitical, cultural and religious status as the covenantal people of God. Against this practice, Pilate brought iconic standards, with their images of Roman emperors. Josephus reports that Pilate sent a company of troops into Jerusalem carrying their standards with the images of their gods on them (*War* 2: 169; *Ant*. 18. 55). The Romans often forced their subjects to acknowledge or worship the army standards, and it was seen as a means of humiliation.

Of all people subjected by the Romans, the Jews would surely have been the ones who were most insulted by the Roman army standards. For the Jews, this action was a subjugation of their God to the Roman gods and it was regarded as a blatant violation the Torah. As Josephus indicates, the Jews considered "their laws to have been trampled underfoot" (War 2: 170b). Thus, large numbers of "townspeople" and "the countryfolk" flocked together (War 2: 170b).[127] The mobs implored Pilate to remove the standards from Jerusalem. Obviously, this assault to the Torah led to an impressive demonstration by crowds from the city and villages at the governor's residence in Caesarea.

"When Pilate refused," Horsley comments, "they fell prostrate around his house and for five whole days and nights remained motionless in that position."[128] Crossan aptly refers to the protest as a "sit-down strike."[129] This was a public protest directed towards Pilate who provoked the Jews by his anti-Jewish action. If it persisted longer, it could have been turned into a severe violent resistance; however, Pilate finally relented. In this remarkably and disciplined mass demonstration, the Jewish protesters had demonstrated their love of and commitment to the Torah that have been the covenantal principle upholding their status as the people of Yahweh.

2.1.1.3. Caligula's Statue in the Temple

In a far more massive and prolonged protest in *ca*. C.E. 39-41, Galilean peasants generated a widespread peasant strike against another Roman provocation. Angered that Jews in Alexandria had not given him the same divine honors as the other subject people, the then new Emperor Gaius (Caligula) ordered his legate in Syria to set up his image in the Jerusalem Temple. If the Judeans resisted, "he was to subdue them by force of arms." Petronius advanced as far

126 Crossan believes that this incident must have happened in the winter of C.E. 26-27 soon after Pilate was appointed governor of Judaea. See, *The Historical Jesus*, 129.

127 Horsley, *Jesus and the Spiral of Violence*, 99.

128 Horsley, *Jesus and the Spiral of Violence*, 99.

129 Crossan, *The Historical Jesus*, 129.

as the city of Ptolemais on the coast west of Galilee with two legions of the Roman troop to prepare the military mission into Judaea. A large number of people came to protest the imminent action. Josephus denotes:

> The Jews assembled with their wives and children in the plain of Ptolemais and implored Petronius to have regard first for the laws of their fathers, and next for themselves. Yielding so far to this vast multitude and their entreaties, he left the statues and his troops at Ptolemais and advanced into Galilee, where he summoned the people, with all persons of distinction, to Tiberias (*War* 2: 192).

This resistance is certainly agrarian in nature. Crossan renders it as "carefully planned activism of the peasantry,"[130] whereas for Horsley, it was a "peasant strike, at least in Galilee."[131] The peasants refused to plant their fields and sustain the strike for weeks. As the nervous high-ranking advisers to Agrippa I—the newly appointed Herodian ruler of Galilee—pointed out, unless the peasants strike ended, there would be no crops later that year, hence there would be no payment of tribute to Romans. Perhaps Agrippa I himself could be the person affected most. The result of Gaius' order and the peasant resistance would inevitably be "a harvest of banditry" (*Ant* 18: 261-274). Petronius was persuaded to defy his emperor. But Gaius's death in C.E. 41 saved him from his suicidal assignment. More significantly, it also saved Galilee and Judaea from what would surely have become a revolt.

2.1.2. Public Assertion of Sanctity of the Temple and Authority of the Torah

For the Jews, their scared scriptures were far more than simply religious. Even under Roman imperial rule, the Jewish society had the authority to govern its internal affairs according to the Torah. Josephus mentions at least two incidents in which the Jewish took stern action against assaults on the Torah by the Romans.

2.1.2.1. Roman Soldier's Indecency in the Temple

Josephus reports that the above incident would have occurred when Alexander was succeeded by Cumanus as the Roman governor.[132] Under Cumanus's regime, an uprising broke out, causing large loss of Jewish lives (*War* 2: 223).[133] Josephus specifies that this incident took place when the crowd gathered to

---

130 Crossan, *The Historical Jesus*, 133.

131 Horsley, "The Zealots, Their Origins, Relationships and Importance in the Jewish Revolt," *NTS* 28 (1986): 39.

132 Cumanus was a governor during 48–52 C.E.

133 Myers considers the violent clashes under Cumanus as "cycle of revenge." See, *Binding the Strong Man*, 57.

celebrate the Passover at Jerusalem (*War* 2: 224). The Roman governor was under the apprehension that the presence of such a huge crowd might stage a platform for uprising. So, he deployed a company of armed soldiers to stand and watch on the roof of the portico of the Temple. Why was the Cumanus the Roman administration anxious about uprising during the Passover? The reason becomes clear once we place the celebration of the Passover in the context of political struggles. The Jewish nation which enjoyed full sovereignty under God's rule was no longer a free nation. In actuality, the celebration of the Passover remained the celebration of liberation in religious fantasy.[134] Horsley denotes, "celebration [of the Passover] had become the last line of defense of their human dignity" for the Jews of Jesus' time.[135] E. P. Sanders mentions that the Roman officials were sensitive enough to public assemblies and kept Jerusalem under military surveillance during celebration of the Jewish major festivals to prevent the huge crowds from political activities.[136] It is evident that the Passover had become a "politically charged occasion" for a religiously sanctioned open resistance.[137]

On such an occasion when even the slightest provocation could evoke explicit protest by the mob, one of the Roman soldiers on duty exposed himself by raising his robe and stooped in an indecent attitude.[138] His gesture was an indecent assault for the Jews who no longer had actual freedom and the celebration of liberation had become the defense of their human dignity.[139] Thus, when the soldier on the Temple porticoes exposed himself to the multitude below, the crowd exploded in protest. During the late C.E. 40s the Jews were hit by severe drought and famine.[140] Considering that they experienced extreme economic hardship, Horsley suspects that the protesting crowds were a combination of the rural folk and the urban poor who were very sensitive to any assaults on their religious celebration.[141] So, the Jews could not take it lightly. This was not only an offense committed against the religious sensitivities of the people of God but rather, it was a blasphemy against God.

The crowd directed their enraged outcry at the governor. Apparently, their action or demand was not a revolutionary. According to Josephus, the

134 Horsley, *Jesus and the Spiral of Violence*, 34-35

135 Horsley, *Jesus and the Spiral of Violence*, 35.

136 Sanders, *The Historical Figure of Jesus,* 23.

137 Scott, *Domination and the Arts of Resistance*, 207.

138 Horsley, *Jesus and the Spiral of Violence*, 35

139 Horsley, *Jesus and the Spiral of Violence*, 35.

140 Takatemjen, *The Banquet Is Ready: Rich and Poor in the Parables of Luke* (Delhi: ISPCK, 2003), 30.

141 Horsley, *Jesus and the Spiral of Violence*, 97.

multitude requested Cumanus to punish the soldier. It must be noted that the protesters did not challenge Cumanus' power or his political system. Their challenge was directed towards the insult. When Cumanus failed to take action against the soldier and the protest intensified, there was an attempt to oust the governor. So, the governor quickly resorted to violent suppression (*War* 2: 226). Many people lost their lives and the festival was turned into mourning for the whole nation.

2.1.2.2. Roman Soldier's Disrespect for the Torah scroll

"This calamity was followed by other disorders, originating with brigands," says Josephus (*War* 2: 228). He, further, tells us that the incident took place at "public road leading up to Bethoron" (*War* 2: 228). This could possible a village about twelve miles northwest of Jerusalem. The space, given in both literary and geographical terms, assumes that this incident is closely linked to the one that preceded one in both time and theme. Since this incident involved brigands, we shall discuss them in detail later. For the time being, what is of interest here is: the Roman disrespect for the Torah and the reaction of the rural masses in the protest against the insulting action. Crossan suggests that "the incident took place during punitive reprisals against villages about a dozen miles northwest of Jerusalem."[142] When some brigands attacked an imperial slave and robbed his baggage, Cumanus sent troops on a punitive expedition around their neighbouring villages.[143] The governor ordered the soldiers on patrol to "bring up the inhabitants to him chains" for not having pursued the bandits. In the course of this operation, one Roman soldier destroyed a Torah scroll that was kept in one of the villages by tearing it off into pieces and throwing them into the fire.

On hearing about the incident, not only the inhabitants of the particular village but the whole country were aroused in anger. Here, Josephus draws our attention to note the vital role that religion played in protest. He writes, "Their religion acting like some instrument to draw them together" (*War* 2: 230c). Even at the first announcement of the news, the multitude hurried to Cumanus at Caesar. They implored him not to leave unpunished the author of such an outrage on God and on their law. As with the previous protest against the indecent insult in the Temple, this protest over the destruction of the Torah was a spontaneous and widespread outcry by the common people. We find no apparent involvement on the part of any high-priestly aristocrats. However, when compared with the previous protest, the present protest was much disciplined. It does not mean that the protesters were less serious in their demonstration than the preceding one. Josephus says, "For, they said,

142 Crossan, *The Historical Jesus*, 134.

143 Roskam, *The Purpose of Mark*, 120-121.

they could not endure to live, since their ancestral code was thus wantonly insulted" (*Ant* 20: 116). Josephus, however, makes no comment on how long the protest lasted. Since there was no continuing protest reported, we can safely conclude that Cumanus, in contrast to the previous protest, gave the protesters satisfaction to their demand by executing the culprit. This incident clearly exemplifies that the Jews were very sensitive regarding matters that involved disrespect or insult to their religious status.

2.1.2.3. Prophetic Campaigns: The Politics of Disguise and Anonymity

Aside from public assertion of worth, the agrarian Jews evidently mounted covert resistance while taking the form of disguised or infra-politics. Our assumption here is that when open protest like the previous ones was not possible, the protest took a different form which had a similar goal. Scott argues that disguised resistance is "the silent partner of a loud form of public resistance."[144] There are times when the Jews could not firmly and openly stand up to defend their status against the hegemonic forces. This happened especially when the Jews were put under the direct rule of Rome. Geographically speaking, the Jews could be situated in this kind of situation when—following the death of Agrippa I in C.E. 44—the Jewish areas were re-constituted as a province who were directly ruled by Rome through the procurators. In such a political scenario, we can assume that the masses of the Jewish populace continued to struggle with assaults or insults upon their status.

However, the subalterns in Judea and Galilee moved their struggles against the Roman domination while crossing the borders of their regions. As they moved their struggle against domination beyond the confines of their sequestered sites into public, Scott denotes that "a politics of disguise and anonymity" had taken place. Some of the significant principle modes of the politics of anonymity, according to Scott, are symbolism, rumor, and creation of an autonomous social space for assertion of dignity.[145] The popular prophetic movements that emerged during the mid-first century C.E. could fit in this category.[146] The protest movements led by the "Samaritan," Theudas and the "Egyptian" in Judea which involved large number of peasants will be analyzed here.

2.1.2.4. The Samaritan Prophet

According to Josephus, there was a resistance movement among the Samaritans during the time of Pontius Pilate (*Ant* 18: 85-87). Yet it differs from other

144 Scott, *Domination and the Arts of Resistance*, 199.

145 Scott, *Domination and the Arts of Resistance*, 198.

146 Myers, *Binding the Strong Man*, 61.

movements in Judea in that—at least according to Josephus—it bears clear military traits and led to an armed revolt. The leader of this movement, whom Josephus calls the "Samaritan" gathered his followers on Mount Gerizim and promised them that he would display there the "holy vessels" buried by Moses.[147] Myers proposes that "this was a symbolic articulation of Samaritan secession from the Jerusalem temple-based order, into which Samaritan had been unwillingly incorporated since the time of the Maccabees."[148] This resistance was put down by the Romans.

2.1.2.5. Theudas

According to Josephus, Theudas appeared during the time of the procurator Cuspius Fadus.[149] Josephus accords him two designations: γόης and προφήτης (*Ant* 20: 97-98). The term γόης refers to a sorcerer, wizard, or impostor.[150] In addition to this, Josephus tells us that Theudas persuaded the majority of the masses to take their possessions and follow him to the Jordan and witness the river which parted at his command (*Ant* 20: 97). Fadus acted decisively upon this movement by sending "a squadron of cavalry" to prevent Theudas from proceeding further. Many of the people who followed him were taken prisoners and Theudas was beheaded (*Ant* 20: 98-99). At a superficial level, as portrayed by Josephus, Theudas was a false prophet who "deceived many" (*Ant* 20: 98).

However, Theudas is also mentioned in Acts 5: 36, though chronologically out of order, being placed before Judas the Galilean (Acts 5: 37). Yet, it is notable that Luke, the writer of Acts places Theudas with this armed resistance fighter, who was the founder of the so-called Fourth Philosophy. Theudas should not be simply rated as "non-violent movement" as some scholars denote.[151] So, unlike Josephus who depicts Theudas to be a false prophet, Luke pictures him as a leader who led peasants to take their right for liberation. In both Acts and Josephus, Theudas' movement involves a large numbers of peasant masses. Theudas' promise to the people—to separate the Jordan River—moreover, implies the crossing of the river to enter into the Promised Land as it happened under the leadership of Joshua (Jos 3). Theudas reasserted

---

147 Craig believes that this Samaritan uprising was in connection with the Samaritan hope for the emergence of the *Teheb* ("restorer") as prophesied in Deut. 18: 15-18). See, *Jesus and His Contemporaries*, 74.

148 Myers, *Binding the Strong Man*, 61.

149 There was apolitical development in Judea after the death of Agrippa I in C.E. 44. Judea became a province of the Roman Empire governed by procurators and Cuspius Fadus was the first procurator.

150 Feldman, *Josephus*, 97, especially footnote b.

151 For instance, Sanders, *The Historical Figure of Jesus,* 30.

that the Israelites were a free nation in covenant with God.[152] He called the people out so that they would symbolically re-cross the Jordan and to re-enter into the land promised by God.[153] With his symbolic action, Theudas attempted to attack the socio-political order on its very ideological basis that had betrayed the peasant masses. Furthermore, according to Josephus, the followers of Theudas were supposed to take all their possessions with them. Arguably, this is a clear pointer that Theudas had in mind a communitarian or egalitarian society that shared all their possessions. Theudas' ideology was meant to reassert the notion of Israel sovereignty as a chosen people and to preserve a sense of Israel's communitarian identity which was distinct from the social practices of the imperial cultures, and to promote the notion that life and the land were gifts of God, which the people must share with God and with each other. His strategy—calling people back to the Jordan River and to part the river at his command—was done in order to make people re-experience the past and to reclaim the same for the present.

One aspect that Josephus greatly emphasizes upon is the decisive action that Fadus had promptly taken. Fadus acted decisively when Theudas led a large following to the Jordan River, where, he claimed, he would part the waters. The Roman procurator sent his cavalry to put the movement to an end. Some of the crowd were killed and captured and Theudas was executed. It must be questioned as to what prompted Fadus to take such military action against what seems to be a mere religious phenomenon? There is a suspicious political motive behind Fadus' action. It must be recalled that Fadus was the first Roman procurator when Judea was constituted as a province of the Roman Empire in C.E. 44.[154] Fadus attempted to place the vestments of the high priest in Roman custody as they had been before the time of Agrippa I, but Jewish protest prevented this. Though there is no clear evidence, yet it is likely that Theudas was part of the protest group and possibly from a subaltern section.

2.1.2.6. The Egyptian Prophet

A similar movement was that of the "Egyptian" in the time of the procurator Felix, who is likewise mentioned by Josephus (*War* 2: 262ff; *Ant.* 20: 169 ff.) and also appears in the New Testament (cf. Acts 21: 38). Most probably, this unnamed Egyptian was a Jew who came from Egypt to Jerusalem and announced himself as a prophet. He was accompanied by a gigantic crowd that followed him in a roundabout manner through the wilderness to the Mount of Olives, and wanted them to bring down the walls of Jerusalem at his command. There are two important things that can be perceived from this movement. On

152 Craig, *Jesus and His Contemporaries*, 74.

153 Myers, *Binding the Strong Man*, 61.

154 Jagersma, *A History of Israel from Alexander the Great to Bar Kochba*, 131.

the one hand, the story recalls the exodus event; on the other hand, it was a resistance movement that was created by the mobilization of the masses. This movement, according to Josephus, was countered by the Roman troops who wiped out the movement and the people themselves.[155] Why did such counter-resistance arise against this? Josephus presupposes that the Egyptian, as like the Maccabeus, wanted to enter Jerusalem, overpower the garrison on the temple mount, and exalted himself as ruler of the people (*War* 2). This reveals that the Egyptian, at the ideological level, had in mind a new ruler for the masses.[156] This corresponds to the fact that in Acts 21: 38 the Egyptian is characterized as one who stirred up a revolt with four thousand "assassins."

These three prophets operated variedly in a different space and time. The movements led by Theudas and the Egyptian were dated mid-century in Judea, whereas the movement led by the Samaritan was dated earlier in Mount Gerizim in Samaria. In both, the movements led by Theudas and the Egyptian involved large numbers of peasants, and the movements led by the Samaritan involved an armed insurgent group. What is common to these movements is the remarkable collective anticipation of divine deliverance. These groups were all powerless and they moved their struggle against ideological domination much beyond their confines. As their struggles moved out of their confines, they became public movements. Thus, the form of their resistance took the "politics of disguise and anonymity" to shield either the meaning or their identity. Recent New Testament scholars have variedly labelled these movements as apocalypticism. Their leaders are called the "sign prophets"[157] or the "action prophets"[158] because they promised to perform symbolic acts that heralded liberation.

2.1.2.7. Summary

These sizeable protests against the provocative Roman actions that touched them are clear indicators of the intractable conflict between the Roman imperial rule and the subject peoples. Although the Judean and Galilean peasantries were powerless against overwhelming Roman military might, they nevertheless mounted sustained demonstrations to insist upon their status being maintained though their covenantal way of life.

155 Myers, *Binding the Strong Man*, 62.

156 Evans, *Jesus and His Contemporaries*, 76.

157 P. W. Barnett, "The Jewish Sign Prophets – A.D. 40-70: Their Intentions and Origins," *NTS* 27 (1980-81): 679-697.

158 Myers, *Binding the Strong Man*, 61-62.

2.2. Resistance to Ideological Domination

The ancient Romans were known for their conquest and victory over other nations. In reading the history of domination and resistance in the Roman period, one must be watchful to see what were the underlying ideologies and strategies of the Romans behind their conquest and victory. Carter highlights a set of ideologies and ideas that expressed and legitimated Rome's empire and power, when he writes:

> The gods have chosen Rome. Rome and its emperor are agents of the god's rule, will, and presence among human beings. Rome manifests the god's blessings–security, peace, justice, faithfulness, fertility–among those that submit to Rome's rule.[159]

We must be critical about the Roman imperial ideologies as they evidently clashed with that of the subalterns in Galilee and Judea. Undoubtedly, some scholars have blindly reaffirmed that the Roman ideological motive behind the conquest was in terms of God's ordained justice, peace and development for the spreading of the good news of Christ. Only a handful of recent historians have broadened our understanding of the attitudes, policies, and practices by which the *Pax Romana* was engineered. We must be skeptical about the ideology or ideologies by which the Roman imperial order was established and maintained. Central to our investigation is the assumption that Roman imperialism created sites for resistance including the belief that Jesus ministered to the rural Galileans who lived under the Roman ideological structures.

The assumption cited above urges us to re-read the ancient texts to see if the Roman imperialistic ideology had generated any counter-ideology that negated the Romans. Some of the historical incidents led by the revolutionary leaders are indicative of the fact that the Jewish peasants developed counter-ideological strategies to the Roman hegemonic ideology. Josephus—our chief historical source for the Herodian-Roman period—is, however, biased and tending to denigrate the agents of resistance in the line as deceivers, impostors and brigands. To quote,

> And so Judaea was filled with brigandage. Anyone might make himself a king as the head of a band of rebels whom he felt in with, and then would press on to the destruction of the community, causing trouble to few Romans and then only to a small degree but bringing the greatest slaughter upon their own people (*Ant* 17: 285).

To what extent the uprisings which the revolutionary leaders led were in a strict sense regarded to be resistance with an ideology is a difficult question to answer. In spite of Josephus' pejorative assessment, several of these aspirants in all probability were counter-ideological movements whose goal was the

159 Carter, *The Roman Empire and the New Testament*, 83. Arrangement is mine.

liberation of Israel. Various popular Jewish resistances during the Herodian-Roman regime led by bandits, prophets, and messiahs will be discussed from this viewpoint.

2.2.1. Public Counter-Ideologies to Roman Ideology

Much of those movements of protest and resistance that have already been discussed under the overt resistance to status domination can be partially public counter-ideologies as they propagated the fundamental Jewish faith and doctrine over and against that of the Romans. In this instance, we shall see some individual figures[160]—who were at the same time the heroes of the subaltern classes—to ascertain how far these heroes negated the ruling ideology. There were a number of sociopolitical and religious phenomena in the Roman-Herodian period that are interpretative of ideological reactions which are reflective of the socio-economic and religio-political disorder brought about by the order of the Roman rule in Judea and Galilee.

2.2.1.1. Simon of Perea: A Former Royal Servant

Simon was an opportunist who arose after Herod's death. Josephus depicts him as a handsome man of great size and strength (*Ant* 17: 273-276; *War* 2: 57-59). This is a natural charismatic gift that lifted him to claim the power.[161] Simon's claim to kingship was even noted by Tacitus (*Hist* 5: 9). Perambulating the country with the brigands whom he had collected, he burnt down the royal palace at Jericho and many other stately mansions. Such incendiaries provided him an easy opportunity for plunder. He attacked the royal palace in Jericho and plundered and took away things that had been kept there. Josephus denotes that Simon also set fire to many other royal residences in many parts of the country (*Ant* 17: 274). No house of any respectability would have escaped the flames, had not Gratus, the commander of the royal infantry, with the archers of Trachnitis and the finest troops of the Sebastenians, gone out to encounter this rascal (*War* 2.57-59; *Ant* 17.273-277).

2.2.1.2. Athronges: The Shepherd in Judea

Athronges was known for his great stature and feats of strength. Though a mere shepherd of no special ancestry or character, he aspired for the throne. Having put the diadem on his head, Athronges began giving orders, exercising

160 I refer here to the figures that are usually referred to as "royal pretenders" or "messianic claimants" by previous scholars. For scholarly discussion on the issue, see Horsley and Hanson, *Bandits, Prophets, and Messiahs*, 88-134; Evans, *Jesus and His Contemporaries*, 53-81; E. W. Stegemann and W. Stegemann, *The Jesus Movement: A Social History of Its First Century*. Minneapolis: Fortress Press, 1999), 137-178, etc.

161 Evans, *Jesus and His Contemporaries*, 62.

and retaining power for a while [4-2 BCE], for he was called king (*Ant* 17: 278-284; *War* 2: 60-65). He was supported by his four brothers and a large number of people had also gathered around them. According to Josephus, the main aims of this armed band are "to kill any who submitted to Roman domination and forcibly to suppress those who voluntarily accepted servitude" (*War* 2. 264). Athronges and his brothers eventually surrendered to Archelaus.[162]

2.2.1.3. Jesus ben Ananias: An Uneducated Villager

Another individual figure has been mentioned by Josephus. His name was Jesus, son of Ananias. He has more than just the name in common with Jesus of Nazareth (*War* 6: 300ff.). He was "an uneducated man from the country" who, four years before the First Jewish Revolt, came to Jerusalem in connection with a pilgrimage to the Feast of Booths and, beginning in the Temple district, he repeatedly prophesied the demise of the temple, the city, and the people. Apparently, he had based his prophesy on Jeremiah (Jer 7: 34; 16: 4). Attempts made by "respected citizens" to silence him culminated in a complaint that had been lodged with the governor. Albinus—who after subjecting the prophet of doom to a scourging and a brief hearing—set him free again because he was held to be insane. E. W. Stegemann and W. Stegemann denote, "He would hardly have been able to escape execution had he—unlike Jesus of Nazareth—not been a loner with no disciples and followers, for such always evoked Roman suspicions of revolutionary activities."[163] According to Josephus, Jesus ben Ananis persistently lamented with his prophecies of disaster until he was killed by a projectile during the siege of Jerusalem by the Romans.

2.2.2. Social Banditry: Agrarian Counter-ideology

Apart from the open counter-ideologies which we have discussed, there are covert forms of counter-ideology that negate the ruling power in Judea and Galilee. Modern social scientists have offered us some insightful thought to understand "social banditry" as a form of political resistance in the ancient world. The term "social banditry" was first employed by E. Hobsbawm in his study of the primitive social movements in the 19th and 20th centuries.[164] Hobsbawm sees some ideological truth behind the social banditry and rural revolutionary movements, such as: the millenarianism, religious sects, rituals, and revolutionary organizations as their strategies.[165] It was further developed by A. Blok by reconsidering the concept of social banditry in the light of

162 See Hengel, *The Zealots*, 328; also Evans, *Jesus and His Contemporaries*, 62-63.

163 Stegemann and W. Stegemann, *The Jesus Movement*, 165.

164 E. Hobsbawm, *Primitive Rebels: Studies in Archaic Forms of Social Movement in the 19th and 20th Centuries* (New York: Norton, 1959).

165 E. Hobsbawm, *Primitive Rebels*, 1.

peasant experiences.[166] In his 1984 article, "Bandits in the Roman World," B. D. Shaw has depicted that social banditry was a widespread incident in the Roman world.[167] The works of the recent past sociopolitical scientists are acceptable to recent Biblical scholars and were found very fruitful for the analysis of the Jewish rural movements during the Roman rule. Scholars like Horsley, Myers, Crossan, Stegemann and Stegemann, *et al.* have brought forth fruitful discussions in the context of early Christianity.[168]

Scott advocates a new dimension which is capable of facilitating any discourse on social banditry in the context of subjugated peasants who have experienced domination. Scott presents social banditry as one of the dissident sub-cultures—along with millennial religions, slave "hush-arbors," world-upside down imagery, myths of the "good" king, *etc.*—more or less "compelled performances" engendered by domination.[169] In other words, social banditry, according to Scott, is a hidden transcript of the powerless developed in sequestered sites off the public stage to counter the domination of the power-holders. Scott helps us to understand that social banditry is not merely regarded as activities of the "peasant outlaws" who resisted material appropriation, but also as counter-ideological stance that propagated justice and equality in negation of the ruling ideology. We take the point raised by Scott to establish if, and to what extent, the brigands and their activities in Judaea and Galilee reported by Josephus negated the imperial powers at an ideological level.

2.2.2.1. Social Banditry in Judea and Galilee

Social Banditry in Judea and Galilee is as old as the history of Israel. There are at least three important things to remember when we discuss social banditry in these regions: the civil war at the end of the Hasmonean rule, the arrival of the Romans, and Herod who was on his way to power.[170] The first major instance of the social banditry under the Roman rule is that of the bandits who operated in northern Galilee.[171] Josephus reports,

---

166 A. Blok, "The Peasant and the Brigand: Social Banditry Reconsidered," *Comparative Studies in Society and History* 14 (1972): 494-503.

167 B. D. Shaw, "Bandits in the Roman Empire," *Past and Present* 105 (1984): 5-52.

168 Horsley and Hanson, *Bandits, Prophets, and Messiahs*, see especially the second chapter (48-87) and *Jesus and the Spiral of Violence*, 37-43; Myers, *Binding the Strong Man*, 58-64; Crossan, *The Historical Jesus*, 168-206; Stegemann and Stegemann, *The Jesus Movement*, 173-186.

169 Scott, *Domination and the Arts of Resistance*, 108-135.

170 Stegemann and Stegemann, *The Jesus Movement*, 175.

171 Belo, *A Materialist Reading of the Gospel of Mark*, 82.

> Herod, energetic by nature, at once found material to test his metal. Discovering that Ezekias, a brigand-chief, at the head of a large horde, was ravaging the district on the Syrian frontier, he caught him and put him and many of the brigands to death" (*War* 1: 204).

As it appears in this report, Ezekias organized a brigand band in the district on the Syrian frontier at least until Antipater's consolidation of power ended the period of central governmental weakness. Herod, appointed by his father to govern Galilee, soon caught and killed Ezekias and many of his brigands. However, this account neither reveals the origin and nature of organization nor establishes the purpose of the bandit movement. It focuses on the military campaign led by Herod who at the same time was on his way to power and made himself prominent in fighting this social banditry led by Ezekias. In order to attain a deeper understanding of this social banditry movement, we must look into the socio-political conditions.

Pompey's arrival in 64 B.C.E. to the eastern Mediterranean brought a new era of new imperialism for the Jews. Pompey settled the Jewish political turmoil with a violent conquest. This conquest was followed by a generation-long period of turmoil as rival Hasmonean factions and rival Roman armies vied for control of the area. This brought a situation similar to the civil war which resulted in the devastation of land, extraordinary levies of taxes, and general social turmoil. The situation became worse when Gabinius—the proconsul in Syria known for his extortions—granted the local nobility governing power in their respective regions in 57 B.C.E. This new political structure disadvantaged the peasants in many ways. Horsley and Hanson believe that it gave the peasantry direct pressure from the local rulers.[172] Many of the agrarian populace disserted Hyrcanus to take side with Aristobulas, the rival Hasmonean local ruler. Gabinius suppressed the rebellion and in 48 B.C.E., Antipater, a loyalist of Hyrcanus, consolidated his power to rule the Jews. Antipater appointed his son Herod to govern Galilee in 48 B.C.E (*War* 1: 203).

We can hardly speak of the Galileans as being submissive to Herod. However, we can imagine that there was at least opposition at an ideological level which was unobtrusive. This opposition must have been established before Herod was crowned, at least a decade before him. Herod's coming into power brings the bandits into political focus and also Josephus. The first action of Herod, as the governor of Galilee, was to eliminate the band of the "bandit chief" Hezekias, who operated in northern Galilee. This is suggestive of the fact that there were protests to the Romans and their client-kingship. Herod's action implies that he felt the bandits were more threatening than the Hasmonean priestly rulers. Josephus' account, in many ways, assumes that

172 Horsley and Hanson, *Bandits, Prophets, and Messiahs*, 63.

Hezekias found support, popularity, and even the sympathy of the Galilean rural populace. A decade later we find Herod once again suppressing bandits along with other rebels in Galilee. "… and then started on a campaign against the cave-dwelling brigands, who were infesting a wide area and inflicting on the inhabitants evils no less than those of war" (*War* 1: 304). This group of bandits was known as "cave bandits." Some scholars including the most recent ones have identified these brigands simply with "the first followers of the deposed Hasmonean."[173] But Horsley and Hanson would reject this assumption on the ground that it fails to note seriously the situation of the Galilean peasant resistance.[174] They have rather suggested that these cave bandits were the products of the economic and political hardship brought about by the renewed civil war and the Roman imperial rule that dominated the peasants in Galilee. For them, the brigands holed up in the cave were not the political faction but were those who were "continuing an extensive popular resistance to Herod."[175] In the vicinity of the village of Arbela, northwest of Tiberias, the bandits were defeated, but the escaped bandits offered stubborn and lengthy resistance from their cave fortifications.

After the cave bandits, Josephus reports no other social banditry during the reign of Herod. It was only when Judea was made a Roman province in C.E. 6, we are informed about resistance movement. Josephus narrates about the founding of the Fourth Philosophy by Judas the Galilean and Zaddok the Pharisee. But the Fourth Philosophy may not be regarded to be in the category of bandits. The canonical Gospels also witnessed the presence of bandits during the time of Jesus, namely: Barabbas (Jn 18: 40) and the two bandits (Gr. *lestai*) who were crucified with Jesus (Mk 15: 27). Josephus, however, does not mention social banditry until C.E. 44. When Agrippa I died, Judea was again under the direct rule of Rome. There appeared under Cuspius Fadus a certain Tholomaeus who operated in the border region (*Ant* 20: 5). Again under Cumanus, there was an attack on an imperial slave named Stephen, allegedly by a bandit near Beth-horon (*War* 2: 228ff). Cumanus launched an action against the souring villages of Beth-horon to capture the culprit. The fact was that the governor presumed there was complicity among the rural communities in the nearby villages.

Another incident took place under Cumanus' rule. Under the leadership of two bandits by name: Eleazar, son of Dinai and Alexander, a pilgrim from Galilee to Jerusalem was murdered by Samaritans. Eleazar, as was typical of social bandits, was hid himself in the mountains (*Ant* 20: 121). This incident had affected the intensity of the traditional rivalry between the Galileans and

173 Stegemann and Stegemann, *The Jesus Movement*, 175.

174 Horsley and Hanson, *Bandits, Prophets, and Messiahs*, 64.

175 Horsley Hanson, *Bandits, Prophets, and Messiahs*, 64.

Samaritans almost to the extent of open war between the two nations. Judeans—comprising both Jerusalem as well as rural masses were—also involved in that crisis. This situation forced Jonathan, the then high priest and some of the Jerusalem aristocrats to calm down the mobs. This attempt was not successful, for Josephus says, "Many of them, however, emboldened by impunity, had recourse to robbery, and raids and insurrections, fostered by the more reckless, broke out all over the county" (*War* 2: 238). The disorder continued until the Syrian governor Quadratus took rigorous action. Quadratus executed the insurrectionist Jews, deported the high priest and other prominent Judeans and Samaritans to Roman in chains, and called the governor and the chiliarch Celer for explanation about action to Rome. Agrippa II also intervened to convince Rome to punish the Samaritans. This exemplifies how the rural resistance and social banditry have had a great impact on the powers in Rome.

Felix was appointed as procurator of the rest of Judea. Activities of social banditry continued under Felix (*War* 2: 253, 264-265; *Ant* 20: 160-161). But, the government evidently stood firm against any anti-Roman activists. Felix captured and killed the bandits. He also punished the villagers as they complied with and sympathized with the bandits. Felix, moreover, took Eleazer the brigand chief "who for twenty years had ravaged the country, with many associates, and sent them for trial to Rome" (*War* 2: 253a) and they were crucified (*War* 2: 253b). Their numbers were high, as Josephus says "incalculable." (*War* 2: 253). As the Romans stood strong against the bandits, the social banditry took a new and different form in its resistance to the powers. Judging from Josephus' report, a coalition emerged between the prophetic groups and brigands. There was also a new quality in the social banditry itself. In this context, the emergence of the Sicarii should be discussed. Fetus is said to have captured and killed many robbers (*War* 2: 271). According to Josephus, Gessius Florus also joined forces with the brigands (*Ant* 20: 255ff.). Social bandits were also involved in the First Jewish War. John of Gishala seems to have recruited his army from them. Menachem, the Sicarii also drew on this reservoir of freedom fighters. Yet, they also appeared on the other side, for the residents of Sepphoris, who wanted to remain true to Rome and they appealed to the robber chief Jesus and his band who operated in the border region of Ptolemy, for help against the commandment of the rebellion in Galilee (*Life* 104ff.).[176]

2.2.2.2. Social Banditry as Ideology at Work

Interestingly enough, each of the activities of social banditry in Judea and Galilee had been connected with a particular land or space. Hezekias and his large gang occupied "the district on the Syrian frontier" (*War* 1:204), the

176 Stegemann and Stegemann, *The Jesus Movement*, 177.

so-called "brigand cave" were said to have "infesting a wide area" at Arbela (War 1: 304), the bandits which attacked the imperial servants presumably occupied Beth-horon and the nearby villages, Eleazar used the mountain as his stronghold. These were the social spaces for the bandits and the peasants in which their dignity and assertion may have been freely denoted. Each of the spaces that they occupied was perhaps neglected by the Roman administration. They became safe places for the subjugated people, free from surveillance from above. However, the creation of a social site served to be more than just a safe place. It involved ideological negation. It provoked the development of more or less equally elaborate replies in the hidden transcript.

2.2.3. Summary

We assume that the principal ideologies of Roman imperialism had privileged those of power and privilege and it was experienced as disruptive and disorienting for many of the subject people. This assumption re-orients our understanding of the *Pax Romana*, the imperial new order, various developmental projects including the constructions of buildings and a network of roads were regarded as justification and a means of the ruling Romans for their oppression and slavery. As we continue to discuss the resistance movements in Judea and Galilee of the Herodian-Roman rule, we shall look into those movements that have bearings upon counter-ideologies to the Roman imperial ideologies. In fact, the ideal of God's reign which Jesus proclaimed could have been a counter ideology to that of the Romans.

2.3. Resistance to Material Domination

So far we have focused upon the aspects of Roman domination as spheres related to both status and the ideological. To understand how the Roman imperial order impoverished and ruined the peasants, we must explore the material aspect as well. We have substantial evidences to denote that the Jewish peasants had been badly affected by the appropriation of land, grain, taxes, labour, *etc*. John depicts a growing material exploitation accompanied by an unprecedented oppression of agrarian masses culminating in the disruption of ecological systems during the Roman imperial rule.[177] This does not mean that the Romans and their client-rulers were the ones who started all these practices. With perhaps partial exception in the Hasmonean period, concentration of ownership land in the hands of a few large land owners as well as leasing of taxes to individuals had already been in practice since the Ptolemaic regime. The unbroken link of these practices can be established from the Ptolemies through the Seleucids to the Hasmoneans and the Romans.

177 John, *The Ecological Vision of Jesus*, 119-152.

Some historical sources, particularly Josephus, Rabbinic literature, and the Gospels, assume that large ownership of land were concentrated in the hands of the upper spectrum of the society during the Roman-Herodian period and the people at the lower stratum were engaged as tenants, day laborers and slaves.[178] This made the Romans wealthy and powerful while ruining the subaltern masses. Our task here is to determine how the subalterns responded to this material domination. Again, Scott makes us aware of that the powerless people resisted material domination at two levels – overt and covert. According to him, overt forms of resistance were publicly declared, such as: petition, demonstration, boycott, strike, land invasion and open revolt; whereas, the covert form of resistance were undeclared resistance, namely: everyday forms of resistance and direct resistance by disguised resisters.[179] Keeping Scott's theory in mind, we shall analyze historical sources that are relevant to the issue in order to determine how the Jewish peasants had reacted to the material domination.

2.3.1. Petition for a Reduction of Taxes

The Roman conquest in the middle of second century B.C.E. brought the Jews back to the burden of taxes. Under the Romans and the Herodians—as it was in the pre-Hasmonean period—they were obliged to pay tributes.[180] Taxes and tributes were not just a matter of money, but were criteria of sovereignty. For the Romans and for their vassals, taxes and tributes were for the maintenance and enlargement of positions and powers. The high-priestly aristocracy who shared the power with the Romans can also be linked to the same interest. We do not have exact figures about the extent of the burden of taxation. The various religious taxes, tributes and direct taxes, indirect taxes, duties, fees, and compulsory labour (Mat 5: 41), which were imposed on the Jewish population in Judea and Galilee were brought together under the term taxes. Stegemann and Stegemann rightly observe that "the kind and degree of burden imposed by these taxes were naturally different, yet structurally the system remained relatively the same from the Ptolemies to the Romans."[181] It was Herod who created an additional tax burden for the people. He paid tributes to the Romans, made a gift of a gigantic sum of 800 talents out of gratitude for confirmation as ruler (*Ant* 15: 200), and sponsored massive construction projects throughout his realm.

---

178 Myers, *Binding the Strong Man*, 49.

179 Scott, *Domination and the Arts of Resistance*, 198.

180 Myers, *Binding the Strong Man*, 51-52.

181 Stegmann and Stegamnn, *The Jesus Movement*, 113.

At the end of Herod's long oppressive reign, the Jewish multitude came with their triple petitions to Archelaus. Josephus reports, "One party clamoured for a reduction of the taxes, another for the abolition duties, a third for the liberation of the prisoners" (*War* 2: 4). Considering the reality of the agrarian communities, especially at the sphere of material appropriation, making a demand or petition before the ruling class could have been one form of resistance on the part of the subaltern people.[182] There is nothing to doubt that after the death of Herod the Great, the agrarian masses petitioned Herod's successor for relief from taxes.[183]

2.3.2. Refusal to Pay Tribute to the Romans

One of the most significant public resistance movements against the imperial rule was led by the "Fourth Philosophy." When the Romans installed the "direct rule" of the Roman governors over Judea and re-imposed the tribute in C.E. 6, Judas a Galilean organized a resistance to pay tribute to the Romans (*War* 2: 118). Josephus makes it clear that Judas, a Galilean and sophist (Gr. σοφιστὴς) was the founder of this philosophy. With his words "having nothing in common with others," Josephus attempts to distinguish this group in question, from the others – Pharisees, Sadducees, and Essenes (*War* 2: 119). These people had to pay a huge amount of money to the Romans. Tribute is a mark of slavery and humiliation. Being a nation that originated as free peasantry in covenant with God, the Jews longed to regain their freedom. Josephus' parallel account in *Jewish Antiquities* suggests this:

> As for the fourth of the philosophies, Judas the Galilean set himself up as leader of it. This school agrees in all other respects with the opinions of the Pharisees, except that they have a passion for liberty that is almost unconquerable, since they are convinced that God alone is their leader and master. They think little of submitting to death in unusual forms and permitting vengeance to fall on kinsmen and friends if only they avoid calling any man master (*Ant* 18: 24).

The statement that "God alone is their leader and master" is fundamental to this resistance group.[184] They understood God literally as their leader and master in their struggle for justice.[185] Judas and his group were motivated by

---

182 T. Rajak discusses how burdensome debt was throughout the Greek world. Social protest usually took place in the form of demanding the abolition of debt. See T. Rajak, *The Historian and His Society* (Philadelphia: Fortress Press, 1983), 139.

183 Fenn, *The Death of Herod*, 163.

184 Crossan discusses this movement as nonviolent resistance to establish God's rule, not Caesar's. See, *God and Empire: Jesus Against Rome, Then and Now* (New York: HarperSanFrancisco, 2007), 91.

185 Crossan, *God and Empire*, 92; Horsley, *Jesus and the Spiral of Violence*, 87.

their "passion for liberty that is almost unconquerable" to take direct action in the hope that God would be acting decisively through their action to re-establish their liberty. Their commitment to suffer and their confidence that God would vindicate them are suggestive of the fact that this Fourth Philosophy had many aspects in common with the people of Modein who resisted the Seleucid aggression earlier.

2.3.2.1. Judas of Sepphoris, Galilee

After Ezekias, his son Judas emerged as a great leader of resistance in Galilee in the wake of Herod's death in C.E. 4. Josephus portrays Judas as a powerful person with a large number of followers who operated in Sepphoris. Judas plundered the royal palace in Sepphoris and seized all the weapons that were stored there. Judas armed his men with seized weapons. According to Josephus, Judas "became an object of terror to all men by plundering those he came across in his desire for great possessions and his ambition for royal rank, a prize that he expected to obtain not through the practice of virtue but through excessive ill-treatment of others" (*Ant* 17: 272).

While Josephus leaves us with negative comments about the activities and ambitious of Judas, he advocates us some clues to reconstruct the ideology behind him and his movement. Josephus' comment, "a man of great power" depicts the strong support which he gained from the masses who were at the same time the victims of the Roman ideology of victory. In all probability, these would have been from the Jewish peasantry. The site of his operation in Sepphoris assumes that this phenomenon was against the Roman administration in Galilee for it was the Roman capital in Galilee that was surrounded by the agrarian villages. Josephus conveys the information that Judas collected "a large number of desperate men" (*Ant* 17. 271). It is likely that the agrarian communities around the Sepphoris had little hope in their daily occupation and were ready to do anything without worrying about danger to themselves or the rulers. Thus, it became a strong resistance movement and Herod captured him "only with great difficulty" (*Ant* 17: 271).

2.3.2.2. Galilean Cave Bandits

Even though this group of bandits was known as "cave bandits," the cave was not their permanent space of operation. According to Josephus, they occupied a wide area of fertile land in and around Gennesaret (*War* 1.304; *Ant* 14.414). As Herod launched a campaign against them, they took refuge at Arbella which was located in the northwestern part of Tiberias.[186] Scholars like Scott take

186 The village of Arbela is one of the well-known villages in the lower Galilee. It is known for nearby cave complexes which have been used for refuge throughout the centuries

"piecemeal squatting" as an "overt of resistance to the material appropriation which is equivalent to an open land invasion"[187] Josephus depicts details about their mode of operation. As Josephus denotes, Herod made serious attempts by getting himself involved in the campaign to capture them and it could be that this group of brigands created continual problems for the Roman imperialists to establish their domain in Galilee.

If Herod's military campaign against this band of bandits is dated correctly in 37 B.C.E., their existence could be defined as the product of more two decades of oppressive rule of the Romans. As it has been mentioned, appropriation was largely the purpose of any imperialism, especially for the Roman rulers. The very material appropriation had possibly entailed systematic social relations of subordination that imposed indignities of one kind or another on the powerless agrarian community in Galilee. To be more specific, social experiences of indignities, control, submission, humiliation, force deference and punishment for failure to do so could have been the result of material appropriation by the Roman regime. These indignities of various colours are the seedbed of the anger, indignation and frustration that nurtured the hidden transcript. The theoretical assumption of Scott that devises the hidden transcript of the subordinates are not "just behind-the-scenes griping and grumbling." The so-called cave bandits could have had a lot of activities that involved theft, pilfering, and careless labour.

2.3.3. The Sicarii: Direct Resistance by Disguised Resisters

In contrast to bandits who based their movement in rural areas, Josephus reports that a different form of banditry emerged in Jerusalem. These were the Sicarii named after their curved-bladed daggers. Mark refers to the Sicarii twice in his Gospel both in the context of "implied subversive activity" (14: 48; 15: 27).[188] Crossan refers to them as "urban terrorism" invented by anti-Roman Jewish rebels.[189] Like the fourth Philosophy, the Sicarii consisted of, or were led by, scribal scholar-teachers. It is highly possible that the leadership of the Sicarii could have continuity with that of the Fourth Philosophy.[190]

However, it must be noted that the tactics of the Sicarii were different from the Fourth Philosophy. While the Fourth Philosophy openly resisted the imperial rulers by refusing to pay tribute; the Sicarii directly and violently

(*Ant* 14: 415-430; *War* 1: 305-3013; 2: 573; *Life* 188, 311). M.A. Chancey believes that "occupation in the nearby villages may go back to this time." See, *The Myth of a Gentile Galilee*, Society for NTS Monograph Series 118 (Cambridge: Cambridge University Press, 2002), 101.

187 Scott, *Domination and the Arts of Resistance*, 199.

188 Myers, *Binding the Strong Man*, 59.

189 Crossan, *God and Empire*, 89.

190 Horsley, *Jesus and Empire*, 42.

resisted but disguised their identity. It is important to note that the Sicarii movement came into existence in order to get their attention of the powers. The Sicarii's campaign in Jerusalem, their choice of festivals as "special seasons" and "mingled with the crowd" are all significant hints for agrarian resistance standpoint. Scott reminds us that on occasion, groups of subordinated people move their continuing struggle against domination beyond the confines of their specially sequestered sites into "a politics of disguise and anonymity that takes place in public view but is designed to have double meaning to shield the identity of the actors."[191] Most scholars do not acknowledge this significant strategy of anonymity.[192] It is unlikely what Josephus had in mind when he denotes "a new species of banditti" as reference to the Sicarii who are projected as a completely new group which are different from the prevailing bandit movements as some scholars suggested.[193]

Perhaps, Josephus hints that the rural agrarian people's struggles arrived at a new phase as they came out from their sequestered site to let their voices be heard in Jerusalem. This argument is more acceptable when we link the emergence of the Sicarii to economic hardships that were suffered by the peasants. In the late 40s, the Judean and Galilean peasants were hit by a drought and famine and the ruling elite had taken no steps to their relief. It is evident that the people had mounted numerous protests, but the high priestly rulers paid no attention. The Roman governors had been unleashing their military forces on both peaceful protests and unarmed movement in the wilderness that were led by popular prophets. For instance, Cumanus (C.E. 48-52) attempted to crush the spreading banditry that was supposedly fueled by the recent drought and famine by crucifixion (*War* 2: 253). The Jerusalem high-priestly aristocracy was in collaboration with the governor rather than protest against his cruel actions. Hence, beyond doubt, this movement was regarded to be public resistance that was directed to the powers. Josephus calls the Sicarii choice of festivals as "special seasons." In this regard, Scott denotes, "The moment when the dissent of the hidden transcript crosses the threshold to open resistance is always a politically charged occasion."[194] The occasion of "the politically charged occasion" in the case of Sicarii, moreover, was itself the politically and religiously charged occasion of the festivals.

Josephus also mentions that the Sicarii committed murders and in some cases even within the temple (*Ant* 20: 164-165). The reason why the

191 Scott, *Domination and the Arts of Resistance*, 18-19.

192 For instance Crossan argues that "with large crowds in a small space within the temple, the assassinations had both maximum anonymity and maximum publicity." See, *God and Empire*, 90.

193 Horsley, *Jesus and the Empire*, 42.

194 Scott, *Domination and the Arts of Resistance*, 207.

Sicarii committed murders in temple is not difficult to explain. The Jerusalem temple-state was from its origin the local face of the imperial order that was established by the Persian regime and perpetuated by the Ptolemies, Seleucids, and the Romans. The Sicarii chose both the centre of power (*i.e.* Jerusalem and the temple) and the highly charged time (*i.e.* festivals) to carry their concealed assassinations.[195] The Sicarii signaled to the powerful elites that the subaltern people were desperate enough to take extreme actions. Perhaps, the Sicarii wanted to stop the powerful elites from the material exploitation of the masses and warned them about further mistreatment of the people. In the entire operation, the identity of the leaders and their cohorts were kept anonymous. This insight urges us to inculcate the Sicarii movement as direct resistance by disguised resisters.

3. Concluding Remarks

This chapter now comes full circle. No single factor can be said to have been the decisive cause of the war. While the corrupt government of various Roman procurators was very crucial, the hatred of many Judeans and the Galileans towards the Romans cannot be over looked. Social, political and economic factors must be pushed to the front in analysing the root cause of the revolt. As for its immediate causes, we can state that "a combination of events sparked off the war."[196] The events leading to the Great Revolt were: (a) when the court verdict on the 'Synagogue blocked' case was announced in favour of the Greeks in C.E. 61, conflict arose in Caesarea and this led to street fighting in the city after five years. (b) Florus's lust for money sent him to Jerusalem and seized some of the temple's treasure; consequently, this act made the situation very tense. When the Jerusalem crowd protested, he ordered his army to plunder the entire city. This was the only way to wake the peoples' fury and the procurator himself had, to return to Caesarea. The Great Jewish Revolt broke out under his rule in C.E. 66.

Horsley & Hanson assert that the revolt was basically "a peasant revolt."[197] This view can be justified from the analysis of those who participated and fought in the war. Sicarii and Zealots, who had tremendously increased in number over the years, were the ones who begun to fight against the Romans. The majority of the population of Judea and Galilee soon joined them. Along with them, the lower priests and some other Jerusalemites participated. Later on, in C.E. 67, the Idumeans and the Samaritans alike also joined the resistance movement.[198]As far as the participation of the chief priests, elders, and leading

195 On the activities of Sicarii, Horsley, *Jesus and the Spiral of Violence*, 40-42.

196 Jagersma, *A History of Israel from Alexander the Great to Bar Kochba*, 138.

197 Horsley & Hanson, *Bandits, Prophets, and Messiahs,* 43.

198 Jagersma, *A History of Israel from Alexander the Great to Bar Kochba*, 139.

Pharisees are concerned, as Josephus denotes, they attempted to implement a "moderating and mediating strategy."[199] Presumably, they did not actually participate in the resistance movement as long as they could negotiate with the Romans. It was evident that they could not control the situation. Many Jewish notables or chief priests deserted to the Romans for safety. One such prominent example is Josephus himself, who was the General in command of Galilee, who simply deserted to the Romans after the initial battles, and assisted the Romans in conquering his own Jewish people.[200] It is reported that the places of Agrippa, Bernice and the high priests were set on fire by the Zealots.[201] This action denotes that the movement, at least at the initial stage was also targeted upon the Jewish leaders. For P. *Schäfer*, the burning of archives in Jerusalem was connected to the social and economic aims of the Zealots and their support which were to achieve a redistribution of land.[202] M. Goodman relates the actions to do away with the discontent over the disparity between the wealth of Jerusalem and the poverty of the rest of the country.[203]

The agrarian nature of the revolt has always been overlooked by scholars including.[204] For many reasons, the great revolt can be referred to as agrarian anxiety and rural resistance upon the imperial rulers and their agents. The economic situation got steadily worse in the period after C.E. 44 when Judea, Galilee and its environs were under the direct rule of Rome. It is certain that the ill governance of many of the procurators, were based on greed and corruption. Such policy aroused rural opposition and therefore provoked disturbances. As a result, the people in the agrarian sectors were the worse victims. More taxes ware collected than what was required, because too much of it disappeared in the hands of intermediaries. The devastating famine which was reported to have taken place during Tiberias was the culmination of the economic hardship that was suffered basically by the agrarian communities. Of the main areas in

199 Horsley and Hanson, *Bandits, Prophets, and Messiahs,* 43.

200 Horsley and Hanson, *Bandits, Prophets, and Messiahs,* 43.

201 Jagersma, *A History of Israel from Alexander the Great to Bar Kochba*, 139.

202 As cited by Jagersma, *A History of Israel from Alexander the Great to Bar Kochba*, 139.

203 M. Goodman, "The First Jewish Revolt: Social Conflict and the Problems of Debt," *Essays in Honour of YigaelYadin,* JJS 33 (1982): 417-427. See also his book, *The Ruling Class of Judaea: The Origins of the Jewish Revolt against Rome, A.D. 66-70* (Cambridge: Cambridge University Press, 1987), which examines the background of the C.E. 66 Judean revolt against Rome. Goodman attempts to explain both the revolt itself and its temporary success by discussing the role of the Jewish ruling class in the sixty years preceding the war and in the independent state that lasted until C.E. 70. The author depicts that the revolt's ultimate cause was a misunderstanding by Rome regarding the status criteria of Jewish society.

204 A. Berlin and J. A. Overman, *The First Jewish Revolt: Archaeology, History, and Ideology* (London: Routledge, 2002); S. Sorek, *The Jews against Rome: War in Palestine AD 66-73* (London: Hambledon Continuum, 2008).

the so-called Palestine, Judea and its capital Jerusalem were still by far the most important places in this period. The aristocrat priestly families lived there along with the most prominent people and rich landowners. At the same time, Galilee seemed to have been a relatively prosperous place in the last decades before the Great Revolt with the coming up of cities like Sepphoris and Tiberias. There are some evidences which denote the Sepphoris had maintained good relations with Rome and it further alienated the rural population. In this regard, there were many important socio-political developments in Galilee that made the region the cradle of the anti-Roman movement.

Chapter 3

The Domination and Resistance in the Gospel of Mark

Modern Biblical historiography has a tendency to confuse the politics of urban elites with that of the rural farmers. Our survey on the history of protests and resistance movements in the previous chapter establishes the fact that the struggles of the rural farmers in Judea and Galilee had a history that was prior to the advent of the dominant groups (*e.g.*, Pharisees, Sadducees, Essenes, *etc*) and continued to move throughout the Hellenistic and Roman regimes in parallel with or perhaps opposite to that of urban elite movements. Even when these two groups nominally came together in a nationalistic movement (*e.g.*, Modein Resistance), a religious faith (Judaism), and a political agenda (freedom), their stakes, interests, and understandings were diverged widely. The Scribes, ancient historians for the most part, wrote history from the urban centres (*i.e.* Jerusalem, Rome, others) and from the perspective of rural elites. The agrarian rural population was generally treated as passive recipients of projects and politics that were implemented by the rural elites. They otherwise received attention only when they broke the standard of the powerful elites in the form of rebellion, social banditry, millenarian movements, land invasions, and the like.[1]

Mark's Gospel—which is supposedly about the agrarian-resistance—was catalysed by Jesus' campaign and it is assumed in this research that it has been written from the perspective of rural farmers—could be the potential historical resource of our knowledge about the rural resistance movements of the first century C.E. This chapter aims to explore whether and how Mark indicates that the rural population in Galilee had resisted the Roman domination. We shall discuss some of the issues that are pertinent to an academic investigation

1 Crossan's discussion on "Aristocrat and Historian" is enlightening in this regard. See, *The Historical Jesus*, 91-102.

of the Gospel and then we shall proceed to explore the varieties of political discourses of the subalterns within the scale of Jesus-in-movement.

1. Rereading Mark's Gospel in the Context of Resistance Movements

Scholarly quests for the historical Jesus since the nineteenth-century have made Mark's Gospel prominent in the last century Gospel studies. However, modern scholars are slow in realizing the political significance of Jesus and his campaign. Most of the approaches designed after enlightenment viewpoint in investigations of the historical Jesus compounded "the depoliticizing effects of modern Western individualism and the separation of religion from political-economic life."[2] Consequently, we are still far from an understanding of the Gospel origins within power relations. There is an urgent need to reclaim the Gospels as a reliable source for the historical Jesus especially as the major interpreters of historical Jesus and Mark's Gospel have evidently tended to ignore, obscure, or trivialize the rural or agrarian resistance motifs embedded in the Gospel. However, this does not mean that the entire issue of the sociopolitical aspects of Jesus' movement has been left out. It is a fact that the pioneering works of great social scientists such as M. Weber, E. Durkheim and K. Marx which take texts and ideas relating to their sociopolitical contexts are lately applied to Gospel researches. But now, increasingly, perspectives offered by these great social scientists have begun to make their way upon the interpretation of the Gospels. Contemporary analyses of rural resistance by prominent authors have increasingly enriched the field of rural or agrarian-resistance studies. Some articles contained in *The Global Resistance Reader* (2005), have suggested that the conceptualization of resistance must be situated within understanding of power, power being comprised within the relational interplay of dominance and subordination.[3] As scholars have engaged more in domination and resistance, we realise that resistance is often more intricate than it is generally made out to be and less obvious than commonly understood. Indeed, it can be—as many western scholars in the past did—flat-out ambiguous since resistance itself is constitutive and reflective of, and embedded in, sociopolitical and cultural life. There has been a tendency among the Gospel scholars to emphasize upon certain forms of resistance that are more overt while overlooking others. In fact, this is one of the motivating criticisms that have brought about this chapter.

Our purpose here is not to convey a lengthy survey on Markan studies during the last centuries. We, rather, attempt to pinpoint major issues in the critical analysis of Mark's Gospel which have given rise to scholarly debate

2 Horsley, *Jesus and Empire,* 55.

3 L. Amoore *The Global Resistance Reader*, ed. A. Moore (London: Routledge, 2005), especially the articles by L. Amoore, "Introduction: Global Resistance: Global Politics," 1-11 and M Foucault, "Method," 86-91.

and to re-examine those issues afresh. In his article entitled, "The Interpretation of Mark: A History of Developments and Issues," W. R. Telford identifies four major issues on which the modern interpreters of Mark have extensively debated upon, such as: orality versus textuality, *Gattung* (or genre), source of Mark and the creativity of Mark.[4] Apart from Telford's discussion, the social context and structure of the Gospel are decisive aspects in academic investigation. Our task here is to re-address these issues in the context of Roman imperialism and resistance by the subjugated Jews.

1.1. Mark as Oral Performance

One serious question among many upon which Markan scholars have debated about is the issue of "the relation of Mark as written text to the oral tradition which preceded it."[5] The emergence of Markan priority theory had firmly established Mark, as being the most primordial Gospel and it contains dependable historical accounts of Jesus' ministry. Mainstream scholars in the eighteenth-century had considered that it was probable to construct a sketch of Jesus' ministry based on Mark. Both Markan priority and historical reliability had been well accepted. However, the scholars at the turn of the twentieth-century began to question the dependability of Mark. The earliest major work that challenged the historical reliability of Mark is W. Wrede. In his *The Messianic Secret in the Gospels* ([1901] ET. 1971), Wrede credibly argued that each Gospel was deeply dogmatic in its understanding of Jesus and it was no longer achievable to build a picture of Jesus' ministry that was based upon the priority of Mark.[6] No less so than the other Gospels, he claimed "the Gospel of Mark belongs to the history of dogma."[7]

Consequently, Wrede's rejection of the historical reliability of Mark encouraged the separation of historical Jesus from any Gospel portrayal of him and it facilitated the removal of Jesus' words from their contexts in the Gospels as a necessary perquisite to establishing their meaning as actual sayings of Jesus.[8] Mark, thus, along with others had not been trusted to offer historical information. This removal of the historical Jesus and his ministry from the Gospel frameworks gave a new impetus to the study of the Gospel. Scholars after Wrede had to seriously engage themselves in searching for a

4 W. R. Telford, "The Interpretation of Mark: A History of Developments and Issues," in *The Interpretation of Mark*, ed. W. R. Telford, 2nd edition (Edinburgh: T&T Clark, 1995), 1-62; esp. 14-40.

5 Telford "The Interpretation of Mark," 14.

6 W. Wrede, *The Messianic Secret*, trans. J.C.G. Grieg (Greenwood, SC: Attic; London: Clarke, 1971).

7 Wrede, *The Messianic Secret*, 131. Wrede's conclusion implies that Mark's interest was theological rather than historical.

8 Cf. Herzog, *Parables as Subversive Speech*, 41-42.

new context within which Jesus' tradition could be understood and in bridging the gap between the historical Jesus and the Jesus of the Gospel.[9] In the field of Gospel studies both M. Dibelius[10] and R. Bultmann[11] are the major contributors who devoted themselves to the work of isolating and classifying the various forms,[12] establishing the *Sitz-im-Leben* of the piece of oral gospel tradition in the community and reconstructing as far as possible the traditional history of the pericope. Thus, the classical form criticism proposed certain answers to these questions by claiming that Mark drew upon a lively oral tradition and, assumed continuity between orality and textuality and posited a relatively linear development from an oral tradition to the written Gospel.

Many scholars seemingly accepted the idea that was proposed by the form-critics that "Mark's Gospel stands on the borderline of oral and written literature."[13] Earlier works of W. H. Kelber,[14] A. Stock,[15] E. Best[16] have maintained that Mark wrote his Gospel based upon the pre-written oral structure. Recent studies on Mark 13 and Mark 4 by E. Brandenburger[17] and P. Sellew[18] respectively have denoted that Mark uses a combination of oral and written sources. The discussion at this stage was limited around the transmission process and its socio-historical context. As Telford highlights, scholars differed in their response over the question regarding whether pre-Markan traditions were transmitted in a "controlled environment" or a "fluid environment" and if the latter, whether the quest for the original or even earlier form of the tradition is legitimate?[19] Some scholarly works, for instance, B.

9 The most useful tool for such task is form criticism; and it has flourished and heavily influenced the study of the Gospels. The form-critical analysis between the first and second world wars seriously tried to recover and examine the tradition behind the Gospel in its pre-literary or oral phase.

10 M. Debelius, *From Tradition to Gospel*, trans. B. L. Woolf (London: Ivor Nicholson and Watson, [Ger. 1919] 1934).

11 R. Bultmann, *The History of the Synoptic Gospel*, trans. J. Marsh from 2nd German Edition ([1st Edition 1921] 1931), 2nd English Edition with corrections and additions from 1962 (Oxford: Blackwell, 1968).

12 For examples: apophthegms, gnomic or wisdom sayings, prophetic or apocalyptic sayings, legal sayings, community rules, Christological sayings, parables, miracle stories, historical stories and legends, a passion narrative

13 Telford "The Interpretation of Mark," 14.

14 W. H. Kelber, "Mark and Oral Tradition" *Semeia* 16 (1979): 7-55; Also his monograph on *The Oral and Written Gospel* (Philadelphia: Fortress Press, 1983).

15 A. Stock, "Chiastic Awareness and Education in Antiquity" *BTB* 14 (1984): 23-27.

16 E. Best "Mark's Narrative Technique" in *JSNT* 37 (1989): 43-58.

17 E. Brandenburger, *Markus 13 und die Apokalyptik* (Gottingen: Vandenhoeck & Ruprecht, 1989).

18 P. Sellew, "Oral and Written Sources in Mark 4: 1-34," *NTS* 36 (1990): 234-67.

19 Telford, "Introduction," 14-15.

Gerhardsson's *The Origins of Gospel Traditions* (1986) have argued for the controlled environment of the master/disciples context rather than variability of the folk tradition which is the common form-critical position.[20] With regard to the question of whether there is continuity between orality textuality or between the oral tradition and the written Gospel, some recent scholars, for example M. Hengel, still support the traditional view.[21]

In spite of volumes of literature having been written on the issue, there is still a lack of certainty among scholars regarding the precise nature and reliability of the pre-Markan tradition, namely the character of its tradents, the medium of its transmission and the process which brought the Gospel itself into its present form. Since the early 1980s, modern oral studies have been much advanced with various publications and a few notable ones are: W. J. Ong,[22] R. Thomas,[23] D. R. Olson & N. Torrance, T. M. Tentz,[24] J. Watson.[25] These works had already exerted their influence on the Gospel studies to challenge the long standing idea that Gospel material existed in oral form before being included in written Gospels. W. H. Kelber's *The Oral and the Written Gospel: The Hermeneutics of Speaking and Writing in the Synoptic Tradition, Mark, Paul, and Q* (1983) has been the pioneer in challenging the field of New Testament studies to note seriously as to how the assumptions of print culture have limited and twisted modern interpreters' ability in order to discern how communication and environment and the transmission of Jesus traditions worked in a predominantly oral communication environment.[26] Kelber describes the differences between how people appear to think and to express themselves before they had learnt how to write and read and how to do so when the art of writing and reading has had time to penetrate their thinking

20 B. Gerhardsson, *The Origins of the Gospel Traditions* (Philadelphia: Fortress Press, 1979); Also see his book *The Gospel Tradition* (Lund: Gleerup, 1986) and his recent article on "The Secret of the Transmission of the Unwritten Jesus Tradition" in *NTS* 51/1 (January 2005): 1-18.

21 M. Hengel, *Studies in the Gospel of Mark,* trans. J. Bowden (Philadelphia: Fortress Press, 1985).

22 W. J. Ong, *Orality and Literacy: The Technologizing of the Word* (London: Methuen, 1982).

23 R. Thomas, *Literacy and Orality in Ancient Greece* (Cambridge: Cambridge University Press, 1992).

24 T. M. Tentz, *Orality and Literacy in Hellenic Greece* (Carbondale: Southern Illinois University Press, 1989.

25 J. Watson, *Speaking Volumes: Orality and Literacy in the Greek and Roman World* (Boston: Brill, 2001).

26 See his groundbreaking work *The Oral and the Written Gospel: The Hermeneutics of Speaking and Writing in the Synoptic Tradition, Mark, Paul, and Q* (Philadelphia: Fortress press, 1983), esp. chapters 1-2 on pre-Markan materials; and his article on "Jesus and Tradition: Words in Time, Words in Space," *Semeia* 65 (1994): 139-167, esp. 140-141.

and speech. According to Kelber, the differences between orality and textuality are enormous. As Markan studies have advanced along this line, more and more scholars begun to realize the significance of oral performance in oral culture. Many scholars are now convinced that long after the earliest discernible Gospel documents existed in written forms, those texts still functioned as oral communication, in performance before groups or communities.[27]

K. E. Bailey—who lived more than three decades in Lebanon, Syria and Iraq—has studied rural culture in villages particularly with regard to how oral tradition operated there and he notices that in these regions, pithy proverbs, poems and stories of different kinds are retold at regular nightly gatherings, where the villagers celebrated their identity and history.[28] Even though, we do not know whether or not the Jewish peasants of Jesus' time practiced the same, we can assume that parables, proverbs and poems could have had a larger role to play in rural culture in terms of protecting their identity and history. A recent work of J. D. G. Dunn[29] is incredibly important as it attempts to explain the making of the gospel tradition and its transmission before the oldest extant written versions. Dunn argues that our modern thinking functions as "a default setting" when we attempt to understand Jesus and the New Testament. Having adopted a 'literary, print-dominated mindset', we cannot understand how the Jesus tradition functioned at the beginning. Dunn urges the modern reader to seriously study how differently minds and thoughts generally operate in a pre-literary society, if they really wanted to understand the gospels historically.[30] Horsley draws our attention to the fact that outside a few aristocrats and scribes in ancient Greece, Rome and in Israel, practically no one could read and write.[31] He tries to maintain a link between writing and oral communication in Markan studies, by stating, "If the vast majority of people in the Roman empire were

27 M. A. Beavis who describes her perspective as "reader-response" analysis denotes that Mark may have been composed for or used in oral performance. See, *Mark's Audience: The Literary and Social Setting of Mark 4:11-12* (Sheffield: JSOT, 1989). D. E. Aune's *work* is an eye-opener in terms of considering Mark and it displays a "popular literary style." See, *The New Testament in Its Literary Environment* (Philadelphia: Westminster, 1987), 47.

28 See his articles, "Informal Controlled Oral Tradition and the Synoptic Gospels," *AJT* 5 (1991): 34-54; "Middle Eastern Oral Tradition and the Synoptic Gospels," *ExpT* 106 (1995): 563-567; and also his book, *Poet & Peasant and Through Peasants Eyes: A Literary-Cultural Approach to the Parables in Luke* (Grand Rapids, Michigan: Eerdmans, 1984).

29 J. D. G. Dunn, *Jesus Remembered* (Grand Rapids, Michigan: Eerdmans, 2003); "Altering the Default Setting: Re-envisaging the Early Transmission of the Jesus Tradition," *NTS* 49/2 (April 2003): 139-175.

30 Dunn, "Altering the Default Setting," 170-175.

31 R. A. Horsley, *Hearing the Whole Story: The Politics of Plot in Mark's Gospel* (Louisville/ London: Westminster John Knox Press, 2001), 53-59.

illiterate, then we must obviously rethink the relationship between the Gospel of Mark and its audience."[32] A joint article by T. Morgan, R. A. Horsley, J. A. Draper and J. M. Foley, "Performing the Gospel: Orality, Memory and Mark" published in *Journal of Theological Studies* (2007) is in fact an eye-opener to denote the debris of orality and memory in Mark.[33]

A reading of Mark's Gospel from a rural peasant perspective strongly supports this view that in the predominantly oral communication environment of antiquity, there is no significant great divide between orality and literacy. As Horsley observes, literacy was rare among the rural masses of the ancient Graeco-Roman.[34] In Judea and Galilee around the time of Jesus, as in the rest of the Roman empire, literacy was evidently concentrated in the political and cultural elite. The scribal class, officials in the Herodian administrations, in Jerusalem and the towns and Galilean cities were presumably trained in Greek, although probably not in Hebrew and Aramaic. M. Bar-Ilan has estimated that the literacy rate in Judea and Galilee of Roman rule as low as three percent.[35] The stance of the past understanding that treated the sayings of Jesus as artifacts that have meaning in themselves cannot be accepted any longer. In actuality, no one communicates in isolation, for communication involves other people in a particular sociopolitical context. In isolating Jesus' sayings from their literary context in the Gospels, however, the standard procedure dispenses with our principal guide to "the historical contextual and relational meaning of Gospel materials."[36] Jesus' campaign as a historical figure would have been remembered in the first place only if they had significance for someone. The significance is laying in the communication between Jesus and those with whom he interacted in a historical context. The Gospels are the principal result and record of such communication.[37] With this insight, we reclaim Mark as a reliable historical source.

---

32 Horsley, *Hearing the Whole Story*, 55.

33 T. Morgan, R. A. Horsley, J. A. Draper, and J. M. Foley, "Performing the Gospel: Orality, Memory and Mark" in *JTS* 58/ 2 (2007): 638-640.

34 Horsley, *Hearing the Whole Story*, 54.

35 M. Bar-Ilan, "Illiteracy in the Land of Israel in the First Centuries C.E.," in *Essays in the Social Scientific Study of Judaism and Jewish Society*, ed. S. Fishbane and S. Schoenfeild (Hoboken, N.J.: KTAV, 1992), 46-61.

36 Horsley, *Jesus and Empire*, 62.

37 Waetjen who looked into "the rustic character of Mark's Greek" finds evidences for the orality of the Gospel in the use of conjunctions at the beginning of sentences and change of verb tenses. In Waetjen's translation of the Gospel, those probable evidences are printed in bold. See, *A Reordering of Power*, xi, 27-61.

1.2. Mark as Resistance Story of Subalterns

When we read Mark, what kind of story are we reading? Modern scholars have intensely debated upon this issue and it may be aptly called the "*Gattung* debate." This debate has focused mainly upon the question of the literary model or models by which the author may have been influenced in the overall conception of his work.[38] Given the individualistic orientation of the modern Western culture, the studies employing the historical-critical frameworks have tended to be taken as biography.[39] Still recently, the literary-critical analyses have reinforced the view that Mark is a biography of Jesus.[40] A closer examination of the pattern and function of Mark's Gospel and the literature to which it has been compared requires us to rethink the question of Mark's *Gattung* or genre. There has been a generalization of view that suggests that Mark's Gospel is not a new genre, but one with parallels in Jewish literature (*e.g*., apocalyptic, wisdom literature or the Old Testament stories of the prophets) or the wider Hellenistic world. But this view seems to be unsatisfactory to those who looked for parallels in Greco-Roman literature. C. H. Talbert's *What is the Gospel? The Genre of the Canonical Gospels* (1978)[41] and D. E. Aune's *The New Testament and Its Literary Environment* (1987)[42] are the scholarly attempts to place Mark within the framework of what Telford terms "ancient historio-biography" and to study the Gospel as an example of Graeco-Roman biography.[43] Similarities between Mark and Hellenistic-Roman biographies or "lives" have attracted particular consideration. C.W.

---

38 For the meaning and significance of "genre," I refer to B. Witherington III, *The Gospel of Mark: A Socio-Rhetorical Commentary* (Grand Rapids, Michigan: William B. Eerdman, 2001), 2.

39 For the detail discussion, see Roskam, *The Purpose of Mark,* 219-321.

40 W. Egger (1979), David Rhoads (1982), A Stock (1982), F. Hahn (1982), J. Drury (1987), W. H. Kelber (1987) – has laid emphasis upon the unity of the narrative created by Mark and the importance of reading it as a narrative whole. Kelber's book on *Mark's Story of Jesus* (1979) and David Rhoads & D. Michie's *Mark as Story* (1982) have strongly argued that the Gospel should be read as a "story." Narrative critics have analysed the Gospel in terms of its rhetoric, structure, story-line, settings and characters. While some scholars have examined a number of Mark's literary devices, others have approached particular sections of the narrative from a literary point of view – the prologue, little apocalypse or Markan ending, the passion narrative or even parenthetical comments.

41 C. H. Talbert, *What Is a Gospel? The Genre of the Canonical Gospels* (Fortress Press, Philadelphia: 1977). See the review by R. T. France "Review: Charles H. Talbert, What Is a Gospel? The Genre of the Canonical Gospels (Fortress Press, Philadelphia: 1977; SPCK, London: 1978) 47 Pp. + Xi. 3.50" in *JSNT.* 2/3 (1979): 73-76.

42 D. E. Aune, *The New Testament and Its Literary Environment* (Cambridge: Clarke, 1988).

43 According to Telford, there were three main types – life or *bios*, *memorabilbia* or *apomnemoneumata* and the aretalogy. See Telford, "Introduction," 16.

Votaw[44] was the first to advance the initial discussion on the significance of ancient biography on the Gospel genre; however, this aspect has been further developed by M. Hadas and M. Smith in their book, *Heroes and Gods* (1965)[45] and in numerous monographs. Meanwhile, D. O. Via, Beavis and others have tried to link Mark and Greek tragedy.[46] More recently, in *Sowing the Gospel: Mark's World in Literary-Historical Perspective* (1989), M. A. Tolbert argues that Mark's Gospel is best understood as belonging to the realm of popular culture and popular literature in the Greco-Roman world.[47]

A second and widely denoted view is that Mark's Gospel is a new genre and would argue for its uniqueness. W. Schneemelcher opines that the Gospel represents a form which we do not elsewhere meet with in ancient literature.[48] W. Barclay says, "In Mark we have the oldest surviving example of a type of literature which was an invention of Christianity."[49] According to S. Schulz, Mark's chief significance resides in the fact that he was the first and only one to create a "Gospel" in the strict sense of the word,[50] although his highly original literary creation was to provide a structural model for many successors.[51] A. Y. Collin also suggests that the Gospel be read as a historical monograph.[52] A third modified position is that since a literary genre which has no roots in antecedent literary types does not exist, the most possible suggestion is that

---

44 C. W. Votaw, "The Gospels and Contemporary Biographies," *ATJ* 19 (1915): 45-73, 217-249. These essays were reprinted in the Facet Book series as *The Gospels and Contemporary Biographies in the Greco-Roman World* (Philadelphia: Fortress Press, 1970).

45 Moses Hadas and Morton Smith, *Heroes and Gods; Spiritual Biographies in Antiquity* (New York: Harper & Row, 1965).

46 D. O. Via, *Kerygma and Comedy in the New Testament: A Structuralist Approach to Hermeneutic* (Philadelphia: Fortress Press, 1975); In *Marks' Audience: The literary and Social Setting of Mark 4: 11-12*, Beavis' maintains that the original audience would have perceived Mark's story of Jesus along the line of a Greek tragedy form of *chreia* (short narrative) that constitutes the larger part of the Gospel.

47 She argues that Mark's Gospel belongs by way of its literary genre with the ancient Greek novels – Chariton's *Chaereas and Callirhoe*, Xenophan's *An Ephesian Tale*, Longus' *Daphnis and Chloe*, Achilles Tatius' *Leucipippe and Clitophon*, and Heliodorus' *An Ethiopian Tale*. See M. A. Tolbert, *Sowing the Gospel: Mark's World in Literary-Historical Perspective* (Minneapolis: Fortress Press, 1989), 24-26.

48 W. Schneemelcher, *New Testament Apocrypha Vol.1, Gospels and Related Writings,* ed. Edgar Hennecke (London: Lutterworth, 1963), 76.

49 W. Barclay, *The First Three Gospels* (Philadelphia: Westminster Press, 1966), 150.

50 S. Schulz, "Mark's Significance for the Theology of Early Christianity," in *The Interpretation of Mark*, ed. W. R. Telford (Edinburgh: T&T Clark, 1995), 197-206.

51 Naickanparampil, *The Gospel of Mark*, 3.

52 A. Y. Collins, *The Beginning of the Gospel: Probings of Mark in Context* (Minneapolis: Fortress Press, 1992), 1-38.

Mark's Gospel represents a new type of "evolved" literature.[53] The innovative feature of the Markan redactor was hence to provide an existing pre-Markan passion narrative with an extended introduction. This view of the Gospel's basic structure was first suggested by M. Kähler and has operated as a major premise for a number of subsequent studies.[54] V. K. Robbins's *Jesus the Teacher: A Socio-Rhetorical Interpretation of Mark* published in 1985 argues that Mark inculcates a fusion of Biblical Jewish and Greco-Roman traditions and standards. He tries to understand Jesus as a composite aspect towards the Jewish prophets and of the Greco-Roman philosopher-teachers.[55]

However, a closer examination of Mark's Gospel suggests that many of those similarities are not apparent and very partial. For Horsley, the differences between the "lives" and Mark's story seem more fundamental.[56] Evidently, the Hellenistic-Roman "lives" were portrayed upon three types of famous figures: kings, general, and other prominent political figures, famous poets or orators, and famous philosophers.[57] Mark has Jesus, a village carpenter, as the hero of his story (Mk. 6: 3).[58] Horsley rightly observes, "far from fitting any of those types, Mark's Jesus is "a charismatic peasant prophet."[59] The literary function of the Hellenistic-Roman "lives" is to display the dominant cultural values as exemplified in the hero. But Mark presents Jesus as a protagonist who, in bringing special revitalizing powers to the people and challenging the dominant order, inaugurates a change in the historical situation.[60] Rather, Mark is narrating instances of how Jesus launched a movement of resistance among the rural agrarian communities that was spread in the surrounding areas.[61] It is suggested that Mark's Gospel is the grounding history of origins that Jesus

53 Naickanparampil, *The Gospel of Mark*, 4; M. Hengel, *Studies in the Gospel of Mark*, trans. J. Bowden (London: SCM Press, 1985), 56.

54 M. Kähler, *The so-called Historical Jesus and the Historic: Biblical Christ* (Philadelphia: Fortress Press, 1964), 80.

55 V. K. Robbins, *Jesus the Teacher: A Socio-Rhetorical Interpretation of Mark* (Philadelphia: Fortress Press, 1984), 5.

56 Horsley, *Hearing the Whole Story*, 22.

57 See Aune, *The New Testament in Its Literary Environment*, 33; also C. Bryan, *A Preface to Mark* (Oxford: Oxford University Press, 1993), 37.

58 While agreeing that Mark's Gospel is a biography, I do not think it as similar to Plutarch's Lives, or Suetonius's narratives about Caesar, or Tactitus's Agricola, or Josephus' autobiography. These are all stories of powerful elites and should be read as public transcripts of the powerful elites.

59 Horsley, *Hearing the Whole Story*, 22.

60 Horsley, *Hearing the Whole Story*, 22.

61 This assumption argues against the general view that Mark wrote the Gospel in response to the threat of persecution in the period just before or after the Jewish Revolt. Roskam, *The Purpose of Mark*, 236.

movement was a resistance movement of the agrarian community or the subaltern peoples over and against the Jerusalem rulers and Roman imperial rule.[62]

1.3. Sources of Mark and the Concept of Hidden Transcript

What is the origin of Mark? Considering the individual effort being responsible for the present form of Mark's Gospel and considering that Mark is the collector and redactor, the historical-criticism never abandons its quest for a specific written source or sources behind Mark or at least of extensive connected cycles of pre-Markan traditional material since the nineteenth-century. Redaction criticism, focusing attention on the creative acts of the evangelists themselves, has reinforced that Mark is a collection of various written or oral traditions.[63] Unlike redactional-critical studies of Matthew and Luke, it is impossible to compare Mark's finished work with a document which was assumed to be his source. An alternative approach was to examine Markan concerns. Generally speaking, source critical analysis mainly examines the miracle materials (Mk 4:35–8: 26), controversies stories (Mk 2: 1–3: 6; 7: 1-23, 11-12, 14-16), saying sources (Mk 9: 33-50–10: 1-52) apocalyptic discourse (Mk 13: 1-37), and passion narrative (Mk 14–16). Considering the orality of the Gospel and especially the limits of the literary within a few aristocrats and scribes in Judea and Galilee of Jesus time and situating the oral communication performed in the context of the Galilean agrarian community—who were not literate, and thus left no records of their own views and actions—it is imperative to denote a quest for the sources behind Mark and propose a manner in which to discern the origin of Mark's Gospel. In order to appreciate the depth of the agrarian-resistance in ancient Galilee and Judaea and to meaningfully read the Gospel of Mark in that context, we must recognize that all forms of protest and resistance, hidden or overt, are rooted in what has been called the "hidden transcript" of the subject people.[64] Evidences from a wide variety of ancient Jewish historical sources including the Gospels indicate that regular domination had generated a set of counter-values. Scott enlightens us to realize that the regular dominations of various forms such as status, material and ideology have generated a "hidden transcript" of the agrarian masses determined to preserve their own dignity, and resists the worst effects of domination and insist upon justice.[65] Scott further encourages us to examine

62 Horsley, "Submerged Biblical Histories and Imperial Biblical Studies," in *The Bible and Postcolonialism*, ed. R. S. Sugirtharajah (Sheffield: Sheffield Academic Press, 1998), 157.

63 Witherington believes that Mark is presenting the story of Jesus by gathering sources. See *The Gospel of Mark,* 16.

64 Horsley, *Jesus and Empire*, 53.

65 Scott, *Domination and the Arts of Resistance*, 114.

that Jesus' ministry was a popular ideology that comprises an alternative to the values and views that were articulated in the temple-state in Jerusalem and that it was controlled by dominant aspects that were possibly embedded in Mark's story of Jesus.[66]

Scott mentions several interrelated features of the "hidden transcript" which can be effectively used for our purpose here. When read within this perspective, Mark's Gospel in many respects analyses the features of what Scott discusses as "hidden transcript." Horsley observes,

> Not only do the earliest gospel sources, Mark and Q, portray Jesus as delivering most of his teachings as hidden transcripts, but the gospel texts themselves can only be understood as hidden transcripts, albeit very well-cooked ones.[67]

We must appreciate Horsley's observation as it renders light to read Mark's Gospel as the hidden transcript. At the same time one must note that Jesus, on certain occasions, addressed the public as well as the ruling classes. Those passages cannot be considered as the hidden transcript. We must be watchful not to confuse what was addressed to the agrarian communities off-stage as well as what was addressed to the ruling classes on-stage.

Broadly speaking, Mark reveals at least two possible sources in the composition of the Gospel. First of all, private or hidden discourses of Jesus are recognizable in various Markan passages. There are four groups of passages in which the hidden motif is embedded in Mark: (a) Jesus' command to be silent as addressed to the demons (3: 12; cf 1: 25, 34), to those who had been healed (5: 43; 7: 36), and to the disciples 8: 30; 9: 9); (b) the parables (4:10-12, 33); (c) the lack of understanding by the disciples (9: 28); (d) certain individual features which betrayed a tendency against publicity (e.g. 9: 30).[68] It is a fact that the secrecy motif pervades the whole Gospel.[69] The recognition of this motif is as old as New Testament criticism itself; yet it has never been attended to as the sources of the Gospel. Wrede's *The Messianic Secret* (1901) sees Mark not as an objective report but as the theologian of the *Messiasgeheimnis* ("messianic secret" or "messianic mystery"). According to Wrede, Jesus himself did not claim to be the Messiah, rather it was the church that regarded Jesus to be the Messiah in the light of its resurrection faith. The Church explained the paucity of messianic claims by Jesus by framing stories that Jesus had secretly

66 Scott, *Domination and the Arts of Resistance*, 118.

67 Horsley, *Jesus in Context*, 189.

68 For general discussion on Jesus' commands to silence in Mark's Gospel, See, Roskam, *The Purpose of Mark*, 172-188.

69 For detailed discussion on the Markan theme of mystery, M. Boucher, *The Mysterious Parable: A Literary Study*. CBQ Monograph Series 6 (Washington D.C.: The Catholic Biblical Association of America, 1977), 64-85.

revealed his messiahship to the disciples and had forbidden them to broadcast it. One must notice that Wrede's concern is not to see the hidden or secret motif as the source of the Gospel; rather he sought sources for the secrecy motif in the early church. Wrede, thus, regarded Mark as the originator of the messianic secret.[70] While Wrede's theory has not survived in the very form in which it was presented, his stress upon Christological motivation at work, in the composition of Mark has had a great impact upon the succeeding scholars. We need to convey special attention as to why Jesus or Mark wanted to hide the messiahship of Jesus. This must be done not in the context of the early church, but in the context of Jesus-in-movement.

Second, Mark also records the public discourse of Jesus as well. Much of the conflict stories (2: 1–3:6; 7: 1-23; 11-12; 14-16) and part of the Parable Discourse (4: 3-24) can be categorized under this. The Source-critical analysis, that focused upon the controversy stories with an aim to probe into the issue with regard to the conflict stories, has claimed to have sufficient evidence to suggest aspects that they are derived from non-Markan sources. M. J. Cook, *Mark's Treatment of the Jewish Leaders* (1978) proposes three written sources upon which the Markan redactor drew for his accounts of the conflict between Jesus and his opponents, such as: an early passion source, a source which focuses only on scribes in Jerusalem, a source which focused on Pharisees in a Galilean context.[71] J. Dewey's *Markan Public Debate: Literary Technique, Concentric Structure and Theology in Mark 2: 1–3:6* (1980) offers a different conclusion by stating that 2: 1–3: 6 is not pre-Markan source, rather it is a product of Mark's redaction upon a previously independent united tradition.[72] More recent discussion that was led by prominent scholars like J.D.G. Dunn[73] and Dewey left the matters unresolved. Mark (also Q) does indeed portray Jesus as pronouncing God's condemnation of the rulers and their representatives to their face in public. But these ostensibly public declarations of the people's real feelings in the face of power are components of overall 'text' performed in communities of resistance movements. In other words, the Gospel of Mark, as suggested by Horsley, is no longer simply the usual examples of the "hidden transcript."[74] Apart from the conflict stories, the Parable Discourse in 4: 1-34 is another public discourse in Mark. Yet, within the discourse is the private discourse. As far as the Parable Discourse is concerned, there is no further

70 Roskam, *The Purpose of Mark*, 172-176.

71 See M. J. Cook, *Mark's Treatment of the Jewish Leaders* (Leiden: Brill, 1978).

72 J. Dewey, *Markan Public Debate: Literary Technique, Concentric Structure and Theology in Mark 2:1-3:6* (Chico, Calif: Scholars Press, 1979).

73 J. G. D. Dunn, "Mark 2:1–3: 6: A Bridge between Jesus and Paul on the Question of the Law," *NTS* 30 (1984): 395-415.

74 Horsley, *Jesus and Empire*, 71.

improvement from Jeremias' assumption that supposes the existence of an underlying pre-Markan collection with 4: 11-12 as an alien insertion.[75] There may have been a consensus on the possible existence of the original document sources as redacted by Mark, but no scholarly consensus has emerged about the meaning and purpose of Mk. 4: 11-12 as Telford rightly observes,

> Nothing illustrates better the difficulties in separating tradition from redaction in 4: 1-34 than the lack of consensus in particular over the origin of the logion 4: 11-12 with its statement concerning the purpose of Jesus' parabolic teaching.[76]

While most scholars would agree that 4: 11-12 is an editorial insertion, some have viewed it as a genuine, if misplaced, saying of Jesus (*e.g.* Jeremias) and others have rendered it as post-dominical but taken from Mark's tradition (*e.g.* Schweitzer, Carlston), while others still note that it is a redactional construction, reflecting Mark's own conception of the function of the parables (*e.g.* Marxsen, Lambrecht and Räisänen).[77] Recent studies are far from rendering an adequate explanation of the hidden motifs embedded in the parable discourse of Mark. In *Mark's Audience: The Literary and Social Setting of Mark 4.11-12* (1989), Beavis argues that Mark 4: 11-12 is not only Markan but also programmatic for the whole Gospel.[78] Given that Mark conveys a resistant story of subaltern people, we must recognize that 4: 11-12 is a 'hidden transcript' that represents a critique of power behind the back of the dominant in a sequestered site.

1.4. Apocalypticism and Agrarian Politics

As we continue to consider the sources of Mark, we shall take up the issue of the source of the Apocalyptic Discourse (Mk 13) in a separate chapter. The Discourse, for many historical critics, is the incorporation of pre-Markan material. However, to what extent and level the traditional elements do remain is a matter of debate and disagreement among the scholars. One view—popularly known as "little apocalyptic" theory—is that the discourse was built around the nucleus of an apocalypse or apocalyptic fly-sheet of independent origin which had originally been circulated in the early Jewish Christian circles, either during the reign of the Emperor Caligula (37-41 C.E.) or at the time of the Roman-Jewish War. This theory has been criticized by G. R. Beasley-Murray (1954) as conveying that the teachings of chapter 13 have represented an authentic discourse of Jesus which began to circulate as

75 See Jeremias, *The Parables of Jesus,* 77-79.

76 Telford, "The Introduction," 53.

77 Telford, "The Introduction," 53, see endnotes 74.

78 M. A. Beavis, *Mark's Audience: The Literary and Social Setting of Mark 4.11-12* (Sheffield: Sheffield Academic Press, 1989).

a document within the first decade of the Church's existence.[79] J. Lambrecht has denoted that Mark had depended upon traditional elements and most notably on Q and the Old Testament. He argues for the Markan redactional activity that is evident throughout it.[80] As more and more scholars argued for Markan dependence on written sources, or at least a combination by oral tradition, many scholars have gone ahead to link Mark 13 with prophetic and apocalyptic passages, particularly Daniel, Micah, Joel, and Zechariah. In *Prophecy Interpreted* (1966), L. Hartman argues that Mark 13 was based on an exposition or meditation upon the book of Daniel.[81]

In spite of the growing awareness of the influence of Jewish scriptures on the composition of Mark 13, we should be cautious enough to note that the concept of "apocalyptic" is problematic in the modern interpretive category. It is important to discern the difference between the Judean apocalyptic literature and the modern concept of apocalypticism. Mark's Gospel cannot be simply interpreted by using the modern concept of apocalypticism which has time as its basic hermeneutical principle. It is Horsley (2001) who draws our attention in this regard. He alleges that European scholars are developing the concept of apocalypticism as "a synthetic construct composed of what they deemed typical elements abstracted from a variety of Jewish 'revelatory' literature from different historical situations ranging from the third B.C.E. to the late antiquity."[82] Under what circumstances and in what regard, then, might apocalyptic literature composed in scribal circles be possible sources for what agrarian people were thinking and doing? Identification of the political crises that the agrarian people were facing under the imperial rule that apparently led to the composition of apocalyptic literature may provide the answer. One must try to decode the subaltern politics lying beneath the apocalyptic texts. In this regard, T. B. Liew's analysis of "Mark's politics of apocalyptic time" becomes our source of inspiration.[83] Situating Mark in the context of resistance and reading it as a resistance story that was addressed to subordinated agrarian

---

79 G. R. Beasley-Murray. *Jesus and the Future: An Examination of the Criticism of the Eschatological Discourse, Mark 13, with Special Reference to the Little Apocalypse Theory* (London: Macmillan, 1954).

80 J. Lambrecht, *Die Redaktion der Markus-Apokalypse: Literarische Analyse und Strukturuntersuchung* (Rom: Päpstliches Bibelinstitut, 1967).

81 L. Hartman, *Prophecy Interpreted* (Lund: Gleerup, 1966).

82 Horsley, *Hearing the Whole Story*, 124; also "Kingdom of God and the Renewal of Israel," 303-344.

83 Liew analyses three major aspects in Mark's Gospel such as: authority, agency and gender to understand what he denotes the "politics of apocalyptic time" in the Gospel. Liew poses certain valid and positive questions against traditional conclusions. See, "The Gospel of Mark," 105-131.

communities sounds less apocalyptic.[84] Mark's Gospel is concerned with opposition to the Roman imperial rule. Horsley rightly argues that Mark's story is not received by divine "revelation" (ἀποκάλυψις).[85] Many features of Mark 13 that have been labelled "apocalyptic" are not distinctive to apocalyptic literature. A more attentive reading of Mark's Gospel in its historical context suggests that "apocalyptic" features were not determinative in Mark.

As indicated in the previous chapter, the Judean apocalyptic literature was written in connection with the Modein Resistance and the Hellenistic persecution under Antiochus Epiphanes. The Scribes, who were responsible for the final form of apocalyptic literature, were controlled by the authority of the high priests in accordance with the tradition and the law to which the temple-state was governed. When the governing high priests, collaborating with the imperial rulers, compromised or abandoned the indigenous Judean way of life, scribal circles were inevitably caught in the middle. Remaining loyal to the traditional Judean culture and laws, of which they were the very guardians, could lead to breaking with, and even opposing, their high-priestly aristocracy. This is precisely what is evident in early apocalyptic literature such as the dream-visions of Daniel 7–12 and sections of I Enoch.[86] Thus, in the very circumstance that evoked apocalyptic literature, certain scribal circles came to experience not only a subjection to foreign rulers but also opposition from and to their own rulers in ways similar to what peasantry had experienced most of the time. These similar experiences may well have evoked similar responses from those who were rooted in the same cultural tradition.[87] It is with this insight that we put forth an analysis of Jesus' speech to the disciples about the future (Mk 13) which is the main basis on which Mark has been deemed as "apocalyptic." The principal motive for modern interpretation of Mark 13 as a "little apocalypse" or an "apocalyptic leaflet" was the concern to discover the source behind Mark and to determine the redactional activities of the evangelist. We need to abandon the modern concept of "apocalyptic" and take a fresh look at the manner in which the earliest Gospel documents portray Jesus' pronouncement of Judgment in Mark 13.[88] If Mark 13 is an exposition of the Book of Daniel as Hartman argues, we must try to find how Jesus—who "taught them as one who had authority, not as the scribes" (Mk. 1: 22)—reads the apocalyptic literature in the context of agrarian politics.

84 Horsley, *Hearing the Whole Story*, 122.

85 Horsley, *Hearing the Whole Story*, 123.

86 Horsley, "Wisdom and Apocalypticism," 228-230.

87 Horsley, *Hearing the Whole Story*, 126.

88 Horsley, *Jesus and Empire*, 81.

1.5. Mark in the Social Context

Our investigation into the domination and resistance in Mark's Gospel has brought us to conclude that Jesus was spearheading a movement of protest and resistance among the rural agrarian communities against urban elites in Jerusalem. Since Jesus mainly dwelt and moved in and around Galilee, it appears that the scale of resistance in Mark's Gospel is limited within Galilee and Jerusalem. Many historical-critical scholars have investigated the significance of the Markan spatial designations Galilee and Jerusalem. Recent literary-critical studies like E. S. Malbon's *Narrative and Mythic in Mark* (1988) have continued to discuss Jesus' movement within the geographical scale of Galilee and Jerusalem, and shifted focus upon the literary and theological whole. A closer reading of Markan story, especially its sub-plot and characters urges us to re-examine Jesus' movement with a multi-scalar approach. The relation between Galilee and Jerusalem which J. Svartvik has termed as "North-south Axis"[89] has generated much discussion and debate for almost over a century. Most scholars who studied the issue have labelled Galilee as "the land of receptor" and Jerusalem as "the city of rejection."[90] In this regard, the influence of the historical-critical studies by E. Lohmeyer, R. H. Lightfoot, Marxsen, Kelber, *et al.* are quite enormous. In *Galiläa und Jerusalem* (1936), Lohmeyer has initially postulated a historical context for the theological dichotomy by denoting that Galilee is the "locale for the eschatological manifestations" while Jerusalem is "the city of foes and sin."[91] For Lohmeyer, Galilee is the centre of Jesus' ministry and the future centre of the fulfilled God's reign, the "holy land" of Mark's Gospel. Jerusalem, on the other hand, was the centre of opposition to 'Mark's' Jesus.[92]

More and more Markan scholars after Lohmeyer have claimed that Galilee and Jerusalem were in opposition to each other. In *Locality and Doctrine in the Gospels* (1936), Lightfoot has made a significant statement regarding the Galilee-Jerusalem axis when he says, "Galilee is the scene of revelation, Jerusalem the scene only of rejection."[93] For him, Galilee and Jerusalem stand in opposition to each other, as the story of the Gospel runs in Mark.[94] In *Mark the Evangelist* (1969), while accepting the historical and eschatological emphases of Lohmeyer and Lightfoot, Marxsen goes further to

89 Svartvik, *Mark and Mission,* 229.

90 Svartvik, *Mark and Mission,* 236.

91 E. Lohmeyer, *Galiläa und Jerusalem* (Göttingen: Vandenhoeck & Ruprecht, 1936), 34-35.

92 Lohmeyer, *Galiläa und Jerusalem*, 34-35.

93 R. H. Lightfoot, *Locality and Doctrine in the Gospels* (London: Hodder & Stoughton, 1936), 81-84.

94 Lightfoot, *Locality and Doctrine in the Gospels*, 124-125.

elucidate upon what both have overlooked as the importance of distinguishing tradition and redaction in Mark. Marxsen argues that the redactional activity of Mark is found basically in the framework – that is, "topical" which is Galilee.[95] In using this framework, Marxsen's exegetical studies on Markan texts is much weighted by Galilee alone, while to a large extent losing the sense of Galilee-Jerusalem relations were stressed upon by Lohmeyer and Lightfoot. Marxsen, one of the earliest redaction critics, acknowledges the significance of Galilee, when he comments: "Galilee is not to be taken strictly as the area west of the Sea, but as including the territory around the Sea."[96] Galilee as a "theological symbol" or "more than just the geographical area" was significant for recent scholars who have employed a sociopolitical framework of reading.

Kelber's *The Kingdom in Mark: A New Place and A New Time* (1974) is an attempt to analyse a balance between the previous studies. Analysing the "kingdom" passages in Mark's Gospel within the framework of Galilee-Jerusalem relations, Kelber has come out with the conclusion along with Lohmeyer that "Mark is representative of a northern Christianity which is in opposition to a southern Jerusalem-type Christianity.[97] Kelber has offered much with his study, for example, that while "in Galilee-Jerusalem polarity is the most conspicuous dynamic" operating within the scale framework of the Markan narrative, it does not represent the full extent of that special framework.[98] Kelber appears to maintain that the Galilee-Jerusalem conflict as historical reality reflects the hostility between Jerusalem Christians and Galilean Christians. Kelber further acknowledges Galilee as "the locus of the Kingdom of God" and the place where "the Kingdom began and where in Mark's own generation it will be consummated."[99]

In the same vein, Freyne, who is widely known as a "connoisseur of the social world of Galilee in the first century"[100] places Galilee as the distinct context in which Jesus revealed the message of salvation and the people of Galilee, who were on the margins of society, became the percipients of the Gospel, while Jerusalem became the city that rejected Jesus.[101] While accepting the significance of Galilee as the spatial basis for Jesus' movement, one must be mindful nevertheless that "scale" has become increasingly problematized in the sociopolitical movement literature. Geographers, such as R. H. Schein, have

95 Marxsen, *Mark the Evangelist* (New York/Nashville: Abingdon, 1969), 56-62.

96 Marxsen, *Mark the Evangelist*, 67.

97 W. H. Kelber, *The Kingdom in Mark: A New Place and a New Time* (Philadelphia: Fortress Press, 1974), 64-65.

98 Kelber, *The Kingdom in Mark*, 129.

99 Kelber, *The Kingdom in Mark,* 130.

100 Svatvik, *Mark and Mission*, 232.

101 Freyne, *Galilee,* 269.

argued that traditional views on scale as "nested spatial hierarchy consisting of fixed, bounded and reified levels—local, regional, national, global—have been challenged by more fluid approaches to special relations, focused upon connections and oppositions and the processes that construct scale in the first place."[102] Hence, it is no longer possible to take sides with the traditional view that bounded Jesus' campaign within the scale of Galilee-Jerusalem. Rather, as D. Masson explains, "scale should not be thought of in void or in the abstract, but always as a dimension of social process."[103]

With such a perspective, the scale of the Markan Jesus' movement might be conceptualized as Galilee being the focal setting at which spatial boundaries namely – Judea, Idumea and beyond Jordan are defined for a specific social claim, activity, or behaviour. Based upon what Lohmeyer has established in terms of the presence of two centres of Christianity, one in Galilee and other in Jerusalem, most studies on Mark have delineated that the two centres had differed in their messianic understanding as well as theological concerns. As pointed by Joy, many scholars including Lightfoot, Marxsen, Kelber and Malbon have argued that Galilee maintained the Son of Man eschatology whereas in Jerusalem it was a nationalistic eschatology.[104] In their expectation of parousia the two centres differed.

As Svartvik rightly observes, the conflict has been rekindled by the new literary critics and postcolonial critics in more recent times.[105] Joy argues that Jerusalem-centred authorities addressed the political issues which affected their survival while forgetting the struggles of the peasants in Galilee.[106] Freyne indicates that Galilee was a stronghold of a powerful resistant movement, *viz*. Zealotism and it was a province with social and political unrest that was provoked by Roman exploitation and an apocalyptic outlook.[107] Freyne believes that the ideas of resistance in the movement of Jesus were easily understood and accepted by the lay people of Galilee.[108] The subalterns in Galilee became part of the resistant movement against Roman colonialism and went as far as opposing the religious authorities in Jerusalem.[109]

---

102 R. H. Schein, "The Place of Landscape: A Conceptual Framework for Interpreting an American Scene," *AAAG* 87/4 (1997): 662.

103 D. Masson, "Transnationalizing Feminist and Women Movements: Towards a Scalar Approach," in *Transnationalizing Women's' Movements: Solidarities without Borders*, ed. P. Dufour, D. Masson and D. Caouette (Vancouver: University of British Columbia Press, 2010), 23.

104 Joy, *Mark and Its Subalterns,* 67.

105 Svartvik, *Mark and Mission,* 229.

106 Kelber, *The Kingdom in Mark,* 68.

107 Freyne, *Galilee,* 5.

108 Freyne, *Galilee,* 5.

109 H. W. Hoehner, *Herod Antipas* (Cambridge: Cambridge University, 1972), 112.

However, not all the Markan scholars have agreed with those arguments that were postulated by the scholars cited above. Svartvik is skeptical about labeling Galilee as "the land of reception" and Jerusalem as "the city of rejection," by earlier scholars and later pursuers of structural and narrative criticism. After examining various antitheses, such as the historical-theological, structural, narrative, he concludes that "the importance of the Galilee-Jerusalem relation has been exaggerated" and for him "Mark does present such a geographical north-south tension as has been suggested."[110] Svartvik also has no doubt that, in contrast to the connotations of Jerusalem, Galilee is connected with "positive symbolic values" yet he insists that "the difference should not be exaggerated."[111] In spite of such a strong caveat voiced by Svartvik, one should not overlook Mark's efforts to bring the conflict between Galilee and Jerusalem.

It is undeniable that Galilee, in the context of Mark's Gospel, is a significant territory as far as colonial domination and resistance are concerned.[112] It is argued that the social context of Mark, which reflects the situation of Galilee during the early period of the first century C.E., has many layers. Most possibly, the struggle against social oppression could be an ideological strategy by the movement of Jesus in Galilee. Elizondo also pointed out that Galilee witnessed "multiple invasions" and "infiltration and migration."[113] This makes the region a place of cultural and economic interaction due to the presence of many ethnic-linguistic groups. As a result Galilee was "rejected and despised by the Judeans because of the racial mixture of the area and its distance from the temple in Jerusalem."[114]

1.6. The Structure of Mark's Gospel

Endeavours to explain the structure of Mark's Gospel generally recognise a similar pattern of development of the plot. The most widely made observation is that in chapter 8 there is a watershed created by Peter's confession of Jesus as Messiah (8: 29) and by Jesus' subsequent declaration that his messianic mission is to culminate in rejection and death (8: 31), a fate which those who follow him must expect to share (8: 34-38). Up to this point, the story has been of Jesus' ministry in and around Galilee, and of the opposition from the Scribes and Pharisees who were supposedly deputed from Jerusalem. After this point, Mark's story moves towards Jerusalem where the public and direct opposition to the powers in Jerusalem are to take place and the focus is less on public

110 Svartvik, *Mark and Mission*, 236.

111 Svartvik, *Mark and Mission*, 236.

112 Joy, *Mark and Its Subalterns*, 64.

113 Elizondo, *Galilean Journey*, 53.

114 Elizondo, *Galilean Journey*, 53.

ministry than on the teaching of the disciples in sequestered sites for what lies ahead. A further turning point comes at the end of chapter 10, when Jesus and his disciples arrived in Jerusalem and the direct confrontation with the powers began. As a result, Mark's Gospel[115] is often understood as consisting of three main stages that are focused on three geographical locations: in and around Galilee (1: 14–8: 21), on the road to Jerusalem (8: 22-10: 52), and in Jerusalem (11: 1 onwards).[116]

Within each of these main stages, there are various sub-sections recognized by modern scholars. Besides this, there are various ways of understanding and handling these sub-sections. Those scholarly works can be broadly divided into two. On the one hand, we have quite a few scholars who have taken the micro-structures within the chapters of Mark's Gospel. The most common examples for the micro-structures are: chiasm,[117] sandwich technique,[118] and doublets.[119] On the other hand, there are scholars who have outlined the Gospel as based upon macro-structures. The rationale behind macro-structures seems to be one of establishing the biographical identity of Jesus. Witherington observes that the structure of Mark's Gospel has been divided into several parts by three questions: Who is Jesus (1: 27, 2: 7, 16, 24, 4: 41; 6: 2; 7: 5), what is his mission (8: 31; 9: 31; 10: 32), and how will the mission be accomplished (chaps. 11-16).[120] Myers proposes that the three major events in Jesus' life—baptism, transfiguration, and death—are narrated in order to focus the reader's attention upon the identity of Jesus.[121] Above all, this three-stage geographical progression is widely noted by Markan interpreters to be the principal structural basis of Mark's Gospel.[122]

---

115 The reference here is the story of Jesus after the prologue (1: 1-13).

116 Some scholars such as Naickanparampil would divide this aspect into five. See, *The Gospel of Mark*, 18.

117 J. Dewey (1980) has outlined the controversy stories of Mark 2: 1–3: 6 by using the chasm. The literary unit is framed by two healing stories (2: 1-12; 3: 1-6), and it has two units of controversies in evolved eating (2: 13-17; 2: 23-27). It would then provide as a centrepiece for a rationale for the behaviour of Jesus and His disciples (2: 18-22). See, J. Dewey, "The Literary Structure of the Controversy Stories in Mark 2:1–3: 6" in *The Interpretation of Mark*," edited by Telford, 141-151.

118 Witherington has listed seven examples that are widely accepted by scholars. The purpose of this technique, according to him is "to encourage the reader to read the two stories in the light of each other, with the one interpreting the other." See, *The Gospel of Mark*, 36-37.

119 Examples of doublets in Mark are: two stories on feeding narratives (6: 30-44; 6: 45-52); two discourses (4: 1-34; 13: 3ff).

120 Witherington, *The Gospel of Mark*, 38-39.

121 C. Myers, *Binding the Strong Man: A Political Reading of Mark's Story of Jesus* (Maryknoll, N.Y.: Orbis, 1988), 390-391.

122 For other suggested structures of Mark, see Robbins, *Jesus the Teacher*, 19-48.

The conclusion, however, is all the more probable when we take note of the detailed whereabouts of Jesus. We can see how this geographical outline is artificial and general. Instead, Mark portrays that Jesus' ministry is beyond geographical borders as Jesus moves back and forth while directing towards Jerusalem.[123] Right from the very outset of Jesus' ministry in and around Capernaum, his fame began to spread throughout Galilee (1: 28); people great in numbers from Judea, Jerusalem, Idumea, Tyre and Sidon came to Jesus (3: 8); and twice the Scribes and the Pharisees from Jerusalem confronted him while Jesus was in Galilee (3: 22; 7: 1). Moreover, given that most Galileans made regular visits to Jerusalem at Passover time, Jesus could have been in Jerusalem before the final week of his ministry. Mark's own narrative indicates such visits to Judea.[124] Mark's outline of an extensive ministry in and around Galilee was followed by a lengthy journey southwards that had culminated in a single climatic visit to Jerusalem and owes more to his dramatic reshaping of the story than to a naive recording of events just as they occurred.[125] We need to consider if this 'Galilee and Jerusalem' schema may properly be understood to have political significance for Mark. In this research, we shall try to understand Mark's Gospel in terms of power relations. Otherwise, the spatial progression of Jesus' ministry, as a purely geographical datum, looks like a structure that has been deliberately imposed upon the story.[126]

In the previous section, we have argued upon the possibility of Mark's Gospel as a resistance story of subalterns. This helps us to consider the political discourses lying in Mark's Gospel as an alternative way of structuring the Gospel. Scott offers us four interrelated political discourses among the subjugated people.[127] Among these four political discourses, three of them are perhaps helpful to our task of discovering the structure of the Gospel. This is not meant to suggest that Mark's Gospel has been designed for performance in three sections. We must thoroughly note how Mark structures the story of Jesus-in-movement to counter-resistance that he received from the urban powerful elites. This leads us to take into consideration the interaction between Jesus and those of the powerful elites. Only after this consideration do we have the exploration of how Jesus speaks truth to powers. It is an observation about how we discern the development of the plot and this may or may not be in keeping with how Mark had devised the structure of his story of Jesus.

---

123 For detail, see Iersel, *Mark: A Reader-Response Commentary*, 76-86.

124 Such as His already existing links with his hosts in Bethany, with the owners of the donkey and of the guest room in Jerusalem that were used for the Passover meal (Mk. 10-11).

125 France, *The Gospel of Mark*, 12.

126 France, *The Gospel of Mark*, 12.

127 Scott, *Domination and the Arts of Resistance*, 18-19.

2. Some Methodological Issues Involved in the Study of the Domination and Resistance in Mark's Gospel

Having identified Mark's Gospel as the story of resistance by the subalterns and having reviewed the Gospel in the context of resistance movement, we shall now attempt to understand the texts in the light of what has been discussed. Before we analyse deeper into the texts, we must bring out a brief report on how Markan scholars have dealt with the issue of domination and resistance in the past. This is to assess how the issue can be studied from a different perspective. The aspect of domination and resistance in Jesus' ministry has been the focus of New Testament research as early as during the modern critical analysis of New Testament. However, right from H. S. Reimarus (1774–1778) to Bandon (1967), until the publication of Horsley's *Jesus and the Spiral of Violence: Popular Jewish Resistance* in 1987,[128] the resistance motifs embedded in the ministry of Jesus had been viewed either in terms of violence/revolutionary or non-violence/non-revolutionary.

Attempts have been carried out mainly to view Jesus' movement in the light of the revolutionary movement led by the Zealot party. E. Bammel's survey on "The Revolution theory from Reimarus to Brandon" published in *Jesus and the Politics of His Day* (1984) reveals that every investigation that assumes revolutionary motifs in the Gospels was counter acted by non-revolutionary ideologists each time.[129] The theory that Jesus was mixed up in the movement or party armed resistance to Rome commonly called the "Zealots" has already been popularized since the publication of R. Eisler's *The Messiah and John the Baptist* published in 1929. It has never lacked proponents especially as prominent scholars like M. Hengel and Brandon have pursued this further.

However, as Horsley & Hanson, and Myers observe, this theoretical assumption could not convince the European and American scholars who were responding to domestic protest and Third World movements of national liberation. There had been strong attempts to "ward off any implication that Jesus had advocated active resistance of any sort to the established order by contrasting Jesus with the Zealots" from the western scholars.[130] The prevailing view that maintained and strongly insisted that there was no organized revolutionary movement at the time of Jesus is a blow to those who viewed Jesus as a revolutionary. The rise and fall of resistance theory being witnessed in the above tinted history of the interpretation of historical Jesus' movement is largely due to the inadequacy of methodology. There is no

128 Horsley, *Jesus and the Spiral of Violence* .page

129 E. Bammel, "The Revolution Theory from Reimarus to Brandon" in *Jesus and the Politics of His Day*, ed. E. Bammel and C. F. D. Moule (Cambridge: Cambridge University Press, 1984).

130 Horsley, *Jesus and the Spiral of Violence*, xi; Myers, *Binding the Strong Man*, 463.

proper conceptualization of resistance which is relevant to the historical Jesus in his sociopolitical milieu. Resistance and dominance should be understood as relational and not separable into distinct categories or levels, whereas the past studies of historical Jesus—especially, under those historical criticism and new literary criticism—largely analyse Jesus or Mark's Gospel out of its political domination. It is assumed that from everyday forms of resistance to sociopolitical and religious movement that has become trans-national in scale, Jesus' movement in Galilee has produced and resulted complex shapes and forms of covert and overt defiance and resistance.

However, extensive literature on the historical Jesus and Mark's Gospel have accumulated over centuries and have been limited within two major approaches: the first emphasizes the violent or revolutionary nature of Jesus' movement that often places Jesus in the company of Zealot resistance fighters. Such a school of thought is probably represented by Reimarus, R. Eisler[131] and Robertson, Brandon,[132] and others. The second stream covers an even larger body of literature and is concerned with the theological and ethical aspects of Jesus' movement. It had also proposed Jesus' movement as non-violent and a few notable ones such as – Schweitzer, Kalthoff, Bultmann and his followers, A. Trocmé, O. Cullman, R. R. Beck and others have depicted this perspective. What these two bodies of stream reveal is a dichotomous typology that has tended to typecast forms of resistance of Jesus' movement as inherently opposite.

What is missing in the past analyses of resistance in both Jesus' movement and Mark's Gospel is, most seemingly, an analytical and comparative framework that highlights the spectrum of the types of resistance from hidden, ordinary and often at times passive to more overt, extraordinary and actively defiant forms of agrarian collective action. At the same time, we need to focus upon the interconnectedness of different scales of collective action across the individual and community levels to local, regional, national, and trans-national. As it has been pointed out, Mark's Gospel encloses potential materials that depicted public and private discourses of Jesus. This public-private dichotomy is indicative of Mark's hermeneutical tool in the composition of the story of Jesus' campaign. While the contemporary analyses of rural resistance, such as: Gramsci, Polanyi and Caouette & Turner have increasingly enriched the field

131 In *The Messiah and John the Baptist* (1929, ET. 1931), R. Eisler has launched a departure in Jesus studies based on source material outside the Gospels and the revolutionary ambition and failure of Jesus. Eisler locates nascent Christianity in the wider context of the social unrest of the time.

132 Brandon, *Jesus and the Zealots*, 355. This work is built on his earlier book, *The Fall of Jerusalem and the Christian Church* (London, 1951). Brandon did not claim that Jesus was actually a Zealot, a member of the party, but that His disciples were in fundamental sympathy with the ideals and aims of the Zealot movements.

of rural/agrarian resistance studies, they are not helpful towards analyzing the theological and political implication of the interrelationship between public and private discourses in Mark's Gospel. We shall basically employ Scott's thesis of the private-public interaction in order to understand the complexities of dominion and resistance with the scale of Jesus' campaign in Capernaum and the nearby villages pertaining to wider Galilee and beyond, as well as in Jerusalem.

3. The Agrarian-Resistance Motifs in Jesus' Campaign in Capernaum and the Nearby Villages (Mk 1:14–3:6)

Mark 1:14–3:6 covers Jesus' campaign narrowly in Capernaum and its neighbourhood. This part of the Gospel begins with the proclamation of the kingdom of God (1: 14) and ends with the Jewish leaders who had to kill him as a result of their strict surveillance (3: 6). In between, Mark arranges various activities of Jesus-in-movement as well as people's wide ranging reaction to those activities of Jesus. Considering the geopolitical situation of Capernaum and its relationship with Jerusalem, many of the Jesus' materials assume a discourse of dignity and indignation of the Galilean villagers. We assume that the public actions and behaviour of any popular resistance movements in Galilee and Judea were coerced by the forces of Roman-Herodian domination that were arrayed against them. This aspect of the Gospel shall be analyzed as the "hidden Transcript" of agrarian dignity and the indignation that developed in sequestered sites of the public stage to counter the regular indignities of domination.

3.1. Jesus-in-movement on the Move: Proclaiming a Hidden Transcript

3.1.1. The Kingdom of God (Mk 1: 14-15)

"Jesus enters the world fearlessly with his message amidst State terrorism that arrested John the Baptizer."[133] This is an introductory remark in a recently published *One Volume Dalit Bible Commentary* (2010). Mark summarizes the message of what Jesus has proclaimed as "the good news of God."[134] The core message of the proclamation is: the kingdom of God has come. People must repent and believe in the good news (1: 14-15). A major change in scene and message has been rendered from that of John's preaching and baptism in the Jordan valley to the preaching of the kingdom

133 M. Goretti, M. Daniel, and A.M.A. Raja, "The Gospel According to Mark," in *One Volume Dalit Bible Commentary: New Testament*, ed. T. K. John (New Delhi: Centre for Dalit/Subaltern Studies, 2010), 171.

134 Crossan, *The Power of Parables*, 159-161.

of God in Galilee.[135] France puts it, "Down here [Jordan valley], people had had to make a special journey to John, but now Jesus is going to where people are, in the inhabited areas of his own province."[136] Most possibly, Jesus wanted to escape the tyranny of the Herod in that moment of the arrest of John and Galilean villages could be a better site therefore to begin his ministry.[137] Jesus, according to Mark, proclaimed τὸ εὐαγγέλιον τοῦ θεοῦ to the Galileans (Mk 1: 14-15). The εὐαγγέλιον which was announced in v.1 as the subject of Mark's Gospel is now proclaimed by Jesus. Some scholars have identified "the coming of Jesus Christ, the Son of God" as the content of the εὐαγγέλιον.[138] Mark maintains in his Gospel that Jesus is the subject of preaching and not the content or the central message of the preaching (Mk 1: 14, 38-39). The kingdom of God stands as its central message (1: 14-15). Simon maintains that Jesus' proclamation "creates an avenue for a subjected community to perceive the *imperium* of God emerging on their behalf."[139] The "good news of God" assumes well prepared and sophisticated politico-cultural forms.

This is the first public action of Jesus. Being a Galilean, like any other Galileans, Jesus was one of those who lived under the regular indignities of domination. His action and behaviour could have been coerced by the forces of domination. Thus, Jesus' central message—the kingdom of God—should be perceived as something that has come out of the experiences of the subjugated people, rather than arriving from another world.[140] Evidences from the historical situation of the book of Daniel indicate that the Seleucid domination and exploitation had generated the ideal of God's reign (Dan 7: 13-14). Jesus' central message combines the declaration of the arrival of the "kingdom of God" and sharp command to repent and believe in the kingdom of God (Mk 1: 14-15). In other words, it is a sharp declaration of God's judgment against the forms and practices of domination and hopeful declarations of the sufficiency and justice that was possible under the reign of God. Jesus' speech resonates vibrantly with Israelite popular tradition. Far from being pure

135 Naickanparampil maintains the difference in the content of proclamation by John the Baptist and Jesus. See, *The Gospel of Mark*, 51; also see Iersel, *Mark: A reader-Response Commentary*, 129-130.

136 R. T. France, *The Gospel of Mark: A Commentary on the Greek Text* (Grand Rapids, Michigan: Eerdmans and Carlisle: The Paternoster Press, 2002), 90.

137 Here I refer to H. E. Wicke who suggests that Jesus moved the thrust of His campaign in Galilee when opposition to the martyr of John the Baptist was mounted in Jerusalem. See, *Mark*, The People's Bible Series (Milwaukee, Wisconsin: Northwestern Publishing House, 1988), 21.

138 France, *The Gospel of Mark,* 91.

139 Samuel, *A Postcolonial Reading of Mark's Story of Jesus*, 121.

140 For Waetjen, it is "the new moral order." See, *A Reordering of Power*, 78.

thought or theology, Jesus' teaching displays features of regular performance in community settings and even in some cases within aspects of performative speech.

3.1.2. Exorcism and Healing: An Expression of Anger and Dignity (1: 21-39)

Healings and exorcisms of some occasions must also be analyzed as hidden transcripts, as they supposedly express anger and resentment of the subaltern people in sequestered sites. Mark 1: 21-39 is a short collection of scenes in and around Capernaum. It is apparently constructed within the framework of a day or two (vv. 29, 32, and 35). Mark portrays Jesus as performing exorcism and healing in village communities, particularly in the synagogues (1: 21-27; 3: 1-5), private houses in Capernaum (1: 29-34; 2: 1-12) and in one unidentified place (1: 40-44). Many western scholars would take healings and exorcisms of Jesus merely as spiritual miracles that marked the arrival of God's reign while neglecting the socio-political and economic aspects. Carter's *The Roman Empire and the New Testament* (2006) brings out interesting discussions upon economics, food and health in the context of Roman imperialism.[141] He denotes that the imperial control of access to food and the imperial food system stand behind the sickness, psychosomatic illness and demonic possessions that were found in the Gospels. Carter concludes, "Jesus' healings and exorcisms are the direct confrontation with the effects of Roman rule."[142] We shall treat the healings and exorcism found within the first political discourse of Mark (1: 14–3: 6) as "dignity-restoring counter-ideology" that negates the dominant paradigm and as one that expresses anger, revenge and worth assertion.[143] They can be grouped into two: On the one hand, we have those that are performed beyond the effective reach of the eyes and ears of power (1: 21-28, 29-34); and those that are performed in the sight of the Scribes and the Pharisees on the other hand (2: 1-12; 3: 1-6). We shall read them in relation to how Jesus uses these occasions to speak truth to powers. The first miraculous work of Jesus in Mark is the encounter with the man with the unclean spirit (1: 21-28). The incident occurred in a synagogue of Capernaum on Sabbath. Mark is silent about the scribal presence.[144] Jesus, or at least Mark, capitalizes this

141 Carter, *The Roman Empire and the New Testament*, 100-136, especially 116-136.

142 Carter, *The Roman Empire and the New Testament*, 117.

143 J. R. Donahue finds a series of strong emotions, such as: pity (1: 41), violent displeasure (1: 43), anger (3: 5), *etc.*, but he considers this simply as the "realism of Mark" drawn from common life. See, his article, "Jesus as the Parable of God in the Gospel of Mark," *Interpretation* 32/4 (1978): 379.

144 Iersel, *Mark: A Reader-Response Commentary*, 135.

occasion to Jesus in terms of expressing his self-worth.[145] It was an accusation for Jesus to be "one having authority, and not as the scribes" (vv. 24, 27) and his fame spread throughout Galilee because Jesus restores that man to fuller humanity.[146]

This incident is followed by the single healing of Peter's mother-in-law. Mark tells us that on leaving the Synagogue, they went the house of Peter and Andrew and James and John went with them (v. 29). The place was Peter's house in Capernaum, therefore, it was a sequestered site beyond the control of powers. Thus, there is no one to question the action of Jesus.[147] Mark denotes that the general people in Capernaum had waited till the sun set, *i.e.*, the end of the Sabbath to bring people who are ill, to Jesus.[148] Thus, the individual healing is followed by mass healing. Mark says "they brought to him all who were sick or possessed with demons" (v. 32). C. S. Mann is right in commenting, thus, "There are no details of any words of Jesus, no account of the symptoms of the sickness, and no mention of any amazement on the part of the bystanders."[149] At any rate, Mark uses the incidents to express the worth of Jesus, saying, "the city was gathered around the door" (v. 33).

3.1.3. Coming Out from Hidden: A Mission of Jesus-in-Movement (1: 35-39)

Up to this point, Jesus operated at a micro level in Capernaum. Mark informs us that Jesus passed along the Sea of Galilee (1: 16), then went to Capernaum" (1: 21), and stayed in Peter's house (1: 29). Mark 1: 35-39 bring us to the end of the scene begun in v. 21. The scene is still Capernaum, but at the outskirts or "a quiet place near the town."[150] The people of Capernaum wanted Jesus to stay and the disciples brought that hope to Jesus. However, Mark's story of Jesus opens a new chapter as Jesus' sense of mission compels him to leave the successful ministry in Capernaum in order to extend his proclamation of the "good news of God" to the rest of Galilee. Thus, Jesus moves on to the next villages (Gr. κωμοπόλις). Jesus invited to his disciples, "Let us go on to the neighbouring towns [Gr. κωμοπόλεις], so that I may proclaim the message there also; for that is what I came out to do" (v. 38). And He went throughout all Galilee, preaching in their Synagogues and casting out demons

145 This comment is made from the observation that Jesus, at that stage, was a new teaching with unheard authority.

146 Samuel, *A Postcolonial Reading of Mark's Story of Jesus*, 123-124.

147 The issues of healing on Sabbath will be raised in Mk. 3: 1-6.

148 France, *The Gospel of Mark*, 107.

149 C. S. Mann, *Mark: A New Translation with Introduction and Commentary*, The Anchor Bible Vol. 27 (New York: Doubleday & Company, Inc., 1986), 214.

150 France, *The Gospel of Mark*, 111.

(Mk 1: 38). Mark's use of the term κωμοπόλεις is highly significant.[151] There have been various interpretations. For Waetjen, it denotes market towns,[152] whereas scholars like Myers regard it to be a "country town."[153] Considering the economic and political context of Galilee, Freyne's description of the word as village "synoecisms" must be given priority in our search for the political meaning of Mark 1: 38.[154] Besides, here is an important mission statement of Jesus that is politically significant to the Gospel: "for that is what I came out to do" (v. 38b).[155] This is a clear and explicit purpose of Jesus' preaching tour in a wider Galilee. The Greek word ἐξῆλθον carries the original idea of Jesus' mission which is from rural to urban.[156] A similar use of ἐξῆλθον in Mark's Gospel in 2: 17; 10: 45 expresses this essential mission suggesting Jesus' departure from Capernaum or leaving Nazareth onto the open (1: 14, 38b).[157] In the words of Scott, the hidden transcript developed by the subaltern people in sequestered sites in villages was now set for public declaration in the rural towns of Galilee. Mark introduces to us the mission paradigm of Jesus as one of coming out from the hidden to the public, and from the rural to the urban in terms of speaking truth to powers.

3.1.4. Testing the Limits

The first round of Jesus' preaching tour ended with a general remark: "And he went throughout Galilee, proclaiming the message in their synagogues and casting out demon" (v. 39). Up to this point, we have Jesus—"a charismatic popular leader and his cadre"[158]—pleasantly moving from village to village, proclaiming new ideology and dealing with the village and its problems.[159]

---

151 This word is not found in LXX.

152 Waetjen, *A Reordering of Power*, 13.

153 Myers, *Binding the Strong Man*, 150.

154 Freyne denotes that κωμοπόλεις is an economic construct in which clans banded together for survival. This finds support from the geopolitical setting of the major Greek cities in Galilee which formed a circle. Freyne, *Galilee*, 146. Cf. Myers, *Binding the Strong Man*, 150-151.

155 Myers believes that Jesus was compelled to leave Capernaum for the neighbouring country towns due to the Synagogue conflict. See, *Binding the Strong Man*, 150.

156 This idea clashes in many ways with the traditional understanding of mission as the coming into the world of the pre-existent Son of God. It is different from the Johannine sense that indicates a mission from above. What Mann suggests; "came to Galilee" is unlikely because Jesus was a Galilean. See, Mann, *Mark*, 217.

157 Naickanparampil, *The Gospel of Mark*, 51; Myers, *Binding the Strong Man*, 141.

158 Horsley, *Hearing the Whole Story*, 1.

159 Myers discusses this incident as a nonviolent assault upon the symbolic order of Judaism and the ideological hegemony of priest and scribe. See, *Binding the Strong Man*, 152-154.

From here on, we can expect a certain amount of obstacles and problems. Here is a story that changes the whole course of Jesus' itinerary:

> [40]A leper came to him begging him, and kneeling he said to him, "If you choose, you can make me clean." [41]Moved with pity, Jesus stretched out his hand and touched him, and said to him, "I do choose. Be made clean!" [42]Immediately the leprosy left him, and he was made clean. [43]After sternly warning him he sent him away at once, [44]saying to him, "See that you say nothing to anyone; but go, show yourself to the priest, and offer for your cleansing what Moses commanded, as a testimony to them." [45]But he went out and began to proclaim it freely, and to spread the word, so that Jesus could no longer go into a town openly, but stayed out in the country; and people came to him from every quarter (Mk 1: 40-45).

Among many other issues, we concentrate upon a couple of interrelated problems which require academic investigation. There is a serious textual problem in v. 41 as to whether we should read ὀγρισθεις ("anger" or "indignation") or σπγχνισθεὶς ("pity" or "compassion").[160] The latter has by far the better manuscript support,[161] whereas the textual support of the former is relatively weak.[162] The difficulty of ὀγρισθεις, however, lends stronger supports to it being the original reading.[163] If we are to read as ὀγρισθεις, we still need to explain what makes Jesus angry? Most often, the Greek work ὀγρισθεις is explained as Jesus' response to the leper ἐαν θέλῃς. Some scholars believe that Jesus is annoyed and that anyone should doubt his willingness to help. If ἐαν θέλῃς is merely a natural polite word, as some scholars suggest, another cause for Jesus' anger must be sought.[164]

Second, Jesus' words in v. 43 such as ἐμβριμησάμενος αὐτῷ ("sternly charged him)[165] and ἐξέβαλεν αὐτὸν ("sent him away at once") are equally unexpected and they need careful analysis. It is proposed that Jesus was annoyed at an interruption to his preaching mission, but this seems totally out of the question, for preaching and healing always go hand in hand in Jesus' ministry. Another suggestion is that Jesus objected to the leper's 'unlawful'

160 Mathew, *Temple-Criticism in Mark's Gospel*, 185; Witherington, *The Gospel of Mark*, 103.

161 Such ℵ A B C K L W ΔΘΠ and the great majority of the MSS.

162 D it.

163 It is natural to observe that the more difficult reading of "indignation" can be easily changed to "compassion" rather than changing "compassion" to "indignation." Most of the modern translations e.g. RSV, NRSV, NIV, NAB) favour σπγχνισθεὶς, but REB and NEP prefer ὀγρισθεις.

164 Witherington has more suggestions for the aspect of anger. See, Witherington III, *The Gospel of Mark*, 103.

165 This strong verb is rare. Mann feels that there is no satisfactory English equivalent. See Mann, *Mark*, 219.

approach. This aspect cannot be right in view of his response by an equally 'unlawful' touch and immediate healing. Besides, if Jesus was displeased at being asked to breech the 'messianic secret' his immediate compliance is hard to explain. Here, Scott's dichotomy of the "great tradition" and "little tradition" finds relevance in terms of a solution of the problem. We have the Judean law being imposed on a Galilee villager and it makes him the victim. Most possibly, Jesus would get angry when he personally met with the victim and his circumstance. This could possibly be how Mark exhibits that the anger was not directed against the man himself. Rather, it was directed against Jerusalem temple-state aristocracy of which this man is a victim.[166] If so then, the immediate gesture of "stretched out and touched" is perhaps not the compassionate response (v. 41) of Jesus, but a public assertion of worth for the leper. The entire episode can be seen as encompassing dignity-restoring ideology that negates the dominant suppressive ideology as generated in the urban elite culture. Perhaps, Jesus sternly warned him and sent him to the priests to speak the truth to them. By his bold act of negation to the Judean-priestly law that isolates lepers, Jesus also emboldened the man to resist the Judean priestly domination publicly. This man's disobedient proclamation was recognised as good news. At the same time, his joyful celebration and refusal to perform the ritual have added a new important dimension in Jesus' ministry.

The consequences of this resistance, according to Mark, are of three dimensions, namely: Jesus "could no longer go into a town openly,"[167] he "stayed out in the country,"[168] and instead, "people came to him from every quarter" (v. 45). This statement of Mark on Jesus being restricted open entry into a city and his stay in the village provides us with a theoretical framework to read the Gospel in terms of rural-urban relations.[169] People who came to Jesus were most likely Galileans. As Mark stresses "from every quarter" (v. 45b), we can expect both villagers and urban dwellers to make their presence. Being the expression of anger, this healing episode ushers a new period which Scott would term "testing the limits" of the hidden transcript.[170] With this significant event in Jesus' campaign, what R. F. Capon labels as "the ministry before the parables" is over.[171] Hereafter, Mark presents us Jesus' ministry under surveillance and how Jesus defends the same.

166 Myers, *Binding the Strong Man*, 153; Mathew, *Temple-Criticism in Mark's Gospel*, 189.

167 Mark's stress on φανερῶς ("openly") suggests Jesus could enter into a city in secret.

168 Waetjen feels that the verb may intimate "a retreat in the face of danger." See, *A Reordering of Power*, 95.

169 Roskam, *The Purpose of Mark*, 182; Liew, "The Gospel of Mark," 124-125.

170 Scott, *Domination and the Arts of Resistance*, 192-197.

171 R. F. Capon, *The Parables of the Kingdom* (Grand Rapids, Michigan: Eerdmans, 1985), 53-60. Waetjen discuses this section under the heading, "Reordering the World and Conflict with the Guardians of Society." See, *A Reordering of Power*, 86-95.

3.2. Jesus' Campaign under Surveillance: Defending the Hidden Transcript (2: 1-3:6)

Mark 2: 1 denotes that Jesus returned to Capernaum (2: 1). With the verb εἰσελθὼν, Mark indicates that Capernaum is not the same place where Jesus "stayed out in the country" (v. 1: 45). Jesus seems to remain here for some time. He performed many things which Mark remarks about in great detail. The social sites found in 2:1–3: 6[172] are no doubt sequestered sites. However, unlike earlier, in each of Jesus' actions recorded by Mark, we have Scribes and Pharisees watching him and also posing a threat to Jesus' movement. We assume that Mark 2: 1–3: 6 denotes Jesus' story of his growing popularity as well as an initial political response from the scribal classes.[173] Mark has far more complex narratives of Jesus, with several conflicts that are overlapping and interwoven.

3.2.1. The Healing of a Paralytic (2: 1-13)

Mark 2: 1-13 is one of the most famous miracles of Jesus. As we have discussed in the previous section, Jesus performed exorcism (1: 21-28) and both individual and mass healings (1: 29-34). Jesus, after his successful and seemingly pleasant preaching tour, came back to Capernaum. This village was a rural headquarters located in lower Galilee. When the people came to know that he was at home, many were gathered.[174] Even though some English renderings have "He was preaching the word to them," the Greek words ἐλαλει αὐτοῖς τὸν λόγον could mean that Jesus was giving the report on his preaching tour. The people in Capernaum gathered to hear Jesus' report and it suggests that Jesus who "came out" for their discourse rendered dignity to the public. The bringing of the paralytic to Jesus confirms their trust in him. Unlike the previous healing stories, this famous story has τινες τῶν γραμματέων ("some of the scribes") hiding amongst the crowd (v. 6). Mark presents these scribes as "questioning in their hearts" about Jesus' words. Jesus used this important occasion to manifest his authority. Most of the interpreters of this story render emphasis on either the faith of the ones who brought the paralytic man or the authority of Jesus.[175] It is true that Mark clearly exhibits those two dimensions beautifully in this miracle. However, many of them considered this healing as

172 Such as: private home (2: 1, 15), "beside the sea" (2: 13), grainfields (2: 23) and village synagogue (3: 1).

173 Kingsbury's interpretation of this section as "human ignorance concerning Jesus' identity" is unlikely. See, *Conflict in Mark*, 37-42.

174 Waetjen observes that the house resembles the rural houses of Mark's audiences instead of an actual house in Capernaum. See, *A Reordering of Power*, 4.

175 Roskam speaks of this miraculous healing as Jesus' authorization by God. See, *The Purpose of Mark*, 148.

a mere religious faith healing story. When we locate power relations regarding the rural and urban into consideration, the healing narrative raises a deeper and larger ideological issue.

Myers finds an "attack on the debt system" in this narrative. For him the statement of Jesus in v. 4 is a pronouncement of debt.[176] Because of his bodily disabilities, this man was denied of full humanity. Mathew assumes, "Oppressive taxation could leave the poor physically malnourished or hysterically disabled."[177] Jesus not only healed him but released him from all debts by declaring forgiveness for him. As Myers observes, this was a restoration of his physical wholeness as well as his social wholeness.[178] Scribes' complaint that "none but God can remit debt (2: 7b) is not a defence of the sovereignty of Yahweh, but their own social power."[179] Henceforth, they were watchful to Jesus' campaign and the same aspect appeared again in 3: 22 as officials who were deputed from Jerusalem.

3.2.2. Eating with Sinners and Tax-Collectors (2: 13-16)

Mark denotes that Jesus went out beside the sea and the crowd gathered about him (2: 13). He depicts Jesus as teacher who teaches the crowd in a private place.[180] From this private site, Mark shifts the site to "tax office." Mann suggests that the tax office would be "a tax-collection service for Herod Antipas, collecting taxes on goods passing through his territory from the neighboring jurisdictions of Herod Philip and the Ten Towns."[181] If the village is still Capernaum, the tax office that Jesus visited could be the regional tax office for the entire region. Surprisingly, the purpose of his visit is not to resist the tax system, but to change the officer and his colleagues who were a part of the dissident sub-culture that was on the move (2: 13-14). Now, there is a further shift in Mark's narrative from the public to private as Mark reports that Jesus sat at the table in a Levi's house. Mark indicates that many tax collectors and sinners were sitting to have a meal with Jesus and his disciples (v. 15). A distinction must be maintained between τελωναι, the officials and ἀρχιτελωναι (Lat. *publicani*), the tax famers whose responsibility was to forward taxes when collected.[182] Mark here refers to the former one. But in either case, the

176 Myers, *Binding the Strong Man*, 155.

177 Mathew, *Temple-Criticism in Mark's Gospel*, 204.

178 Myers, *Binding the Strong Man*, 155.

179 Myers, *Binding the Strong Man*, 155.

180 Naickanparampil, *The Gospel of Mark*, 54-58.

181 Mann, *Mark*, 229 (see note no. 14).

182 Waetjen classifies the collection as "fish tax imposed by the Herodians on all fishing in the Sea of Galilee." See, *A Reordering of Power*, 89. On the possible meanings for the term "sinners," see Mathew, *Temple-Criticism in Mark's Gospel*, 190. Also T. A. Friedrichsen,

employment of a Jew would have been treated by strict Jews such as Pharisees as disgraceful. Carter discerns that the tax collectors were widely despised by the Jewish elites as "extortionists and thieves" and labelled as "sinners."[183] The tax collectors, in the words of Belo, were "hated by the masses and condemned by the intellectual leaders."[184]

Mark conveys the picture of the social subaltern class in Galilee—people from fishing trade, sinners and the staff of the local tax office—meeting in a private house convened by a village carpenter turned charismatic leader.[185] This could be a real threat to the ruling classes.[186] As expected, "the scribes of the Pharisees" appeared and asked the disciples, "Why does he eat with tax collectors and sinners" (2: 16).[187] "On the earlier occasion scribes kept their ideas about Jesus' activities to themselves, now they express their thought openly," says Iersel.[188] Their question reveals that they had serious apprehension about Jesus and what he was doing with the groups which they never could put under their control. Many western interpreters have considered this text narrowly within the religious realm neglecting the political aspect.[189]

In general, there has been a strong tendency among the modern scholars that the Pharisees were separatists. It may be true that the Pharisees had separated themselves from the process of Hellenization; yet we hardly found the Pharisees being separated from the people of the land. Especially after losing their political power, it could be that they tried to pretend to be people-friendly parties. As Mark identifies these scribes as belonging to the Pharisaic party, they were the losing group in the Jewish political arena that was dominated by the Sadducees. In order to gain power or at least to maintain their status quo, the "scribes of the Pharisees" would have imposed strict observance of the Law upon the people. There were groups within the Jewish society—elsewhere including rural Galilee—who associated with the Roman rulers. Apparently, the Pharisees were not on good terms with them. The tax

---

"The Temple, a Pharisee, a Tax Collector, and the Kingdom of God: Rereading a Jesus Parables (Luke 18: 10-14a)" *JBL* 124/1 (Spring 2005): 107-109.

183 Carter, *The Roman Empire and the New Testament*, 114.

184 Belo, *A Materialist Reading of the Gospel of Mark*, 64.

185 Cf. Myers, *Binding the Strong Man*, 156-157.

186 Samuel interprets Jesus' action as a disruption of the socio-religious status quo. See, *A Postcolonial Reading of Mark's Story of Jesus*, 124.

187 For discussion on the socio-economic role of the Pharisee, see Myers, *Binding the Strong Man*, 160-161.

188 Iersel, *Mark: A Reader-Response Commentary*, 153.

189 Schweizer interprets this episode in the context of the Jew-Gentile relationship to argue that "righteousness of the occupied the church for a long time." See, *The Good News According to Mark*, 63-64. Mann discusses it in the context of Jews and the early Christian relationship. See, *Mark*, 228-229.

collectors were despised by them as the task involved the handling of coins with pagan symbols and even human representations on them and the work was also being performed for the Herodian family and ultimately for Rome. They labelled people as "sinners" whose observance of the Law and its oral traditions were regarded as unsatisfactory in their sight.[190]

Jesus practiced rather radically inclusive and non-hierarchical table fellowship as a central strategy in his ministry among the Galileans. Although, a few authors have challenged the historicity of Jesus' actually eating with "many tax collectors and sinners" in Levi's house (Mk 2: 15), the evidence as well as the reason for such an intentionally exclusive table fellowship is quite strong as multiple sources including Mark (2: 15-17), Q (Mat 9: 9-13 & Lk 5: 29-32), and the Gospel of Thomas (64) have denoted the same. Myers who distinguishes "tax collectors" from "tax farmers" identifies the former as employed by the Jews under the Roman or Herodian administration to handle "the myriad of local transportation taxes and tariffs."[191] As "bureaucratic representative of the oppressive politico-economic order," their reputation for dishonesty could have been widely known among the agrarian community in Galilee. It is highly probable that Jesus did associate frequently with such immoral people, at table and elsewhere. Jesus' open table fellowship was a strategy that was used to resist social and religious exclusivism wherever it was accepted as normal or officially sanctioned. The boundary of Jesus-in-movement embraces the socially outcaste and is thus a contrast to the Pharisaic programme of maintaining identity through separation.[192] Jesus' reply to the scribes has two parts that are equally important. The first part, "Those who were well have no need of a physician, but those who are sick" (v.17a) is a proverbial saying that might have originated in the context of the subalterns struggling against the dominant who claimed themselves to be righteous. The second part, "I have come not to call the righteous, but sinners" (v. 17b) expresses Jesus' own mission towards the people at the margins.

3.2.3. Fasting: Rituals of Aggression (Mk 2: 18-19)

Fasting, in its socio-political sense, is not a mere religious ritual, rather it is a form of resistance.[193] All the protest or resistance groups during and prior to Jesus had practiced fasting. Mark's Gospel too observes that the Pharisees and John the Baptist groups practiced the same. Mark reports that the Pharisees,

---

190 Waetjen, *A Reordering of Power*, 89-90; Goretti, Daniel, and Raja, "The Gospel According to Mark," 173.

191 Myers, *Binding the Strong Man*, 157.

192 Myers, *Binding the Strong Man*, 157.

193 T. Hagerland, "Jesus and the Rites of Repentance" *NTS* 52/2 (April 2006): 166-187, esp. 181-184.

whose disciples practice fasting, challenge Jesus' disciples' of not observing the fast, to which Jesus responds that in his mission something new and special is happening. Here is a clear indication that Jesus, though he does not reject the practice of fasting, ignores it for the time being in this context.

3.2.4. Plucking Heads of Grain on Sabbath (Mk 2: 23-28)

In contrast to what Myers denotes the incident of plucking the heads of grain in Mark 2: 23 by Jesus' disciples is regarded as "civil disobedience,"[194] and it fits well with what Scott terms as "pilfering" or "petty theft." Is plucking the heads of grain a mere response to a hunger pangs, is it done for the pleasure of adventure, or is it meant to chasten the Pharisees? It could be any of these and more. One must question both the Israelite "common law" (Deut 23: 24-25) that permits snacking on one's neighbour's grapes or grains when walking through the field and the rules on "gleaning rights" for the poor if they really worked out for the rural poor. Supposedly, the laws or customs were at the backdrop ever since rich people from the city took over the ownership of land and had control over them. Jesus' response to the accusation leveled by the Pharisaic party on his disciples' on the Sabbath can be seen at two levels. First, Jesus apparently denotes that the action of his disciples was "an act of hunger"– for he cited "what David did when he and his companions were hungry and in need of food" (2: 25b).[195] This incident reminds us of how the hungry people collectively, yet not openly, would have resisted the impact of agrarian transition in the life of Galilean villages at local or micro level in their everyday life.[196]

At the deeper and ideological level, Jesus resists the hegemonic interpretation of the Torah by the Pharisees in terms of concerning the meaning and purpose of the Sabbath (2: 27). Jesus knows, or even shares the experiences with the poor villagers with regards to how much they had suffered unnecessary troubles under the strict rules that were laid down by the urban elite religious groups like the Pharisees. Publicly, of course, the Pharisees' definition of "theft" or "breaking the law" prevailed in this narrative. However, behind the scenes, the action of Jesus' disciples is seen as simply taking back the product of one's labour, thus – becomes a form of protest or resistance from below.

3.2.5. Healing on Sabbath (Mk 3: 1-6)

Another aspect of resistance at the local level that found its place in the Gospel story is the healing of a withered hand on Sabbath (3:1-6). The site

194 Myers, *Binding the Strong Man*, 159.

195 Samuel sees Markan Jesus employing "a contrapuntal reading of the Jewish discourse on David." See. *A Postcolonial Reading of Mark's Story of Jesus*, 125.

196 Waetjen, *A Reordering of Power*, 93.

of the story is now shifted from the grainfield (2: 23)—the power house of the peasants—to the Synagogue (3: 1), the basis of village assembly led by the village elders. This episode involves a tactic of foot dragging. For Mark adds, "They [Pharisees, v. 2: 23] watched him, to see whether he would cure him on the sabbath, so that they might accuse him" (3: 2). Here, the arena is the very power house of the village, the Pharisees watched Jesus to see whether Jesus would cure a withered hand on the Sabbath. Jesus asked them, "Is it lawful to do good or to do harm on the sabbath, to save life or to kill?" (3: 4). Jesus could have waited for the next day to heal the paralytic man, and saved himself from Pharisaic harassment;[197] yet he chose to resist with the form of noncompliance. Jesus confronts them with a hermeneutical key question about the just observation of the sabbath. Mark tells us that the Pharisees were silent (v. 4). Some scholars were tempted to interpret that Jesus silenced them. But this is unlikely. The Pharisees seem to silent not because they had no answer to Jesus' question, but because they had another answer to Jesus. Mark presents the behaviour of Jesus in this manner: "And he [Jesus] looked around at them with anger; he was grieved at their hardness of heart" (v. 5a). Noticeably, Mark presents Jesus' response as anger and grief.[198] Mark's portrayal of Jesus assumes an escalating conflict between Jesus and the Pharisees. Under this strong opposition, Jesus heals this man with a withered hand (v. 5). On the first occasion, the meeting of the village community in a private house where Jesus presented his report on his preaching tour, where "some of the scribes" were sitting in the house, questioning in their hearts about Jesus (2: 7). For the second time at the house of Levi, "the scribes of the Pharisees" raised their concern about Jesus, but directed it to the disciple (2: 16). Thirdly, "people" came and asked Jesus about his disciples and their lack of fasting. This Markan systematic presentation of the intensifying opposition mounted against Jesus-in-movement becomes clearer from the agrarian-resistance stance.

3.3. Summary

From our discussion, it is clear that Mark 1: 14–3: 6 depicts the first phase of the political discourse in the ministry of Jesus. Within this first phase of political discourse, there are at least three decisive aspects that should be taken into consideration in any academic investigation. First of all, Mark portrays Jesus' authority over and above that of the scribes. Within the locality of Capernaum and its neighbourhood, to put it in the words of Liew, Jesus replaced "the scribes as a reliable mediator of divine wisdom, divine forgiveness, and divine power."[199] Second, Mark tells us that Jesus' "fame began to spread throughout

197 Waetjen, *A Reordering of Power*, 94.

198 Goretti, Daniel and Raja, "The Gospel According to Mark," 174.

199 Liew, "The Gospel of Mark," 107.

the surrounding region of Galilee" (1: 28) with the proclamation of the "good news of God" (1: 14), forming a small band of disciples along the Sea of Galilee (1: 16-20), and exorcism in the synagogue of Capernaum (1: 21-27). Then, Jesus continued his healing ministry in a private house in Capernaum (1: 29-34). Jesus also launched a preaching tour in Galilee.

In this preaching tour, according to Mark's generalization, Jesus "went throughout Galilee proclaiming the message in their synagogues and casting out" (1: 39) seemingly without any opposition from the urban ruling classes. Third, with a particular healing of a leper, Jesus "could no longer go into a town openly, but stayed out in the country" (1: 40-45, esp. 45b). Henceforth, Jesus' ministry was under surveillance from above. Every aspect of his deed, such as: healing (2: 1-12), eating with sinners (2: 15-17), non-practice of fasting by his disciples (2: 18), plucking of grains on Sabbath (2: 23-27), and healing of a withered hand (3: 1-5) were strictly observed. However, there are no reports of serious obstacles until the Pharisees allied with the Herodians to conspire Jesus-in-movement and plotted to destroy him (3: 6).[200] This implies that the Pharisees wanted to destroy Jesus by capital punishment. If J. P. Meier is correct, it is possible that the Pharisees required the cooperation of Antipas who held power over Galilee.[201] In many respects, this section of the Gospel resonates what Scott devises as a "hidden transcript" developed by Galilean subaltern masses in sequestered sites off the public stage to counter the regular indignities of domination.[202] In the next section, we shall critically analyse the words and deeds of Jesus in this section to see if they were "dignity-restoring counter-ideology" that negated the dominant paradigm and also expressed anger, revenge and self-assertion.

4. Jesus' Campaign in Galilee and Beyond and the Politics of Disguise and Anonymity (Mk 3: 7–8: 30)

As we move on to read the Gospel, we see a lot more about Jesus struggling against the powers. Mark, indeed, presents a considerable historical verisimilitude on how Jesus' preaching and healing in Galilean villages touched off a seemingly spontaneous movement of resistance that generated divinely inspired popular power that was opposed to and threatened by the dominant rulers and their representatives. If Mark 1: 14–3: 6 resonates Scott's concept of

200 S. Dowd and E. S. Malbon, the Pharisees and the Herodians were the powers that claimed to represent God, yet they were the losers when Jesus proclaimed God's kingdom. See, "The Significance of Jesus' Death in Mark: Narrative Context and Authorial Audience," *SBL* 125/2 (2006): 276. On the various explanations of the identity of the Herodians, J. P. Meier, "The Historical Jesus and the Historical Herodians," *JBL* 119/4 (2000): 741.

201 Meier, "The Historical Jesus and the Historical Herodians," 743.

202 If Meyers' observation is correct, after the incident in Mark 3: 6, Jesus never enters a *polis* until his approach to Jerusalem. See, Myers, *Binding the Strong Man*, 151.

the hidden transcript, Mark 3: 7–8: 30 must be analyzed as a politics of disguise and anonymity. Having analyzed Jesus' campaign in a comparatively smaller region in and around Capernaum (Mk 1: 14–3: 6) as the hidden transcript of the Galilean villagers, we shall now move on to discuss Jesus' campaign in the larger area of Galilee and beyond. This seems imperative as Mark considerably denotes space to this part of Jesus' story. At the same time, it also provides the context for many of the parables. This section mainly attempts to understand the activities of Jesus that were found in Mark 3: 7–8: 30 as a political disguise and anonymity.

4.1. Geopolitical Shift in Jesus' Campaign

The scale of Jesus' campaign is obviously a Markan construct. Mark's portrayal of Jesus conveyed the picture that he started off his campaign quietly in the wilderness (1: 12-13), but he was actually building for himself a storm of movement. Indeed, for Mark, Jesus needs only a few days and a few people to launch the powerful movement in the villages of Galilee. However, Jesus unleashed himself into a movement without warning. Liew rightly labels Jesus as "a rising star with the rising sun of a brand new day in Capernaum."[203] Mark indicates a significant shift from micro to macro in the scale of Jesus' campaign and it reads:

> 7Jesus departed with his disciples to the lake, and a great multitude from Galilee followed him; 8hearing all that he was doing, they came to him in great numbers from Judea, Jerusalem, Idumea, beyond the Jordan, and the region around Tyre and Sidon (3: 7-8).

According to these verses, Mark not only notices that the fame of Jesus spread throughout Galilee and beyond, he even takes note of how the crowds increased in size and soon expanded into "great multitudes" and "great numbers" from various corners of Judea, Idumea to the south, and even from the region around Tyre and Sidon to the north (Mk 1:27-28, 32-33, 37-39, 45; 2: 1-2, 13; 3: 7-10, 20; 5: 20-21, 24; 6: 33, 54-56).[204] Mark renders the picture that as Jesus moved further from Capernaum towards the larger area in Galilee, a great multitude from the regions beyond Galilee also came to him. Jesus' campaign which had once operated outside the "intimidating gaze of power" and found itself in the "words of anger, revenge and self-assertion" is now in public view.[205] Scott tells us that the hidden transcript does not confine itself to the secured sites in which it is cultivated. Rather, the subaltern people's

---

203 Liew, "The Gospel of Mark," 124.

204 Naickanparampil, *The Gospel of Mark*, 63-64.

205 Scott, *Domination and the Arts of Resistance*, 18.

indignation overflows the borders of their villages in other forms of popular politics, which are usually found in the forms of disguise and anonymity.[206]

We shall discuss this section of the Gospel with two basic assumptions. First, it is assumed that Mark 3: 7–8: 30 recalls Jesus' campaign in a wider Galilee and beyond. Mark's presentation of Jesus' campaign suggests that the hidden transcript of dignity and indignity spills over the borders in two ways: people coming to Jesus by crossing the border and Jesus himself crossing the border. The social site of Jesus' campaign—Capernaum and its surrounding villages—thus, apparently became the public space while gradually losing its significance as social sites for the hidden transcript (Mk 6: 1-4). Jesus-in-movement is more defenseless and exposed to ruling classes as he leaves for an outer space. Our main concern here is to unfold how Jesus addressed that crowd in public and conveyed the "discourse of dignity" to the powers which he had freely spoken about in the sequestered context.

Second, most of the public life of Jesus-in-movement this section is supposed to be found neither in an open defiance of power-holders nor incomplete hegemonic compliance. Mark portrays him as dwelling in between these two polar opposites. We rarely find Jesus' direct proclamation of the kingdom of God in plain words (cf. 1: 14), or his anger (cf. 1: 41; 3: 5) in this section. Mark no longer records of Jesus' self-assertion such as his authority to forgive sin (2:10) and lordship over the sabbath (2: 28). Rather, we enter into the world of rumour, gossip, disguises, parables, ritual gestures, and anonymity. In many respects, this stage resonates of Scott's politics of disguise and anonymity. This takes place in public view but is designed to have double meaning or to shield the identity. In our attempt to recognize the elements of the politics of disguise and anonymity in Mark 3: 7– 8: 30, we shall be selective in focusing upon those texts that have a direct bearing to the powerful elites to whom Jesus supposedly speaks the truth. With these assumptions, we do not mean that previous scholars never acknowledge these presuppositions. However, they ostensibly considered various strands of politics of disguise and anonymity motif in the Gospel of Mark that occur narrowly within the religious realm. Such investigations mainly ended up in negligence of the resistance motifs that are embedded in the Gospel. This study re-examines the same concerns as politics of disguise and anonymity. Thus, we call for three elementary forms of disguise: anonymity, euphemism and grumbling for consideration.

4.2. Rumour, Crowd, and God's Kingdom

As discussed above, crowds from various corners of Jewish settlement flocked together at Jesus' campaign. Our answer to who or what communicated to the

206 Scott, *Domination and the Arts of Resistance*, 18-19.

distant crowds with words about Jesus-in-movement and convinced them to flock at the feet of Jesus could be crucial for the understanding of this part of the Gospel. In view of the situation before the development of electronic mass media, rumour could be virtually the only means that was communicated about Jesus in terms of both his actions and sayings. Scott opines that rumour is integral to the revolution that sparks off violent acts.[207] This study assumes that rumours played a vital role in spreading Jesus-in-movement as well as the arrival of the big crowds to Jesus. The hermeneutical significance of rumour must be spelt out in an academic investigation such as this. Once it is clear that rumor plays a significant role in Jesus' campaign, we must ensure how exactly rumour works among the subaltern masses. First of all, we must note that rumour has no author but that it effectively delivers the message. This quality of anonymity needs to be appreciated in any study of resistance from below. This is to say that rumour can be an effective instrument to spark revolt among the subalterns as it hides the actors. Scott, by citing several illustrations, discusses how rumour travels in a process of elaboration in which it is adapted to the hopes and fears of those who hear and retell it.[208] Scott's illustrations,[209] in the words of Horsley, are "suggestive for the Gospel of Mark and, through Mark, for Jesus and the movement around him."[210]

Second, we must also note that a "politically charged rumor can easily spark violent acts."[211] Mark's description of the crowd—"hearing all that he was doing" (v. 8a)—interestingly assumes a speedy popular response to Jesus' preaching of the kingdom of God and manifestation of God's power in exorcism and healings.[212] Though Mark does explicitly mention in his presentation that the crowds came with urgency, it also implies the political emotions of the great multitude that joined Jesus' campaign. It is possible they have hope in Jesus for their deliverance. Our previous chapter reveals that some resistance movements in the first-century C. E. Galilee and Judea—*viz*. Theudas, the Egyptian, and Judas of Galilee—remarkably involved the collective anticipation of a divine deliverance. These movements might have

---

207 Scott, *Domination and the Arts of Resistance*, 144, 147.

208 Scott, *Domination and the Arts of Resistance*, 145.

209 One of Scott's illustrations explains how the Dalits of colonial India "are prone to read their hopes into rumor." Some cases of the peasant movements in Judea and Galilee led by Theudas, Judas of Galilee (Acts 5: 36), Theudas the Egyptian (Ant. 20: 97-98) and others are good reminders that during the time of Jesus, collective anticipation of God's new acts of deliverance were not uncommon; the political impulse provided by rumor was so integral to the peasant resistance movements. See Scott, *Domination and the Arts of Resistance*, 144-152.

210 Horsley, "The Politics of Disguise and Public Declaration of the Hidden Transcript," 69.

211 Scott, *Domination and the Arts of Resistance*, 144.

212 Horsley, *Jesus in Context*, 193.

been relatively small in reality; yet they spread like wild fire with rumours of anticipated divine deliverance. Thus, these movements became mass movements that threatened the Roman imperial rule. Many previous studies on Jesus' campaign in Galilee and beyond have tended to neglect this aspect.[213] We must look into the Gospel of Mark to see if there is any evidence of the collective anticipation of God's new act of deliverance that was spread through rumour.

Third, we must also recognize that rumours survive only in a fertile land. There is a general presumption that rumours are "false or at least probably false."[214] The historical and scientific investigations of the Gospel in the past have never raised historical questions concerning the Markan detail regarding information about the rapidity of people's response to Jesus and their emotional expressions. It was as if they had no historical value. In their 1947 book, *The Psychology of Rumor*, G. W. Allport and L. Postman have established the idea that rumours cannot survive "without secure standards of evidence being present."[215] What Allport and Postman did not bring out is the socio-political implication that rumours could have possessed in the society. Rumour is not an individual experience alone, but is a collective one.[216] It is T. Shibutani's *Improvised News: A Sociological Study of Rumor* (1996) that gives us light to realize the sociological concerns of rumours. Shibutani maintains that rumor flourishes especially in situations that are characterized by disasters or social unrest.[217]

Scott believes that rumour is an effective instrument for the subordinated people's resistance to domination beyond their sequestered sites. Mark gives us a clue to assume that the pathetic situation of the Jewish agrarian communities under the Roman imperial rule provided the most fertile social site for a generation of rumours. The powerful but suppressed desire for relief from the burdens of subordination seems not only to infuse the religious life of the oppressed Jewish peasants, but it also strongly colours their interpretation of the "good news of God" that are touched off by the power of God's reign as manifested in exorcisms and healings. Horsley observes, "Mark's portrayal of Jesus' mission in Galilee and beyond thus resembles where other peasants

213 For instance, Naickanparampil considers "His authoritative teaching, His healings and other acts of power" as the reasons for the popularity and fame of Jesus. See, *The Gospel of Mark*, 63.

214 Suh, *Discipleship and Community*, 68.

215 G. W. Allport and L. Postman, *The Psychology of Rumor*, (New York: Henry Holt and Company, 1947), ix.

216 Suh, *Discipleship and Community*, 70.

217 T. Shibutani, *Improvised News: A Sociological Study of Rumor* (Indianapolis and New York: The Bobbs-Merill Company, Inc., 1966), 32.

movements that spread through rumor."[218] Mark evidently emphasizes the rapidity of the widening popular response to Jesus' mission (1: 28)[219] and the power of emotions that are expressed by the crowd in their strong aspiration or yearning for liberation.[220] Right from the beginning, people kept their ears close to Jesus, Mark states, "They were all amazed, and they keep on asking one another, 'What is this? A new teaching–with authority!'" (1: 28). As they kept on asking one another about the "new teaching" that emerged with Jesus; hence the rumour travelled far and wide in a powerful form of anonymous communication adapting to the hopes and fears of those who heard it and later retold it. Scholars like E. Trocmé, Waetjen, *et al.* have identified the crowds to be "dispossessed lower classes" who were eager to experience God's deliverance.[221]

Finally, we must perceive that not only the subjugated masses, but the Roman rulers and their Jewish collaborates were attentive to the rumours though with their vested interests. Hence, we must not suppose the crowd as exclusively consisting of lower classes, rather we can expect people from the higher strata. R. Guha notes, "Roman emperors were sensitive enough to rumor to engage an entire cadre of officials–*delatores*–in collecting and reporting it."[222] Such different responses to Jesus and the movement around him created new sites of struggle in which counter-hegemonic movements and resistance were taking place. Thus, Jesus' campaign which had already been under surveillance from above could have been encompassed by elements of anonymity that were designed to have double meaning or to shield the identity of the actor in this part of Mark's Gospel.

4.3. Euphemism and Spirit Possession: The Case of "My name is Legion"

If the anonymity in the form of rumor is what veils the messenger, it helps Jesus to effectively speak truth to powers. One might imagine that without anonymity Jesus' campaign would revert to one of submissive deference. The alternative to submissive powers is to disguise the message to avoid vengeance. If anonymity (*i.e.* veiling of the messenger) helps the delivery of unveiled message, their veiling of the message would equally render the

218 Horsley, *Jesus in Context*, 195.

219 With the expression, "At once his fame began to spread" (1: 28) Mark indicates the rapidity of Jesus' fame.

220 People came bearing their friends and relatives for healing (e.g. 2: 33; 5: 21-23), a woman who had been hemorrhaging for twelve years touched Him from behind (5: 25-34), etc. are good examples in this regard.

221 E. Trocmé, *The Formation of the Gospel According to Mark*, trans. P. Gaughan (Philadelphia: Westminster Press, 1975), 88-93; Waetjen, *A Reordering of Power*, 95.

222 R. Guha, *Elementary Forms of Peasant Insurgency*, 251.

purpose. For Scott, euphemization is the technique that disguises the message and he declares:

> Euphemization is an accurate way of to describe what happens to a hidden transcript when it is expressed in a power-laden situation by an actor who wishes to avoid the sanctions that direct statement will bring. Although subordinate groups are by no means the only persons to use euphemisms, they resort to it frequently because of their greater exposure to sanctions.[223]

Certain words and phrases that are found in Mark 3: 7–8: 30 are surely "varnished" to veil the message. The use of euphemism as disguise is the most striking genre of all the parables in Mark. This elaborate form of veiling will be taken up separately in the next chapter. There are many other incidents that exhibit which the characters of the Gospel did euphemize while maintaining socio-linguistic boundary. The words and expressions, such as: "He has gone out of his mind" (3: 21b); the Scribes from Jerusalem used "he has Beelzebul" to accuse him of being spirit possessed (3: 22, cf. 30). Jesus' caution "beware of the yeast of the Pharisee and the yeast of Herod" (8: 15), referring the agrarian community in Galilee to as "sheep without shepherd" (6: 34b),[224] can be taken as examples of euphemisms in the Gospel. But, one of the most significant and interesting example is the reference to "Legion" in Mark 5: 1-20. We shall discuss this account as it seems to represent Jesus' telling of the truth to the region beyond Galilee in Decapolis.[225] Mark presents the casting out of Legion as one among the other major activities of Jesus. Even at a cursory reading, we can make out that this miraculous story assumes bitter conflict between the people of the city (vv. 14-15) and the poor man living among "the herd of swine" (vv. 1-12) at the city suburb. Evidences, as we shall analyze, assume that this man appears to effectively launch a social protest. But, supposedly, as his message was veiled by the spirit possession, nobody could find out his resistance till the complete destruction of their intensive pig farming projects. In this, we shall discuss this aspect of spirit possession to ascertain if it is an elementary form of disguise resistance.

G. Theissen's *The Miracle Stories of the Early Christian Tradition* (1983) agrees that imperial subjugation sometimes appears as possession by a foreign spirit.[226] This political aspect cannot be neglected in engaging with

---

223 Scott, *Domination and the Arts of Resistance*, 152-153.

224 Myers indicates that there is an implied political criticism in Jesus' saying regarding the sheep without the shepherd. See, Myers, *Binding the Strong Man*, 208.

225 In his socio-rhetorical commentary on Mark, Witherrington convincingly argues that the story is the beginning and establishment of Jesus' mission in the Gentile world. See, *The Gospel of Mark*, 178-184.

226 G. Theissen, *The Miracle Stories of the Early Christian Tradition* (London: T&T Clark, 1983), 256.

Mark's miracle stories. Mark, apart from the general mission statements, has four different stories of spirit possession in the Gospel (1: 21-28; 3: 22-30; 5: 1-20; 7: 24-30; 9: 14-29). The frequency of occurrence alone suggests that spirit possession was common among the peoples that were subjugated by Rome. Each of the spirit possession stories has its own context and purpose. As already been discussed, the first exorcism (Mk 1: 21- 8) was set in the Sabbath gathering of a Synagogue in Capernaum which is beyond the intimidating gaze of power in Jerusalem.[227] Mark's portrayal of the synagogue community in Capernaum was seen as asserting Jesus' authority against the scribes (vv. 23, 27) and it assumes that negative attitudes were depicted towards the highly priestly aristocracy in Jerusalem. This found support in terms of the counter-resistance by the scribes from Jerusalem by accusing him of possessing Beelzebul. Mark clearly says, "For they [the scribes] had said, 'He [Jesus] has an unclean spirit'" (Mk 3: 30). Assuming that the next three stories of spirit possession have the element of resistance, we shall discuss them by situating them within power relations.

Mark 5: 1-20 provides us the most dramatic violent exorcism as found in the Gospel. Myers calls it as "the second inaugural exorcism" probably due to the linguistic similarities of the first exorcism in Mark 1: 21-28.[228] Yet, the first exorcism is a public assertion of worth for Jesus in the Jewish village assembly and the other ends with destruction of pig farming in the neighbourhood. Political disguise is assumed in the latter one as Mark situates it beyond the border of Galilee. We must render direct attention to unfold the subaltern politics that were assumed in this spirit possession narrative. Many of the modern interpreters have analyzed the stories of exorcism narrowly within the realm of religion while neglecting the political dimension.[229] The impression that prevails is that Jesus did not condemn Roman rule. The traditional view is that Jesus was preaching a spiritual kingdom, while Caesar headed the temporal kingdom. We shall take another look while following our sociological reading. Recent studies have recognized that Jesus' exorcism in the Gospels indicate that exorcism defeats Roman rule. Crossan's *The Historical Jesus: The Life of a Mediterranean Jewish Peasants* (1991) labels Jesus' exorcism as magic, but however it tends to obscure the political dimension both in demon possession and in the manner in which exorcism is interpreted in the Gospel tradition.[230]

227 Stein, *Mark*, 83.

228 Myers, *Binding the Strong Man*, 192-193.

229 Among recent studies of this particular text, Joy's discussion conveys special attraction as the scholar has analyzed the text in the light of the issues of class, nationalism and subalternity. See, *Mark and Its Subalterns*, 168-178.

230 Crossan, *The Historical Jesus*, 313-320.

Some recent critics have attempted to understand the aspect of spirit possession in the context of the imperial domination. For instance, Myers sees "political liberation from the might of Rome" in this story.[231] Waetjen attempts to understand the Latin military term "Legion" and its demoniac link to Roman colonialism. He blames colonialism for creating "an atmosphere of living death which fosters a systematic breakdown of human personality" by its oppressive nature and denial of humanity to its people.[232] Incigneri's *The Gospel to the Romans* (2003) also identifies the demonic forces with Roman forces.[233] More recently, Horsley—who employs medical anthropology—considers that spirit possession is related to invasive outside forces.[234] He believes that the Roman military conquest and other pressures of colonial rule had affected the health condition of the Galileans and Judeans. For him, the casting out of Legion (Mk 5: 1-20) refers to conquering the Roman troop.[235] Horsley is hopeful that one can see through medical anthology lenses as to how spirit possession and other illness were understood in ancient Galilean and Judean culture. Horsley becomes our source of inspiration to read the spirit possession stories in the Roman imperial situation.

However, medical anthropology may not help in decoding subaltern politics that were embedded in the spirit possession stories of Mark's Gospel. From our reading of Scott's discussion on this matter, we shall argue that spirit possession represents a disguised form of social protest of the subaltern class in many pre-industrial societies where open protest would be dangerous.[236] Mark 5: 1-20 could have been a sort of resistant act that was produced by domination.[237] Mark refers to him as "a man out of the tombs with an unclean spirit" (v. 2b). Mark's description about him conveys the impression that this man had created a lot of problems and social unrest for the neighbourhood.[238] Mark situates this exorcism in the "country of Gerasenes" (v. 1). ἐξελθόντος αὐτοῦ ἐκ τοῦ πλοίου ("when he had stepped out of the boat") in v. 2 introduces Jesus' campaign in the Decapolis. The campaign beyond Galilee will be

231 Myers, *Binding the Strong Man*, 194.

232 Waetjen, *A Reordering of Power*, 115.

233 Incigneri, *The Gospel to the Romans*, 190-194.

234 Horsley, *Jesus and the Powers*, 113-129. Koester links the composition of the Roman Legion with what he calls "philosophical marketplace." He says, "In the imperial period the army of the wandering missionaries and philosophers had become legion." See, *History, Culture and Religion of the Hellenistic Age*, 355-356.

235 Horsley, *Jesus and the Powers*, 126-129.

236 Scott, *Domination and the Arts of Resistance*, 140-142.

237 Waetjen reads this passage as "a narrative of the destruction of demonic powers of living death and dehumanization." See, *A Reordering of Power*, 113.

238 Stein, *Mark*, 251-252.

resumed in 7: 24–8: 10, and Jesus would return to the Decapolis in 7: 31-37.[239] Given the little or no welcome that he received on his return to the city even after becoming a new human "clothed and in his right mind" (v. 15), the man who possessed Legion could have been a person from a subaltern class.

A little survey on the political situation of Decapolis may be enough to illuminate us upon his political status. The region of Decapolis (lit. "ten cities") was a group of ten cities on the eastern frontier of the Roman Empire.[240] The ten cities were not an independent political unit, but they were grouped together because of their culture, language, location, and political status, with each possessing a certain degree of sovereignty.[241] It is extremely important that we understand the multi-ethnicity of the region. It was a region where two cultures—that of Greek colonists and the indigenous Semitic—interacted. Frequent conflict is envisaged between the two.[242] Various elements of Semitic dissident towards the dominant and assimilative nature of the Greek culture gradually culminated during the Roman domination. Most possibly, the point of conflict between Semitic inhabitants and Greek colonists could have been on the matter of swine.

For the Jews, pork is something to be avoided.[243] The Torah classifies the pig as an unclean animal; and so it is regarded as forbidden for food (Lev 11: 7-8; Deut 14: 8; cf. Isa 65: 4; 66: 17). The Jews of the post Modein Revolt in particular must have been very sensitive about the pig, because Antiochus Epiphanes attempted to force Jews to sacrifice and eat pigs. The Jews strongly rejected the king's effort (1 Macc 1: 47; 2 Macc 6: 2-5; 6: 818-7: 42). Evidences in the Gospels reveal that the pig had become the symbol of paganism among the Jews (Mat 7: 6; Lk 15: 15-16). For the Romans, however, the pig was a ceremonial animal that was used for purification.[244] The ethnic identity of the man who was possessed by the unclean spirit is not clear. Mark mentions that this man considers Jesus to be "the Son of Most High" (v. 7). This could be a clue to trace his religious identity as an adherent of Semitic religion. Besides, Mark records that this man pleaded that he would be with Jesus (v. 18). This denotes his affinity towards the Jews. But, Jesus' words of refusal, "Go home to yours friends" (v. 19) makes it clear that he was neither a resident of Galilee nor Judea. It seems safe to conclude that this man belonged to the Semitic

239 Stein, *Mark*, 251.

240 Myers, *Binding the Strong Man*, 190-192.

241 Witherington believes that the Decapolis was formed as a "defense league about A.D. 1 to protect themselves." See, *The Gospel of Mark*, 178.

242 R. Dormandy, "The Expulsion of Legion: A Political Reading of Mark 5: 1-20," *ExpTim* 111/10 (2000): 335. Joy states that "there were many unsuccessful rebellions by the marginalized native population." See, *Mark and Its Subalterns*, 170.

243 Witherington, *The Gospel of Mark*, 179.

244 Incigneri, *The Gospel to the Romans*, 192.

community in the Decapolis that was in continual conflict with the Greek colonists. Mark tells us that they begged Jesus "earnestly not to send them out to the country" (v. 10). Rather, they suggested, "Send us into the swine; let us enter them" (v. 12). Why was the man earnest in his appeal with regard to sending them out of the country? Why does he want them to enter the swine? An answer to these questions could be decisive in determining the meaning of this narrative. Mark's portrayal of the character and the behaviour of this man assume that there is a political disguise beneath the story. Presumably, there was perhaps a growing demand of supply of pork in the Roman world.[245] A part of the Decapolis had taken measures towards the growing need, by intensive pig farming in the countryside. Mark's reference to "a great herd of swine" feeding in the hillside (v. 11) assumes that a large number of lands were acquired for pig farming. This man could possibly be the victim and was evicted from his own land. Most possibly, he was doomed to residential segregation and was divorced from normal civil life.[246] His behaviour, actions, words and strategies can be interpreted as what Scott calls "host of down-to earth, low-profile stratagems designed to minimize [material] appropriation."[247]

From Mark's description about this man, he managed to resist in two ways: "squatting" and "sabotage."[248] Mark denotes that the spirit possessed man occupied public places. The geographical space needs to be clarified. Mark's opening statement "to the country of the Gerasenes" (v. 1) specifies the geographical location of the incident. However, the textual problems associated with the site are well known.[249] While France suggests that the "territory of the Gerasenes" functions as a loose term for the whole of the Decapolis;[250] Edwards suggests that the territory of Gerasa extended to the Sea of Galilee.[251] Although, the textual evidence favours "Gerasenes," this is only a "C" rating.[252] Mark's use of the genitive absolute in v. 2 suggests the proximity of the eastern shore of Galilee and the geographical description of the incident. B. M. Metzger (1994) draws our attention to Gadara, a city of Decapolis about five miles southeast of the Sea of Galilee. Metzger's finds support from ancient

245 Waetjen argues that pigs were probably sold at a good profit to the Roman army in order to furnish the tables of the legionnaires. See, *A Reordering of Power*, 118.

246 Goretti, Daniel and Raja "The Gospel According to Mark," 177.

247 Scott, *Domination and the Arts of Resistance*, 188.

248 These are the two important items in the list of Scott's everyday form of resistance. See, Scott, *Domination and the Arts of Resistance*, 188.

249 Along with Γερασηνῶν or Gerasenes (א* B D it vg cop^{sa}), we also have Γεδαρηνῶν or Gadarenes (A C K Π 33), and Γεργεσηνῶν or Gergesenes(א^{c} L Δ Θ f^{1}, etc)

250 France, *Mark*, 227;

251 Edwards, *Mark*, 153.

252 B. M. Metzger, *A Textual Commentary of the Greek New Testament*, 2nd edition (Stuttgart: Deutche Bibelgegesellschaft, 1994), 121.

coins bearing the name of Gadara and often portray a ship, indicating that its territory was seen as bordering the Sea of Galilee.[253] Mark reveals that the man dwells upon the tombs and on the mountains. From here, he was "howling and bruising himself with stones" (v. 5). On the other hillside was a feeding place of a great herd of swine. A large numbers of pigs being drowned as a result of exorcism (v.13b) suggests that the city mentioned in v. 14 was big enough to demand a huge amount of pork. Surprisingly, the people of the city wanted Jesus to leave their city in spite of his miraculous work (v. 17). The people's decision to drive away Jesus from their neighbourhood suggests that they were worried about Jesus because his powerful act killed their pigs.[254]

Considering the plurality of ethnicity and the subaltern politics among the inhabitants, we may not do justice if we simply read the incident as Jesus encounter with the demon possessed man who called himself Legion; the name of Roman forces. It is safe to conclude that this man was perhaps a victim of the Roman massive pig faming policy that was evicted from his land and lived in the mountain and tombs. Since he had such a lowly status, he was not equipped with the power to resist the official policies and practices of the powers. So he seems to disguise himself in the form of spirit possession and he would disturb the people who were coming to the highway. This is an euphemistic strategy to resist the imperial powers.

4.4. Grumbling: Some Cases in Jesus' Campaign

Grumbling is a covert form of protest and complaint. The intention of grumbling, according to Scott is "to communicate general sense of dissatisfaction without assuming responsibly for an open, specific complaint."[255] Scott conceptualizes communicative gestures in order to convey dissatisfaction or animosity, thus: "Providing such a message was imparted, almost any means of communication might serve the purpose: a groan, a sigh, a moan, a chuckle, a well-timed silence, a wink, or a stare."[256] Mark does not give us the full account of Jesus' communicative act or gesture when he is in confrontation with the powers. Still then, there are some gestures that resonate to what Scott devises as grumbling.

---

253 Metzger, *A Textual Commentary of the Greek New Testament*, 18. According to Witherington, Gerasa was a city of Decapolis which is thirty-seven miles southeast of the Sea of Galilee. He argues that it is far enough for the pigs to run into the sea from there. See, *The Gospel of Mark*, 179-180.

254 On the attitude of the inhabitants of the locality towards Jesus and the transformation that He brought about, see Goretti, Daniel and Raja, "The Gospel According to Mark," 178.

255 Scott, *Domination and the Arts of Resistance*, 154.

256 Scott, *Domination and the Arts of Resistance*, 155.

4.4.1. Shake off the Dust (6: 11)

First of all, it seems evident that Jesus instructed his disciples on how to grumble in front of those who would oppose them. While sending them out into village two by two, Jesus declared:

> [11]He said to them, 'Wherever you enter a house stay there until you leave the place. If any place will not welcome you and they refuse to hear you, as you leave, shake off the dust that is on your feet as a testimony against them' (Mk. 6: 10-12).

Mark arranges this story concerning the mission of the disciples after Jesus was rejected in his own village (6:1-6). The rejection at home, however, ushers a stage where Jesus' campaign would go further into other regions.[257] The mission discourse ends here negatively because of misunderstanding and opposition from local rulers who were influenced by the scribes from Jerusalem. We may also recall the previous incident of rejection in 3: 6 where the Pharisees and the Herodians conspired to kill Jesus.[258] The succeeding account is the death of John the Baptist (6: 14-29). Mark's long and detailed story of the martyrdom of Jesus' forerunner assumes a difficult situation. Stein observes that thematically, Jesus' rejection in Nazareth (6: 4-6a) is linked to his warning of the disciples regarding his missionary precepts. Stein believes that the disciples might have had a similar experience (6: 11a), and thus Jesus gave the instructions to them (cf. 6: 11b with 6: 5a).[259] The mission of the disciples is one of the best attested facts in the life of Jesus.[260] It is not surprising to see him conveying instructions in this manner before they go.

Jesus' instruction that follow in Mark 6: 8-9 are concerned with what they should not take, such as: bread, bag, money, two tunics. Scholars like Taylor and Guelich have noticed that the charge "to take/not take" is proceeded by a ἵνα, which introduces not a purpose, but the content of the command.[261] However, ἵνα seems to take care of both the messengers as well as the message. The charge—both to take and not to take—thus involves political disguise. The exclusion of normal travelling needs and supplies (bread, bag, money, extra tunic) is not likely that the disciples were to travel light.[262] Rather, they

257 For detailed discussion on the rejection of Jesus in Nazareth, see Myers, *Binding the Strong Man*, 211-212.

258 For the mission and misunderstanding in Mk. 6: 6b–8: 21, I use Stein, *Mark*, 287.

259 Stein, *Mark*, 289.

260 There is a debate as to whether the present account was constructed by Mark out of diverse materials or whether it existed much in its form before Mark. See, Taylor, *The Gospel According to St. Mark*, 302 and Best, *Following Jesus*, 190-192.

261 Taylor, *The Gospel According to St. Mark*, 304; Geulich, *Mark 1–8: 26*, 321.

262 Goretti, Daniel and Raja feel that the motive behind this is "solidarity with the dispossessed." See, "The Gospel According to Mark," 179.

were to proceed on their campaign in disguise and anonymity.[263] Crossan beautifully puts it, "reaction to rejection."[264] This provides a more possible rationale for the campaign in the context of resistance by the subaltern class. Jesus also gave instructions on how they should react with the opposition from the villagers and perhaps even the local rulers. To consistently remain in a house where they entered is the prerequisite. This could possibly prevent the disciples, as Stein suggests, from "moving up to the social ladder to better and more luxurious housing."[265]

Now, we come to the crux of the point of grumbling. Jesus prepares the Twelve in Mark 6: 11 for two possible responses which they may encounter in their campaign. Mark's presentation of Jesus' instruction assumes that any village that does not receive them and where the people do not listen to their message is to receive the parabolic act of the disciples "shake off the dust … as a testimony against them" (v. 11). Truly, "shake off the dust that is on your feet" simply belongs what Scott renders as a "communicative act" that intends to "convey an indistinct and deniable sense of ridicule, dissatisfaction, or animosity."[266] This act of shaking dust off the feet is completely different from the foot-washing ritual that was a common practice among the people of the east. Till recently, scholars have failed to consider this act of grumbling as they took the text out of its original agrarian-resistance context. This may be taken as a symbolic act that terminated contact with the place. In *Binding the Strong Man* (1988), Myers has established the view that Jesus' instructions were "social strategy" for the purposes of mission and travel in villages.[267] Edwards interprets this act as to how the disciples should treat the Gentiles.[268] Given the dynamics of power relations in Galilee, Jesus' instruction might have assumed veiled complaint without assuming responsibility for further retaliation.

4.4.2. Eating without Washing Hands (7: 1-6)

Mark has already mentioned Jesus' direct contact with the Pharisees and the Scribes (2: 16; 24; 3: 6, 22).[269] Here, the narrative is largely characterized by the disciples' failure to comply with the hand washing law and the response

263 Some scholars like Waetjen would take this verse to denote a sense of identification with the people to whom they are ministering. See, *A Reordering of Power*, 124.

264 Crossan, *The Power of Parable*, 187.

265 Stein, *Mark*. 293.

266 Scott, *Domination and the Arts of Resistance*, 155.

267 Myers, *Binding the Strong Man*, 214.

268 Edwards, *The Gospel According to Mark*, 181.

269 For detailed discussion on the issue of purity in Mark, see J. H. Neyrey, "The Idea of Purity in Mark's Gospel," in *Social-Scientific Criticism of the New Testament and its Social World*. Semeia 35. Decatur, GA: SBL 1986, 105-124.

from the ruling class. This account is important for academic investigation as it involves a probable case of grumbling. In the entire course of his campaign in the sequestered site, Mark portrays Jesus as having aggressively confronted the powerful ruling elites regarding their practices of the Law. However it was perhaps no longer possible to be as aggressive as before. As he confronted the Pharisees and the Scribes from Jerusalem, concerning their strict observance hand washing, even at the market place, we have Jesus-in-movement and his disciples grumbling regarding the practice. The incident in Mark 7: 1-4 is interesting as Mark situates the action possibly in the "market" (6: 56). "Market" presents the peasant subsistence economy, as well as traditional social relations, with a number of risks.[270] For Myers, Mark has special interest in mentioning the word "marketplace" in 6: 56 and 7: 4. He felt that this social site of narrative represents the economic sphere.[271] Myers also acknowledges that Mark later refers to it as the public site of scribal "piety" that oppresses the poor (12: 38ff.).[272] In other words, market is "the privileged site of anti-hegemonic discourse."[273] Scott argues that the peasants will often resist the market, being risk-averse and concerned predominantly with survival. During the first century of the Roman imperial rule in Judea, the scribal community in Jerusalem mounted *ad dhoc protests and organised a resistance to the imperialism by way of avoiding the Gentiles in the marketplace. Mark denotes, "they do not eat anything from the market unless they wash it" (7: 4). For Myers, Mark 7: 6-13 in which Jesus attacks the purity code is a "vigorous counteroffensive that attempts to delegitimize Pharisaic authority altogether."*[274] The purification law is one of the finest examples of everyday forms of resistance for the contemporary Judeans of Jesus' time.

Ironically, some of Jesus' disciples were "eating with defiled hands" (7: 2). Jesus' defense of their deed in 7: 6-23 strongly indicates that it was not accidental. This incident is a clear representation of the conflict between the "little tradition" and the "great tradition." Mark reports with a vivid explanation that the Pharisees were serious when they noticed some of the disciples eating food without washing their hands (7: 3-5). Here lies another point to indicate that Jesus and his disciples were not in compliance

270 Scott, *Domination and the Arts of Resistance*, 122.

271 Koester discusses how philosophy was associated with marketplace. He argues that during Roman rule, "the real life of 'philosophy,' left the schools and had gone into the marketplace and onto the streets of the big cities." See, *History, Culture and Religion of the Hellenistic Age*, 355-356.

272 Myers, *Binding the Strong Man*, 219.

273 This are the words of Mikhail Bakhtin, as paraphrased by Scott in his *Domination and the Arts of Resistance*, 122. For details, see M. Bakhtin, *Rebelais and His World*, trans. Helene Iswolaky (Bloomington: Indiana University Press, 1984).

274 Myers, *Binding the Strong Man*, 220.

with the norms of the "traditions of the elders" as cultivated by the Jerusalem elites. Historically, the "traditions of the elders" is linked to the Pharisees who were experts in the Law and propounded rulings for the society beyond those in the Mosaic Law in a few decades after the Modein Revolt.[275] As Josephus denotes, John Hyrcanus, the Hasmonean high priest rescinded these rulings as part of official state law (*Ant 13: 296-297). Thus, traditions of elders – especially hand washing are alien rules to the Galileans. The Pharisees defended the purity code (i.e. hand washing) as fundamental to national identity. This act of non-action in a market place must be appreciated in the light of subaltern political experiences. If the market is where the religious elites—viz. Pharisees and the Scribes who are at the same time seeking political power—declared their public transcript, it should also be the right place for Jesus-in-movement to declare the hidden transcript of the dignity. Mark says, "And wherever he [Jesus] went into, villages or cities or farms, they laid sick in the marketplaces ... were healed" (Mk 6: 56). Here, we have a clear manifestation that the agrarian-resistance was fighting the domination on two fronts. On the one hand, we come across Jesus-in-movement claiming the space in marketplace of the people from margins; and on the other hand, his disciples were practicing "behind-the-scenes griping and grumbling"*[276] by eating meals without washing their hands in the sight of those who prohibited the same. As the incident took place in public and in the very presence of the representatives of the high-priestly aristocrats in Jerusalem, we should consider that both the actions involved veiled complaint from the part of Jesus and his disciples. These are the aspects in which Jesus and his disciples speak truth to the powers. We shall pick up this issue again when we discuss the Parable of defilement in the next chapter.

4.4.2.1. Sighed Deeply (8: 11-13)

> [11]The Pharisees came and began to argue with him, asking him for a sign from heaven, to test him. [12]And he *sighed deeply* in his spirit and said, 'Why does this generation ask for a sign? Truly I tell you, no sign will be given to this generation.' [13]And he left them, and getting into the boat again, he went across to the other side (8: 11-13).[277]

Mark has another conflict story that was initiated by the Pharisees. According to Mark, the Pharisees came and disputed with Jesus about what he was saying and doing, and then tested him. This incident happens right after the great feeding of the four thousand (8: 1-10). Jesus, who performed many might

275 Horsley, *Hearing the Whole Story*, 153.

276 Scott, *Domination and the Arts of Resistance*, 188.

277 Emphasis is mine.

words and signs, was denying a sign to the Pharisees. Previous scholars mainly debated upon the extent to which this account existed as an independent, pre-Markan story rather than an integral part of subaltern resistance story. In Q material (Mat 12: 38-39; Lk 11: 29-32), the sign is specified as a "sign of Jonah." The absence of such specification in Mark assumes that the present one is a Markan creation. However, scholars like R. Edwards and Geulich and others have argued for pre-Markan tradition behind this text.[278] Interestingly enough, only Mark has an unusual gesture by Jesus καὶ ἀναστενάξας τῷ πνεύματι ("sighed deeply") in 8: 12.[279] The term ἀναστενάξας has been interpreted in various ways by scholars. Witherington proposes two possible meanings for the word. First, the term may refer to "some deep emotional reaction" that is similar to "Jesus' anger in Mark 1: 41" caused by "lack of faith of the Pharisees in relationship to Jesus." Second, the term may also reflect "the sort of deep movement of the Spirit within a prophetic person."[280] To some extent, it may have been true to consider the behavior of the Pharisee to be a radical denial of faith. This account entails more than their personal faith in miracle or sign.

Even in the next section, Jesus warned his disciples to beware of the yeast of the Pharisees and of Herod (8: 14-21). In various contexts, "yeast" is used in relation a "synonym for corruption" (1 Cor 5: 6-8; Gal 5: 9).[281] It could be more acceptable to consider this incident as a continuing political struggle between Jesus and the corrupt Jewish leaders. Myers' political commentary reveals that this gesture is an action that refuses to provide the signs that were demanded by the Pharisees.[282] Jesus seemingly hides his message—sayings and deeds—from them and escaped by "getting into the boat" (v. 13). Mark, by mentioning the inattention of Pharisees "to test him" (v. 11b), situates this narrative in the context of a political situation that was unfavorable for the Jesus-in-movement. Crossan comments, "Jesus is asked to give a sign from heaven proving his identity and validating his proclamation."[283] In such a situation, Mark may have aspects other than emotional reaction or prophetic spirituality in retaining the gesture of Jesus, *i.e.*, ἀναστενάξας. We may possible take this gesture as a politics of disguise and anonymity. This involves "refusal of any proof sign."[284] This is, indeed, one among the communicative acts which Scott

---

278 R. A. Edwards, "The Sign of Jonah in the Theology of the Evangelists and Q," *SBL* 2/18 (1971), 75; Geulich, Mark 1: 1 – 8: 26, 411.

279 Donahue, "Jesus as the Parable of God in the Gospel of Mark," 379.

280 Witherington, *The Gospel of Mark*, 237; also Goretti, Daniel and Raja, "The Gospel According to Mark," 183.

281 Witherington, *The Gospel of Mark*, 237.

282 Myers, *Binding the Strong Man*, 223.

283 Crossan, *The Power of Parable*, 189.

284 Crossan, *The Power of Parable*, 189.

devises as the act of grumbling.[285] As Mark puts it in the context of Jesus addressing the Pharisees, it is worth considering a low form of resistance.

4.5. Summary

That Mark's Gospel is a story about the resistance of agrarian community in Galilee as catalyzed by Jesus of Nazareth is evident in three-fold political discourses. Having been generated in the sequestered sites of Capernaum and its neighbourhoods, the hidden transcript of dignity and indignation has been carried more widely into other parts of Galilee and beyond. Mark does provide how the political discourse on how Jesus proclaims the "hidden transcript" that was cultivated in the villages of Galilee to the larger Galilee and beyond. Jesus, thus, seems to be creatively adapting the popular ideology that comprises an alternative to the values and views as articulated in the official transcript controlled by the dominant scribal class. We have discussed the probability of how Jesus brings political expression of the hidden transcript to the public expression and public view. Crossan is right in commenting the text, "That is a simple but very emphatic refusal to give any proof—but without any name-calling."[286] At this stage, we are convinced that Jesus' manner of speaking truth to powers in public, evidently takes upon a sense of disguise and anonymity.

5. Jesus' Campaign in Jerusalem and the Declaration of the Hidden Transcript in the Face of Power (8: 31–16: 20)

That Jesus is spearheading the agrarian-resistance movement in opposition to the rulers in Jerusalem and that he is also opposed by them is evident is the final part of Mark's Gospel (8: 27–16: 20). The ideology that is lying beneath the hidden transcript and disguise form of resistance obviously pose direct challenges to the Jerusalem temple-state. The ideal of God's reign—which is at the same time the central message of Jesus—addresses the rural needs, and it thus profanes the great tradition as cultivated by the urban ruling powerful elites. The rural power that expels unclean sprit and praised by local community sounds like the "Beelzebul" to the urban aristocrat community in Jerusalem (1: 21-28; 3: 22). The healing and forgiveness of sin at the centre in Galilee seem to provoke the power-holders at the centre (2: 1-12). Likewise, the Scribes and the Pharisees—representatives of the temple-state who "come down from Jerusalem" (3: 22; 7: 1)—challenged Jesus throughout his campaign in Galilee. Mark tells us that the Pharisees "conspire with the Herodians … to destroy him" (3: 6).

We now proceed to the final political discourse in Mark 8:22–16: 20. In this part of the Gospel, we have Jesus-in-movement marching up to

285 Scott, *Domination and the Arts of Resistance*, 155.

286 Crossan, *The Power of Parable*, 189.

Jerusalem to directly engage the high priests, scribes and elders in a series of confrontation, beginning with a demonstration of God's condemnation of the Temple (11: 15-19).[287] In response to his bold action, Jesus was arrested, trailed and executed. This stage is similar to what Scott calls, "the rupturing of the political order with direct attack and challenge." It is unfortunate that modern western interpreters convey an interpretation of Jesus as politically innocuous.[288] Jesus' confine was seen largely in cultural-religious affairs, and his bold public declarations that might seem politically challenging are effectively depoliticized. As a result, Jesus' entry into Jerusalem was only a fulfillment of the prophecy in Zechariah 9: 9; and the obstructive prophetic demonstration against the temple becomes a cleansing; and it was a rendering of 'unto God and Caesar' that was reduced to church versus state. We pose the question as to how those actions and declarations of Jesus in the temple have been remembered unless they have had historical impact? Horsley, who encourages an understanding of the final actions of Jesus in Jerusalem as his confrontation with the rulers in Jerusalem, says:

> Jesus' confrontation with rulers in Jerusalem, perhaps mainly his condemnation of the temple and high priests, as compounded by his crucifixion, appears to have been the breakthrough event that led to the sudden expansion of the movement he had inaugurated in Galilee, ensuring that he became a significant historical figure. And the expansion of that movement, in turn, did not merely remember his teachings and deeds, but perpetuated, cultivated, and consolidated his speech and program of societal renewal.[289]

Assuming that these are declarations and actions that are in public confrontation to the rulers and the ruling institutions in Jerusalem, we shall attempt to read this portion of the Gospel by Scott's position of the fourth variety of the politics of resistance. Scott's fourth political discourse takes on the public declaration of the hidden transcript in the face of power. For Scott, this politics is "the rapture of the political *cordon sanitaire* between the hidden and the public transcript."[290] We will examine such actions and declarations for the insights that they offer into the dynamics of a political breakthrough.

5.1. The Portent of Political Breakthrough (8: 27–9: 50)

In the previous section, we have focused upon Mark 3: 7–8: 26 seeking the political dynamics of the conflictual relations between the dominant and the

287 Kingsbury, *Conflict in Mark*, 42-43.

288 Horsley, "Politics of Disguise and Public Declaration," 73.

289 Horsley, "Politics of Disguise and Public Declaration," 73.

290 Scott, *Domination and the Arts of Resistance*, 19.

subaltern that was developed and interacted in public in the form of disguise and anonymity. In this part of the Gospel, we find that those essentials of disguise and anonymity were gradually moving away as Jesus moves closer to Jerusalem. As we carefully follow Mark's story of Jesus, we reach a state where Jesus of Nazareth cannot take anymore aspects of speaking truth to powers. Such moments of challenge and overt defiance is preceded by certain events taking place on Jesus' way to Jerusalem. Those events can be better understood if explicated in terms of taking away of the shields from the messenger and the message. Jesus is the carrier of the hidden transcript of dignity and indignation. However, his identity as the Messiah was veiled in public until Peter acknowledges him (8: 27-30). Hereafter, as Mark denotes, Jesus began to prepare his disciples for a direct and open confrontation with the powers (8: 31). Modern scholars generally interpreted this aspect as discourse on discipleship in religious sense. When we analyze them in the context of political domination and resistance; we can see them as preparation of the direct or overt resistance. Jesus foretold his death and resurrection in three separate geographical locations.[291] First, it happened while he was possibly still in Caesarea Philippi. Jesus told his disciples that he must undergo great suffering, rejection by the elders, the chief priests, and the scribes (8: 27, 31-31). Mark has a special remark on this, "He said all this quite openly" (8: 32). Again, Jesus foretold his death when they "passed through Galilee" (9: 30a). Unlike the previous confession, "He [Jesus] did not want anyone to know it," says Mark (9: 30b).[292] Mark, thus, adds that even his disciples also did not understand (9: 32). Finally, "when they were on the road, going up to Jerusalem" Jesus depicted again his fate (10: 32-34). This time, Jesus foretold exclusively to the twelve (10: 32b). Jesus' unveiling of his identify takes place in a supernatural way. This is what we generally regard as "transfiguration" (9: 2-8). We are not informed about the specific geographical location, but it was on a "high mountain" (9:2). It was not a public incident. It so happened that while Jesus and three of his selected disciples were together in that high mountain, not only the messenger but the message also comes back unveiled. The nearness of the kingdom of God, which was proclaimed freely and openly at the beginning, had disappeared. In a form of an elaborate form of anonymity, Jesus denoted the secret of the kingdom of God to the public. In 9: 1, as Jesus prepared his disciples for what was ahead, he spoke about the kingdom of God as coming with power.

---

291 cf. S. Dowd and E. S. Malbon, the Pharisees and the Herodians were the powers that claimed to represent God, yet were the losers when Jesus proclaimed God's kingdom. See, "The Significance of Jesus' Death in Mark: Narrative Context and Authorial Audience," *SBL* 125/2 (2006): 279-280.

292 Roskam, *The Purpose of Mark*, 158.

As he blessed the children brought to him, Jesus made a specific statement, thus:

> [14b]Let the little children come to me; do not stop them; for it is to such as these that the kingdom of God belongs. [15]Truly I tell you, whoever does not receive the kingdom of God as a little child will never enter it. [16]And he took them up in his arms, laid his hands on them, and blessed them (10: 14b-16).

Mark picks up the theme of kingdom of God. Here, it is linked with those "undervalued in society."[293] The story that follows is a story of rich man who "went away grieving" (10: 17-22). Jesus made a contrasting statement while referring to the kingdom of God, thus: "How hard it will be for those who have wealth to enter the kingdom of God" (10: 23). Liew comments, "Jesus uses children as an object to teach his disciples that their service and sacrifice should benefit those who have little power or no power in society."[294]

5.2. The Rupture of Political Cordon Sanitaire (Mk 11:1-11)

Jesus' entry into Jerusalem posed a significant threat to the Roman imperial order.[295] We must consider why Jerusalem was the final destination of Jesus. It is evident that the Synoptic tradition does convey that Jesus was living and working in Galilee, a region under Herod Antipas, and not the Jerusalem with the high priests. If Jesus' intention was simply to oppose the ruling house, as Horsley suggests, he could have gone either to Antipas' capital Sepphoris or Tiberias which most directly exploited the people of Galilee.[296] Jesus seems to have a broader agenda beyond Galilee. With the methodological individualism of Gospel studies, the meaning of Jesus' entry into Jerusalem has also been sought apart from its socio-political context. Even though the essential historicity of Jesus' entry into Jerusalem with a crowd has never been doubted by critical scholars, yet issues have been raised concerning the political significance of the event for the agrarian communities in Galilee.[297] Issues being raised were concerned simply regarding how much those who handed

293 Dowd and Malbon, "The Significance of Jesus' Death in Mark," 279.

294 Liew, "The Gospel of Mark," 110.

295 According to the geographical organization of Mark, the present account records the first and only time Jesus enters Jerusalem. John, on the other hand, refers to several such visits in 2: 13–4: 45; 5:1- 47; 7: 1-10; and 12: 12 – 20: 30. Luke suggests more than one such visit to Jerusalem in 13; 34 (cf. Mk. 14: 49).

296 Horsley, *Jesus and the Powers*, 168.

297 Some scholars have suggested that the present account is an early Christian myth that was created and it read back into the life of Jesus on the basis of the church's reading of Zechariah 9: 9. See, Bultmann, *The History of the Synoptic Tradition*, 261-262; Dibelius, *From Tradition to Gospel*, 121-122. Stein is not convinced by these form critics as there is no quotation of Zach 9: 9 in Mark's Gospel. See, *Mark*, 501.

on the tradition shaped the story in order to make it a vehicle for expressing the allegedly later belief of the early church, in the light of the fact that Jesus was the fulfillment of the Jewish hope for a messianic deliverer in the form of a Davidic king. For example, Bultmann—while not denying that the story has a historical fact—labels it as "a Messianic legend under the influence of Zech 9: 9."[298] D. R. Catchpole argues that the story fits the pattern of accounts in Jewish literature of "the celebratory entry to a city by a hero figure who has previously achieved his triumph."[299] Catchpole cites as evidence, entries of heroic figures in the Jewish literature such as: Alexander, Apollonius, Jonathan, Antigonus, Marcus Agrippa and Archelaus. If we take Jesus' entry into Jerusalem as that of these heroes, the incident could not be interpreted as a subaltern political discourse in which Jesus challenged the power structure of the Jewish temple-state. Instead, we should assume that the incident is not an acknowledgement of the status that Jesus had already achieved. Brandon argues that Jesus' action is "obviously calculated to cause the authorities, both Jewish and Roman, to view him and his movement as subversive."[300] Brandon's argument sounds more significant to the present investigation. From the agrarian-resistance viewpoint, Jesus' entry into Jerusalem can hardly be the event that was celebrated as "triumphal entry" in recognition of the kingship that he had previously won. Rather, it seems that Jesus entered into the city to declare the hidden transcript in the face of the powers.[301] It is envisaged that the issue can be better addressed after a survey of the presentation of Jesus' entry into Jerusalem in the Gospel itself from this perspective.

To the reader of the Gospel of Mark which may be rendered as a story of subjugated people, it is clear that Jesus entered Jerusalem to take direct opposition to the rulers and ruling institutions. Horsley opines that "the importance of structural factors" is essential in understanding the political significance of the event.[302] In recent years, we have learnt much about the history of Galilee and its relations with Jerusalem from socio-political historians. Jesus' travel from Galilee to Jerusalem brings the prophetic spokesperson and the leader of the agrarian movement from Galilee and the high priestly aristocrats in the temple who had taken Galilee and ruled for

298 R. Bultmann, *The History of Synoptic Tradition*, Rev. ed. (New York: Harper & Row, 1969), 262; Samuel, *A Postcolonial Reading of Mark's Story of Jesus*, 136-137.

299 D. R. Catchpole, "The Triumphal Entry," in *Jesus and the Politics of His Day*, ed. E. Bammel and C. F. D. Moule (Cambridge: Cambridge University Press, 1984), 319.

300 Brandon, *Jesus and Zealots*, 324.

301 Waetjen discusses Jesus' entry into Jerusalem under the sub-heading "negation of the temple institution and confrontation with the ruling elite." See, *A Reordering of Power*, 179-196. Witherington argues that Jesus chooses to ride a donkey rather to walk as "some sort of prophetic sign act." See, *The Gospel of Mark*, 310.

302 Horsley, "Politics of Disguise and Public Declaration," 74.

a century before the time of Jesus. This pilgrimage stages the significant juxtaposition of the spokesperson of the subaltern masses from Galilee and the dominant rulers. Here, Scott's idea of the emotional dynamics of domination and subjugation finds its relevance. The status domination that had been imposed by the ruling class in Jerusalem upon the subjugated Galileans has produced a certain oppositional ideology. However, the agrarian communities in Galilee were blocked by the coercive power of the dominant Judeans. This indignation needs expression. A spokesperson's bold defiance of the dominant can transform the collective indignation into an energy that drives events and create a political breakthrough that can escalate rapidly into a significant movement. Scott believes that such charismatic acts "gain their social force by virtue of their roots in the hidden transcripts of a subordinate group."[303]

Scott's statement, "The moment when the dissent of the hidden transcript crosses the threshold to open resistance is always a politically charged occasion"[304] has hermeneutical significance for the explication of the meaning of Jesus' entry into Jerusalem. In Jesus' case "the occasion of the politically charged occasion" could be the occasion of the Passover (Mk14: 1-3, 12). Modern studies on Jesus' overt confrontation with the Jewish leaders at the Passover time have never challenged its historical reliability. The theological significance of Jesus' declaration of the hidden transcript in the face of powers during the occasion of the Passover requires further investigation. As discussed in the previous chapter, there was a riot and massacre under the governor Cumanus during the celebration of the Passover. Jesus' bold declaration of the hidden transcript of dignity and indignation of the subalterns at Passover time can be noted as the celebration of liberation from foreign domination.

Mark's presentation of Jesus' entry into Jerusalem is largely characterized by the presence of the crowd. *One Volume Dalit Bible Commentary* (2012) aptly calls it "People's March into the Temple with Their Leader."[305] Scott rightly argues, "Large, autonomous gatherings of subordinate are threatening to domination."[306] In *Terror in the Mind of God* (2000), M. Juergensmeyer denotes how in ancient Jerusalem, without modern instruments of democracy, demonstrations or riots by urban mobs constituted the principal means by which the economically dependent populace could clamour to their rulers for redressal of grievances.[307] Mark 11: 8 reads: "Many people spread their cloaks on the road, and others spread leafy branches that they had cut in the fields."

303 Scott, *Domination and the Arts of Resistance*, 203.

304 Scott, *Domination and the Arts of Resistance*, 207.

305 Goretti, Daniel and Raja, "The Gospel According to Mark," 189.

306 Scott, *Domination and the Arts of Resistance*, 65.

307 M. Juergensmeyer, *Terror in the Mind of God* (Berkeley: University of California Press, 2000), 131-133.

There is no explicit reference to the identity of the crowds. The spreading of leafy branches cut from the field implies that they were a rural crowd. This signifies that Mark keeps the "rural crowds and the urban elites" in contrast.[308] Myers sees the peasants brandishing Jesus with only their weapons in this passage.[309] The slogan "Hossana!" is Hebrew for "Save now!"[310] Its use in Psalm 118 means a cry for God to now save the people of Israel from their enemies.[311] This perhaps suggests that the "many people" were the subordinated ones.[312] Jesus' use of the donkey still involves politics disguise and anonymity. For Zachariah 9: 9 mentions that the donkey is the animal that God or God's Messiah is to ride into Jerusalem when those who resist God's purposes are defeated. Carter is of the opinion that Mark leaves the political significance of Jesus' use of donkey as disguised.[313]

The significance of Jesus' entry into Jerusalem lies not only in Jesus, but also on the crowd who paraded into the city.[314] It is important to note how the participants among the "many people" are subordinated people who might feel emboldened by the act of massing itself. There is the visual impact of collective power that a vast assembly of agrarian subordinates conveys both its own number and to its adversaries. Obviously, it renders hope to those suffering under the Roman imperial rule. In the words of Carter, Jesus' entrance is a kind of "street theatre or acted parable."[315] Such an assembly provides each participant with a measure of anonymity or disguise, thereby lowering the risk of being identified personality for the action of that day. They would have realized that there is power in numbers. From this moment onwards, we find Jesus' direct confrontation with the ruling order as a bid to expose its exploitation. This is the most explosive realm of politics. Mark depicts this event as the rapture of the political *cordon sanitaire* between the hidden transcript and public transcript.

---

308 Myers, *Binding the Strong Man*, 296.

309 Myers, *Binding the Strong Man*, 296.

310 Some scholars interpret this as a cry for God's final intervention. For example, Naickanparampil, *The Gospel of Mark*, 168.

311 For scholars like Carter, Ps. 118 signifies the celebration of God's victory over the nations. See, Carter, *The Roman Empire and the New Testament*, 130.

312 Rejection to my stand, for instance, Stein, *Mark*, 505, is acknowledged.

313 Carter, *The Roman Empire and the New Testament*, 130.

314 Stein comments that for the disciples and the crowd the incident was an "exuberant experience that brought much excitement." See, *Mark*, 506. Lane conveys excitement as general enthusiasm of the pilgrim going up to Jerusalem. The feast is compared with one whom they regarded to be a great prophet and teacher, one who comes in the Lord's name. Lane, *The Gospel of Mark*, 397-398.

315 Carter, *The Roman Empire and the New Testament*, 130.

5.3. Jesus' Demonstration in the Temple (11: 15-19)[316]

Mark 11: 15-17 is often called "cleansing of the temple." Myers denotes that this passage is a "pretext for debates" about whether Jesus' protest was "pro or anti-Zealot."[317] While is it important to read the incident in the light of what is to happen, it is also important to read it in the light of what had happened in Galilee. Recent postcolonial critics like Liew would link entering Satan's house in 3: 7 with Jesus' entering the temple in 11: 17.[318] In both cases, we shall try to squeeze out a deeper meaning by reading the event as an obstructive prophetic demonstration against the powers.[319] Mark portrays Jesus' demonstration in the temple as forcible if not violent, with Jesus physically "overturned the tables of the money changers and the seats of those who sold doves" and not allowing "anyone to carry anything through the temple [courtyard]" (11: 15).[320] Beck argues that this temple action was "nonviolent prophetic confrontation."[321] Samuel reads this incident as "decisive, drastic and disruptive activity" of Jesus in the temple.[322] Recent studies by Myers, Horsley and Herzog have clearly explained this temple demonstration episode as Jesus' direct or prophetic action and speech of God's impeding judgment of the temple. For these scholars, Jesus was effectively blocking the normal operation that was integral to the functioning of the religious political-economy of the Temple, such as money changing and the selling of doves.[323] We should not overlook the economic and political aspect lying underneath Jesus' demonstration. Waetjen rightly labels the temple as "the hub of all commercial enterprise and activity."[324] The temple in Jerusalem was not merely a religious place; rather it had functioned as the centre of collection and redistribution of taxes and tributes that were

316 Scholars like Stein clubbed this passage together with the previous incident of the cursing of the fig tree to form "Jesus' judgment of the fig free and the temple." See, Stein, *Mark*, 508.

317 Myers, *Binding the Strong Man*, 299.

318 Liew, "The Gospel of Mark," 105-106.

319 Jesus' action seems to disapprove how the temple was functioning. John, *The Ecological Vision of Jesus*, 155.

320 For a possible implication of the text, see, Waetjen, *Reordering of Power*, 181; Mathew, *Temple-Criticism in Mark's Gospel*, 145-146.

321 R. R. Beck, *Nonviolent Story: Narrative Conflict Resolution in the Gospel of Mark* (Maryknoll, New York: Orbis Books, 1996), 159-163.

322 Samuel, *A Postcolonial Reading of Mark's Story of Jesus*, 138-139.

323 See Horsley, *Jesus and the Spiral of Violence*, 285-300; also W. R. Herzog II, *Jesus, Justice, and the Reign of God* (Louisville: Westminster John Knox, 2000), 137-143; also Incigneri, *The Gospel to the Romans*, 140, footnote no. 85; also Mathew, *Temple-Criticism in Mark's Gospel*, 141.

324 Waetjen, *A Reordering of Power*, 183.

appropriated from the agrarian surpluses of the rural masses.[325] The temple also received vast income from the temple tax which the law required every Jew to pay annually; gifts from individuals, revenues from its land-holdings, and its profits from the sale of sacrificial animals and money exchange.[326] The temple, according to Waetjen, was the central bank of worldwide Judaism controlled and administered by the priestly aristocracy.[327]

Obviously, Jesus' prophetic act could be safely considered as public resistance to material domination. In explaining his violent action, the Markan Jesus recites a prophecy saying, "Is it not written, 'My house shall be called a house of prayer for all the nations'? But you have made it a den of robbers" (Mk 11: 17).[328] Jesus' dramatic disruption of temple business was a symbolic prophetic demonstration as that of Isaiah who walked barefoot and naked for three years to enact symbolically the prophecy that the Assyrian Empire would lead away Egyptians as captives (Isa 20).[329] Jeremiah had worn an ox on his neck around Jerusalem to dramatize God's demand that the Judean monarchy should submit to the yoke of the Babylonian emperor (Jer 27–28).[330] Jesus was thus symbolically acting out a new prophetic condemnation not just of the building but of the temple system, because of its oppression of the people, as indicated in the reference to Jeremiah's original condemnation of the temple system.[331] The high priests and scribes knew what Jesus had done and thus, from this point of time "they kept looking for a way to kill him; for they were afraid of him" (Mk 11: 18a; cf. Jer 26).[332] Freyne, who tried to understand Jesus' entry into Jerusalem as pilgrimage, insists that Jesus' prophetic demonstration must be understood "in the light of the festival's expectations and tensions."[333]

---

325 Myers, *Binding the Strong Man*, 49.

326 Myers, *Binding the Strong Man*, 51-52, 300-302.

327 Waetjen, *A Reordering of Power*, 183.

328 For Horsley, Jesus prophecy appears to be a combination of a line from Isaiah 56: 7 with one from Jeremiah 7: 11. This almost certainly indicates that the prophecy was being recited from popular tradition. The second line, "you have made it a den of robbers" would have been an unmistakable reference to Jeremiah's famous prophecy against the original Temple in Jerusalem (7: 1-15). Jeremiah had prophesied that God had condemned the original Temple because its officials were stealing from the people, in violation of the Mosaic covenant commandments, and then presuming to use the Temple as their hideout on their bandits' den. The first line of Jesus' prophetic statement, "my house shall be called a house of prayer for all peoples," as indicated by its original context in Isaiah 56, was part of a prophetic appeal to make the second Temple a center where God could gather the outcasts of Israel and other peoples (Isa. 56: 8). See *Jesus and Empire*, 92.

329 Incigneri, *The Gospel to the Romans*, 143.

330 Carter, *The Roman Empire and the New Testament*, 69.

331 Horsley, *Jesus and Empire*, 92-93; also Roskam, *The Purpose of Mark*, 163.

332 Waetjen, *A Reordering of Power*, 183.

333 Freyne, *Galilee*, 290-293.

Freyne further argues that the action, for the Jerusalemites, was "a direct attack by a country outsider."[334]

However, we must not think of Jesus' presence in Jerusalem as merely a "pilgrimage to Jerusalem" but as a political discourse of the rural community. For Myers, this incident signifies "the apocalyptic struggle to bind the strong man and plunder his house."[335] Above all, Mathew's conclusion that Jesus' action was "a criticism of the economic exploitation by the Temple authorities and their agents" cannot be turned down.[336] Another aspect that one must take into account is the manner in which Markan narrative frames the demonstration. The prophetic action is sandwiched by the narratives of the withered fig tree.[337] Just before the demonstration in the temple, Jesus cursed the barren fig tree saying, "May no one eat fruit from you again" (Mk 11: 14).[338] Then immediately after the demonstration, Jesus, responded to Peter's report; "the fig tree that you cursed has withered," makes a declaration with a word of power faith in God, thus: "Have faith in God. Truly I tell you, if you say to this mountain, 'Be taken up and thrown into the sea', and … it will be done for you" (Mk 11: 20-24).[339] By the phrase "this mountain" Jesus might have referred to the mountain on which the temple stood. One can trust that God would have the temple removed.

5.4. The Question about Paying Tribute to Caesar (12: 13-17)

The Pharisees and Herodians attempted to entrap Jesus with "a precarious political question" about whether the tribute to Rome is lawful (Mk 12: 13-17).[340] Meier's rejection of incidents in Mark 3: 1 and 12: 13 as reliable historical information needs to be reviewed.[341] It is important that we read Jesus' response to this question in its historical context of the Israelite peoples under Roman imperial rule.[342] As discussed in the previous chapter, Judas of Galilee had incited resistance against proposed Roman taxation in Judea in C.E. 6 (*Ant* 18: 23; cf. *War* 2: 118). These two groups, Pharisees and Herodians (cf. Mk 3: 6) would have presumably known very well that it was not lawful

334 Freyne, *Galilee*, 291.

335 Myers, *Binding the Strong Man*, 303-304.

336 Mathew, *Temple-Criticism in Mark's Gospel*, 155.

337 Roskam, *The Purpose of Mark*, 162; Stein, *Mark*, 510.

338 Incigneri's insistence that fig trees as Rome is acknowledged. See, *The Gospel to the Romans*, 143.

339 Myers, *Binding the Strong Man*, 305.

340 Samuel, *A Postcolonial Reading of Mark's Story of Jesus*, 140. Waetjen puts it "a votile political issue." See, *A Reordering of Power*, 189.

341 Meier, "The Historical Jesus and the Historical Herodians," 746.

342 Liew, "The Gospel of Mark," 109.

to mosaic covenantal law to pay tributes to Rome. They would equally have been familiar with the law that not to pay tributes would have been taken by the Romans as tantamount to rebellion.[343] Indeed, it would have been suicidal, since the Romans might well have again slaughtered and enslaved people in vicious retaliation, as they had in 4 B.C.E. In fact, in a little more than two decades prior to Jesus' mission in Galilee and confrontation in Jerusalem, some of the Pharisees processors had helped organize resistance to the tribute as leaders of the Fourth Philosophy.[344]

This passage deals with issues of power.[345] Myers considers it as "the harshest criticism for the Jewish social order" for Jesus.[346] This is a difficult moment for Jesus to speak truth to powers as it directly confronts the matter of Roman imperial rule. In his response, Jesus subtly avoids the trap in their search for an excuse to arrest him as a rebel.[347] Jesus did not give a direct answer to the question.[348] But Jesus' response—"Give to Caesar the things that are Caesar's, and to God the things that are God's"—would have been understood in a just manner by every Israelite listening "including the Pharisees." Samuel treats Jesus' response as "a postcolonial strategy of Jesus and his community" that lived in-between Caesar and God.[349] For Carter, paying tax is an expression of hidden resistance.[350] It will be better to assume that Jesus took the same stand as the earlier Fourth Philosophy. Jesus was clearly and simply reasserting the Israelite principle that Caesar, or any other imperial ruler, had no claim on the Israelite people, since God was their actual king and master.[351]

5.5. Pronouncement of the Destruction of Jerusalem Temple (13: 1-2)

After his prolonged confrontation with the Jewish leaders that shared power in Jerusalem, Jesus announces to his disciples that "these great buildings" would be destroyed (Mk 13: 1-2).[352] Jesus' long discourse about the future

---

343 Samuel, *A Postcolonial Reading of Mark's Story of Jesus*, 140.

344 Horsley, *Jesus and Empire*, 99.

345 Incigneri, *The Gospel to the Romans*, 201.

346 Myers, *Binding the Strong Man*, 310.

347 Naickanparampil, *The Gospel of Mark*, 182.

348 For Incigneri sees the astuteness of Jesus that re-affirms the sovereignty of God while maintaining the acceptability of paying taxes. See, *The Gospel to the Romans*, 195.

349 Samuel, *A Postcolonial Reading of Mark's Story of Jesus*, 140-141.

350 Carter, *The Roman Empire and the New Testament*, 28, 133.

351 For detailed discussion, see Horsley, *Jesus and the Spiral of Violence*, 306-317; also Herzog, *Jesus, Justice, and the Reign of God*, 219-232; Naickanparampil, *The Gospel of Mark*, 182.

352 On the accuracy of Mark 13: 2, see Incigneri, *The Gospel to the Romans*, 120-122.

is introduced by his announcement of the destruction of the temple.[353] In Mark's Gospel, the open opposition of Jesus to the Jerusalem temple-state ruled over by the priestly aristocrats begins with the demonstration against the temple, and the pronouncement of God's condemnation of temple, high priests, Sadducees and scribes which would now be complete with destruction. Interestingly enough, the confrontation that began with Jesus' symbolic prophetic demonstration of God's judgment of the temple would be realized in its destruction. Jesus evidently pronounced and symbolically acted out God's condemnation of the temple and high priests. With this pronouncement of the destruction of the temple in Jerusalem, we come to the final stage of Jesus' public declaration of the hidden transcript of the Galileans in Jerusalem. In chapter 11, Mark demonstrates that the temple was no longer a place of contact with God. In chapter 12, Mark condemns the powerful elites of the temple-state. Here, we find that Mark pronounced the "complete destruction" of the temple.[354] Incigneri comments: "Jesus never shows reverence for the Temple, offers no sacrifice or prayer in it, and proclaims the end of its function."[355]

5.6. Summary

We should take special note of Scott's point that the breaking act of resistance must be public in order to have any impact. We have seen the passage under consideration as turning to the most visible forms of dissent in the Gospel of Mark. Resistance to oppressive rulers and conditions of endemic sociopolitical conflict exacerbated by Graeco-Roman rule have suggested that the people whom Jesus addressed would have expected and welcomed a condemnation of the high priests and perhaps the temple itself, as well as of Roman rule. Was Jesus totally different from other popular leaders and movements and dissent scribal circles? Or was Jesus distinctive mainly in the particular mode of his pronouncement of God's judgment against the Roman colonial rule? The Roman colonial rule that was presented in Jesus' time was that of its client rulers, the Herodian "tetrarch" Antipas in Galilee and in Judaea the high priests based in the temple in Jerusalem. A prophetic programme of God's reign against the imperial rule in order to bring justice for the agrarian communities would, in the first place, have to focus on the Roman client rulers of Israel and the high priesthood that were based in the temple.

---

353 Roskam, *The Purpose of* Mark, 165; Naickanparampil, *The Gospel of Mark*, 189; Hengel, *Studies in the Gospel of Mark*, 14-16; Myers sees Jesus declaring judgment upon the temple, *Binding the Strong Man*, 318.

354 J. S. Kloppenborg, "*Evocatio Deorum* and the Date of Mark," *JBL* 124/3 (2005): 427.

355 Incigneri, *The Gospel to the Romans*, 204.

6. Conclusion

In this chapter, we have attempted to explore the theme of domination and resistance in the Gospel of Mark. The study began with a rereading of certain issues that were pertinent to Markan studies, such as: orality, genre, source, apocalyptic idea, social context and the structure of Mark's Gospel in the context of agrarian politics. We are convinced that Mark's Gospel has been performed before a group; hence it is to a great extent a reliable historical source of how the agrarian subjugated people in Galilee resisted Roman imperialism. The study reveals that Mark's Gospel in its present form depicts three major scales of Jesus' campaign– Capernaum and its neighbourhoods (1: 14–3: 6), wider Galilee and the regions beyond (3: 7–8: 30), and on the road to and in Jerusalem (8: 31–16: 20). When we analyze these three basic scales by using Scott's theory of political discourses among the subjugated groups, we have unlocked three distinguish political discourses of the subalterns in Galilee. First of all, we read the first scale of Jesus' campaign as the hidden transcript of indignation and dignity that had been developed by the agrarian people in the sequestered villages off the public stage to counter the regular indignities of domination. It is evident that Jesus in the relative safely of his locality could speak words of anger and self-assertion. Jesus' campaign within this scale is certainly a form of hidden or undisclosed resistance. We have determined that the kingdom of God is a popular ideology that comprises an alternative to the values and views that have been articulated in the official public transcript that was controlled by the powerful elites of Jerusalem. Thus, healings and exorcism, for instance, are no doubt the expressions of anger and dignity while also being manifestations of God's kingdom. Besides, we also take note of Mark's presentation of Jesus' tour in Galilee (1: 38) and assume that Jesus was the carrier of the hidden transcript within a certain degree of limitation. After the first tour, his fame spread throughout Galilee, Jesus' campaign was under surveillance from the above (1: 39, 45; 2: 6, 16, 18-20, 24; 3: 2, 6) and Jesus had to defend the hidden transcript openly, yet within the sequestered sites.

Second, we marked out the second scale of Jesus' campaign as taking place in the wider regions of Galilee and beyond. As Jesus continued to struggle against the Roman domination beyond the confines of his localities, Jesus' campaign is expected to further develop into the next level of resistance. We have employed Scott's idea of political disguise and anonymity for the analysis of the words and deeds that were found in Mark 3: 6–8: 30. Three elementary forms of disguise, such as: rumour, euphemism, and grumbling are found to be instrumental in exploring the agrarian-resistance motifs that are embedded in this part of the Gospel. We have proposed that rumour played a significant role for the rapidly widening popular response to Jesus' proclamation of God's kingdom and its manifestations in healing and exorcism. We have also established that the spread of rumor of anticipated divine deliverance could be a strong form of a resistance to the domination of various forms while concealing the identity of the actors. Observation has been made regarding hidden forms of resistance in terms of euphemism. Taking the case of the healing of Legion (Mk 5: 1-20), we have suggested that the public or overt movement of political opposition was dangerous under the Roman rule. The man, seemingly evicted by the Roman pig farming policy, had been protesting under the disguise of spirit possession, later named as Legion. This man effectively resisted the appropriation of land while concealing his message. Jesus' mission instructions; "shake off the dust" (Mk 6: 11), eating without washing hands (Mk 7: 1-6), and Mark's description of Jesus' gesture at the time of responding the Pharisees, *i.e.*, sighed deeply (8: 11-13) are all illustrative of the infra-politics that are inherent of subalterns groups.

We have also analysed the third scale of Jesus' campaign in Jerusalem. After Peter's confession of Jesus' identity, Mark conveys Jesus-in-movement while focusing upon the struggle against the powers in Jerusalem. This study elucidates that there was a great political breakthrough as Jesus entered into Jerusalem (Mk 11:1-11). Jesus' foretelling of his sufferings in the hands of the Jewish leaders reveals that his direct confrontation with those leaders was purposeful. All his actions and especially his demonstration in the Temple (11: 15-19) along with confrontation regarding the question about paying tribute to Caesar (12: 13-17), pronouncement of the destruction of Jerusalem temple (13: 1-2) have been understood as Jesus' bold declaration of the hidden transcript in the face of powers.

Chapter 4

The Agrarian-Resistance Motifs in the Parables in the Gospel of Mark

In the previous chapter—based upon Scott's theory of resistance by subjugated people—we laid down two interrelated theses pertaining to the Gospel of Mark that (a) it is a story of resistance by the subalterns; and (b) it is composed of three varieties of political discourse—*viz*., the hidden transcript developed by the rural communities in Galilee (1: 14–3: 6), the politics of disguise and anonymity (3:7–8: 30), and the declaration of the hidden transcript in the face of power (8: 31 onwards). It has been argued that these political discourses assumed how Jesus-in-movement insinuated the agrarian-resistance to the powers. These theses have been established within the scale of Jesus' campaign in Galilee and beyond which moved back and forth between the public and the private, while moving out from Capernaum and the neighbourhoods towards Jerusalem. Up to this stage, our exploration of the resistance motifs in Mark's Gospel is vague in a sense that we have been working only theoretical at a level in order to gain an overview of the agrarian-resistance in Mark. It is assumed that the parables of Jesus are potential resources for our knowledge of the resistance to the Roman imperialism by the agrarian masses of the first-century C. E. Galilee. Hence, our study must evolve into a detailed exegetical analysis of the parables in Mark's Gospel. However, because of its intricate nature and other reasons, there have been a lot of discussions and debates concerning the meaning and purpose of the parables. First of all, we shall attempt to understand the meaning and purpose of the parables in the context of Jesus-in-movement and then bring out the study of texts that are identified as parables. Our purpose here is to explore and analyse the agrarian-resistance motifs that are embedded in the parables of Jesus in Mark's Gospel. This crucial task will be carried out mainly through an exegetical analysis of all texts in Mark's Gospel that have been identified as parables.

1. Understanding the Parables in the Context of Jesus-in-Movement

The context of the parables can be more decisive in the understanding of the meaning of Jesus' parables than what the Greek term παραβολή or what the Hebrew משל themselves regarded. For the term παραβολή as well as the parables themselves in Mark's Gospel are presumably context-dependent and reflective of, and embedded in Jesus' campaign that resisted various forms of domination. Assuming that the parables in Mark's Gospel are socio-political constructs as well as a reflection of the agrarian communities in Galilee of Jesus' time, we shall try to understand the parables in the context of Jesus-in-movement. Prior to the exegetical study, by way of introducing our view on parables, we shall consider some basic questions concerning the meaning of the parable, classification and distribution of the parables in Mark's Gospel.

1.1. Meaning of the Word "παραβολή"

When studying Jesus' parables, one should be mindful about how the Greek word πἀραβολή is defined. Witherington has pointed out the possibility that the Greek themselves treated parables as "comparisons or comparative illustrations that could be used for rhetorical purposes, that is, the purpose of persuading someone about something."[1] This raises crucial question as to whether Mark while—writing the political discourse of the subalterns—might have understood the term and applied it to Jesus' campaign. Our presumption is that the parables in Mark, be it proverbial sayings or similes or short stories, take public form in elements of folk or popular culture. We try to understand that the parables of Jesus in their oral rather than written form could also possibly be cultural expressions of the subaltern masses. Simply being originated in oral culture, they offer a kind of hiddenness and even anonymity that make them ideal vehicles for political resistance. In this sense, the parables of Jesus to a great extent resonate of what Scott calls "the elaborate forms of disguise."[2] Considering the political situations in Galilee under which the bearers of this folk culture (*i.e.* the rural agrarian communities) habitually operated, its public expression possibly wore a political mask. Therefore, this study partly denotes that the parables of Jesus are an ideal vehicle for political resistance, developed and cultivated among the subjugated Galilean villagers and used by Jesus as a

---

1 Witherington, *The Gospel of Mark*, 161.

2 Scott divides the arts of political disguise into "elementary forms of disguise" and "elaborate forms of disguise." See, *Domination and the Arts of Resistance*, 138-172. The former has been discussed in the previous chapter in relation to Jesus' campaign in Galilee and beyond. We propose the latter to have many things in common with the parables of Jesus.

response to the rapidly widening reaction to his preaching of the kingdom of God and as manifestation of God's enabling power in exorcism and healings. Scholarly definitions of the word "parable" in the past rarely addressed this concern.

Attempts to define the word in any standard dictionary or encyclopaedia can be traced back to spring from the literary connotation of the Greek word παραβολή. For instance, M. Mowry has defined the term parable as "an extended metaphor, or simile, frequently becoming a brief narrative, generally used by men [sic.] of Biblical times for didactic purpose."[3] In the same vein C. L. Blomberg also defined parable as "a metaphor extended to a short narrative; in biblical contexts almost always formulated to reveal and illustrate the kingdom of God."[4] These definitions always confine the parable within a literary and didactic sphere and hardly bring out the parables as collective representation of agrarian masses. Thus, we must be very careful not to misuse the literary meaning of the Greek παραβολή. This compound word (lit. "setting beside")[5] may rhetorically carry an aspect of comparison in its Greek classical sense, but in the agrarian context of Galilee, it may not quite reflect what it would convey to Jesus or Mark.

However, scholars who rhetorically understand the word as comparison or even symbol tend to take parables as concrete tools which are drawn from daily life to explain the abstract reality of something. For instance, Stein argues that the Greek word παραβολή is "an illustration, a comparison, or analogy, usually in story form, using common events of everyday life to reveal a moral or spiritual truth."[6] Even though some parables in Mark are indeed stories that are drawn from daily life of Galilee, yet many of them share the nature of the proverb, riddle, and even word of derision. Dodd's frequently quoted definition is also not free from this, thus: "…parable is a metaphor or simile drawn from nature or common life, arresting the hearer by its vividness or strangeness, and leaving the mind in sufficient doubt about its precise application to tease it onto active thought."[7] In a similar thought, T. W. Manson argues, "A parable is literary creation in narrative form designed either to portray a type of character for warning or example or to embody a principle of God's governance of the world and men [sic.]."[8] When we look into the parables, we hardly find any

3 L. Mowry, "Parable" in *IBD* Vol. 3, ed. G. A. Buttrick, *et at.* (New York and Nashville: Abingdon Press, 1962), 649.

4 C. L. Blomberg, "Parables" in *ISBE*, Vol. 3 K-P, ed. G. W. Broimley, *et. al.* (Grand Rapids, Michigan: Eerdmans, 1986), 655-659.

5 F. Hauck, "παραβολή" in *TDNT* 5 (1967), 744; Scott, *Hear Then the Parable*, 19.

6 Stein, *An Introduction to the Parables of Jesus*, 16.

7 Dodd, *Parables of Kingdom*, 16.

8 T. W. Manson, *The Teaching of Jesus* (Cambridge: Cambridge University Press, 1939), 65.

strong evidences to revere them as earthly stories with a heavenly meaning. This study will also look into the Greek preposition παρα (lit. behind, beside, by) to take in its meaning in terms of political disguise and anonymity so that we may be able to read those images that are drawn from nature or daily life, more meaningfully in the context of the agrarian protest and resistance. It is M. I. Boucher who draws our attention to note carefully if the English term "parable" and the Greek term "παραβολή" fully define what the term "parable" signifies for Jesus.[9] This Greco-English parabolic thought obviously determines Jesus only as a moral teacher who drew illustrations from the daily life of the Galileans in order to illustrate the moral or spiritual truths that were entailed his preaching. It is true that Jesus' parables denote the real life situation of Judea and Galilee of the first-century. We assume that Jesus delivered his parables in the age of opposition and resistance.

As scholarly debate continues, attempts to define the parable in terms of its Hebraic rendering emerged. In his famous book, *The Parables of Jesus*, Jeremias insists that the parable should be understood in the light of the Hebrew משל. For Jeremias the Hebrew משל, along with the Aramaic *mathla*, encompasses all types of forms: "parable, similitude, allegory, fable, proverb, apocalyptic visions, riddles, symbol, pseudonym, fictitious person, example, theme, argument, apology, refutation, jest."[10] In order to drive home the parable, Jeremias devotes a large section of his book to the issue of returning to "Jesus from the primitive church."[11] In doing so, Jeremias drives home Jesus' parables from the Greco-English to their Semitic origins. In the years subsequent to Jeremias, in one way or another, the Hebrew משל persistently continues to play a leading role in the scholarly quest for the appropriate definition of the parables of Jesus. The reason of its persistence is not in line with our understanding of the meaning of parable.[12] These scholars are still far from revealing the politics of those subalterns who lie beneath the parables of Jesus. Yet, they are inclined more to accept the nature of disguise and anonymity of the parables of Jesus. Stein, in his survey of the Old Testament usage of the term, conveys that the Hebrew משל was used diversely to convey; simple proverb, by word, satire, taunt or word of derision, riddle and short story or allegory.[13] In spite of its varied possible meanings, the Hebraic rendering points to the intrinsic idea of concealment. In contemporary Jewish and early Christian writings,

9 Boucher, *The Parables,* 15-19.

10 Jeremias, *The Parables of Jesus*, 20.

11 Jeremias, *The Parables of Jesus*, 23-103.

12 We are not negating the value this contribution. We acknowledge that once the intrinsic meaning of parable has been discovered through the Semitic framework, the interpreters of the parables of Jesus could situate them in the life of historical Jesus which the Greek rhetorical meaning of illustration could never permit.

13 Stein, *An Introduction to the Parables of Jesus*, 16-18.

as G. H. Boobyer argues, the term parables could also extend to include "any utterance which was something of a riddle, in the sense that it contained a hidden meaning clear only to specially privileged eyes."[14] Boobyer finds that in Mark "any cryptic form of speech, intentionally enigmatic, could be named a 'parable.'"[15] He then analyses Mark 4: 11-12 and 8: 17-21 (cf. 6: 52) and arrives at the conclusion that in this context the word "parable" has a broader significance.[16]

While many historical critics in Europe were busy with the terminological usage in order to arrive at what the word "parable" could possibly mean to the historical Jesus, scholars in North America—largely influenced by the work of M. Heidegger—began to ask as to what kind of a world has been established by the parables.[17] A. N. Wilder's *Early Christian Rhetoric: The Language of the Gospel* (1971) has made a significant influence upon the American school of parable interpretation. For Wilder, the parables reflect certain basic assumptions about existence and a worldview which regard the historical process as moving toward the completion. There is a revelatory quality in the parables which deem it to be both prophetic as well as apocalyptic in teaching.[18] He seems to admit the reality and humanity while accepting the moral and religious perspective as the application of the parables. The parables thus unveil mysteries in a prophetic way. In the 1970s, as Perkins observes, more and more scholars begin to emphasize upon the "poetic and aesthetic qualities of the parables a means of presenting the hearer with Jesus' experience of faith in God."[19] For them Jesus' parables disclose a religious dimension to common, human experience. Perkins further comments, "They might be described as a poetry that seeks to establish God's rule in our lives."[20] The immediate aim of a parable is to be compellingly interesting, and in being interesting it diverts attention and gradually disarms. For N. Perrin the parables of Jesus are "artistic creations of a very high order, and they embody a distinctive vision of reality."[21] At any rate, the ultimate aim of the parables is to awaken insight, stimulate the conscience and move to action. We shall take the primary reason

---

14 G. H. Boobyer, "The Redaction of Mark IV. 1-34," *NTS* 8 (1961-62): 62.

15 Boobyer, "The Redaction of Mark IV. 1-34," 63.

16 Boobyer, "The Redaction of Mark IV. 1-34," 63.

17 R. H. Stein, "The Genre of the Parables," in *The Challenges of Jesus' Parables*, ed. R. N. Longenecker (Grand Rapids, Michigan: Eerdmans, 2000), 34.

18 A. N. Wilder, *Early Christian Rhetoric: The Language of the Gospel* (London: SCM Press,), 87-88.

19 P. Perkins, *Hearing the Parables of Jesus* (New York: Paulist Press, 1981), 2.

20 Perkins, *Hearing the Parables of Jesus*, 2.

21 N. Perrin, "Historical Criticism, Literary Criticism, and Hermeneutics: The Interpretation of the Parables of Jesus and the Gospel of Mark Today," *The Journal of Religion* 52/4 (October 1972): 362.

which is Jesus' parables as stories with intent and are prophetic in nature and are regarded to be a vehicle for speaking truth to the powers.

1.2. The Genre of the Parables

The genre of the parables has been interpreted by scholars in various ways. Jülicher's introduction of a new genre in the interpretation of the parables has ushered in the modern interpretation of parables. When Jülicher rescued the parable from the methodological abuse of allegory, he appears to resort to Aristotle's *Rhetoric* in dividing literary form of the parable into "similitude," "parables" and "exemplary story." The reason of Jülicher's dependence on the Greek usage is obvious. In its classical usage, the παραβολή is understood basically as "comparison" with a single point of comparison in each parable while the plurality of forms of comparison is also well taken care of. His acknowledgment of the various forms of comparison led Jülicher to a new classification of παραβολή into similitude and parable. This categorization is inevitable for Greek rhetoric, as F. Hauck observes, the word is used technically for "similitude" and "parable."[22] Apart from his famous differentiation of the term "parable" and "allegory," Jülicher offers a new way of rendering the literary form of parables into three: similitude, parable, exemplary story.[23]

Jülicher's threefold divisions of the genre of parables have further attained a new phase when the form critics—*viz*. Dibelius and Bultmann—have defined types of parables with careful, detailed analyses of their form. While retaining Jülicher's threefold division of parables, Bultmann subdivided the similitude into three parts: figurative sayings, metaphors, and similitude proper.[24] Dodd also follows Jülicher and groups the parables into three main categories.[25] Dodd refers to the threefold division of the parables in the same manner as Jülicher and Bultmann, and he defines parables differently by importing the English meaning of the parables. C. A. Bugge is known to be the first to criticize Jülicher's use of the Aristotelian and Greek view of parables.[26] Bugge opted for Jewish rhetoric and the Hebrew משל rather than the Aristotelian and dogmatic understanding of parable as proposed by Jülicher which obscured the historical situation of the parables.[27] The modern approach

22 Hauck, "παραβολή," 745. He cites Aristotle, such as: Rhet. II. 20, 1393a, 22.1394a, 18.

23 Cited by Stein, "The Genre of the Parables," 30.

24 Bultmann, *History of the Synoptic Tradition*, 166-179.

25 Dodd, *Parables of the Kingdom*, 5-7.

26 C. A. Bugge's book entitled *Die Haupt-Parabeln Jesu* (Giessen: J. Richer'sch Verlagsbuchhandlung, 1903) was published four years after Julicher's book. Since Bugge's work has never been translated into English, I am indebted to the review made by W. Kissinger, *The Parables of Jesus: A History of Interpretation and Bibliography.* ATLA Bibliography Series No. 4 (Lanham, Maryland: *ATLA*, 1979): 77-80.

27 Kissinger, *The Parables of Jesus*, 79.

to the parables in the Gospels at the earliest phase—*i.e.,* grouping them into various forms—tends not to ask questions of the historical significance.

Even though Jülicher, Bultmann, and Dodd have analysed much about the significance of the historical context in which the parables were delivered, yet they speak of the parables in terms of the normal culture of the agrarian Jews of Jesus' time; and thus, failed to bring out the agrarian-resistance motifs embedded within. There are two fundamental problems that are interrelated to each other. First, a classification of the parables according to their literary genre simply isolates the parables from its context. Jesus does not communicate in the parables in isolation. Also the focus upon the artificial fragments could not constitute the parables as means of communicating the truth to others. Second, since the meaning of a saying or story always depends on the meaning in context, the modern practice of taking the parables of Jesus out of their literary context leaves the scholars with no indication that the original historical context, were their original meaning.

In order to appreciate the political significance of the genre of the parables, this research tries to relate the various genres of parables as the hidden transcript of dignity and indignation. Insofar as Mark indicates that all these genres were rendered by Jesus, who himself belonged to the social class, we should consider them as the collective representations of a culture of subordinate groups that contradict the official views and values. Scott mentions three reasons as to why the culture of the subalterns should reflect the smuggling of the portions of the hidden transcript onto the public stage. First of all, Scott argues that "folk or popular culture is the property of a social class or strata whose social location generates distinctive experiences and values."[28] Jesus' parables—be it parabolic or proverbial sayings or similitude or story—must have been the property of the Galilean villages.[29] What survives and flourishes with Jesus' campaign is largely dependent on the dominant values that are imposed upon the rural masses. Second, Scott discerns agrarian-resistance as taking its expression in cultural life as "a riposte to an official culture."[30] Mark seems to portray all genres of parable as a quick and clever response to criticism. In his 1975's published article, G. Theissen has already argued that some sayings in Mark represent folklore from certain groups of early Christianity.[31] We must examine these aspects to ascertain if Mark's representation of the culture of the priestly aristocrats distinguishes

28 Scott, *Domination and the Arts of Resistance*, 157.

29 Scott, a profound parable commentator, discerns that "Jesus' parables draw on the conventions of village life for their repertoire." See, Scott, *Hear Then the Parable*, 85.

30 Scott, *Domination and the Arts of Resistance*, 157.

31 G. Theissen, "Itinerant Radicalism: The Tradition of Jesus Sayings from the Perspective of the Sociology of Literature," *Radical Religion* 2 (1975): 84-93.

these ruling groups from the subaltern masses. In this respect, Robbins' thesis that the folk-sayings in Mark perpetuated the identity of socio-religious group over against the powerful elites within Jewish society could be used as one of the various concepts among other useful principles in our study of the parables in Mark.[32] Thus, we can note that the parables of Jesus have placed the critics of Jesus in a position that denies their respect. Finally, Scott proposes cultural expression (*e.g.* symbolism and metaphor) as an effective weapon for the subalterns to undermine powers. He states,

> Finally, what permits subordinate groups to undercut the authorized cultural norms is the fact that cultural expression by virtue of its polyvalent symbolism and metaphor lends itself to disguise. By the subtle use of codes one can insinuate into a ritual, a pattern of dress, a song, a story, meanings that are accessible to one intended audience and opaque to another audience the actors wish to exclude.[33]

In this way, Scott emboldens us to read various genres of the parables as effective weapons for Jesus and the community around him.

1.3. The Distribution of the Parables in Mark

Insofar as parable is an ideal vehicle of speaking truth to powers, we can expect parables wherever Jesus-in-movement was in his encounter with the powers. Three political discourses in Mark's Gospel that have been identified and discussed in the previous chapter can be decisive in sorting out the distribution of the parables in this Gospel. First of all, during his campaign in Capernaum and the nearby villages (Mk 1: 14–3: 6), Mark has a lesser number of parables from Jesus. As Jesus was under surveillance from above and he was probably in need of defending the hidden transcript, he began to use some proverbial sayings as ready answers to his critics. The saying, "Those who are well have no need of a physician, but those who are sick" (2: 17) is the first parable in the Gospel of Mark. This is followed by a series of parabolic sayings which is given in response to question about fasting (2: 18-22). We shall analyze these parabolic sayings to see if they are given in defence of the hidden transcript. Significantly, in the second political discourse in Mark (*i.e.* 3: 6–8: 30), many of Jesus' parables are found in this part of the Gospel. Mark begins to use the word "parables" (3: 23) along with a series of riddles (3: 22-27). He includes the Parable Discourse (4: 1-34), the Parables of Defilement (7: 15), and the Parable of Yeast (8: 15). In all these, Mark portrays Jesus-in-movement as ways of expressing dissonant views through the parables. Finally, in the third political discourse (*i.e.* Mk 8: 31 onwards), Mark cites only a few parables. Some of the parables found in this section are: the Parables of the Camel and

32 Robbins, *Jesus the Teacher*, 8.

33 Scott, *Domination and the Arts of Resistance*, 158.

The Eye of the Needle (10: 25), The Parables of Tenants in Vineyard (12: 1-12), and the Parables of The Fig Tree and the Door Keeper (13: 28, 34).

2. The Parables in the First Political Discourse (Mk 1: 14 – 3: 6)

We shall analyse the parables as the means of defending, disguising and declaring the hidden transcript of the popular indignation and dignity. There are four parables found within the first political discourse such as: Physician (v. 17) Wedding Guests (v. 19), Unshrunk Cloth (v. 20) and New Wine (v. 21). Since Mark places them as explanations of "non-conforming actions,"[34] we shall treat them as an instrument of defending the hidden transcript.

2.1. The Parable of the Physician (2:17)

> When Jesus heard this, he said to them, 'Those who are well have no need of a physician, but those who are sick; I have come to call not the righteous but sinners' (v. 17).

2.1.1. The Context, Setting and Genre of the Parables

This is the first parabolic saying in Mark's Gospel. Mark fits this saying in the context of Jesus' calling of Levi (vv. 13-14) and eating with the sinner and tax-collectors (vv. 15-17).[35] The place is "Levi's house."[36] Apart from many tax-collectors and sinners, Mark includes "many who followed him" to be those sitting with Jesus for the dinner (v. 15). The phrase "sitting ...for the dinner" is literally reclining at the table. Jews, Greeks, and Romans, especially at festive gatherings, ate "at couches, lying on their left elbow."[37] Jesus' action would have been noticed by "the scribes of the Pharisees" who separated themselves from anything assumed ritually unclean.[38] The scribes asked Jesus' disciples as to why Jesus ate with tax-collectors and sinners and this indicated the emerging hostility towards Jesus. Thus, Mark situates this saying in the context of a hostile situation. Recent scholars have accepted this saying as a proverb that has numerous parallels in Greek and Jewish literature.[39] Iersel observes that this proverb is "built up round a metaphor in keeping with the preceding cures

34 Liew, "The Gospel of Mark," 111.

35 Dodd, *The Parables of the Kingdom*, 90.

36 Mann opines that this can be read as meaning the Levite's house, or a house Jesus was using in Galilee. See Mann, *Mark*, 229. J. R. Donahue and D. J. Harrington argue this house is Jesus' own house. See, *The Gospel of Mark*, Sacra Pagina Series 2 (Collegeville, MN: Liturgical Press, 2002), 101.

37 Donahue and Harrington, *The Gospel of Mark*, 101.

38 Stein, *Mark*, 130. Borg, *Conflict, Holiness & Politics*, 82.

39 Geulich, Mark 1-8: 26, 104; Donahue and Harrington, *The Gospel of Mark*, 102-103.

than the meal."[40] Acknowledgement of the popular element in this proverb could perhaps enable us to decode the subaltern politics beneath the saying.

2.1.2. Explanation of the Parable

Mark shows this proverb was uttered in response to the scribal indignation. The word κακῶς is commonly translated as "physician" or "doctor." Greek literature often portrays the philosopher as κακῶς (or physician).[41] The oἱ ἰσχύοντες ("Those who are well") should not be taken narrowly as medically well, rather it could refer to those who were socially and politically strong or mighty. The mighty and the powerful ones have no need of Jesus. The corresponding word "the sick" might have symbolized the powerless. This proverb functions as a defence of Jesus' action.[42] Its corresponding statement, "I have come to call not the righteous but sinners" (v. 17b), is another mission statement (cf. Mk 1: 38b). Witherington believes that the term "righteous" meant "the so-called righteous."[43] The term "sinners" may not be taken as "Christian sense of all fallen human being."[44] They were not primarily people who committed crimes, but those who lived outside the great tradition in a constant and fundamental way.[45] In this manner, the term would have included the subaltern masses in Galilee who were at the margins.[46]

2.1.3. A Series of Parabolic Sayings (2:18-22)

2.1.3.1. The Context, Setting and Genre of the Parables

The context is situated in terms of people who questioned the status of a newly founded Jesus movement. Some unidentified people (Gr. ἔρχονται) came and posed a question to Jesus: "Why do John's disciples and the disciples of Pharisees fast, but your disciples do not fast?" (2: 18b). This question sounds simple and casual. However, we see some suggestive elements that are capable of producing the plausible meaning of the parables when read in the spatial setting of Jesus-in-movement. This episode belongs to what is termed as the "first political discourse" of Jesus. At this stage, as argued before, Jesus and the movement around him had begun to struggle against domination within the confines of its sequestered sites. Myers' analysis of events found in 1: 21-3: 35 as "the first direct action campaign"[47] is applicable as the events assume acts

40 Iersel, *Mark: A Reader-Response Commentary*, 154.

41 See, Dio Chrysostom, *Orations* 32.14-30; Epictetus, *Discourses* 3.23, 30.

42 Donahue and Harrington, *The Gospel of Mark*, 103.

43 Witherington, *The Gospel of Mark*, 123.

44 Witherington, *The Gospel of Mark*, 123; Waetjen, *A Reordering of Power*, 89-90.

45 Donahue and Harrington, *The Gospel of Mark*, 103.

46 Waetjen, *A Reordering of Power*, 90.

47 Myers, *Binding the Strong Man*, 137-167.

of defending. However, Jesus' campaign is now in transition. Mark, thus, begins to keep the identity of the inquiring party obscure to his readers.[48] Mark plainly states ἔρχονται και λέγουσιν (v. 18; lit. "they come and said").[49] Before and after this incident, Jesus is confronted by a group who were identified as "the scribes of Pharisees" (v.16) and "Pharisees" (v. 24) respectively. While the earlier exegetes of Mark are skeptical enough to identify the subject ἔρχονται (third person, plural) as referring to certain persons,[50] there is a strong tendency that identifies the enquiring group as the Scribes or the Pharisees.[51] If this opposing party belonged to the Pharisaic party, they could have asked Jesus, "Why do John's disciples and 'our' disciples fast, but 'your' disciples do not fast?" Besides, the Pharisees have never been depicted to have disciples at the time of Jesus. However, those inquirers are quoted as uttering "disciples of Pharisees." Since there is a significant lack of knowledge about the Pharisees and their movement, they are incompatible to consider them as scribes or Pharisees. It is more unlikely that Mark represents the inquirers as the Pharisees, but referred to the practice of fasting by the Pharisees as a point of comparison. The identity of the opposing group remains anonymous. These anonymous people compared the newly founded Jesus' movement with the Pharisaic sect and also the followers of John with the intention to put them down.[52]

What the inquiring party could perhaps have in mind is with regard to the new movement led by Jesus of Nazareth all about? Was it going to be the re-enactment of the traditions of liberation that fired the hopes of the oppressed Jewish classes, or a kind of ascetic life practiced by the Pharisees and the Baptist group? Previously, Mark conveys that the people were pre-occupied with the question regarding the status of the Jesus-in-movement (Mk 1: 27). The same question was repeated here, but in a new situation perhaps led by a different group, possibly with a different interest of their own. Given that the reference point of comparison is the non-practice of fasting by the disciples of Jesus and the practice of fasting by the disciples of John and the Pharisees, we must know what fasting meant for the Jews. Here, Mark uses imperfect

48 Luke has οἱ δὲ εἶπαν, *i.e.*, the scribes and Pharisees (5: 33); and Matthew οἱ μαθηταὶ Ἰωάνου, with the question in the first person, "Why do we …?" (9: 14).

49 For some scholars ἔρχονται και λέγουσιν are "impersonal verbs." The indefinite subject assumes "people" as English versions like NRSV have translated it. Guelich, *Mark: 1-8: 26*, 109.

50 Taylor indicates that scholars like– E. Klostermann (1926), C. H. Tuner (1928), and M. J. Lagrange (1937) take the subject as referring probably to "impersonal." See Taylor, *The Gospel According to St. Mark*, 209.

51 Guelich, *Mark: 1-8: 26*, 109-110.

52 Myers, *Binding the Strong Man*, 159.

(lit. "...were fasting") to express habitual action.[53] According to the Biblical tradition, the Law requires the Jews to fast on the Day of Atonement (Lev 16: 29; cf. Acts 27: 9). Taylor (1963) suggests that extra traditions of fasting: "additional fasts" observed by the Pharisees twice in the week on Mondays and Thursdays, and "traditional fasts" were observed in commemoration of historical events (Lk 18: 12).[54] It is possible that the disciples of John observed fasting in commemoration of the martyrdom of their master.[55] In spite of the absence of explicit references, we can assume that this group wanted to play down the status of Jesus' disciples on the ground of their non-practice of fasting. It was as though they had attempted to scale down the religiosity of Jesus' disciples below the line of John's disciples and the Pharisees. In response to the challenge, Jesus uttered his longest discourse so far in Mark's Gospel, but it was of a different genre. While the first parable takes the form of a simile, the latter two are proverbial sayings. Given that Jesus' response to the challenge takes the form of the public assertion of worth, there was a certain element of status domination in the process. This insight would clash with what form-critics have previously read; regarding the parabolic sayings and not as form-critics who took them simply as "pronouncement-stories" connected with those which precede and follow.[56]

2.1.3.2. The Bridegroom's Guest (2: 19-20)

> Jesus said to them, "The wedding-guests cannot fast while the bridegroom is with them, can they? As long as bridegroom is with them, they cannot fast. The days will come when the bridegroom is taken away from them, and then they will fast on that day (vv. 19-20).

Jesus wasted no time in defending his disciples against the charge that they were not observing a recognized fast day (vv. 18-22). This Parable of the Wedding-Guests comes as the immediate Jesus' response to the question regarding as to why Jesus used this wedding imagery to respond to the challenge. For sure, fasting as it appears in Jesus' parable is not the primary issue. Because Jesus assures that there will be a time to fast for his disciples when the bridegroom departs "on that day" (v. 20b). What concerns us most in this parable perhaps is Jesus' display of the status of his disciples. This parable compares the disciples to οἱ υἱοὶ τοῦ μυνφωνος (lit. "Sons of the bride-

53 Donahue and Harrington, *The Gospel of Mark*, 106.

54 Taylor, *The Gospel According to St. Mark*, 209.

55 Other options like that of Guelich (1989) who argues that fasting of John's disciple could be that of an act of ascetic lifestyle (See "Mark 1-8: 26," 109) is acknowledged here.

56 Dibelius, *From Tradition to Gospel*, 43; Bultmann, *Jesus and the Word*, 17.

chamber").[57] For some scholars, the phrase is a Semitic form of expression which signifies a deeper meaning than its Greek rendering. E. P. Gould bases it upon its Hebraic form and tries to establish the expression as the "friends of the bridegroom" and their duty as "to provide for the nuptials whatever was necessary."[58] Jesus' public assertion of his disciples as the invited closest-friends of the bridegroom is really of worthy status. At that moment they were those who witnessed the joyous moment with feasting and not fasting. Mark uses the strong words "οὐ δύνανται νηστεύειν" (lit. "cannot fast") to shield their failure to fast. Cranfield observes that "to expect the disciples to fast now that the new age has come is as unreasonable as to expect wedding-guests to fast during a wedding."[59]

There is a tendency to explain this parable within the framework of eschatology. For instance, Heil suggests that the wedding imagery of the parable symbolizes "the joyous festivity of the eschatological age of God's salvation."[60] Heil even portrays Jesus as characterizing the "bridegroom" of the eschatological marriage feast and his disciples as the "wedding quests."[61] It is hard to believe that Jesus the Bridegroom is being taken away from the Church, (as Bride in the eschatological wedding). Myers opines that the images of "bridegroom" and "on that day" both are drawn from the apocalyptic category that points to the death of Jesus.[62] It is no doubt that Jesus refers to his fate in future when he says, "the bridegroom is taken away from them." However, we must consciously read the text in the context of Jesus-in-movement while bearing the indignation and dignity of the subjugated agrarian communities in the villages of Galilee. Jesus envisages the date as to when his disciples are to fast in terms of when he is taken away. This foresees Jesus' bold declaration of the hidden transcript in the face of the power and the severe reaction thereupon. By using this wedding imagery, Jesus-in-movement depicted the third party who challenged the status of his closest friends. He indicated that a new family was in the process of creation through his mission. His disciples have the vital role as the closest friends in this process. Thus, Jesus' pedagogy in this parable depicts respect towards their integrity and freedom.

---

57 C.E.B. Cranfield suggests that this word takes a Semitic form of expression. See his commentary, "The Gospel According to Mark" in *Cambridge Greek Testament Commentary*, edited by C.F.D. Moule (Cambridge: Cambridge University, 1959), 109. Literally, it means "sons of the wedding hall and can mean the wedding guests or the groom's attendants."

58 E. P. Gould. *A Critical and Exegetical Commentary on the Gospel According to St. Mark*. ICC Series (Edinburgh: T&T Clark, 1901).

59 Cranfield, *The Gospel According to Saint Mark*, 109.

60 Heil, *Mark as a Model for Action*, 67-68.

61 Heil, *Mark as a Model for Action*, 67-68.

62 Myers, *Binding the Strong Man*, 159. Cf. Waetjen, *A Reordering of Power*, 91.

2.1.3.3. Unshrunk Cloth (2: 21)

> No one sews a piece of unshrunk cloth on an old cloak; otherwise, the patch pulls away from it, the new from the old, and a worse tear is made.

Here, we have double parabolic sayings that are added to the discussion, and this thus denotes a broader response to the question about fasting.[63] There are various opinions as to the origin of sayings of patches and wineskins. Taylor suggests that these sayings have an "independent existence" before Mark incorporated into this.[64] Heil even denotes that these two proverbial sayings apply to the new circumstance of the breaking of God's kingdom in and through Jesus, as illustrated not only by his disciples who do not fast, but also by his authoritative declaration of God's healing forgiveness (2:1-12), and his table-fellowship with public sinners (2:13-17).[65] The central idea in both these parabolic sayings is of the incompatibility of the new and the old.[66] ἐπιβλημα is used with the meaning "patch." But in classical Greek, in accordance with its derivation, it can mean a "coverlet" a "bedspread" "tapestry" or a "bandage" and in the LXX a "mantle" or "covering."[67] On an old garment one does not sew a patch of new unshrunken cloth, which will tear or pull the old cloth as soon as it gets wet. For Donahue and Harrington, this saying reflects "a social location of ordinary people who must mend their clothes rather than the rich who dress in fine robes."[68] Way back in 1928, Buttrik had a question which every interpreter must deal with: "Is this a hint of the poverty of his [Jesus] boyhood home?"[69]

2.1.3.4. New Wine (2: 22)

> And no one puts new wine into old wineskins; otherwise, the wine will burst the skins, and the wine is lost, and so are the skins; but one puts new wine into fresh wineskins.

This second parable appears several times in ancient literatures and evidently is proverbial. One does not put new wine into old and brittle wineskin, for when it ferments, it will burst the skins. The central point of these sayings

63 Donahue and Harrington that that these two parabolic sayings were independently joined here by the theme of new versus old. See, *The Gospel of Mark*, 107; Dodd thinks Mark appended these parables to the controversy about fasting, *The Parables of the Kingdom*, 90.

64 Taylor, *The Gospel According to Mark*, 212.

65 Heil, *Mark as a Model for Action*, 68.

66 Waetjen, *A Reordering of Power*, 92; Liew, "The Gospel of Mark," 111.

67 Taylor, *The Gospel According to St. Mark*, 212.

68 Donahue and Harrington, *The Gospel of Mark*, 107.

69 Buttrik, *The Parables of Jesus,* 6.

seems rather damaging with regard to what the new does to the old. As Taylor rightly comments, the general sense of this saying is "the incompatibility of combining the new and old."[70] The patch of undressed cloth shrinks, and so the old garment is torn further. Many commentators comprehend the saying as referring to the Pharisees or to the disciples of John. Rawlinson denotes that it was as if "it had proved impossible for the Christian Church–or, at least, for the Gentile-Christian Church–to express its religious life though the ancient forms of Judaism, without being cramped thereby."[71] But it seems more probable that the two sayings in vv. 21-22 were appended by the Evangelist to vv. 18-20. As Rawlinson asserts, "we do not know – and it is idle to guess – in what context they were spoken. They are characteristic sayings of Jesus, unforgettable in their homely vividness and power."[72] Heil considers the two proverbial statements as "metaphorically express the incompatibility of the new radically new situation of God's salvific intervention."[73] But for Taylor the sentiments expressed are "revolutionary" since they affirmed that "a new message must find a fresh vehicle, if it is not to perish and to destroy existing institutions."[74]

2.1.3.5. Summary

Mark situates this series of parables in the context of the surveillance of Jesus' campaign in and around Capernaum. The first four parables, all taking the genre of proverb, served as Jesus' quick response to the conduct of Jesus and his disciples. The first proverb is given in response to the question about Jesus' eating with people who were despised by the society. The remaining three sayings responded to the question about fasting. Insofar as the first political discourse in Mark (1: 14–3: 6) is considered as Jesus' campaign in the sequestered sites, the freedom that the dissident subculture developed in Capernaum and its neighbourhood can be seen as under pressure. The pressure comes from two sides, *i.e.*, from the top (Scribes and Pharisees) and from below (people), of two extreme and contrasting views, *i.e.*, eating and fasting. The opposition is both from the Jewish leaders and the people of undeclared identity. Mark places these four parabolic sayings in the context where people getting confused about the newly launched Jesus' movement that had taken the crowd by storm. Finally, Mark seems to preserve these parabolic sayings to illustrate that Jesus came out to declare the hidden transcript that was cultivated by the victims of the oppressive rituals and traditions of the established powers.

70 Taylor, *The Gospel According to St. Mark*, 213.

71 Rawlinson, *St. Mark with Introduction,* 32.

72 Rawlinson, *St. Mark with Introduction,* 32.

73 Heil, *Mark As a Model for Action*, 68.

74 Taylor, *The Gospel According to St. Mark*, 212.

3. The Parables in the Second Political Discourse (Mk 3: 7– 8: 30)

As already discussed in the previous chapter, Mark 3: 7–8: 30 mainly focuses upon Jesus' campaign in wider Galilee and beyond. The shift from Capernaum and its neighborhoods to the wider Galilee is considered as the Galilean subalterns' struggle while crossing the confines of the sequestered sites into a politics of disguise and anonymity that takes place in public view. Thus, we shall read the parables in this section of the Gospel as the politics of disguise and anonymity.

3.1. Question about Jesus' Authority and the Parables (Mk 3: 19b-22)

> [19b]Then he went home; [20]and the crowd came together again, so that they could not even eat. [21]When his family heard it, they went out to restrain him, for people were saying, "He has gone out of his mind." [22]And the scribes who came down from Jerusalem said, "He has Beelzebul, and by the ruler of the demons he casts out demons." [23]And he called them to him, and spoke to them in parables, "How can Satan cast out Satan? [24] If a kingdom is divided against itself, that kingdom cannot stand. [25]And if a house is divided against itself, that house will not be able to stand. [26]And if Satan has risen up against himself and is divided, he cannot stand, but his end has come. [27]But no one can enter a strong man's house and plunder his property without first tying up the strong man; then indeed the house can be plundered.

3.1.1. Context, Setting and Genre of the Parables

The context in which Mark situates the second cluster of parables in Mark's Gospel resonates what Scott discusses as "politics of disguise and anonymity." Various elementary forms of disguise–gossip, rumor, spirit possession, euphemism, *etc.*–exhibited in this episode are at the same time the context of the parables.[75] The crowd here is qualified with πάλιν (v. 20) referring to the same "great multitude from Galilee" added by the "great numbers" from Judea, Jerusalem, Idumea to the south, beyond the Jordan to the east, and the region around Tyre and Sidon to the north (3: 7-8). Mark's portrayal of Jesus' mission in Galilee thus gathered more people of diverse backgrounds who possibly belonged to agrarian communities. Perhaps, these were the subjugated peoples who came out of their long-suppressed situations for liberation.[76] Their indignation overflowed the borders of their villages and regions and they gathered around Jesus-in-movement. The scale of Jesus' movement right here

---

75 Scott, *Domination and the Arts of Resistance*, 138-156.

76 Goretti, Daniel, and Raja depict the crowd as "faceless and voiceless unorganized people." See, *The Gospel According to Mark*, 176. Also Rhoads, *Israel in Revolution*, 47-60.

cannot be viewed simply as fixed and bounded–local, regional, national–but as a dimension concerning the socio-political process.

There is an exegetical problem concerning the spatial setting of the parables. Mark simply states ἔρχεται εἰς οἶκον (v. 19b) without identifying place of the house. Given that there has been no change of spatial setting hinted since the focus on Capernaum (Mk 1: 21; 2: 1), we can safely situate this within a house in the locality of Capernaum. However, there are two houses that were specifically identified so far–the house of Levi (2: 15) and the house of Simon and Andrew in Capernaum (1: 29). Besides, G. D. Kilpatrick has established the idea that Jesus had his own house in Capernaum, and was separated from his family back home in Nazareth.[77] Since, it was the house of Simon and Andrew where Jesus initially based his Capernaum campaign, it probably could have been this same house where Jesus returned after a cycle of campaigns. Jesus returns to the earlier sequestered site of "the house" only to find that it is no longer a safe place for him.[78] This very private house which provides a space for the hidden transcript of villages in no time became a public space. Mark portrays it as a meeting point of the big crowd while encompassing people of various regions, close-relatives of Jesus and the scribes from Jerusalem. Both function as the intersection of surveillance from below and above to Jesus-in-movement respectively. The large crowd gathered around Jesus could not be a new one, as πάλιν suggests (v. 20). The word πάλιν can refer to either a local crowd as in 2: 2 or a global crowd as in 3: 7-8. However, here the crowd not only blocked the access to Jesus, but was so persistently invasive to the privacy of Jesus (3: 20).[79] The swollen crowd is suggestive that Mark presents a story of how the spontaneous resistance movement was touched by Jesus' proclamation of "the good news of God." Thus they had tremendously increased in numbers to become a threat to the dominant rulers and their representatives. Recognizing this, the dominant groups—both from local and centre—had also developed a disguised form of counter-movement while facilitating open criticism and attacked Jesus in the form of gossip, spirit possession and euphemism.

Mark mentions two malevolent stories about Jesus—"He has gone out of his mind" (v. 21b) and "He has Beelzebul and by the ruler of demons he casts out demons" (v. 22)—were certainly in the air. Scott's *Hear Then the Parable* (1989) states that "gossip and criticism, rampant in the village, keep others from taking advantage of one's weaknesses."[80] The Greek ἐξέστη is used in

77 G. D. Kilpatrick, "Jesus, His Family and His Disciples," *JSNT* 15 (1982): 3-8.

78 Myers, *Binding the Strong Man*, 164.

79 France, *The Gospel of Mark*, 165.

80 Scott, *Hear Then the Parable*, 86.

classical Greek for being out of one's mind.[81] The people who said ἐξέστη were not specified. It is very unnatural to take "his family" as the subject of this malicious saying about Jesus. Mark simply puts it ἔλεγον; thus, he keeps the subject to remain anonymous. This malicious story (*i.e.* ἐξέστη) assaulting Jesus' dignity is, at the same time, popular aggression against Jesus-in-movement to ruin his reputation. Scott gives us the clue to render this nasty gossip as "a discourse about social rules [imposed by the Pharisees] that have been violated" by Jesus-in-movement.[82] Jesus' reputation would have been damaged—at least in the sight of those who opposed him—by the stories about his alleged case of blasphemy (2: 7), his view of the Sabbath (2: 27-28; 3: 2), his fellowship with sinners and tax collectors or his insulting words (2: 15-17). There is no reason why we should deny the reality of Mark's picture of people who spread the gossip: "He has gone out of his mind." (3: 21). In view of the stereotypical village tyranny of the majority in Galilee, it is undoubtedly justifiable that οἱ παρ' αὐτοῦ believed and acted upon this gossip (v. 21).[83] The prepositional phrase οἱ παρ' αὐτοῦ (lit. "those of him"[84]) is vaguer than the usual English rendering, for example: "his family" (NRSV), "his own people" (NIV), *etc*. Interpreters vary in the degree to which their translations are visible. Many of the earlier liberal interpreters of Mark suggested οἱ παρ' αὐτοῦ to mean "his friends" or "the disciples"– not necessarily Jesus' own family.[85] Taylor envisions "deep personal concern for Jesus" of his family at Nazareth when he takes it as "family."[86] France suggests "his envoys" or "his associates" as the normal meaning of this unusual phrase; however, he thinks the context is decisive of "who are comprised under this phrase."[87] Edwards opines the phrase to have mean "associates, kin, or followers as well as friends or family."[88] As Taylor suggests, the circumstances in which "envoys" or

---

81 E.g., In *Ant*. 10: 114, Josephus reports that the people ridicule Jeremiah as if he is out of his mid.

82 Scott, *Domination and the Arts of Resistance*, 142.

83 Wilson, "Mark," 803.

84 Edwards, *The Gospel According to Mark*, 118.

85 E. P. Gould, *The Gospel According to St. Mark*, ICC Series (Edinburgh, 1896), 61; H. B. Sweete, *The Gospel According to St. Mark*, 3rd edition (London, 1928); 63; A. E. J. Rawlinson, *The Gospel According to St. Mark*, Westminster Commentaries, 7th edition (London, 1949), 41; J. V. Barlet, *St. Mark*, Century Bible (Oxford: The Clarendon Bible, 1926), 152; A. Plummer, *The Gospel According to St. Mark* (Cambridge: Cambridge University Press, 1914), 110; B. H. Branscomb, *The Gospel of Mark*, The Moffat New Testament Commentary (London: 1937), 68; Wilson, "Mark," 803.

86 Taylor, *The Gospel According to St. Mark*, 236; see also Waetjen, *A Reordering of Power*, 99.

87 France, *The Gospel of Mark*, 166.

88 Edwards, *The Gospel According to Mark*, 118.

"associates" of Jesus ἐξλῆθον (lit. "came out of") are indicated by ἀκούσαντες and their purpose by κρατῆσαι αὐτόν.[89] What Mark seems to say is the family of Jesus, on hearing the gossip–"people were saying" (v. 21a)–about Jesus "He has gone out of his mind" (v. 21b)[90] came out of Nazareth to Capernaum in order to "restrain him." It would be hard for the closest ones back home in Nazareth to ignore the popular aggression against Jesus that was in the air. This situation suggests that the Greek word κρατῆσαι used not "in the sense of attempting to bind Jesus and deprive him of freedom,"[91] but "to take in hand for his own sake and for the family's reputation."[92] Before they could arrive to take action, as Mark assumes, a more damaging accusation came from the Scribes from Jerusalem.[93] Myers comments, "Jesus' family believes that he has gone too far and demands that he gives up his mission … their caution is too late, already government investigators from the capital come already to press charges (3: 22)."[94]

Mark indicates this second parallel accusation—"He has Beelzebul and by the ruler of demons he casts out demons" (v. 22)—to be more potentially and extremely oppressive to Jesus' status.[95] Mark obviously reveals two important things. First, these scribes neither simply posed insinuating questions (2: 7) nor repeated what others said. They boldly confronted Jesus with a "virulent judgment"– "He has Beelzebul" and "by the ruler of demons he casts out demons" (v. 22).[96] It is a case of what Gould once calls "charge of diabolism."[97] Spirit possession was not uncommon in the world of Jesus. Branscomb finds references to "Jesus as a sorcerer" in the rabbinic writings.[98] Scott discusses spirit possession as "dangerous expressions of hostility" and "quasi-covert form of social protest" where overt resistance would be impossible.[99] It represents a critique of Jesus-in-movement with the intention "to brand Jesus as a messenger not of God but of Satan."[100] Second, another ominous aspect of the text is the source of the critique.

---

89 Taylor, *The Gospel According to St. Mark*, 236.

90 Explaining this phrase in the light of Jewish purity law, Neyrey comments "out of line and dangerous." See, "Idea of Purity in Mark's Gospel," 109.

91 Edwards, *The Gospel According to Mark*, 118.

92 France, *The Gospel of Mark*, 167.

93 France, *The Gospel of Mark*, 167; Belo, *A Materialist Reading of the Gospel of Mark*, 117.

94 Myers, *Binding the Strong Man*, 164.

95 France, *The Gospel of Mark*, 168.

96 Edwards, *The Gospel According to Mark*, 119.

97 Gould, *The Gospel of Mark*, 60.

98 Branscomb, *The Gospel of Mark*, 69.

99 Scott, *Domination and Arts of Resistance*, 141.

100 France, *The Gospel of Mark*, 168.

Mark identifies this opposing group as οἱ γραμματιες ἀπὸ Ἱεροσολύμων. This presumes that Mark's portrayal of the scribes is officially deputed by the powers in Jerusalem.[101] Here, Mark anticipates the place of Jesus' bold declaration of the hidden transcript in the face of powers. It is assumed that their view on Jesus-in-movement is highly partisan and controlled by Jerusalem temple-state. Mark represents Jerusalem as a place of hostility for Jesus.[102] Until now, Jesus has met with "some of the scribes" (2: 6) and "the scribes of the Pharisees" (2: 16). They represent "the real core of the hostility" towards Jesus-in-movement.[103] These local scribes and Pharisees in Galilee accused Jesus and his disciples and the opposition culminated in a plot against his life, (3: 6), which was no easy task to carry out as Jesus remained popular in the region.[104] In this given context of the double-accusation that attacked his own personality to sabotage his mission, Jesus delivered a series of parable sayings. Myers sums up the situation and says, "To his extended family, and to his political opponents he is demonic."[105] Mark states that Jesus' fame spread Jesus beyond Galilee.

Mark's editorial comment that "he [Jesus] called them to him and spoke to them in parables" (v. 23) prepares the readers' mind that Jesus has the superior counter-questioning and argumentation over the double euphemistic accusation that were leveled against Jesus. The phrase προσκαλεσάμενος αὐτοὺς introduces a dual aspect of Jesus' actions.[106] Mark's portrayal of Jesus' authority excels that of the scribes.[107] More importantly, it implies that the scribes were speaking about Jesus rather directly to him, and that Jesus now initiates direct confrontation.[108]

With ἐν παραβολαῖς, Mark assumes the purpose of Jesus in using parables was meant for confrontation. It is in this sense that we read the parables of Jesus. Since his critics used elementary forms of disguise, such

---

101 Branscomb discusses that since Galilee was under a different political power, religious matters would have been directed by the council of scribes which met in the "Hall of Hewn Stones" on the temple mount. For Branscomb, it is uncertain whether these scribes sent by official authority, or a voluntary group who were interested in Jesus' mission. See *The Gospel of Mark*, 69-70.

102 Guelich, *Mark 1-8: 26*, 174.

103 Schweizer, *The Good News According to Mark*, 85.

104 France, *The Gospel of Mark*, 168.

105 Taylor, *The Gospel According to St. Mark*, 212.

106 Edwards reports that the Greek verb προσκαλεομαι "occurs in eight instances when Jesus makes solemn and important pronouncements." See Edwards, *The Gospel According to Mark*, 121.

107 Johnson argues that this editorial remark portrays Jesus as a "monarch or a teacher of unquestioned authority." See, *A Commentary on the Gospel According to St. Mark*, 82.

108 France, *The Gospel of Mark*, 171.

as: gossip and spirit possession and euphemism in their resistance, Jesus' response took a quite public form in presenting elements of folklore or popular culture. The literary beauty with all the encompassing "intricate parallelism and cross-referencing of images" like kingdom, house and Satan in this series of parabolic sayings is obvious.[109] But, why did Jesus use these sayings as a riposte to the official judgment that is invariably demeaning him? There is no doubt that the genre of the sayings belongs to folk-sayings which is part and parcel of the Hebrew לשמ. This series of parables involves elaborate forms of disguise and thus obscurity is expected. In this sense, Mark 3: 20-35 is far from what Myers presumes in that: "Jesus declares ideological war."[110] Rather, we can only expect "undeclared war" that is also not at the level of ideology, but of status domination. Insofar as these folk-sayings are the property of Jesus-in-movement who represented the hidden transcript of indignation and dignity of the Galilean peasants, we should expect that the ideas, beliefs and opinions expressed in this series of sayings are regarded as real in the socio-political and religious context of villages in Galilee.

3.1.2. How can Satan cast out Satan?

France argues that the basic argument of the sayings is grounded on the theme: "strength depends on unity"[111] By using this hypothetical theme, we can say that "How can Satan cast out Satan?" (v. 23b)—a saying which is peculiar to Mark[112]—conveys the theological principle that "Satan cannot cast out Satan."[113] This principle is further illustrated by the two parallels (vv. 24-25). Interestingly enough, Jesus did not use the name Βεελζεβούλ, even though he was charged by the Jerusalem scribes that "Βεελζεβούλ ἔχει."[114] Instead, Jesus used the name of Satan. It is unlikely that Jesus changed the name with the intention to make it more derisive.[115] It is argued that Βεελζεβούλ was a foreign god who was worshipped in Syria and Ekron.[116] This presumes that

---

109 Myers, *Binding the Strong Man*, 166.

110 Myers, *Binding the Strong Man*, 164-167.

111 France, *The Gospel of Mark*, 171.

112 Its parallel form with a slight modification in Mat. 12: 25 and Lk. 11: 17 is acknowledged.

113 Taylor, *The Gospel According to St. Mark*, 241.

114 Neither Jesus repeated the idea of the prince of demons. This does not mean that Jesus disagreed with the contemporary Jewish belief in "the reality of Satan as the lord of the kingdom of evil." See, Taylor, *The Gospel According to St. Mark*, 239; A. Busch, "Questioning and Conviction: Double-voiced Discourse in Mark 3: 22-30," *JBL* 125/3 (2006): 479.

115 Wilson, *Mark*, 803.

116 According to Johnson, the name must be the Aramaic form of *Ba'al z^{e}bhul* (Lord of [high] house' *i.e.*, the Temple). A god bearing this name may have been worshipped in Syria from high antiquity, for in the *Ras Shamra* texts c. 1400 B.C., one of the titles of Aleyan

Jesus' intention is to re-size the issue within the context of Galilee-Jerusalem relations. Jesus' identification of Βεελζεβούλ as Satan is extremely important in the context where the existing religious hierarchical holds out the view that the God of the ruling aristocrats in Jerusalem is largely distinguished from that of the subaltern masses in the Galilee of the Gentiles.[117]

3.1.3. Divided Kingdom and Divided House

From the image of Satan, Jesus shifts to that of divided kingdom and family (vv. 24-25). The purpose of Jesus is perhaps to further illustrate the principle—"Satan cannot cast out Satan"—as he has established terms of the previous saying. Both the statements of Jesus sayings are put in a grammatical framework of conditional clause by introducing with the construction ἐὰν … σταθῆαι (subjunctive):

> [24]καὶ ἐὰν βασιλεία ἐφ'ἑαυτὴν μερισθῇ, οὐ δύναται σταθῆαι ἡ βασιλεία ἐκεινη
> [25]καὶ ἐὰν οἰκία ἐφ'ἑαυτὴν μερισθῇ, οὐ δύνήσεται σταθῆαι ἡ οἰκία ἐκεινη.

Even though these parabolic sayings are clouded by the intricate parallelism and cross-referencing of images (*viz.* βασιλεία and οἰκία), the point of argument was made on the assumption that—strength depends on unity—and it is beautifully exemplified here; and, it shall be fulfilled in future.[118] Donahue and Harrington consider the household of Herod the Great that divided in 4 B.C.E. as the political reality behind this saying.[119]

3.1.4. Satan will not stand

After exemplifying the theme, Jesus referred back to the actual circumstance of his parable in that: Satan could not rise up against himself, if so– he cannot stand. With this simple logic, Jesus makes it clear that his exorcism was an attack to Satan's domain. He has no secret collusive relationship with Satan;

Baal is "*Zebul, baal* of the earth." Most English versions have adopted from the Latin the form 'Beelzebub,' which represents the Old Testament *Ba'al zebub*, 'lord of flies,' who has the god of Ekron; the Hebrews evidently corrupted the name in this fashion to show their contempt (2 Kings 1: 2). See Johnson, *A Commentary on the Gospel According to St. Mark*, 81. See, also Taylor's *The Gospel According to St. Mark*, 238-239 for various explanations of Βεελζεβούλ.

117 This argument stands against the idea the change of Beelzebul into Satan is not a mere the transmissional process, as proposed by Crossan, *The Historical Jesus*, 318-319.

118 Incigneri situates these sayings in their historical contexts of recent upheavals of the civil war. See, *The Gospel to the Romans,* 185-186.

119 Donahue and Harrington, *The Gospel of Mark*, 130; Incigneri's proposal to link this saying with the incident in December A.D. 69 is unlikely. See, *The Gospel to the Romans*, 73-74.

rather he was the threat to Satan's power.[120] These sayings reflect more of folk sayings rather than Jesus' own creation.[121] Since these folk sayings are the culture embedded within the subjugated agrarian communities and are used by Jesus as a riposte to the scribes from Jerusalem, the carefully chosen images of the domain of Satan (*i.e.* βασιλεία and οἰκία) could probably correspond to the temple-state that were controlled by the powerful priestly aristocrats. D. E. Oakman's argument that the images are references to the house of Herod or kingdom of Rome and this can be well accepted.[122] Myers denotes they "bear remarkable correspondence to the ideological foundation of scribal Judaism: the centralized politics of the Davidic state ('kingdom,' 3: 24) and its symbolic centre which is the temple ('house,' 3: 25).[123]

3.1.5. Jesus vis-à-vis the "Strong Man" (v.27)

> But no one can enter a strong man's [ἰσχυροῦ] house and plunder his property [τὰ σκεύη] without first tying up [δήσῃ] the strong man; then indeed the house can be plundered (v. 27).[124]

By using the series of triad-parables to denote who he is not, Jesus now turned to the positive side to reflect who he is. This brief but nuclear parable assumes that Jesus' intention is to bind the strong man.[125] This parable recalls a popular belief of the messianic high priest and his mission to bind Satan.[126] Key-words in the parable may unlock Jesus' meaning. The Greek τὰ σκεύη ("property") refers to the property of various materials and usages. According to Maurer, the word refers to "utensils of various materials ... which are employed for the most varied purposes in home and field, in war and peace, in the secular world and the sacred."[127] It occurs again in Mark 11: 16 in reference to the vessels that Jesus bans to carry through the temple.[128] It is assumed that Mark uses this word in the sense of the sacred purpose.

---

120 France, *The Gospel of Mark*, 171.

121 I argue against Perrin's conclusion that the parables are "artistic creations" and "foundation myth." See Perrin, "Historical Criticism, Literary Criticism, and Hermeneutics," 362, 369.

122 D. E. Oakman, "Rulers' House, Thieves, and Usurpers: The Beelzebul Pericope," *Forum* 4/3 (1988): 115.

123 Myers, *Binding the Strong Man*, 166.

124 Insertion of Greek words is mine.

125 For Dodd, Jesus sees "the end of Satan's kingdom." See, *The Parables of the Kingdom*, 95; Busch, "Questioning and Conviction," 484-486; also Neyrey, "Idea of Purity in Mark's Gospel," 110-112.

126 Edwards discusses this parable in the light the Jewish texts that reflected the messianic high priest. See, Edwards, *The Gospel According to Mark*, 121-122.

127 Maurer, "σκεύη" in *TDNT* 8: 360.

128 Myers, *Binding the Strong Man*, 167.

Another revealing word to the meaning is δήσῃ ("tying up"). Mark uses this word in the contexts of the exorcism (5: 3-4) and the political imprisonment of John (6: 17) and Barabbas (15: 7). Jesus—ό ἰσχυρότερος as heralded by John (1: 8)—intends to overthrow the reign of the strong man's house.[129] Since Mark's use of the word τὰ σκεύη is in relation to vessels of the temple, Jesus' intention assumes the reign of the temple-state or the scribal establishment. This argument is strengthened by another key-word δήσῃ ("binding") in the context of demon possession and political imprisonment. Jesus' tradition bears this aspect of breaking and entering.[130]

3.1.6. Summary

Mark's editorial passage that attributes the accusation to the scribes from Jerusalem is noteworthy in the subaltern marginalised reading. Especially in the context of the Galilee-Jerusalem conflict situation, where Galilee was being looked down by the authorities in the city. Hence, the context provides us the subalternity of the parables. These scribes have used a double euphemism for Satan–Beelzebul and "prince of the demons." With this double-euphemistic accusation, the Jerusalem scribes attacked Jesus. According to Heil, the two-fold accumulations raised against Jesus are "viciously his person as being demon possessed" and "maliciously attribute his exorcistic activity to this demon possession."[131] The result of the accusation would "bring harm rather than healing to the people."[132] Myers puts it "political war of myth."[133] That means when the ruling class felt that its hegemony was being threatened, it tries to neutralize challengers by identifying them with the mythic cultural arch-demon. The logic of the scribes was simple: because they believed themselves to be God's representatives, Jesus' secession necessarily puts him in allegiance to Satan. Mark ends Jesus' response to the "scribes" charge with the warning about the "eternal sin" (vv. 28-29).[134] Liew puts it, "Because of Jesus' unique and authoritative status, those who criticize him are "guilty of an eternal sin' (3: 29)."[135]

3.2. The Parable Discourse (Mk 4: 1-34)

Mark records two extended teachings of Jesus, *viz.* the Parable Discourse (4: 1-34) and the Apocalyptic Discourse (13: 1-37). Even a cursory reading reveals

---

129 The Greek noun ἰσχυρος literally means strong, mighty, powerful.

130 Cf. Mat. 24: 43; I Thess. 5: 2, 4; II Pet. 3: 10; Rev. 3: 3, 16: 15.

131 Heil, *Mark as a Model for Action*, 87.

132 Heil, *Mark as a Model for Action*, 88.

133 Myers, *Binding the Strong Man*, 164.

134 Geulich, *Mark 1-8: 26*, 177.

135 Liew, "The Gospel of Mark," 115.

certain differences between the two discourses. One among such differences is the fact that the former discourse represents Jesus' public interaction with the crowd while revealing the intricate parts of Jesus' interaction with the trusted disciples in private; whereas the latter is entirely the private interaction of Jesus with a few disciples and it was delivered after a series of Jesus' public confrontation with the powers in Jerusalem. This study intends to explore politics of resistance by denoting that the public-private dichotomy occupies a central place in the exegetical analysis of the texts. This insightful dichotomy has always been overlooked for exegetical consideration. For instance, Theissen believes that Mark 4 is about "internal perils of the church" and Mark 13 concerns "external threats to the community."[136] Hence the discourses, for Theissen, are merely "secret instructions to the disciples."[137]

Quite a different perspective is proposed by Perrin who considers the discourses as "Jesus' vision of reality."[138] The discourses are more than Jesus' teaching on internal or external threats to the early Christian community and vision of Jesus. Mark presents the Parable Discourse in a very complex and ambiguous way. Unlike other parables that have been discussed earlier, Mark does not specify any concrete situation to explain as to why Jesus taught in terms of the parables. Mark simply states that Jesus taught "a very large crowd gathered around him" in parables (vv. 1-2).[139] To this crowd, Jesus spoke about the parable of sowing (vv. 3-8). While portraying the Parable Discourse as Jesus' public address to the crowd; however, Mark inserts Jesus' interaction with a smaller group of disciples in private (vv. 10-12; 13-20).[140] Then Jesus narrated the purpose of his parables (vv. 10-12), the interpretation of the parable of sowing, and a series of parabolic sayings. These were clearly an offstage performance of Jesus. Again, Jesus picked up the theme of sowing and this time the parables of growing were referred to (vv. 26-29). Even though Mark does indicate explicitly his editorial comment in vv. 33-34 suggests that two Parables of Kingdom could surely be addressed public. In between the parables of "sowing seed" (vv. 3-9) and "growing seed" (vv. 26-29), Mark has in mind: the purpose of the parables (vv. 10-12), the allegorical interpretation of the parable (vv. 13-20); a series of parabolic sayings (vv. 21-25). This intricate nature of systematic interplay between the public and private discourse within

136 Theissen, *The Gospels in Context*, 125.

137 Theissen, *The Gospels in Context*, 125.

138 Perrin, "Historical Criticism, Literary Criticism, and Hermeneutics," 374.

139 Donahue and Harrington rightly observe that Mark continually stresses the size of the crowd (2: 2, 13; 3: 9, 20, 32). See, *The Gospel of Mark*, 137.

140 Scholars like D. Peters have always defined this text as two classes of people: those who are outside and those who are within. See, "Vulnerable Promise from the Land (Mark 4: 3b-8)" in *Jesus and His Parables: Interpreting the Parables of Jesus Today*, ed. V. G. Shillington (Edinburgh: T&T Clark, 1997), 75.

the Parable Discourse turned the plain agrarian parables of Jesus into the most crucial and debated ones. This interrelationship between the public and private discourses has never been a serious concern of the earlier researches.

A majority of the commentators of this Parable Discourse simply have usually interpreted the structure of the Parable Discourse in terms of the outside-inside binary. Besides, the interpretation of the parable (vv. 14-20) is commonly understood as an allegorical interpretation of the early Church.[141] There is no doubt that the structure of the Parable Discourse in its present form is of the Markan construct. Yet, the political motive behind the construction must be sought in the agrarian politics of the first century Galilee. Our task here is to re-read the Parable Discourse in the light of Scott's understanding of the systematic relationship between the public and private discourses.

3.2.1. The Parable of Sowing on Various Landscapes (vv. 3-9)

> [3]Listen! A sower went out to sow.[4] And as he sowed, some seed fell on the path, and the birds came and ate it up. [5]Other seed fell on rocky ground, where it did not have much soil, and it sprang up quickly, since it had no depth of soil. [6]And when the sun rose, it was scorched, and since it had no root, it withered away.[7] Other seed fell among thorns, and the thorns grew up and choked it, and it yielded no grain. [8]Other seed fell into good soil and brought forth grain, growing up and increasing and yielding thirty and sixty and a hundredfold. [9]And he said, 'Let anyone with ears to hear listen!'

3.2.2. Setting, Context and Genre of the Parables

Mark situates this parable of sowing after the series of parabolic sayings while indicating that it was given by Jesus in response to the Scribes and the Pharisees who had been deputed from Jerusalem. The present parable can be taken as an extension of Jesus' response to such attempts. As for the context and setting of this parable, there are at least two things that must be kept in mind. First, Mark situates it is the context of Jesus' public interaction in terms of the wider Galilee. Unlike the previous parables, Jesus teaches "a very large Crowd" (4: 1) "many things" (Gr. πολλά) in the parable (4: 2). With his editorial note– ὄχλος πλεῖστος gathered around him (v. 1a), Mark establishes "the steady and progressive accumulation of more and more people around Jesus."[142] Thus,

141 Among very few scholars who established the possibility that the interpretation in an earlier form may go back to Jesus himself is R. E. Brown. See, "Parable and Allegory Reconsidered," *New Testament Essays* (New York: Doubleday, 1968), 256-260.

142 Heil, *Mark as a Model for Action*, 94. Mark points out that in 1:33 the "whole city" was gathered at the door; in 2:13 "many" gathered so that there was no room even around the door; in 2: 13 "all the crowd" came to him; in 3: 7-8, a "great multitude from Galilee followed and also from Judea and from Jerusalem and from Idumea and beyond the

Mark impresses upon us that Jesus' parables are intended to communicate with the crowd in public.[143] Recently, scholars have also assumed that the use of the Greek word ὄχλος (crowd) in Mark over against λαός (people) has deep ideological and theological implications.[144] J. P. Louw and E. A. Nida present ὄχλος as referring to "a casual non-membership group of people" whereas λαός refers to "a collective for people who belong to God."[145] This vague and generalized distinction of ὄχλος and λαός does not help much to understand the public-private problem in the discourse. One must discern who the people were and where they came from.

Second, being an onstage performance of Jesus, we can expect a politics of disguise and anonymity that was involved in the parable. As already discussed in the previous chapter, Mark takes note of how the crowds increased in size as the fame of Jesus spread throughout Galilee and beyond. The crowd that Jesus addressed with this, parables were most probably gathered from various regions. Marcus opines that the presence of an extraordinary divine power in the words and deeds is the basic reason as to why Jesus attracted such a large crowd.[146] It is no doubt that the ordinary masses (crowd) inclusive of the second word (people) have had an anticipation of God's deliverance from the oppressive Roman imperialism.[147] Most probably, rumour could be virtually the means that that brought such a large crowd to Jesus-in-movement. In the analysis of this parable, we shall try to spell out the hermeneutical significance of rumour. Third, another significant setting provided by Mark is the seating arrangement. Jesus sat in the boat whereas the entire crowd sat "on the land" (Gr. ἐπὶ τῆς γῆς).[148] This seating arrangement conveys to us that Jesus is in confrontation with a massive crowd as "the authoritative leader" rather than as "the powerful healer."[149] In other words, Jesus is portrayed as the one who spearheaded the agrarian-resistance movement by declaring the hidden transcript of the villager farmers in public.

Jordon and from around Tyre and Sidon; in 3: 20, "the crowd" gathered so that they could not even eat; now in 4:1 a "very large crowd" gathered about him, and also "all the crowd" was beside the sea on the land.

143 Schottroff, *The Parables of Jesus*, 112.

144 Joy, *Mark and Its Subalterns*, 114.

145 J. P. Louw and E.A. Nida, *Greek-English Lexicon of the New Testament* (New York, UBS, 1989), 121-122.

146 J. Marcus, *The Mystery of the Kingdom of God,* SBL Dissertation Series 90 (Atlanta, Georgia: Scholars Press, 1986), 15-16.

147 John, *The Ecological Vision of Jesus*, 164.

148 John acknowledges the seating arrangement as peculiar to Mark. See, *The Ecological Vision of Jesus*, 185.

149 Heil, *Mark as a Model for Action*, 94.

3.2.3. Explanation of the Parable

This parable is certainly agrarian in its nature. It encompasses not only an entire agricultural seasons from sowing to harvest, but also a variety of landscapes.[150] This parable has the sower, the seed and the soil as its major characters. Scholars are divided as to which one of these should be placed at the centre of our understanding of the parable: the sower or the fate of the seed or the various types of ground where the seed fell. A better outcome could be envisaged if the interrelationship between the characters are maintained and analyzed in the context of agrarian politics.

3.2.3.1. Identity of the Sower (v. 3-4)

Mark mentions "Listen! A sower went out to sow" and this sentence was followed by his act of sowing, "as he sowed ..." (vv. 3-4). For many scholars ὁ σπείρων (v. 3a) sounds so central to the parable and it has given rise to the title– the Parable of Sower.[151] Apart from this, nothing is mentioned about the sower in the rest of the parable. It seems obvious that the sower is not at a central point in the parable. However, as Marcus observes, the figure of the "sower is not accidental" in this parable.[152] A majority of scholars have argued that Mark intended his readers to understand that the sower is Jesus.[153] To these scholars, the verb ἐξῆλθεν ("went out" v. 3) is decisive as it perhaps recalls the mission statement of Jesus (1: 38) and Mark's editorial remark (2: 13) in both of which we have Jesus moving out to a wider area in order to carry out his campaign. Mark's use of aorist tense denotes that the act of sowing is the reflection of Jesus' campaign. In one sense, it is possible that the sower represents Jesus of Nazareth. At the same time, we must seek to unearth the identity of the sower in the entire range of Jesus' campaign. Mark indicates that Jesus' fame had travelled faster than his physical presence (Mk 1: 28, 45; 3: 7-8). The crowd at distant places possibly received the proclamation by means of rumor.[154] This supposition is affirmed by the composition of the crowd whom Jesus addressed in terms of this parable.

Apart from Galilee, the members of the crowd were drawn from various regions, such as: Judea, Jerusalem, Idumea, beyond the Jordan, and Tyre and Sidon (3: 7-8). Even though Jesus had unleashed himself into a great movement, yet at this stage, he was yet to cross the border of Galilee. Therefore, an identification of the figure of sower needs to be re-examined within the wider scale of Jesus' campaign where "politically charged rumor"

150 Waetjen, *A Reordering of Power*, 100-101.

151 Dodd, *Parables of the Kingdom of God*, 145-147; Jeremias, *Parables of Jesus*, 11-12, etc.

152 Marcus, *The Mystery of the Kingdom of God,* 37.

153 Marcus, *The Mystery of the Kingdom of God,* 38.

154 Suh, *Discipleship and Community*, 68.

played a vital role.[155] Those who came from afar (*i.e.*, the non-Galilean crowds) most possibly received the sowing of the seed from other mediums apart from Jesus. Given the absence of the modern mass media, rumour could be the most possible medium through these people from far off places. In the light of this, it is possible to note that the least reference to the sower also reveals the anonymity that was involved in Jesus' campaign.

This insight further pushes us to consider the narrative strategy of Jesus in his parable. Mark records Jesus' command to "listen" (Ἀκούετε, Mk 4: 3, 9; cf. 4: 24, 9, 23).[156] The present parable begins and concludes with the urging to "hear" (vv. 3, 9), which occurs ten times in Mark 4. The Greek word Ἀκούετε found in v. 3 is in the imperative mood which underscores its urgency and importance. Why is it still necessary for Jesus to urge the crowd who came from far and distant places to listen to his attractive speech in the parables? Various answers have been proposed to this question. Schweizer argues, "Because kingdom of God is so mysterious that it can only be proclaimed in figures of speech to one who is willing to listen, the subject often strains the metaphor."[157] Jesus' words in v. 11 do not support this view. Myers sees an editorial reflection of Mark on "the paradoxical nature of parable discourse" in this matter.[158] The paradoxical nature of the Parable Discourse must be spelt out in the context of domination and resistance.

Given that Jesus gave this parable as a reflection of this campaign in Galilee that had been spread beyond Galilee through rumour, a thoughtful listening would have been involved from the part of the crowd who arrived across the border. Scott provides us two reasons as to why Jesus commanded his audience to listen. First, Jesus' proclamation of the arrival of God's kingdom and its manifestation in miraculous healing and exorcism are the events of vital importance to the Jewish peoples' interest. The crowds were to keep their ears close to the events and were to repeat avidly whatever news there was.[159] Second, the crowd was to be cautious so as to prevent themselves from embellishment and exaggeration of the message they heard. As Scott observers, "the oral transmission of rumour allows for a process of elaboration, distortion and exaggeration that is so defuse and collective it has discernible

155 Scott, *Domination and the Arts of Resistance*, 144.

156 Donahue and Harrington observe similarity between the Shema (Deut. 6: 4-5) and Mk. 4: 1-34 beyond the phrase "listen." See, *The Gospel of Mark*, 138.

157 Schweizer, *The Good News According to Mark*, 89.

158 Myers seems to base his understanding the parable discourse on "mystery to be obscure" in 4: 10-12 and the parable as "secret to be revealed" in 4: 2-22. See, *Binding the Strong Man*, 170.

159 Scott, *Domination and the Arts of Resistance*, 144.

author."[160] Thus, Buttrick is right in calling for "responsibility of hearing" to the understanding of the narrative strategy of Jesus.[161]

3.2.3.2. Profligate Sowing of Seed

Another aspect of this parable that received scholarly attention is profligate or wasteful sowing of seed. Jesus denotes that some seeds fell on the path (v. 4a), other seeds fell on rocky ground (v. 5a), some among thorns (v. 7a), and some on good soil (v. 8a).[162] This parable leaves its interpreters wondering at the seeming carelessness and randomness of the sower in scattering his seeds. For some scholars this profligate or wasteful sowing of seed reflects the simple farming practices common in Galilee. Jeremias explains this farming system as a result of "sowing precedes ploughing."[163] K. D. White disagrees with this assertion. White points out that the Mediterranean farmers were familiar with the importance of maintaining a summer fallow.[164] He believes that no good farmer in the past or present would deliberately sow upon unploughed stubble.[165] P. B. Payne re-examines the issue and concludes that "ploughing regularly follows sowing in order to bury the seed."[166] This theory of ploughing after sowing is attractive as it denotes why the seed is sown in unpromising places like the path, the rocky ground and even amongst the thorns. However, it must be noted that farming in Judaea and Galilee was a hardscrabble affair (cf. Jer 4: 3) and the farmer sowed unsparingly. According to the standing instructions written in the *Mishnah*, farming was to be orderly and done in a systematic manner and special care was to be given so as not to mix seeds (*m. Kil* 2: 3ff.). The sowing, as reflected in Jesus' parable, was just the opposite, and it was done in a disorderly, unsystematic and above all wasteful manner. This profligate sowing can suitably be equated with how the words of rumor travelled amongst all sections of the Jewish society.

3.2.3.3. The Various Landscapes

This parable is largely contained by the act of sowing and as well as its reaction. The role of the various landscapes is reflected in a larger part of the parable. Jesus mentions the image of four landscapes, such as: way side land with thieving birds, land with thorns, rocky land under the scorching sun and

---

160 Scott, *Domination and the Arts of Resistance*, 144.

161 Butrick, *The Parables of Jesus*, 41-48.

162 John takes them as "different types of soil." See, *The Ecological Vision of Jesus*, 189.

163 Jeremias, *The Parables of Jesus*, 11.

164 K. D. White, "The Parable of the Sower," in *JTS* 15 (1964): 301, 305.

165 White, "The Parable of the Sower," 305.

166 P. B. Payne, "The Order of Sowing and Ploughing in the Parable of the Sower," *NTS* 25 (1978): 127.

one portion of fertile land producing abundantly.[167] Moreover, scholars like Marcus are confused by a series of direct equations in Jesus' interpretation which identifies the seed both with "the word" and with those who hear the words (vv. 15-20).[168] There are various suggestions for the meaning of παρὰ τὴν ὁδόν upon which the first seed fell. Our review on various proposals is indicative of how the previous studies are an attempt to understand narrowly within the context of a local practice of farming. For instance, Gould takes it not as "a wide road" but "a path course to the hardness of the trodden soil."[169] Johnson suggests "the road on the edge of the field" or "the way through it."[170] Rawlison believes that "a trodden path runs across the field, and some seed falls on the path."[171] Taylor believes that behind παρά τὴν ὁδόν lies the Aramaic *'al 'urha* ("upon the path") instead of "alongside."[172] Besides, both "way" and "road" translate Greek ὁδόν the metaphor often used in the Biblical tradition for the journey motif. It describes the activity of God as symbolized by the exodus event. Mark's usage of "on the road" at 8: 27 and 10: 52—standing at the beginning and end which is also the main theme of the central section of Mark's Gospel—assumes the theological significance of the trade routes or the highways.

What did Jesus really hope to convey with this phrase παρὰ τὴν ὁδόν? This needs to be spelt out in the larger historical context of the Roman imperial activities. In the previous chapter (*i.e.* chapter two), we have depicted how the trade routes supposedly helped the Greek and Romans to take control of the socio-economic and politics of Galilee and how it brought about the economic exploitation of the subalterns. Indeed, the famous dictum "All roads lead to Rome" is worthy of quoting here. In every experience of imperial rule, be it ancient or modern, the people who lived by the ὁδός were usually the people who were most affected by the process. The same can be observed in the situation of Roman Galilee. This parable denotes that the problem of the seed sown on the path or alongside is that "birds came and easily ate it up" (v. 4b). In his interpretation of the parable, Jesus connects the seed that fell on the path to the ones from the word which they had heard had been taken away by Satan immediately before the word worked in them (v. 15). Jesus' representation of birds as Satan is worth mentioning.[173]

---

167 Shillington, "Engaging with Parables," 11.

168 Marcus, *The Mystery of the Kingdom of God,* 25-26. This scholar sees a direct equation in the form of x = y in Jesus' interpretation of the parable in Mark 4: 13-20.

169 E. P. Gould, *The Gospel According to St. Mark*, 70.

170 Johnson, *A Commentary on the Gospel According to St. Mark*, 88.

171 Rawlison, *St. Mark*, 49.

172 Taylor, *The Gospel According to Mark*, 252.

173 Crossan, *The Power of Parable*, 23.

There is no doubt that the ἐπὶ τὸ πετρῶδες ("upon rocky ground") refers to the familiar Galilean the condition where a rocky outcropping lies a few inches underground.[174] Given that the depths of soil were not uniform and taking the extensive terracing of the land into consideration, we can assume the widespread presence of rocks. Inadequate clearing of soil could be suspected. Scholars like Nineham, Jeremias and Oakman have pointed out the possibilities of overlooking the rock under the soil until ploughing was underway.[175] Guelich denotes that "rootlessness corresponds to the sudden springing up of the seeds."[176] Lack of root, according to the interpretation of the parable (v.17b), makes the hearers vulnerable to persecution.[177] People made their living by dry farming and the rocky ground of Galilee would realize the vulnerability of their life under the sunny rule of colonial power and they saw themselves as being "scorched." Jesus' interpretation of the parable as found in Mark further suggests that their status had been exposed to a political "trouble or persecution" (v. 17b).[178]

The appearance of τὰς ἀκὰνθας ("the thorns") in the parable is again the result of the poor clearance of the land before sowing.[179] Rawlison explains how the oriental farmers would not be at pains to eradicate the thorns. He says, "They have been cut down or burnt, but the roots are still in the soil and spring up afresh impending the development of the wheat."[180] But in reality concerning people's life in terms of the geopolitical, linguistic, ethnicity of the region, they were in danger of being alienated or assimilated by the thorns. The parable does not end with a discouraging story. Jesus narrates how the "other seed" fell into good soil "growing," "increasing," and "yielding" an extraordinary harvest (v. 8). The harvest of one hundredfold was extraordinary in Galilee and was surely a sign of a divine blessing.[181] Jesus hints that the reason for yielding a breathtaking harvest depended on the seed as well as the quality of soil. In v. 8, in contrast to ἄλλο in vv. 5 and 7, ἄλλα is used of individual seeds. The land (γῆν) is τὴν καλὴν–can be translated as "fair" or "fine" land. The soil of Gennesareth valley, the section around Capernaum was proverbially rich. Hanson and Oakman have spoken of the *Bet Netofa Valley*,

---

174 Branscomb, *The Gospel of Mark*, 80: John, *The Ecological Vision of Jesus*, 195-196.

175 Nineham, *The Gospel of St. Mark*, 135; Jeremias, *The Parables of Jesus*, 12; Oakman, *Jesus and the Economic Questions of His Day*, 106.

176 Guelich, *Mark 1-8: 26*, 194.

177 Guelich, *Mark 1-8: 26*, 194.

178 Roskam, *The Purpose of Mark*, 28-35.

179 Oakman, *Jesus and the Economic Questions of His Day*, 106.

180 Rawlison, *St. Mark*, 49.

181 For Jeremias, it symbolizes "the eschatological overflowing of the divine fullness." See, *The Parables of Jesus*, 150.

the rich agricultural land as the likely locale for many of Jesus' stories.[182] In short, the seeds fell into good land and continued to yield fruit while sprouting and increasing and providing an abundant harvest.[183] In Jesus' interpretation of the parable, the seeds that fell on good soil were the people who heard the Word and accepted it and bore fruit (v. 20).

Earlier studies have largely neglected the decisiveness of landscapes where the seeds were sown and where they fell. There is a strong tendency among the historical-eschatological scholars that stresses upon the aspect of successful harvest (v. 8) as the key to unpack the possible meaning of the parable. For instance, Jeremias sees the temporal contrast, *i.e.*, the contrast between the time of sowing and the time of eschatological harvest, as the main concern of the parable.[184] However, from our analysis, it is probable that the primary concern of the parable is not temporal but spatial, *i.e.*, between the different areas of the field.[185] Jesus-in-movement would have probably in mind the scale of his campaign when he referred to various landscapes in his parable. It consists of rocky ground, uncultivated land covered by thorn, and plain-fertile soil. Indeed, they are suggestive of giving the most probable meaning of the parable. The people of the παρά τὴν ὁδόν could have been the first to hear about the rumor of the good news of deliverance from the oppression. So also the first recipients of gossip about Jesus, *i.e.,* "His disciples do not fast" (2: 18), "He has gone out of His mind" (3: 21), "He has Beelzebul" (3: 22), *etc*. Jesus' proclamation of the good news of God—the central message being the counter-ideology—developed out of domination and exploitation and invited quick response, but it also anticipates "trouble or persecution on account of the word" (4: 17). This is what the seed that fell on the rocky ground seemingly signifies. Jesus' proclamation of the hidden transcript of the subjugated villagers in Galilee does not guarantee a positive effect on all who hear. Yet, the proclamation has also penetrated some who in turn would nurture the message and be productive.[186]

---

182 K. C. Hanson and Douglas E. Oakman, *Palestine in the Time of Jesus: Social Structures and Social Conflicts* (Minneapolis; Fortress Press, 1998), 104.

183 Schweizer believes that the successful harvest is God's achievement of his objective, kingdom of God which is blessing and fullness. See, *The Good News According to Mark*, 90.

184 Jeremias, *Parables of Jesus*, 149-151.

185 Marcus, *The Mystery of the Kingdom of God*, 40. If Schottroff's proposition that the parable "hints at a minimal field size" is correct, the parable gives us valuable historical information to argue that the peasants in Galilee cultivated the smallest bits of field. See, *The Parables of Jesus*, 73.

186 Cf. D. Peters, "Vulnerable Promise from the Land (Mark 4: 3b-8)" in *Jesus and His Parables: Interpreting the Parables of Jesus Today*, edited by V. G. Shillington (Edinburg: T&T Clark, 1997), 73.

3.2.3.4. Summary

Our analysis marks the probability that this parable reflects the public interaction of Jesus-in-movement who moved out with the struggles of the Galilean villagers across the border of Galilee and how people of various regions responded to his campaign. Mark denotes that at the heart of the hidden transcript lies the popular ideology, *i.e.* God's kingdom. It is believed the concept of God's kingdom had been developed as a hidden and disguised form of resistance and it comprises an alternative to the values and that views were articulated in the aristocratic temple-state in Jerusalem, which was further controlled by Rome. Mark's portrayal of the rapidly widening popular response to Jesus' proclamation of the arrival of God's kingdom and manifestation of God's enabling power in exorcisms and healings assumes a "politically charged rumor" that can by far cause violent acts. The various landscapes must be understood in terms of the fertility of each landscape and also in accommodating the declaration that spread to Galilee and beyond through rumor.[187] We can observe that Mark ostensibly intends his readers to understand the parable as a representation of the historical in-breaking of God's kingdom in Jesus. Horsley's suggestion that Jesus' declaration enshrines two dimensions: "sharp declarations of God's judgment against the forms and practices of domination" and "hopeful declarations of the sufficiency and justice possible under the direct rule of God"[188] finds much importance. Such a "sharp" and "hopeful" declaration could not but generate various reactions from the people of various spatial or geographical settings. Thus, Mark's representation of the parable assumes that Jesus was well-informed about the varied responses that were sparked off by his public declaration of the ideology of God's reign over against the reign of the dominants.

3.3. A Group of Parabolic Sayings (Mk. 4: 21-25)

> 21He said to them, "Is lamp brought in to be put under the bushel basket, or under the bed, and not on the lampstand? 22For there is nothing hidden, except to be disclosed; nor is anything secret, except to come to light. 23Let anyone with ears to hear listen!" 24And he said to them, "Pay attention to what you hear; the measure you will give be the measure you get, and still more be given you. 25For to those who have, more will be given; and from those who have nothing, even what they have will be taken away."

187 Landscape has always been taken in terms of "cultural milieu" (*e.g.*, desert, mountains, etc) and "social milieu" (*e.g.*, urban and rural) to mean divisions and groups in the societies. See, G. Theissen, *The Gospels in Context: Social and Political History in the Synoptic Tradition*. Trans. by L. M. Maloney (Edinburg: T&T Clark, 1992), 10.

188 Horsley, *Jesus in Context*, 189.

3.3.1. The Context and Genre of the Parables

As already denoted, Mark structures the Parable Discourse (4: 1-34) upon the dichotomy of public and private discourses. With the preceding passages, such as: the purpose of the parables (vv. 10-12) and the interpretation of the parables (vv. 13-21), this group of parabolic sayings (vv. 21-25) forms the private discourse of Jesus. Mark's portrayal of Jesus as teaching the public in the parables while giving the explanation in private to his trusted disciples (vv. 33-34) should not be taken as cunning or deception. This subtlety is surely linked to the vulnerability of Jesus-in-movement which rarely permitted him overt confrontation. This insight offers us a new framework to read complicated texts like–the purpose of the parable (vv. 10-12), the interpretation of the parable of the sowing on various landscapes (vv. 13-20); and perhaps, the collection of sayings (vv. 21-25).

As far as the genre is concerned, the sayings under consideration are folk-sayings. The main idea in the inserted sayings is about a mystery, of what is to be revealed. The parabolic saying of Jesus (4: 21-22) denotes what is hidden and secret, what is to be and what is to be manifested, which is followed by a strong exhortation to be watchful of what they heard. "For to those who have, more will be given; and from those who have nothing, even what they have will be taken away" (v. 25). In his summary on the use of parables (vv. 33-34), Mark clearly states that "He [Jesus] did not speak to them except in parables, but he explained everything in private to his disciples" (v. 34). The parables were in all probability the property of subaltern classes in Galilee. We shall approach them to ensure whether they were the expressions of their experiences and values over and against the urban power elites in order that we may sharpen our perspective to read the texts as a riposte to the official culture that was so degrading to the rural existence. Considering the collection of sayings in vv. 21-25 is an extension of the offstage performances of Jesus. We shall analyse them as undisclosed resistance to ideological domination.

3.3.2. The Analysis of the Parabolic Sayings

Jesus continues to employ elaborate forms of disguise and anonymity in his declaration of the agrarian-resistance ideology. We shall give closer attention to assure whether these sayings can be considered as an ideological sedition that was intended to encourage the trusted disciples of Jesus to resist the powers.[189]

---

189 Guelich sees the introductory note "he said to them" (v. 21a) could refer to "the private audience" or "the public crowds." He thinks these parabolic sayings (vv. 21-24) fit the former group. See. Guelich, *Mark 1-8: 26*, 228. T. A. Burkill believes that these sayings are a continuation of Jesus' private instruction to the disciples. See, "The Cryptology of Parables in St. Mark Gospel," 248.

3.3.2.1. Image of Lamp, Bushel Basket and Bed (v. 21)

> Jesus asks, "Is lamp brought in to be put under the bushel basket, or under the bed, and not on the lampstand?"

This verse entails a pair of questions. The first question must be answered negatively and the second positively.[190] It seems that Jesus wanted his disciples to realize the absurdity of the lamp which would be hidden from view under "τὸν μόδιον ("the bushel") or under τὴν κλίνην ("the bed" or "couch") rather than displayed on τὴν λυχνίαν ("the lampstand"). The phrase ἔρχεται ὁ λύχνος (lit. "the lamp is come") has always been considered as symbolically alluding either to Jesus' coming or the kingdom's coming.[191] Taylor denies the phrase as the reference to the incarnation of Jesus.[192] We should not think of Jesus merely as the one who "comes" on his "way" of preaching, teaching and healing throughout Markan narrative,[193] but as the one who declares the hidden transcript of indignity and dignity of the villagers. Mark asserts that just as "the lamp comes" to be displayed before all, so is the "secret of the kingdom of God" (Mk 4: 11) *i.e.*, previously hidden to the outsiders to be openly revealed. In a more direct way, Jesus promises a further and deeper revelation of what is hidden and what is secret.[194] Although, the parables may obscure in the revelation of the meaning of the gospel, the obscurity is not their final purpose. The expression, "For there is nothing hidden, except to be disclosed; nor is anything secret, except to come to light" indicates that secrets or mysteries are not permanent, but only held in reserve for future revelation. As Gould says "the ultimate end of the hiding is manifesting."[195] The parables are to make way for a more telling revelation at the right time and the disciples could be sent to reveal the mysteries. G. J. Paul's conclusion that the disciples "be sent back to the crowd as revealers"[196] is enlightening. Jesus has already challenged the crowd to a "true and attentive" hearing in Mk. 4: 3, 9. Again, Jesus summoned the disciples to really "hear" and understand his parables with the solemn challenge: "Let anyone with ears to hear listen!" (v. 23). The idea of the hidden and disclose in this saying supposes that revealing truth to powers was a serious concern for the subjugated subalterns.

---

190 Heil, *Mark as a Model for Action*, 105.

191 Guelich, *Mark 1-8: 26*, 228.

192 Taylor, *The Gospel According to St. Mark*, 263.

193 Heil, *Mark as a Model for Action*, 105.

194 Crossan argues that Mark 4: 22 as pointing to "an imminent future consummation" when what is hidden now will be revealed. See, *Historical Jesus*, 350.

195 Gould, *The Gospel According to St. Mark*, 78.

196 G. J. Paul, *The Gospel According to Saint Mark: Introduction and Commentary*, CSL No. 13 (Mysore: CLS, 1957), 115-116.

3.3.2.2. The Image of Measurement (v. 24b)

To the theme of hidden and revelation, Mark attaches a saying of Jesus about being measured by the standard that one sets for others (v. 24).[197] Jesus presses forward his private teaching to his disciples with yet a more explicit warning about the object of hearing: "Pay attention to what you hear." The word βλεπω conveys "be alert it" or "observe it." The disciples were warned to carefully consider what they hear. The saying "the measure you will give be the measure you get..." which follows, introduced without any connecting link gives the reason as to why they would be alert. The significance of this saying in Mark is obscured for many scholars. For instance, Swete explains it to mean: "Your attention to the teaching will be the measure of the profit you will receive from it."[198] Taylor proposes that "Mark has taken it from a collection and brought it into an unnatural connexion."[199] This saying is considered by some scholars as a popular saying among the Jews.[200] The passive voice of the two verbs μετρηθήσεται and προστεθήσεται are divine passive, meaning, "God will measure it out and add it out to you." The passive voice is used perhaps in order to avoid the name of God for the fear of profaning it.

3.3.2.3. The Saying of Have and Have Not (v. 25)

> "For to those who have, more will be given, and from those who have nothing, even what they have will be taken away."

Even though Matthew and Luke have documented the saying, they are different in terms of content and context and yet all of them encapsulate this saying in the context of the parable.[201] Some commentators have interpreted this saying as God's promises to those who pay attention to what they hear and consequently will be given more understanding.[202] Rather, this saying should be read in the context of material domination. John insists that the social milieu of Mark 4 is an extreme exploitation of natural resources, oppression and marginalization of the agrarian masses.[203] This parabolic saying could have been a popular saying that criticized the political order in a given particular

---

197 Edwards, *The Gospel According to Mark*, 140.

198 As quoted by Taylor, *The Gospel According to St. Mark*, 264.

199 As quoted by Taylor, *The Gospel According to St. Mark*, 265.

200 Donahue and Harrington propose the saying may reflect "folk wisdom." See, *The Gospel of Mark*, 150; Edwards, *The Gospel According to Mark*, 140-141.

201 Matthew and Luke locate this saying at the end of the parables of the talents/pounds (Mat. 25: 29; Lk. 19: 26). For Donahue and Harrington this is more logic. See, *The Gospel of Mark*, 150.

202 Schweizer, *The Good News According to Mark*, 100.

203 John, *The Ecological Vision of Jesus*, 167.

history. This assumption establishes the view that notion of God's reign is an ideology that developed out of material domination. It is less likely that Jesus intended to state that "those to whom the mystery of the kingdom of God is given will receive even greater capacity to enter it" or "those who fail to receive the mystery in Jesus will discover that even what he has will be taken from him/her." A deeper insight can be drawn if this saying is situated in an economic and political power differential.[204]

3.3.2.4. Comment

The parabolic sayings in this passage are scattered in various contexts in the Gospels of Matthew and Luke. The sayings bear different meanings in the Gospels according to the differing contexts in which they are located. Their original meaning and context are seemingly no longer recoverable for some scholars. Considering the secrecy motif that runs throughout Mark's Gospel and particularly in the discourse, analysing the motif in the context of Jesus who assumingly declared the hidden transcript of the subordinated villagers, is best suited to the presentation alternate ideology of the peasants. Some scholars have cast their views in favour of this stance. For instance, Taylor believes that the Markan sayings are intended to refer to the manifestation of the kingdom of God and this may be the original significance.[205] Heil also argues that the identity and the meaning of Jesus' teachings are a part of the mysteries.[206] Jesus declared that God's reign was a part of the ideology that was cultivated in the context of the people who were under the reigning system of oppression. It was not appropriate for Jesus to denote everything openly to the crowd. For Jesus was under surveillance since his declaration of the good news of God. Jesus told his disciples the meaning of the parable as well as the secret of the kingdom and he urged them to listen carefully and to trace out the meaning of what he uttered in parables.

3.4. The Parables of Kingdom (4: 26-34)

Mark concludes his Parable Discourse with two parables about the kingdom of God (4: 26-29; 30-32) and a summary of the purpose of parables (4: 33-34). With these parables, as Waetjen observes, Jesus returned to the public audience.[207] Strictly speaking, these are the parables which carry the kingdom of God as their direct referent. This implies that they are the public performance of Jesus. Thus, we must warrant attention to decipher whether there are any elements of political disguise and anonymity in these parables. Both the parables repeat

204 Cf. Myers, *Binding the Strong Man*, 178.

205 *The Gospel According to St. Mark*, 264.

206 Heil, *Mark as a Model for Action*, 105.

207 Waetjen, *A Reordering of Power*, 107.

the image of a person sowing seed (cf. v. 3ff.), but to completely different effects.[208] Both the parables, according to Edwards, are "stories of surprise."[209] Presumably, in the first parable the main emphasis falls upon the significance of the life giving land; whereas the second parable accentuates the significance of the produce. Keeping this in mind, we shall try to analyse the exact nature of the kingdom of God as proclaimed by Jesus.

3.4.1. The Parable of the Seed Growing Secretly (4: 26-29)

> 26He also said, "the kingdom of God is as if someone would scatter seed on the ground, 27and would sleep and rise night and day, and the seed would sprout and grow, he does not know. 28The earth produces of itself first the stalk, then the head, then the full grain in the head. 29But when the grain is ripe, at one he goes in with his sickle, because the harvest has come."

3.4.2. Explanation of the Parable

This parable is unique to Mark and it is found nowhere else in other Gospels.[210] For the first time in Mark's Gospel, Jesus' parable is directly linked to the idea of the kingdom of God. The kingdom of God is compared here to a seed that was scattered on the ground by a man (v. 26). One must be conscious enough not to overlook the elements of anonymity that are involved in this parable. Jesus' presentation of the idea of God's kingdom situates the common and lowly images of agrarian culture while one expects something grand and glorious. Activities that are basic to the daily agrarian routine, such as: sowing, seed, growing, harvest, *etc.* are mundane clues to the nature of the kingdom of God.

3.4.3. The identity of the ἄνθρωπος

Mark's presentation of the sower and the act of sowing are unusual. The sower is not ό σπείρων as in 4: 3, but simply an ἄνθρωπος who did not "sow" but "would throw" (βάλῃ, subjunctive mood) his seed upon the ground. The NRSV rightly puts it, "as if someone would scatter seed." For Guelich suggests it a βάλῃ sounds a "careless act of simply tossing out the seed."[211] Mark portrays him as quite ordinary. Marcus paraphrases it, "He is not responsible for the growth of the plant indeed does not know how it grows; inactive during the time of growth; at the time of harvest he suddenly springs into action and

208 Edwards, *The Gospel According to Mark*, 142. On possibilities on various interpretations, see Dodd, *The Parables of the Kingdom*, 141-144.

209 Edwards, *The Gospel According to Mark*, 142.

210 Luke omits it altogether and Matthew substitutes for it the Parable of Tares (Mat. 13: 24-30) in the same context.

211 Guelich, *Mark 1-8: 26*, 241.

reaps the grain."[212] Who or what will be the possible candidate for the referent of the "man," remains significant. Under the dominance of allegorical and eschatological interpretations that have dominated the larger part of the history of parable study, the sower is usually equated as Jesus or God. Even in recent times, some scholars insist that the figure of the sower is a representation of Jesus or God. In his monograph, *The Mystery of the Kingdom of God* (1986), Marcus identifies the sower with Jesus. His claim is established upon Mark's identification of the seed with the "word." To identity the sower in this particular parable with Jesus is not without difficulties. The key words ἄνθρωπος and βάλῃ are quite general in order to match up Mark's depiction of Jesus. Mark's characterization of the sower as not knowing how the plant grows (4: 27c) does cope with Jesus who knew what he did.[213] J. Dupont—who based his argument on the citation of Joel 4: 31 in Mark 4: 29—identifies the man with God. He asserts that since this parable is a parable of God's kingdom, God must be the chief actor in the parable.[214] Dupont's insistence must be considered as Mark's portrayal of the farmer as inactive and irresponsible during the time of growth and it does not suit the omnipotent nature of God. It is hard to portray God as inactive in the process of establishing God's kingdom.

Mark's picture of the sower does not assume an expert farmer. Mark seems to have an ill-mannered cultivator who did not maintain the basic technique of farming. This supposition makes us opt for an alternate way of understanding. The alternate way of reading can be established if we consider take the element of political disguise and anonymity in the academic investigation of this parable. As it has been reflected, the message of Jesus had spread to the larger Galilee and beyond through rumor. Therefore, it is possible that Mark might have referred to rumor as the subject of βάλῃ of seeds on the ground. However, rumor is not referred to in a strictly personified sense, but rather to convey the subordinated people's message while veiling the messenger. This insight is able to cope with the notion of the messianic secret in Mark.

3.4.4. The Creative Power of Earth (v. 28)

The anonymous identity of the sower gives us space to look for another concern in the parable. We must imagine how the disenfranchised people in the Roman Galilee were losing land, upon which the entire economy of an agrarian society was based, from the hands of others. The life-supporting land had come under the tyranny of Roman occupation and Jewish religious impotence. In spite of the inactivity and irresponsibility of the sower, Jesus asserts, "the earth produces of itself" (v. 28). The creative power and activity

212 Marcus, *The Mystery of the Kingdom of God*, 171.

213 Marcus, *The Mystery of the Kingdom of God*, 172.

214 As cited by Marcus, *The Mystery of the Kingdom of God*, 171, see footnote no. 27.

of the land is at work. Could this be the aspect that Mark wanted to keep at the centre of this parable? Naickanparampil says, "The earth produces of itself" means "of its own accord" or "automatically" apart from the said farmer.[215]

3.4.5. The Seed as God's Kingdom

The earliest host of modern parable scholars reflected that Jesus taught, with this parable, the gradual evolution of the kingdom in human society. Usually, the seed has been allegorized as the divine seed which Jesus implants in the heart of the church. But there no evidence in the parable that Jesus is referring to himself as the divine seed which he sows. General understanding suggested that the main purpose of the parable was to teach the need for patience. The eschatological interpretation that laid emphasis on the harvest saw the significance of the speedy in-breaking of the kingdom. Dodd, Cadoux, and others related the parable to the immediate situation of Jesus and also to imply that the kingdom was already present. For Jeremias, this phrase expresses the common perception that the germination of seed is God's miraculous activity in contrast to human activity.[216] Mark clearly mentions that the seed sprouts and grows through the creative and activity of the land. The growing, as reflected in the parable, is a gradual process, first a "stalk" then the "head" then the "full grain in the head" (v. 28). It is no doubt that this gradual and steady growth of the seed resembles the kingdom of God.[217] Once the gradual and inevitable growth reaches a point and the "fruit is ripened" the man comes to harvest.[218] Although the man does not know how this happened, he goes with his sickle for harvest (v. 29). Myers sees "the revolutionary patience and hope of the kingdom" in this verse.[219]

3.4.6. Summary

Many scholars have offered various views and insights for the interpretation of this parable. In most cases, the parable is held with reference to the kingdom of God. Previous conclusions regarding this aspect need to be revised in the light of our understanding of the kingdom of God as the ideology of the subjugated peasants made public by Jesus. In spite of the previous studies that raised attention mainly on the process of growth or the harvest in an eschatological category, we recognize that ἡ γῆ ("the earth') lies at the very centre of this

215 Naickanparampil, *The Gospel of Mark*, 122.

216 Jeremias, *Parables of Jesus*, 149, 151-152.

217 Buttrick coins "inherent power" to explain the quality or force of the kingdom of God. See, *The Parables of Jesus*, 18.

218 Meyers alleges Mark to politicize Joel 3: 13 in order to invoke the prophetic-apocalyptic holy war tradition. See, *Binding the Strong Man*, 179.

219 Myers, *Binding the Strong Man*, 179.

parable as the life giving power to the seeds. Mark leaves no or less space for "unworldly characters"[220] in the kingdom of God proclaimed by Jesus.

3.4.7. The Parable of the Mustard Seed (4: 30-32)

> [30]He also said, "With what can we compare the kingdom of God, or what parable will we use for it? [31]It is like a mustard seed, which, when sown upon the ground, is the smallest of all the seeds on earth; [32]yet when it is sown it grows up and becomes the greatest of all shrubs, and puts forth large branches, so that the birds of the air can make nests in its shade."

This parable is found in all three Synoptic Gospels (Mat 13: 31-32; Lk 13: 18-19) and has been variously interpreted by scholars. Some scholars even regarded the parable to be one of the best attested elements in the teaching of Jesus.[221] This parable reveals Jesus' view of the nature of the kingdom of God. Taylor highlights four mainline interpretations of the parable, such as: (a) growth, (b) slow and gradual development, (c) speedy and catastrophic in-breaking of the kingdom, and (d) the kingdom as relevant to the immediate situation of Jesus including Gentiles within its scope.[222] It is likely that the majority of commentators have emphasized the idea of growth, *i.e.*, the essentially tiny mustard seed springs up and becomes a plant which is capable of giving shelter.[223] What is always neglected by the western scholars is the underlying significance of land on which the smallest seed has been transformed into the greatest of all shrubs. What Dodd calls "the fortunes of his [Jesus] work in Galilee"[224] must be sought in terms of space. Jesus continued his public teaching to the crowd by introducing this final parable with a double question: "With what can we compare the kingdom of God, or what parable will we use for it?" (v. 30). Jesus challenged his audience to join him in expressing and communicating yet another taste of God's kingdom through a parable. To compare God's kingdom, Jesus used the phenomenal growth of the small κόκκω σινάπεως (a grain of mustard). The grain of mustard is presented here as "the smallest of all the seeds on earth" but mustard seed may not be literally the smallest seeds of all.[225] Jesus said "the smallest of all seeds" is transformed into "the greatest of all shrubs." This phenomenal transformation happened at a time "when sown upon the ground" (v. 31) and this transforming

---

220 N. A. Huffman, "Atypical Features in the Parables of Jesus," *JBL* 97/2 (1978): 219.

221 Taylor, *The Gospel According to St. Mark*, 268.

222 Taylor, *The Gospel According to St. Mark*, 268.

223 Naickanparampil, *The Gospel of Mark*, 123.

224 Dodd, *The Parables of the Kingdom*, 147.

225 H. Hendrickx believes that this saying could be proverb among the Jews of Jesus' time. See, *The Parables of Jesus* (San Francisco: Harper & Row, 1983), 33; also Scott, *Hear Then the Parable*, 378.

factor is repeated in this context (v. 32). Only because it is sown on earth, the smallest seed of all becomes the greatest of all shrubs. Which means that Mark emphasizes upon the "automatic and inevitable growth"[226] through the life giving power of the earth, he had already depicted this in the preceding parable. That the grown mustard shrub "puts forth large branches, so that the birds of the air can make nests in its shade" (v. 32b) brings the parable to its full grown size.

The mustard plant has often been found growing to a height of 8 to 12 feet and great numbers of small birds alight upon its stalks to pluck the seeds.[227] "Birds" in the Parable of Seeds Sown on Various Landscapes are portrayed as enemies to the seeds (Mk 4: 4, 14). However, in the present parable, the birds are depicted as the beneficiaries of the power of growth. The imagery that has been used here is illustrated in Daniel 4: 12 and Ezekiel 17: 23. In these passages, the tree symbolizes protection which is given to subject peoples by a great nation.[228] This envisions the overthrowing of the mighty Rome and the establishment of God's kingdom as dreamt by the subaltern masses in rural Galilee.

3.4.8. Comment

Jesus fashioned the proverbial mustard seed into an illustration of the kingdom. As with the proceeding parable, this parable presents God's kingdom not as something which is to arrive from somewhere, but is sown and grown on the land. Jesus' parables are not merely primarily the expression of Jesus' own experience of God. They are more reflective of Jesus' proclamation of the hidden transcript of the indignation and dignity of the subjugated peasants in Galilee. The greater point, however, is that the ideology of God's reign arises from obscurity and insignificance.[229] Here again, the land is presented as the transforming power, through which even the smallest thing can be transformed into the greatest one. Though the kingdom as represented by a mustard tree, has a small beginning, it has grown into a world-wide phenomenon and the subjected peoples find protection and can live in safety and security. Both the parables reveal the wonderful and mysterious God activity of God in the world.[230]

---

226 Heil, *Mark as Model for Action*, 111.

227 Taylor, *The Gospel According to St. Mark*, 270.

228 Belo, *A Materialist Reading of the Gospel of Mark*, 124; Myers, *Binding the Strong Man*, 180.

229 Here, I argue against scholars like Hendrickx who proposed that the smallest seed becoming a tree as a symbolization of the protection extended by a powerful king to his subjects. See, *The Parables of Jesus*, 35.

230 Waetjen, *A Reordering of Power*, 108.

3.5. The Parabolic Saying on Defilement (7: 14-15)

> [14]Then he called the crowd again and said to them, "Listen to me, all of you, and understand: [15]there is nothing outside a person that by going in can defile, but the things that come out are what defile.

3.5.1. Context, Setting and Genre of the Parable

Regarding the context and setting of this parabolic saying, its literary and spatial setting requires closer examination. Mark situates this parable as a part of the conflict between the Pharisees and the Scribes from Jerusalem. It is the context of what Herzog (2004) discusses "defining and defending world" of the Torah.[231] Like the previous Parable Discourse (4: 3-34), Mark structures this parable upon the dichotomy of the public and private teachings of Jesus. After his confrontation with the Jerusalem elites, he called "the people" and uttered this parable (7: 14-6). In the words of Scott, it is Jesus' onstage performance. Interestingly enough—as it was in the case of the Parable Discourse—his disciples asked Jesus in private about the meaning of the parable and Jesus rendered the interpretation of his parable (7: 17-23; cf. 4: 19-12, 13-20). This aspect of interaction between public and private must serve as the point of departure.[232] Its geographical setting must be analysed for consideration. Mark indicates that the incident took place in Gennesaret (6: 53), which was the most fertile place in Galilee.[233] Edwards gives us the description of Gennesaret that it was a "fertile plain three miles long by a mile wide on the west shore of the lake between Capernaum and Tiberius."[234] Taylor opines that Gennesaret was the name of a place, and it could either be a town or village.[235] Due to its

---

231 W. R. Herzog II, "Onstage and Offstage with Jesus of Nazareth: Public Transcripts, hidden Transcripts, and Gospel Texts," in *Hidden Transcripts and the Arts of Resistance: Applying the World of James C. Scott to Jesus and Paul*, edited by R.A. Horsley (Atlanta: SBL, 2004), 41.

232 Borg explains the public and private dimensions as two different audiences. See, *Conflict, Holiness & Politics*, 97.

233 Unlike the preceding stories, there is no link between this narrative and the rest, no temporal or spatial expression which tells us the location of the incident. The reference to some of the scribes who came from Jerusalem implies that the incident in Galilee, and the Pharisees mentioned were probably resident here. The last mentioning of specified location of Jesus' mission in Mark is Gennesaret (6: 53). Since there is no change in the location, we assume the spatial setting of the parable to be Gennesaret. Mark presents this village as one of the locations of the summary of Jesus' healing activity (cf. 1: 32-34; 3: 7-12). One recognizable unique feature of Jesus' healing activity here is that Jesus was already well known as a healer. He need not go out to seek for patients.(6: 55b). See also Taylor, *The Gospel According to St. Mark*, 334.

234 Edwards, *The Gospel According to Mark*, 203.

235 Taylor, *The Gospel According to St. Mark*, 332.

strategic significance of being a lake-side fertile area, the incident was said to occur in the home of agrarian communities in Galilee. The presence of Pharisees and the scribes from Jerusalem exhibits that the Jerusalem temple-state had interest in this fertile land. As we have already seen with the Jerusalem ruling class, both the Romans and the high priest office, claimed the lion's share for themselves while leaving barely enough room for peasants to maintain their subsistence. The high recognition given by the inhabitants of this fertile-plain area to Jesus-in-movement at the time of his landing on this place supports the presupposition.[236] Did the urban elites employ the Torah by imposing their interpretation of the Torah upon the villages of Galilee? Attempt will be made to explore whether or not the ruling elites in Jerusalem had used their religious powers to sustain the subjugation and to exact tributes from this most fertile part of Galilee. With regard to the genre, this parable is unobtrusive in its nature. Mark conveys us that the disciples identified Jesus' proclamation in Mark 7: 15 as a parable (7: 17b).[237] This is the lone non-agrarian parable in Mark. It takes the imagery of the human digestive system to illustrate the issue of defilement. The saying is truly a pronouncement which takes the form of the parable. Who pronounces what and why is it rendered as a parable? These are the basic exegetical questions that require serious attention in unfolding the meaning and purpose of Jesus.

3.5.2. Analysis of the Parable (7: 15)

France labels this parable as an "epigrammatic saying."[238] However, it is unlikely because there is no such thing to render amusement to it. This parable assumes a statement of public assertion of worth in the form of pronouncement. Unlike other parables, it is not the vehicle by which Jesus confronted his opponents. Jesus had directly confronted his opponents and denounced them as "hypocrites" who rejected the commandment of God by preserving the "human tradition" that had been cultivated by them. Later Jesus called the people and made this parabolic pronouncement.

The introduction to the pronouncement (v. 14)—consists of common Markan words, such as: προσκάλεσαμενος (3: 1), ὄχλος (2: 4), πάλιν (2: 1; 3: 20)—is certainly Mark's editorial work.[239] The Greek verb uttered in the middle voice προσκαλέομαι (lit. "call to oneself") occurs nine times in Mark with reference to—except in 15: 44 which records Pilate calling the centurion—

236 The Greek *krabbatos* (NIV "mats"), refers to mattresses or pallets used by poor people, indicates that Jesus' influence is extended to the common and poor.

237 Boucher, *The Mysterious Parables*, 64-67.

238 Scholars like France thinks than this parable is "an epigrammatic saying whose potentially wide application is balanced by its epigrammatic form, so that the hearers to work out its significance for themselves." See, France, *The Gospel of Mark*, 288-289.

239 Taylor, *The Gospel According to St. Mark*, 342.

Jesus' calling of his disciples and certain individuals to Him, with the purpose of uttering a certain pronouncement.[240] The private discussion on the issue of purity between Jesus and the scribal delegation was now over. The Pharisees and the Scribes have receded from Jesus while the crowds were calling in. In other words, the scribal accusation has been rebutted by Jesus and turned down as false. Jesus took the step to pronounce publicly that his disciples were clean.[241] Jesus' introductory note: "Listen to me, all of you, and understand" (v. 14b) prepares the crowd for a closer attention to the pronouncement that was about to make.

The parable engages the imagery of the human digestive system by making aspects of εἰσπορευόμενον (lit. "come in" or "enter") and ἐκπορευόμενά (lit. "come out') to explain what defiles and what not. The form of this pronouncement is a combination of parallelism and antithesis that has been beautifully constructed in οὐδέν ... ἀλλὰ ... form. One must be cautious not to overlook the Hebraic usage of parallelism in translating and interpreting any text in the form of antithetic-parallelism such as this including, the present one. France argues that "οὐδέν ... ἀλλὰ ... constructions in Semitic context can sometimes be understood in a more relative than absolute sense."[242] If the parallel lines in the pronouncement are to be taken as relative rather than absolute as suggested, the pronouncement cannot be translated as "Not at all things enter in a person can defile, but only things that come out are what defile." Instead, defilement by things that come in are considered and judged by being compared with the defilement by the things that come out. Thus, the first line in the pronouncement is explained and complemented by the second line (v.15). Even though this parabolic saying focuses upon no specific regulation on purity, it presumes that Jesus' principle of uncleanness comes from within and not from without. This may raise much more fundamental issues of purity which goes far beyond the limited questions of the validity of the scribal rules for hand washing. In His explanation of the parable in private, Jesus condemned the Jewish leaders on account of the uncleanliness in their hearts (vv. 18-23).

3.5.3. Comment

The parable itself is simple and straightforward, yet it is still confusing even to the disciples of Jesus. It seems clear from our study that this saying is Jesus' public statement of assertion of the worth of his disciples who were accused of unclean. On the one hand, Jesus publicly announced the dignity of his disciples who were dis-privileged and insulted by the Pharisees and the Scribes. "There

240 Those references are: Mark 3: 13, 23; 6: 7: 14; 8: 1, 34; 10: 42; 12: 43; 12: 43; 15: 44.

241 Crossan, *The Power of Parable*, 23; also Myers, *Binding the Strong Man*, 219.

242 France, *The Gospel of Mark*, 289.

is nothing outside a person that by going in can defile, but the things that come out are what defile" (v. 15) is surely a public assertion of worth. On the other hand, its geopolitical setting suggests that the parable is a vehicle for resistance to material dominance. The strong execution of the tradition of the elders assumes that the Jewish ruling elites had special interest for the appropriation of grains, taxes and labour, from the fertile valley.

3.6. The Parable of Yeast (8: 15)

> [15]And he cautioned them, saying, 'Watch out – beware of the yeast of the Pharisees and the yeast of Herod.'

3.6.1. Context, Setting, and Genre of the Parable

Mark denotes clues to trace the setting of this saying by recalling three things. First, the reference to "the Pharisees" recalls the Pharisees' demand for a sign in the preceding incident (vv. 10-13). Second, the lack of understanding by the disciples (vv. 16-17, 21) also recalls "the dullness of the disciples" which has been repeated time and again in the Gospel (4: 13, 41; 6: 37, 52; 7: 18; 8: 4, 31-33; 9: 6, *etc*.).[243] Third, this recounts the two feeding miracles which primarily involved material aspect of Jesus' campaign (6: 34-44; 8: 1-9). From these aspects of information from the Gospel, it is quite a difficult task to determine how Mark links the matter of bread with the Pharisees and Herod. Mark conveys that this is an interaction between Jesus and the disciples in private, and it is thus an offstage performance of Jesus (8: 10).

3.6.2. Analysis of the Parable

Mark denotes that this is parabolic warning which is directed to the disciples. The double imperative ὁρᾶτε, βλέπετε (lit. "see, look") indicates that Jesus was emphatic that his disciples should be aware of the yeast of the Pharisees and of Herod.[244] It is not clear what is actually meant by Jesus' caution – "beware of yeast of the Pharisees and the yeast of Herod." Mark provides no explanation. The reference to ζύμης ("yeast" or "leaven") could mean at least three things. First, Mark might have used it the sense of the ordinary bread of the Pharisees and Herod (*i.e*., bread with leaven in it). Second, it could perhaps refer to the teaching of the Pharisees and Herod. In Matthew, it refers to the "teaching of the Pharisees and the Sadducees" (Mat. 16: 12). Matthean editorial notes might refer to which the interpretation of the Law these groups advocated. Third, it might refer to the evil disposition of these parties which lead a people astray. This view is supported by the Lukan parallel where the reference to Herod is dropped and also adds that Jesus meant "the hypocrisy of

243 Stein, *Mark*, 379, 380.

244 Stein, *Mark*, 381.

the Pharisees" (Lk 12: 1). Following Lukan understanding, many scholars are tempted to take the evil disposition of the Pharisees and Herod as the point of reference to the yeast.

Various suggestions that have been proposed interpret what is actually meant by "the yeast of the Pharisees and the yeast of Herod." Based on the previous incident in Mark 8: 11-12, R. H. Gundry, Donahue & Harington have suggested the element of sign-seeking attitude of the Pharisees.[245] This interpretation does not take care of "the yeast of Herod." Mark does not mention Herod or Herodian as seeking for signs. Marcus opines that idea of ζύμης (yeast) is the evil inclination that has hardened the heart of the Pharisees and Herod.[246] Scholars like Quesnell, Guelich, Edwards have interpreted ζύμης as the refusal to recognize and accept the truth and unbelief that is reflected in one's response to Jesus.[247] Despite the fact that there have been various suggestions by the scholars, there is no satisfactory answer as to what the parabolic saying could really mean. One of the principal reasons for this aspect is that the previous studies do not consider this warning as political caution, but simply as religious warning. Stein cites some recent scholars such as E. Lohmeyer, R. Pesch, and J. Gnilka as having proposed "politically dangerous nationalism" as the meaning of "yeast" in relation to the Pharisees and Herod.[248] Besides, many of the interpreters have evidently derived their conclusion either from Matthean or Lukan editorial activities. For many reasons, Mark seems to maintain the original form of the saying.[249] Therefore, we must look for meaning within the theological framework of Mark, especially in the context of the political disguise and anonymity. For Mark, the Pharisees and the Herod or Herodians are political alliances that form serious threat to Jesus-in-movement (Mk 3: 6, 12: 13). Mark must have political reason in inserting the parabolic warning of Jesus into this passage. The phrase "we have no bread" (v. 16) possibly reminds us of the seriousness of the problems of food security in Galilee under the Roman-Herodian regime. When we read this parable in the material circumstance of agrarian politics, the word ζύμης conveys the idea of "the bread of the Pharisees and Herod" which symbolizes power and authority that was the oppressive to the subaltern masses. Mark, in the following verses, emphasizes upon Jesus' great miracle-

245 R. H. Gundry, *Mark: A Commentary on His Apology for the Cross* (Grand Rapids, Michigan: Eerdmans, 1993), 408; Donahue and Herrington, *The Gospel of Mark*, 252.

246 J. Marcus, *Mark 1–8: A New Translation with Introduction and Commentary*, AB 27 (New York: Doubleday, 2000), 510.

247 Q. Quesnell, *The Mind of Mark: Interpretation and Method through the Exegesis of Mark 6: 52*. Analecta Biblica 38 (Rome: Pontifical Biblical Institute, 1969), 254-257; Geulich, *Mark 1–8:26*, 423-424; Edwards, *The Gospel According to Mark*, 239.

248 Stein, *Mark*, 382.

249 Taylor, *The Gospel According to St. Mark*, 367.

working power (vv. 19-21). As Liew observes, "Without doubt, the feedings should have reminded the disciples of Jesus' supernatural ability to provide an overabundant food supply, thus making their worry over bread superfluous."[250]

3.6.3. Summary

Our study indicates that this parable is part of the private discourse of Jesus. As Jesus and his disciples fled away by boat from the presence of the sign seeking Pharisees, the disciples realized that they did not have enough bread for all of them. Jesus directly warned them that they should beware of the yeast of Pharisees and of Herod. The Parable of Yeast can be taken in partnership with the public resistance to the Pharisees which had been rendered in the context of grumbling. This is the last parable that has been cited by Mark within the second political discourse. From the next parable, it can be rendered in a more straightforward manner than these.

4. The Parables in the Third Political Discourse (Mk 8: 31–16: 20)

We now proceed to the final political discourse of Mark which Scott denotes as the rupturing of the political order with direct attack and challenge.[251] In this part of the Gospel, we have Jesus-in-movement and marching up to Jerusalem to directly engage with the powers in Jerusalem. There are four parables in this section. We shall analyse them with the aim to note whether Jesus has used them as a vehicle for resistance.

4.1. The Parable of Camel and the Eye of the Needle (Mk 10: 25)

> It is easier for a camel to go through the eye of a needle than for someone who is rich to enter the kingdom of God.

4.1.1. The Setting, Context, and Genre of the Parable

Mark sets this parable in the spatial setting of Jesus who moved beyond the bounds of Galilee. The parable is situated in Jesus' journey to Jerusalem. We shall explore whether the declaration of the hidden transcript of the Galilean agrarian communities in the face of powers can possibly be Jesus' agenda or not. Mark conveys the impression that Jesus' journey is a "journey unto suffering and execution."[252] The geographical setting envisages the context of the parable to be a politically turbulent atmosphere. Jesus was encountered by a rich man (Mk 10: 17, 22) who is variedly represented by other Synoptic writers as both a "young man" (Mat 19: 22) and "ruler" (Lk 18: 18).[253] The Decalogue

250 Liew, "The Gospel of Mark," 108.

251 Scott , *Domination and the Arts of Resistance*, 19.

252 Suh, *Discipleship and Community*, 92.

253 Myers, *Binding the Strong Man*, 272.

stands at the backdrop of the encounter.[254] It is against this background that we shall analyse the Parable of the Camel and the Eye of the Needle. Once it is clear that Jesus-in-movement is no longer in sequestered sites in Galilean villages, but on the threshold of entering Jerusalem for direct confrontation with the power-holders there, we need to creatively determine its genre, aside from what has been proposed by previous scholars. Both the spatial setting and the literary context of this parabolic saying presume that the genre could not be a general one. With regard to its genre, this parable would be most apt to consider it as pronouncement parable. It is less necessary to reflect upon the saying as Jesus' own composition; rather it could have originated in the popular culture of the agrarian communities in Galilee, who constantly resisted the urban religious elites who were at the same time effectively involved in the colonial activities of material domination. This is one rendering of what Huffman had once labelled as "atypical" or "hyperbolic" parable.[255] We need to concern ourselves with the purpose of Jesus by using this mode.

4.1.2. The Analysis of the Parable

As Jesus drew near to the city, "a man" ran up and knelt before Jesus to ask, "Good Teacher, what must I do to inherit eternal life?" (10: 17). This man labels Jesus a "Διδάσκαλε ἀγαθέ." Myers believes this man flattered rather than respected Jesus.[256] By asking Jesus about a matter like eternal life, the man acknowledges Jesus' status to answer his question.[257] Most commentators regard that the man was attempting to flatter Jesus. For instance, basing on the oriental cultural practice, Bailey argues that this man addressed Jesus with a term of respect while expecting to receive a similar respectful title, such as "Noble Ruler" in return.[258] However, Jesus declined the title "good teacher" for himself! This envisions that Jesus had no didactic purpose ahead of his visit to Jerusalem, but to declare the hidden transcript of the subjugated communities in Galilee before the powers. Jesus said to this man, "τὰς ἐντολὰς οἶδας" ("You know the commandments"). What does this mean for the young man? C. A. Evans opines that Jesus' intention is not to ask this man if he knows the basic teaching of the Torah. But, he knew that he was educated and

254 Herzog compares the two lists of commandments in Exod. 20: 1-17 and Mk. 10: 17-22 to denote what have been omitted and included. He finds out that the first four commandments fundamental to one's own responsibility to God, and possibly the tenth commandment are omitted. Herzog indicates that Mark has a greater concern on the ethical and material or property application of the Decalogue. See Herzog, *Jesus, Justice, and the Reign of God*, 158-167.

255 Huffman, "Atypical Features in the Parables of Jesus," 220.

256 Myers, *Binding the Strong Man*, 272.

257 Herzog, *Jesus, Justice, and the Reign of God*, 159.

258 Bailey, *Through Peasant Eyes*, 161-163.

was an admirer of the Torah as interpreted by the Jerusalem aristocrats and so Jesus perhaps uttered this to start their dialogue.[259] This man claimed that he had been observing the demands of the Torah from his youth (v. 20). The man was challenged by Jesus to sell off his possessions and to give the money to the poor. This idea of liquidating one's possession to join community is seen at Qumran (1 QS and 4QS). However, this man was not impressed by this ideology. Thus, his "face falling" hearing Jesus' word and "went away grieving, for he had many possessions" (vv. 21-22). This man reacted quickly and negatively towards Jesus, whom he had earlier called "Good Teacher."

In this context, Jesus warned his disciples by saying: "How hard it will be for those who have wealth to enter the kingdom of God" (v. 23). Jesus employed the images of the camel and the eye of the needle to confirm the impossibilities. The context in which Jesus pronounced this saying is less likely the context where Jesus taught His disciples about "wealth and its use, helping the poor and the needy,"[260] rather it was a resistance to material domination. The passage, for scholars like Schweitzer, is "discipleship in freedom from possessions."[261] In our analysis of the text, we shall keep the aspect of discipleship to the secondary level. Mark's story of Jesus' dealing with this man involves elements of disguise and anonymity.[262] Mark renders the identity of the anonymous by referring him simply as εἷς (v. 17).[263] However, this man is ὁ νεανίκος "the young man" in Matthew (19: 22) and ἄρχων ("ruler" or "official authority") in Luke (18: 18). Only at the end, Mark conveys that he was rich (v. 22).[264] On the other hand, Matthew and Luke omit the vivid details—the man "ran up," and "knelt" (v. 17), Jesus "looking upon him loved" (v. 20) the man's face fell (v. 22)—all are Mark's unique materials. The combined Synoptic Jesus' tradition pictures him as "a young rich ruler" who could have taken active part in appropriate of material benefits from the rural peasants. His gestures: "ran" and "knelt before him" (v. 17a) and his words: "Good Teacher" and "what must I do to inherit eternal life" (v. 17b) sound an act of flattering.[265] He projected himself as a faithful Torah-observant Jew who wanted to inherit eternal life.[266] Jesus did not assure him of eternal life. This

259 Evans, *Mark 8: 27-16: 20*, 96.

260 Naickanparampil, *The Gospel of Mark: Themes Explored*, 156.

261 Schweitzer, *The Good News According to Mark*, 208.

262 Cf. Schweitzer, *The Good News According to Mark*, 210.

263 Takatemjen opines that "man" as found in Mark is to be original since other synoptic writers changed it. See, *Banquet Is Ready*, 182.

264 Taylor, *The Gospel According to St. Mark*, 425.

265 Schweitzer argues that the address is "not customary for either Jew or Greek." See, *The Good News According to Mark*, 210.

266 Evans, *Mark 8: 27-16: 20*, 97.

man's oppressive character is further exposed in his response to Jesus' question about the commandments. Scott's idea of "public transcript" of the elites helps us to probe deeper into his claim of keeping the commandments from youth as the means to justify his practices of injustice against the poor.[267] At a realistic level, he is unable to produce the practical aspects of his strict observance of the commandments. His desire to inherit the eternal life is weighed down by his love for material wealth. Thus, this aspect falls from what Schweizer once has labelled as "discipleship in freedom from possessions."[268]

This parable is certainly not an independent narrative. It should be studied in connection with the rich man's query. However, Jesus' gesture of looking round the disciples assumes that the pronouncement is made after his departure. Jesus pronounces how difficult is for the rich person to enter the kingdom of God. The man had concerned himself with the conditions by which he could enter into the inheritance of eternal life.[269] Yet Jesus' pronouncement concerns itself about the entrance into the kingdom of God.[270] Jesus warns twice, "How hard it will be for those who have wealth to enter the kingdom of God" (vv. 23, 24). For the third time, Jesus emphasizes upon the difficulty of a rich man's entering into the kingdom of God by the metaphor of the camel and the needle eye. Mark uses the Greek τὰ χτήματα for the man's wealth (v. 22b). This word connotes material riches and it could be translated as "possession," "property," and "piece of land" or "real estate."[271] Herzog appreciably reminds us that "wealth is based on land and controlled of land" in the agrarian world of Jesus.[272] The underlining idea of one entering kingdom of God suggests that the kingdom is more like an area of authority into which one can enter.[273] Jesus uses χρήματα ("monetary wealth"), which is a more general term for rich (v. 25). These two words for wealth are interchangeably used in this passage. Its implication, according to Edwards, is that "wealth in its manifold and more liquid forms is as dangerous to faith as the obvious wealth of great property owners."[274]

Some commentators have tried to eviscerate the image "a camel to go through the eye of a needle" (v. 25) by suggesting that the original Greek is

---

267 Scott, *Domination and the Arts of Resistance*, 18. Schweitzer's position in defense of this man's response to Jesus "not to be expression pride" based upon "Jesus loved him" is acknowledged here. See, *The Good News According to Mark*, 212.

268 Schweitzer, *The Good News According to Mark*, 208.

269 Taylor, *The Gospel According to St. Mark*, 426.

270 Takatemjen, *The Banquet Is Ready*, 189.

271 Myers, *Binding the Strong Man*, 274; Edwards, *The Gospel According to Mark*, 313.

272 Herzog, *Jesus, Justice and the Reign of God*, 90.

273 Schweizer, *The Good News According to Mark*, 47.

274 Edwards, *The Gospel According to Mark*, 313-314.

κάμιλος ("a rope") instead of κάμηλος ("a camel"). But there is no strong and decisive textual evidence to support this view. Another suggestion takes "the eye of the needle" to be "a door in the walls of Jerusalem" through which only with difficulty a camel might perhaps squeeze[275]– as though the rich may enter the kingdom of God if only they humble themselves. There is no evidence for the legendary gate until the ninth century C.E.[276] It is best to stick to the text as it is. Taylor suggests that the saying is a hyperbole.[277] This kind of hyperbole saying is not foreign to Jesus or rabbinic literature. Sayings like "the beam and the splinter" (Lk 4: 41-42) and "the gnat and the camel" (Mat 23: 24) are good examples of the hyperbole sayings of Jesus. A rabbinic parallel speaks of the impossibility of an elephant passing through the eye of a needle (Ber 55b).[278] There is no doubt that wealth is a potential hindrance in order to enter into the kingdom of God. However, wealth is neither categorically condemned by Jesus nor does he make poverty to be a special virtue. Edwards has pointed out that neither the unnamed woman of 14: 3-9 nor Joseph of Arimathea are examples (14: 43) to illustrate that all the wealthy people are not questioned or condemned in Mark.[279] But for this "man" wealth is a potential hindrance in order to enter into the kingdom of God. Not only because it prevents him from selling all his possessions and following Jesus, but the question of how this "man" accumulates all his possessions is doubtful. He could have been involved in the appropriation of taxes, labour, land and others from the rural masses.[280] Scott reminds us that "peasant's anti-urban-elite point of view is important in a number of Jesus' parables."[281] There is no strong reason as to why we should read this parable as a form of resistance saying to material domination.

4.1.3. Summary

Our analysis reveals that this parable is a pronouncement by Jesus-in-movement against a rich man who could possibly belong to the ruling class in Jerusalem. Besides, it also comes to light that this parable is an offstage performance of Jesus. We note that Jesus speaks of humans entering into the kingdom of God, and not *vice versa*. Theologically, it implies that Jesus' understanding of God's kingdom is not something alien to human

275 Taylor, *The Gospel According to St. Mark*, 431.

276 Schweitzer, *The Good News According to Mark*, 212.

277 Taylor, *The Gospel According to St. Mark*, 431.

278 For detail, Myers, *Binding the Strong Man*, 274-275.

279 Edwards, *Gospel According to Mark*, 314.

280 C. I. David Joy's reading of the context, setting and style of Mark 10: 17-27 is enlightening in this regard. See, "Mark 10: 17-27 in the Light of the Issues of Poor and their Representation: A Postcolonial Reading," *BTF* 38/1 (June 2006): 163-165.

281 Scott, *Hear Then the Parable*, 92.

experiences that arrive from somewhere. The kingdom of God, as taught by Jesus of Nazareth, is possibly an ideology which has been developed by the subjugated agrarian communities in Galilee in order to preserve their dignity and to effectively resist the domination under the sovereign rule of God. Therefore, it is not possible to enter into that kingdom of God for a "man" who is of vivid target of this ideology. We must understand what France calls, "the revolutionary values of the kingdom of God" in this passage.[282] Any person which accumulates the riches through appropriation from the subjugated people too is "a camel before the eye of a needle."[283] Mark conveys the impression that the subaltern classes, such as: the leper (1: 40-45), the tax-collectors and sinners (2: 3-17), the Gerasene demoniac (5: 1-20), *etc*. have a better chance of entering into God's kingdom than the wealthy and powerful elites.[284]

4.2. The Parable of Tenants in the Vineyard (Mk 12: 1-9)

> 1Then he began to speak to them in parables. A man planted a vineyard,
> put a fence around it, dug a pit for the wine press, and built a watch-tower;
> then he leased it to tenants and went to another country. 2When the season
> came, he sent a slave to the tenants to collect from them his share of the
> produce of the vineyard. 3But they seized him, and beat him, and sent him
> away empty-handed. 4And again he sent another slave to them; this one
> they beat over the head and insulted. 5Then he sent another, and that one
> they killed. And so it was with many others; some they beat, and others
> they killed. 6He had still one other, a beloved son. Finally he sent him to
> them, saying, "They will respect my son." 7But those tenants said to one
> another, "This is the heir; come, let us kill him, and the inheritance will be
> ours." 8So they seized him, killed him, and threw him out of the vineyard.
> 9What then will the owner of the vineyard do? He will come and destroy
> the tenants and give the vineyard to others.

4.2.1. The Setting, Context, and Genre of the Parable

The spatial setting is highly significant for an understanding of the parable. Mark not only sets this parable in Jerusalem, but in the temple, the powerhouse of the elites (11: 27).[285] This is the first parable which has been told by Mark in Jerusalem. Jesus had launched by now an open and direct confrontation towards the powerful elites and the number of parables has been shown as being diminished. In view of the Galilee-Jerusalem conflict, the parable is regarded

282 France, *The Gospel of Mark*, 385.

283 Cf. Edwards, *Gospel According to Mark*, 314.

284 Liew, "The Gospel of Mark," 110.

285 Takatemjen, *The Banquet Is Ready*, 31-36; John, *The Ecological Vision of Jesus*, 153; Scott, *Hear Then the Parable*, 238.

to be significant in the eyes of the marginalised groups in Galilee, who were racially, economically, and politically looked down upon by the Judeans, and specifically upon the powerful elites in Jerusalem.[286] Dodd situates this parable in the context of revolt, economic crisis and nationalism.[287] Myers discusses it under the sub-tile "The Central Political Parable."[288] Not only that, a larger part of Galilee was "formed into estates that were owned by foreign landlords."[289] It is envisaged that Jesus who championed the God's sovereign reign, the significance of land, and the poor people during his public ministry in Galilee would stand up for the plight of the subjugated groups whom he served them in Galilee. Schottroff denotes, "This parable, in all its details, matches the reality of agriculture in Palestine."[290] It is in this context that one should read and interpret this parable. However, the parable has been interpreted by various scholars in various ways. Those interpretations can be mainly distinguished into three: (a) allegorical,[291] (b) eschatological, and (c) ecclesiological. It is our task to delve into this parable in the context of Jesus-in-movement who resists the material domination.

Mark fits this parable in a context that has been sandwiched by two stories: one which depicts of the chief priests, the scribes, and the elders who questioned Jesus' authority (11: 27-33) and the other which reveals that Jesus is trapped by the Pharisees and Herodians by asking him about paying attributes to Caesar (12: 13-17).[292] The parable can be read as Jesus' quick response to the attack that he had received upon his own authority from the top officials in the temple administration. On the other hand, it could be that Jesus resumes his protest against the material domination which he had already done on his way to Jerusalem. Attention will be given towards the literary arrangement of the parable to examine if Mark strategically arranges to insinuate the agrarian-resistance to the powers in Jerusalem. Mark depicts Jesus as directly

---

286 Horsley, *Jesus and the Powers*, 173.

287 Dodd, *The Parables of the Kingdom*, 96-97.

288 Myers, *Binding the Strong Man*, 308.

289 Recent scholars are convinced that land ownership increased markedly in the first-century C.E. N. F. Fisher, *The Parables of Jesus: Glimpses of God's Reign* (New York: Crossroad, 1990), 127.

290 L. Schottroff, *The Parables of Jesus*, 15.

291 The allegorical method generally relates the "tenants" to Israel's regents and leaders, the messengers to the prophets, the son to Christ; the punishment of the tenant is God's rejection of Israel, and the "others" to them the vineyard now belongs, are the Gentile Church. Cf. Jeremias, *The Parables of Jesus*, 70. Ever since the emergence of A. Julicher's *Gleichnisreden Jesu* (1888), many scholars have regarded the parable as "an allegory constructed in the early Church with reference to the death of Jesus." See, Taylor, *The Gospel According to St. Mark*, 472.

292 Myers opines that Mark 12: 13-17 is crucial in determining Jesus' target of the parable. See, *Binding the Strong Man*, 309.

confronting the ruling elites with land appropriation and then the attributes to Caesar. Does it mean that Mark acknowledge that the Jerusalem powerful elites were directly involved in both the cases? Mark's presentation further assumes that this parable reflects that not only the Roman colonizers, but also their local collaborates, including the Jewish leaders were the landowners.[293] Analysis will be done by assuming that the parable is directed against the temple administrators (Mk 12: 12).[294] The genre of the parable is different from the rest of Jesus' parable in Mark. As a result, its authenticity has been often questioned on the ground that it is an allegory.[295] Some exegetes suspected that this parable is reflective of the theology of the early church. However, the narrative is not purely an allegory. This analysis assumes that this parable is a story which has been developed by the subjugated villagers in Galilee in order to resist the landlords.

4.2.2. Analysis of the Parable

4.2.2.1. The Vineyard, the Owner and the Tenants

Mark begins with the description of a man who had created a vineyard, yet neither Luke nor *The Gospel of Thomas* includes these details. Isaiah also has a story which is similar to this parable (Isa 5: 1-2).[296] Even a cursory reading at the texts reveals both similarity and dissimilarity. It reminds us that the Markan parable is prophetic in nature. The parable impresses us to picture the owner as a wealthy person[297] as he affords of planting a "vineyard" put a "fence" around it, dig a "wine press" and "built a watch-tower" (v. 1). He then leased the vineyard to "tenants" and "went to another country" (v. 1b).[298] Why and how could this happen? The mechanism, according to Heil is that "these 'tenants' will pay their rent to the owner with the produce of the vineyard."[299]

293 Drury, *The Parables in the Gospels*, 66.

294 Roskam, *The Purpose of Mark*, 164.

295 Wilson, *Mark*, 812.

296 For the discussion on the origins of the parable, see J. D. Crossan, "The Parable of the Wicked Husbandmen," *JBL* 90/4 (December 1971): 452.

297 Herzog has a strong argument for this when he says, "it would produce to crop during the four years required for the vines to mature and an unsure harvest in the fifth year, and the owner would need enough capital to pay tenants to nurture and dress the vines, which required constant care." See Herzog, *Parables as Subversive Speech,* 102.

298 Columella, a Roman author of the period is quoted as saying that "for owners of large landholdings advises them that, if owners did not want to live on their lands, they should under no circumstances allow the property to be managed by slaves and a family of overseers." As quoted by Schottroff, *The Parable of Jesus*, 16; also Incigneri, *The Gospel to the Romans*, 73-74.

299 Waetjen points out that many members of the Sanhedrin were absentee landlords of large estates in Galilee and Judea and they were the enemies of the peasants who worked in their land. See, *A Reordering of Power*, 8; also Heil, *Mark as a model for Action*, 235.

J. D. M. Derrett maintains an enlightening idea that building a vineyard was a "speculative investment."[300] If Derrett's claim is real, and as the parable hints, we too can safely conclude that planting a vineyard is "the prerogative of the elite."[301] As Herzog observes, this was "sharecropping arrangement" that displaced the tenants from their own land.[302]

It is an interesting endeavour to explore the identity of the one who planted the vineyard. One clue that the parable provides us is located in the term "went to another country." Even though the Greek word ἀπεδήμησεν, may exactly imply travel to a foreign country,[303] Mark's intention seems to project him as "an international elite."[304] To explore the identity of "tenants" is also highly significant as far as socio-historical research is concerned. The word γεωργός (sing. "farmer," "tenant," and "vinedresser") is used in dative (γεωργοις in vv. 1b, 2,) and genitive case (γεωργων, in v. 2); whereas, all other "wicked verbs" were attributed to him (e.g. ἔδειραν, ἀπεστειλαν, ἐκεφαλαίωσαν, ἠτίμασαν, απέκτειναν, *etc*). It never appears in nominative except in v. 7. Therefore, the farmers or tenants are the subject of the parable rather than the object. Therefore, the tenants can be taken as representation of the subjected people. Almost all the commentators of this parable have designated these tenants as "wicked husbandmen" or "wicked tenants" down through the history.[305] It is important to suspect and challenge this previous designation. Who called these tenants "wicked?" Why did they call him in such a manner? Is it not that Jesus himself refers them simply to "tenants."

4.2.2.2. The Produce of the Vineyard and the Defiance of the Tenants (vv. 2-3)

As anticipated, three slaves were sent to receive the produce of the vineyard "when the season came." Taylor takes the dative noun τῳ καιρῳ ("the season") as "at the time of proper season," *i.e.*, the fifth year (cf. Lev 19: 23-25).[306] As this vineyard is equipped with a winepress, this would not be at the grape harvest, but any time that followed the winemaking.[307] The expression "to

300 J. D. M. Derrett, *Law in the New Testament* (London: Darton, Longman & Todd, 1970), 289.

301 Herzog, *Parables as Subversive Speech*, 103.

302 Herzog, *Parables as Subversive Speech*, 103.

303 For against this view, Waetjen, *A Reordering of Power*, 186.

304 Herzog, *Parables as Subversive Speech*, 104.

305 Bailey suggests that this title assumes that the farmers or tenants are the major players in the drama. See, *Jesus Through Middle Eastern Eyes*, 410. This clearly shows the negligence of the agrarian-resistance by the modern scholarship.

306 Taylor, *The Gospel According to St. Mark*, 474.

307 Gould, *The Gospel According to St. Mark*, 220.

collect from them his share of the produce of the vineyard" recollects the verb ἐχέδοτο ("he leased"). The vineyard is let out on shares, the owner receiving a certain part of the product. Johnson exposes the practices in share-cropping in Judea and Galilee and the methods adapted in this way, to quote:

> Agriculture lands were frequently rented out to tenants on a share-cropping agreement. The farmer paid his own expenses and returned to the owner from one-quarter to one-half the crop. There were men who owned properties in Judea and Galilee, with a wife and a husband in each place.[308]

The first slave is "seized" and "beaten" and is "sent away empty-handed." Verse 2 begins simply with "καὶ" instead of "δέ" which is a contrast to this verse with the succeeding one. Mark probably implies that Jesus anticipated such an act, even before the action occur, and is not surprised by the unkindness of the tenants.

4.2.2.3. Violence Intensified in the Vineyard (vv. 4-5)

The second and third slaves are again sent in succession. The second slave is "beaten" over the head and "insulted." The verb ἐκεφαλαίωσαν has been translated as "wounded in the head" and it is a difficult word to translate and it occurs only here. It can also be translated as "smote on the head."[309] The third slave is "killed." To further intensify the seriousness of the event in the vineyard Mark inserts, "And so it was with many others; some they beat, and others they killed." The involvement of πολλούς ἄλλους (many others), whether they are deputed by the owner or voluntarily or forcefully they offered themselves, is not mentioned; yet however, they were the victims of the violence.

Even the beloved son of the landlord was not spared. The phrase "still one other" points to the last resort. After sending and losing three slaves and "many others" the owner had to send his own "beloved son." The owner hoped that they would respect his son.[310] But the outcome is just the opposite. The tenants said to one another, "This is the heir; come, let us kill him, and the inheritance will be ours." "Inheritance" here means "possession", *i.e.,* the vineyard. This is the most potential reason for the violent actions. The violence has taken place as it is before "they seized him" and "killed him." However, the extraordinary act is that the son is thrown "out of the vineyard." This seems to accord with their intention to take over the inheritance of the vineyard. While the acts of those tenants seem cruel and malicious; their violent acts also picture how pathetic their situation is as they were being landless marginalized people in their own land.

308 Johnson, *A Commentary on the Gospel According to St. Mark*, 195.

309 Cranfield, *The Gospel According to Saint Mark*, 365.

310 Waetjen, *A Reordering of Power*, 187.

4.2.2.4. The Land Belongs to Whom?

With this series of that included the killing of the owner's son, the parable gradually came to an end. At this point, the vineyard and the power over it, is in the hands the tenants.[311] They are in the vineyard, whereas the owner lives afar in a distant foreign country (v. 1). Not only does the owner lose all his slaves and beloved son who would collect his share from the vineyard; he loses all his presumptive heirs. That is why Markan Jesus asks, "What then will the owner of the vineyard do? Two verbs ἐλεύσεται (he will come) and ἀπολέσει (destroy) is the clue to think that status of the vineyard owner.[312] Unless he is a politically sophisticated person, he could not come to his enemies and annihilate them. The expression "to destroy the tenants" does not mean to revoke the lease-agreement, but to kill those tenants who declare an open revolt against him and put the vineyard under controlled. Jesus did not specify to whom the vineyard will be given.

4.2.2.5. Comment on the Parable

Our study reveals that the parable speaks of a palpable conflict between a wealthy landowner and the tenants in the vineyard. This parable, in many ways, matches the reality of life in the agrarian society of Galilee where the rich and the powerful incline to use and misuse their power in ways that are harmful to the peasants.[313] The landowner who leases out his vineyard to the tenants and goes to another country could not be a poor Galilean cultivator, but possibly powerful elite. The peasants are entrusted with the newly planted vineyards belonging to the absentee landlord. They protest violently to pay the landlord from the meager crop of the vineyard. The protest then turns out to be an intensified claim of the ownership of the land. The tenants have survived and won victory for the time being, eventually and inevitably, the landlord would come to do away with them in order to give the land to others. It is highly important for us to recognize the picture that this parable gives us. Finally, it is possible that Jesus speaks the truth to powers regarding what God is going to do with the story which is familiar to them. Mark indicates that the Jewish leaders did not have the support of the masses and they had to find an opportune time for arresting Jesus (v.12).[314] As Liew explicates, "God

311 Scholars like Snodgrass, Fisher and others have argued that there was no legal provision in this regard. The inheritance could be declared ownerless property to be claimed by anyone. Snodgrass, *The Parables of the Wicked Tenants*, 35, 37; Fisher, *The Parables of Jesus*, 127.

312 Scott, *Hear Then the Parable*, 252.

313 Samuel, *A Postcolonial Reading of Mark's Story of Jesus*, 139-140.

314 Goretti, Daniel and Raja, *The Gospel According to Mark*, 192.

will come, God will destroy the Jewish authorities, and God will transfer their positions of leadership to others."[315]

4.3. The Final Parables in the Gospel (Mk 13: 28-36)

Mark clusters two parables at the end of the "Apocalyptic Discourse" (13: 28-29, 34-36). These are the last two parables of Jesus in the Gospel. Mark situates these parables in the context of the destruction of the temple, the persecution of the community and the end times.[316] As discussed earlier, some elements in the discourse assume Mark's representation of the apocalyptic vision of Jesus and reflects more of "the end of the older order"[317] that is to say the imperial regime, rather than the end of the world. With this insight, we shall analyse these parables to see if they contain resistance elements.

4.3.1. Setting, Context and Genre of the Parables

The spatial setting remains Jerusalem. Yet Jesus was no longer in the temple. Jesus and his disciples left the temple and crossed the Kidron Valley to the Mount of Olives.[318] Mark specifically states that Jesus was with a select few disciples "on the Mount of Olives opposite the temple" when he delivered these parables (13: 3). Mark provides us valuable information that four disciples of Jesus—Peter, James, John, and Andrew— "privately" posed a question to Jesus which becomes the immediate context of discourse (13: 3). The spatial setting of the parables is characterized by these select few disciples who secretly asked a question in a secret place.[319] Mark also clearly indicates that Jesus delivered this Apocalyptic Discourse in the context of Jesus' prediction of the fall of the Jerusalem temple (13: 1-2), which is the literary context regarding the disciples asking Jesus vital questions regarding when and how the fall of Jerusalem temple would occur (13: 3-4). In response to the question, Jesus delivered this lengthy teaching (13: 5-37). Mark situates the entire discourse in the literary context of the aftermath of Jesus' direct confrontation to the temple administrators. It is important that we focus on the parables to observe their role in this apocalyptic narrative.

This tradition of apocalypticism entails the "world-upside-down" images. This is to be a time of unprecedented socio-political upheaval in the history of the Jews. As Jesus' open resistance to the Jerusalem temple-state that was controlled by the aristocrats had now reached its culmination in Jesus' prediction of the destruction of the temple, the existing order has come to an

315 Liew, "The Gospel of Mark," 107.

316 Scott, *Hear Then the Parable*, 339.

317 France, *The Gospel of Mark*, 497.

318 France, *The Gospel of Mark*, 495-496.

319 Dowd and Malbon, "The Significance of Jesus' Death in Mark," 290.

end and something new is to take place. France denotes: "Jerusalem, and the temple which is the focus of its authority, is about to lose its central role in God's economy. The divine government, the βασιλεία τοῦ θεοῦ, is to find a new focus."[320] Here, Jesus depicts a topsy-turvy world which will be initiated by disastrous events like rumours of war, earthquakes and famines (vv. 6-8).[321] Notably, this narrative is largely characterized by a series of events which can be highlighted into three major points: (a) persecution of the disciples (vv. 9-13); and (d) setting up of the "desolating sacrilege" in the temple and the persecution of the Judeans (vv. 14-23);[322] and (c) the coming of the Son of Man (vv. 24-27). This series of events features the inversion of the normal relations and hierarchies. The disciples of Jesus, a group of people drawn from villages in Galilee, stand before court to tell justice the powers (vv. 9-11), where brothers betray brothers (v. 12a), fathers rise against children and vice versa (v. 12b). More importantly, Jesus apparently envisages a setting up of "the desolating sacrilege" in the temple that ushers a severe persecution in Judea (v. 14). The people in Judea are advised to flee to hilly areas for refuge (v.14). It is as though those in the fields have better security than those in the buildings (v. 16). False messiahs and prophets would perform signs and miracles and the elected ones would be part of the victims (v. 22).

The state of great confusion adversely would affect even the celestial bodies. The sun would darken, and stars would no longer shine and they would lose their power fallen on earth (vv. 24-25). While the people in Jerusalem and Judea were predicted as undergoing the great distresses, there would be far more reversals with the coming of a new ruler in power and glory. This new ruler, a possibly apocalyptic figure, is expected to come with clouds to collect the people. It is in this context of the coming of the Son of Man that Mark presents the parables. Mark assumes that the disciples of Jesus are a representation of "persecuted and threatened church which is eagerly waiting the parousia of the Son of Man."[323] Before turning to some vital questions about the parables, we must stress that the apocalyptic up-side-down teaching of Jesus stand not in themselves but have been nested and cultivated in the popular culture of the non-elites brimming over with images of reversal.[324]

---

320 France, *The Gospel of Mark*, 497.

321 Theissen, *The Gospels in Context*, 154-156.

322 This verse can be taken in various ways. If the expression "desolating sacrilege" is interpreted with reference to its historical context of the Modein Revolt, it could mean profanation of the temple and the cessation of regular temple activities. Mark depicts that it is "scathing symbol" of the Roman imperial power. See, Suh, *Discipleship and Community*, 143.

323 Hengel, *Studies in the Gospel of Mark*, 41.

324 Such images could be found in the Book of Isaiah, etc.

4.3.2. The Budding of Fig Tree (13: 28-29)

> 28From the fig tree learn its lesson: as soon as its branch becomes tender and puts forth its leaves, you know that summer is near. 29So also, when you see these things taking place, you know that he is near, at the very gates.

Mark depicts that Jesus used the fig tree to convey the message to be ready as the day and hour is unknown. Why does Jesus use the fig tree in particular? Why not other trees? There are obviously two reasons as to why Jesus picked up the image of the fig tree: (a) it is one of the few deciduous trees,[325] and the commonest tree in Judea and Galilee.[326] The fig tree bears leaves in March-April. An early harvest can be expected in May-June. Once the branch of the fig tree becomes tender with the rising of its sap in the spring it begins to sprout leaves, it is common knowledge that summer is near.[327] The Greek term τὸ θέρος means "summer" and it is the time for the fig tree to bear fruits. France thinks that θέρος may have a nuance meaning of ὁ θερισμός ("harvest time").[328] Tendering of the fig leaves which are assured of the promise that harvest—the happiest and moment of joy for the agrarian communities—will follow.[329] The next verse denotes the application of the parable of fig tree. The pronoun ὑμεις is emphatic, distinguishing the restricted "you" as an address only to his disciples. What does this phrase "when you see these things taking place" refer to? According to Gould, the expression ταῦτα πάντα ("these things") refers to "the besieging [Roman] armies" and "the sufferings of the siege" (cf. Mk. 5:14).[330] Edwards suggests ταῦτα πάντα to refer to "the events leading up to the fall of Jerusalem in vv. 5-13."[331] Scott suggests "signs listed throughout the chapter [Mk. 13]."[332] And "at the very gates" is a common figurative expression of nearness. There is no doubt that the fall of the temple is near. The other verse that follows explain in a more vivid way that "these things" will occur in the then generation (vv. 30-31).

---

325 Edwards convincingly argues the uniqueness of the fig tree from other. Trees like olive, oak, terebinth, and other evergreen trees are not capable of announcing the change of seasons as they never lose their leaves in winter. But the leaves of fig tree fall in winter and in the spring, its branches grow tender with buds announcing that the summer is near. See, *The Gospel According to Mark*, 404-405.

326 France, *The Gospel of Mark*, 537.

327 Heil, *Mark as a Model for Action*, 268; Scott, *Hear Then the Parable*, 340.

328 France, *The Gospel of Mark*, 537.

329 On the other possible meaning, see Myers, *Binding the Strong Man*, 345.

330 Gould, *The Gospel of Mark*, 253.

331 Edwards, *The Gospel According to Mark*, 405. For detail discussion, See Suh, *Discipleship and Community*, 49-50.

332 Scott, *Hear Then the Parable*, 339.

4.3.3. The Watchman (13: 34-36)

> 34It is like a man going on a journey, when he leaves home and puts his slaves in charge, each with his work, and commands the doorkeeper to be on the watch.

This is the last parable in Mark's Gospel. Mark sums up the discourse with the word βλέπετε ("look' or "beware") and ἀγρυπνιετε ("be wakeful" or "keep alert" in v. 33). In order to make the imperatives meaningful and more comprehensible to the disciples, Jesus employed this one-line story of the absent household. The story is most likely a combination of Luke's Parable of the Watching Servants (12: 37ff.) with reminiscences of the Parable of the Talents or Pounds (Mat 25: 14-30; Lk 19: 11-27). In this manner, Jesus warned the disciples that they must be as alert as servants who diligently await the return of the lord of the house. The parabolic saying starts with the phrase "ὡς ἄνθρωπος ἀπόδημος" (v. 34a). The word ὡς signifies a "simile" which illustrates the exhortations to watchfulness (vv. 33, 35).[333] After which the simile is combined with the exhortation to "keep awake" within the context of the parable. The phrase ἄνθρωπος ἀπόδημος (lit. "a man away from home on a journey") recalls the figure of the absentee landlord in the Parable of Vineyard (12: 1-12). The figure of the absentee householder is familiar to the Jesus' tradition (Mat 24: 45-51; 25: 14-30; Lk 12: 35-38; 19: 11-27; Mk 12: 1-12). Unlike the other references to the absentee landlord, the householder in this parable represents the Son of Man. The householder left behind his household to his slaves "each with his work" at his departure (v. 34).

Of all the responsibilities that are assigned to slaves, special attention is focused upon the θυρωρῷ ("doorkeeper") by specifying his responsibility of watching.[334] In order to keep the doorkeeper's assignment "to be on watch" at the centre of the parable, Jesus obscured not only the purpose and the destiny of the householder, but also the time of his return. Thus, one thing certain about this householder is the uncertainty of his return. Jesus told the disciples the uncertainty by adopting the Roman time-reckoning. The Romans divided the twelve hours of the night into four quarters or watches–probably three hours each, such as: 6-9 p.m.; 9 p.m.-12 midnight; 12 midnight-3 a.m., and 3 a.m.- 6 a.m.[335] Mark mentions all the watches: "evening, "midnight," "cock crow," and "dawn" (v. 36). The doorkeeper is expected to watch throughout all four watches.[336]

333 Taylor acknowledges an abrupt beginning of the parable. See, *The Gospel According to St. Mark*, 523.

334 Taylor, *The Gospel According to St. Mark*, 523; France, *The Gospel of Mark*, 537.

335 For detailed discussion, T. W. Martin, "Watch during the Watches (Mark 13:35)," *JBL* 120/4 (2001): 685-701.

336 Myers, *Binding the Strong Man*, 347.

4.3.4. Comment on the Parables

From our study, it is clear that the world-upside-down images are something of a resistance to the dominant temple-state which is actually devised by the agrarian rural communities as a symbolic substitute for their present world. Mark brings back here the ideal of God's reign in its real sense. For Mark, Jesus assured his disciples of the glorious coming of the Son of Man which would bring God's reign after the end of the present aeon (vv. 24-27). Jesus, however, kept the date or time of as mystery. No one including "the angels in heaven" and "the son" but "only the father" knows the day or hour (v. 32). However, Jesus directed his disciples to learn the παραβολην (or lesson) from the natural phenomenon of the growth of a fig tree. Both the parabolic sayings and the one-liner story denote watchfulness for the great events that are to come. The last parable in Mark exhibits three different individuals: a man, slaves and a doorkeeper. The man is presented as wealthy. The servants have been "empowered with authority" to do the owner' works. However, the doorkeeper (θυρωρῷ), the least employee of all is commanded that "he should watch." Here the lowest of all ranks—the subaltern—has been given the privilege to be the first to witness the coming of the Son of Man.

5. Conclusion

We have explored the agrarian-resistance motifs in the parables in Mark's Gospel by situating them within the context of Jesus' campaign in Galilee and the regions beyond. Our study reveals the vital role that has been played by the interrelationship between the public and private discourses of Jesus that are displayed in the composition of Mark's Gospel. In Mark's Gospel, fourteen out of twenty-two parables are onstage performance of Jesus; whereas the remaining eight parables belonged to offstage performance. Most of all the parables in public discourse, excepting the Parable of Sowing on Various Landscapes (3: 3-8) are evidently directed against the Pharisees, the Scribes, the Herodians, and the Sadducees who were the ruling elites and the collaborates of Rome. Whenever Mark links those parables directly with the Jewish leaders, these parables served as riposte of Jesus to the imperial values that were demeaning to the rural community. We also find out that Mark maintains the relationship between the public and private discourses. Each of the parables uttered before the public become the silent partner of those parables which are delivered in private. For instance, the Parable of Sowing on Various Landscapes and the Parable of Defilement contains elements of disguise and anonymity, and therefore require interpretations in private (4: 10-12, 13-20; 7: 17-23). Scott's theory of various political discourses helps us to understand the political significance of the interplay between public and private discourses to the subjugated people. It is safe to conclude that the parables in Mark's Gospel are part and parcel of Jesus' campaign as he defended, disguised and declared the hidden transcript of dignity and indignation cultivated in villages to the powers. On many occasions, the parables seem to be the basic instrument for speaking truth to power for Jesus on stage (*e.g.*, Mk 2: 18-22; 3: 20-27; 4: 3-9, 26-34; 7: 14-15; 12: 1-12); but on other occasions they serve as a didactic tool of Jesus off stage (Mk 10: 25; 13: 28, 34). This remark implies that Jesus' parables are not solely meant for didactic purposes, rather they are also meant for politics of disguise and anonymity which the very integral part of agrarian-resistance. Details about the theological meaning of resistance embedded in the parables of Mark will be focused upon in the next chapter.

Chapter 5

The Theology of the Agrarian-Resistance as Reflected in the Parables of Jesus God and the Subalterns

Our study so far, in the hope that it has yielded good results, has been limited within the exploration of agrarian-resistance leitmotifs that are embedded in Mark's Gospel and particularly in the parables of Jesus. The crucial task in the thesis is to spell out the theological meaning of the agrarian-resistance in the parables by linking it with a particular theological theme, and to analyze it within a given political context. Understandings of Jesus' campaign in Galilee and the regions beyond are necessarily influenced by the manner in which one theologizes resistance. Too often, the term resistance has been perceived variedly, sometimes as a synonym for challenge, protest and even renewal. The scholarly works of Horsley is illustrative in this regard. In his *Jesus and Empire: The Kingdom of God and the New World Disorder* (2003), Horsley tries to understand Jesus' movement as a movement of renewal that is based on the Israelite little tradition that had been cultivated in the villages.[1] Horsley emphasizes upon Jesus' loyalty to the old tradition and the subsequent renewal of it while minimizing the subversive aspect.

This chapter tries to explicate the theological meaning of the agrarian-resistance leitmotifs that have been explored in the previous chapters. To carry out the task, we shall link the resistance themes with God's kingdom in Mark's Gospel and see how God's kingdom is set in favour of the subaltern masses in Galilee in the first-century C.E. In the midst of various approaches to and interpretations of God's kingdom siding with apocalyptic and eschatological

1 Horsley's main argument is that the Roman empire was a great factor that brought disorder for the Jewish community and Jesus' message and the kingdom of God is an attempt to re-order. See, *Jesus and Empire*, especially, chapters 4 and 5.

viewpoints, Borg's exploration of the prophetic conflict and mystical aspects in Jesus' understanding of God's kingdom encourages the facilitation and inclusion of political aspects in this endeavour.[2] More importantly, Crossan's thesis of a "brokerless kingdom" helps us to understand the Markan kingdom of the sayings in a subaltern context which is different from the elitist view.[3] Our assumption is that the idea of God's kingdom in Mark is more of counter-ideology that comprises an alternate to the values and views of the urban powerful elites. Special attention shall also be given to find out how Jesus used the parables as a vehicle for resistance to the domination.

1. God, God's Kingdom and the Subalterns in the Interpretation of Parables

The notion of God or God's kingdom remains a primary concern in the interpretation of the parables. The modern parable study has flourished largely due to the contributions of the great anti-dogmatic thinkers—*viz*., F. Schleiermacher, A. Jülicher and W. Wrede—who rendered new meanings to God, parables, and the Gospel of Mark respectively. Schleiermacher gives us the insight that God is not a God of dogma but a God of experience and he brought the notion of God to the centre of theological discourse by minimizing the element of dogma and emphasizing upon the experiential elements of the concept. Jülicher teaches us that the parables of Jesus are not allegory and that they should be understood in their historical context rather than the Christian faith and doctrine of the early church as well as the medieval church. Wrede persuades scholars to claim that each Gospel is heavily dogmatic in its presentation of Jesus, and thus he successfully deconstructed the picture of Jesus' ministry as constructed upon the priority of Mark's Gospel. It is obvious that the modern interpretation of the parables—though gradually and implicitly—is largely deviating from the allegorical approach that was determined by the faith, doctrines and practices of the elite interpreters towards what we envisage as "reading from below." However, since theological discussion on the parables has always been analysed within the values and viewpoints of the western scholars, their other-worldly understanding of eschatology always obscures the political significance of God's kingdom. The parable scholarship suffers a serious setback from the exclusion of politics. Thus, a decoding of subaltern politics to unpack the agrarian resistance embedded in the parables is an evitable task.

---

2 Borg situates Jesus' campaign in the context of Rome's domination and tries to see what it meant to be 'Israel.' See, *Conflict, Holiness & Politics*, especially 17-20, 51.

3 Crossan, *The Historical Jesus*, 224-416.

1.1. Bringing 'God' In

Schleiermacher, the father of the Protestant Liberalism, has been credited for his contribution to the bringing in of the notion of God in modern theological discourse. For him, God is discerned in one's awareness of an absolute dependence upon God. He insists that the task of theology is to explicate the nature and content of this distinctive consciousness. Schleiermacher further denotes Christianity as essentially a redemptive religion which was grounded in "the constant potency of Christ's God-consciousness."[4] However, scholars till the recent past were not critical enough to see what made Schleiermacher minimize the dogmatic character while emphasizing the experiential aspect of God in his theological discourse. Till recently, the scholars hardly put effort to unearth the sociopolitical circumstances that determined Schleiermacher to have arrived at this conclusion. With the arrival of postcolonial frameworks, attempts have been initiated to expose their engagements to powers. For instance, J. Reiger proposes the "emergence of middle class" as the decisive factor in Schleiermacher's experiential understanding of God.[5] Obviously, his political involvement in the resistance movement against Napoleon and the rising of France made Schleiermacher perceive of Jesus as calling people into fellowship and associating him with the kingdom of God. For Schleiermacher the kingdom of God is the corporate human God-consciousness which is the existence of God in human nature and which comes into being as a result of Christ's God-consciousness.[6]

It was Ritschl who brought the concept of the kingdom of God to the modern theological discussions. In his *The Christian Doctrine of Justification and Reconciliation* (1902), Ritschl explicates that the kingdom of God is the outstanding feature of Christian doctrine. That the kingdom of God is the moral principle in the redemptive history of Christianity is evident in Ritschl's discussion. For Ritschl, the kingdom of God is the moral organization of humanity through action which is inspired by love. Moreover, it has a specifically theological aspect and is the common end of God and of Christianity as a community. The kingdom of God is the goal to which the believers direct their spiritual and ethical activity.[7] The theological heritage of Ritschl was carried on and extended by the Ritschlian School. One of the major scholars of the school was W. Herrmann, who insists that the kingdom

---

4 F. Schleiermacher, *The Christian Faith* (New York: Harper and Row, 1963), 385.

5 J. Reiger, "Friedrich Schleiermacher" in *Empire and the Tradition: New Readings of Classical Theologians,* ed. K. Pui-lan, D. H. Compier and J. Reiger (Minneapolis: Fortress Press, 2007), 271.

6 *The Christian Faith*, 723.

7 A. Ritschl, *The Christian Doctrine of Justification and Reconciliation*, Vol. 3 (Edinburgh: T&T Clark, 1902), 11-13.

of God comes as a miraculous act of God from another and not developed out of the present order. Since Hermann's emphasis is upon the role of God in realisation of the kingdom of God, he argues that it is God's gift rather than the result of human achievement.[8] Another Ristchlian scholar, A. v. Harnack has sharpened the dimension of the future and is immanent in his attempt to explicate Jesus' understanding of the kingdom of God. Harnack insists that Jesus retained the dualistic view on two kingdoms; one of God and the other of evil, which are in conflict until God will defeat the devil in future – in his reading of the parables of Jesus.[9] Those who read the Gospels in accordance with Herrmann may emphasize that Jesus never described the kingdom of God in his parables; and those who do the same with Harnack possibly would insist that one must read the parables to know the kingdom of God and its meaning.[10] Unlike Ritschl who regards community as space for the kingdom, Harnack seem to hold the opinion that the kingdom of God would arrived by coming to the individual and entering into his soul and laying hold of it. Harnack renders importance to 'reign' in the hearts of individuals.[11] We must take note of insight from Harnack that the essence of Jesus' message is not found in his apocalyptic imagery, but in his description of God and the soul and the soul to God. The Protestant liberalism presented God's kingdom as supernatural and as a gift from above and not a product of the socio-political experiences of the subalterns, not on the basis of land values, but purely as a religious blessing. They focused upon the inner link with the living God and for them the kingdom of God is the most important experience that a person could have, that on which everything else depends – it permeates and dominants his/her whole existence, because sin is forgiven and mystery is banished. We shall see how their understanding of God and God's kingdom has an impact upon the parable study.

1.2. Imminent Eschatology and the Exclusion of Subaltern Politics

As Crossan denotes, modern scholarship always presents God's kingdom—"in its advent from heaven to earth"—as "an eschatological" or "apocalyptic kingdom."[12] It is Dodd who establishes the perspective of viewing the parables as the parables of the kingdom.[13] It must be noted that Dodd's view is part of the

8 W. Herrmann, "*The Communion of the Christian with God,*" ed. R. T. Voelkel (Philadelphia: Fortress Press, 1971), 94-97; Systematic Theology, ed. N. Micklem and K. A. Saunders (New York: Macmillan. 1927), 43-49.

9 A. v. Harnack, *What is Christianity?* trans. T. B. Saunders (New York: Harper & Row, 1957), 34-37, 51-62.

10 Harnack, *What is Christianity?* 37-37.

11 Harnack, *What is Christianity?* 51-62.

12 Crossan, *The Power of Parable*, 118.

13 Dodd, *The Parables of the Kingdom.*

ongoing eschatological school that had reacted to the Ritschlian school which discussed Jesus' understanding of kingdom of God in the light of "the great tradition" of Jerusalem that rendered emphasis upon an other-worldly character. Earlier, *i.e.*, before Dodd, Weiss and Schweitzer had claimed the "Kingdom as imminent, and in some sense even perhaps proleptically present"[14] with their *consequente Eschatologie* reading of Jesus. Dodd, unconvinced by this claim, argues that the kingdom of God had actually occurred in Jesus' ministry and the eschatology of Jesus was a "realised eschatology." This rendered a necessity for Dodd to take "special account of the Gospel parables, particularly those which deal with the theme of the Kingdom of God."[15] He groups them into two clusters: first, the "parables of crisis"[16] which exhorts their hearers to watchfulness;[17] and second, the "parables of growth"[18] which declare the arrival of the kingdom as a small and seemingly insignificant presence in the world that will, in time, grow to its full stature.[19] Even though Dodd had the skill to handle God's reign satisfactorily in relation to the parables of Jesus, he is much obsessed with the issue of time (*i.e.* present or future) in the proclamation of Jesus. Dodd provides an insight into which one could see that the reign of God had arrived in history. However, Dodd's insight is not sufficient enough to penetrate deep into the layers of the resistance motifs, and to suggest that the motifs were a major key towards an understanding of the parables.

Even so, Dodd's impact is so great that scholars after him could not but be aware of how deeply one's understanding of the parables affected one's interpretation of the kingdom of God in the message of Jesus and *vice versa.*[20] Jeremias was aware of this as it was clearly reflected in *The Parables of Jesus*. Jeremias was also convinced that each parable communicated only a single point. However, as Herzog observes, Dodd had learnt that the meaning of the parable needs not be confined to the moral reading as proposed by Jülicher;

14 As paraphrased in Perrin's *Jesus and the Language of the Kingdom*, 37. Borg accuses Weiss and Schweitzer of being responsible to establish the idea that "politics were of no concern to Jesus." Both of them linked God's kingdom with an imminent end to the world. We must note that they were mere voices reacting to their predecessors who held non-eschatological ideas. See, Borg, *Conflict, Holiness & Politics*, 8.

15 Dodd, *The Parables of the Kingdom of God*, vii.

16 Parables of crisis consist of the parables of the Faithful and Unfaithful Servants, the Waiting Servants, the Thief at Night, and the Ten Virgins. For Dodd, these parables are intended to be referred to directly in terms of the expected second advent of Christ and to inculcate preparedness for that approaching crisis.

17 Dodd, *The Parables of the Kingdom*, 122-138.

18 Parables of Growth are a group of parables that have been distinguished by the idea of growth: those of the Sower, the Tares, the Seed Growing Secretly and the Mustard Seed.

19 Dodd, *The Parables of the Kingdom*, 140-156.

20 Perrin, *Jesus and the Language of the Kingdom,* 98.

rather, it could grow out of the theological themes that were associated with Jesus' ministry.[21] As mentioned above, Dodd limits himself to a theme, *i.e.*, the proclamation that the reign of God has arrived; but Jeremias organizes the parables into ten distinct theological themes. He neither confines the meaning of parables into a single point as suggested by Jülicher nor accepts Dodd's "realized eschatology,"[22] but Jeremias could still apparently reveal his indebtedness to Dodd in aspects concerning the centrality of God's reign in the parables of Jesus. "All nine of his theological themes were basically elaborations of the meaning of the arrival of the reign of God in the person and work of Jesus."[23] Jeremias has also remarked that "the parables are weapons of warfare."[24] This clearly touches upon the resistance motifs, though not necessarily the agrarian ones. He locates the parables in a situation of conflict and was thus able to comment that the parables "correct, reprove, attack."[25] In the same manner, Jeremias' insight into "the hortatory use of parables by the Church"[26] helps us to reflect upon how the parables have been removed from their polemical context in Jesus' ministry and reset them in the Gospels.

On the other hand, Bultmann and G. Bornkamm have pursued this solution by using existentialist philosophy to supply the hermeneutical key that is required to unlock the meaning of the apocalyptic Jesus materials. In both cases, the parables are removed from their Gospel contexts. In their search for the original form of parables and authenticity, form-critics isolated the parables of Jesus from their literary contexts by claiming to find a new context in the actual situation of Jesus. The existentialist approach had removed Jesus from his historical and political context. Herzog comments, "Rather than moving among the peasant villages and traditional culture of Galilee, Jesus moves into the alienated world of Europe after World War I."[27] The modern interpreters of the parables have severely limited the historical impact of Jesus and the historical significance of his parables.[28] While they are helpful as long as they resorted to Jesus' actual situation for the original setting of the parables, they hardly considered that Jesus himself was connected with a movement. Their attempts to situate the parables find no better setting than the Gospel themselves. Gowler rightly observes, "Dodd's 'original setting'—as is every

21 Herzog, *Parables as Subversive Speech*, 10.

22 Jeremias opted for some variation on the theme of eschatology "in the process of realization." Jeremias.

23 Herzog, *Parables as Subversive Speech*, 11.

24 Jeremias, *The Parables of Jesus*, 21.

25 Jeremias, *The Parables of Jesus*, 21.

26 Jeremias, *The Parables of Jesus*, 42-48.

27 Herzog, *Parables as Subversive Speech*, 36.

28 Horsley, *Jesus in Context*, 186.

attempt to postulate an original specific historical event—is a hypothetical and reconstructed context."[29]

On many counts, the study of the parables and the kingdom of God in the last century can be seen largely as a chain of reactions. The works of Jülicher, Wrede and Schweitzer invited reactions from two different lines of thought, *viz.*, eschatological (Dodd, Jeremias, *etc.*) and existential (Bultmann, Bornkamm, *etc*). In the process, we find imminent and existential interpretations that were strongly established as the only interpretation of the parables and the kingdom of God. As a result of both over-emphasis and non-emphasis of the eschatological aspect, the dimension subaltern politics is missing in the interpretation of the Gospels. This insight prompts us to take up the problems and challenges of reading the kingdom passages from the perspective of the subalterns.

1.3. God's Kingdom from the Subaltern Perspective: Problems and Challenges

Apart from the Protestant liberal understanding of God and the dynamics of God's kingdom, the *Sitz-im-Leben* of Jesus remains the most indispensable starting point in terms of the understanding of the theology of Jesus' parables. Most of the prominent parable scholars, who employed the form-critical approach, tried to situate the parables in the context of the historical Jesus. For this is inevitable for the recovery of the original meaning of Jesus' parables. To attain what they assumed in terms of the original meaning and authenticity of the parables, the modern parable scholars have consistently maintained the difference between "the parables of historical Jesus" and "the parables in the Gospels."[30] The goal of their interpretation is to establish the parables in the Gospels back to the historical Jesus. While their works are highly appreciable and widely considered as a great achievement, the historical critics hardly considered the historical Jesus as being connected with subaltern politics. They set a trend that helps us to read the parables in Jesus' own context while leaving us with a task that delineates the subaltern politics in the agrarian context. In this section, we attempt to understand the agrarian-resistance embedded in the parables within the scale of Jesus-in-movement.

Why does the quest for the historical Jesus or at least the *Sitz-im-Leben* of Jesus become a prerequisite task for the parable interpreters? There are three scholars who are responsible for the present state of the parable studies, *viz.* Jülicher, Wrede, and Schweitzer. Jülicher established that the parables of Jesus were not allegories and thus he brought the parables down to their historical contexts. Wrede has encouraged the Gospel scholars to find out the setting

29 Gowler, *What Are They Saying About the Parables?* 7.

30 Gowler, *What Are They Saying About the Parables?* 3.

of the parables in aspects other than their setting in the Gospels, because he felt that Mark is not a reliable historical source of Jesus. Hence, it becomes necessary to separate the parables of Jesus from their literary contexts in the Gospels in order to establish their meaning as parables of Jesus. As observed by Herzog, "The removal historical Jesus and the parables of Jesus from their Gospel frameworks created the need for new contexts within which each could be understood."[31] When Schweitzer looked to the parables for clues in his thoroughgoing eschatological reading of Jesus,[32] he becomes the first to offer a new context in terms of Jesus' parables, *i.e.*, thoroughgoing eschatology. It is obvious from the discussion above that the earliest modern parable scholars had to work within the already established eschatological parameters that had been denoted by the protestant liberal scholars. As a result, many parable scholars have dealt extensively with God's kingdom in relation to imminent eschatology. Seldom does this central message of Jesus, *i.e.*, kingdom of God, receive the treatment which it deserves in the parables, as it depicts God's activity in the history of the subalterns.[33] In this section, we shall discuss the importance of understanding the kingdom of God from the subaltern perspective. First, our task is to sketch out in brief, the subaltern concerns and theories and then we shall highlight the significance of the subaltern perspective.

1.3.1. The Subaltern Reading Theory

As we attempt to re-contextualize the parables in the context of subaltern politics, we must look into the subaltern methodological breakthrough that occurred during the last few decades. The publication of the first volume of the *Subaltern Studies* (1982) series is regarded to be the turning point in scholarly inquiry of the people's movement past and present. It must be recalled that *Subaltern Studies* is preceded by the 1978 release of E. Said's masterpiece, *Orientalism*, a study that linked knowledge, and its construction and dissemination, to power and exploitation. That the alliance between the subaltern and Saidian methods exerted its influence over the following years in the manner in which the academic investigation is conducted in South Asia is evident in Said's *Representations of the Intellectual* that was released in 1994. Said argues that the intellectual's essential role is to 'speak truth to powers,' that is, to speak out against injustice and to stand morally with and advocate

31 Herzog, *Parables as Subversive Speech*, 40.

32 A. Schweitzer maintained that Jesus' understanding of the Kingdom of God was apocalyptic and other worldly and that its advent was imminent. See, *The Quest for Historical Jesus,* 351-397.

33 Dalit interprets the subversive nature of Jesus in proclamation of the kingdom of God. See, Goretti, Daniel, and Raja, "The Gospel According to Mark", 171.

for, the world's dispossessed and marginalized.[34] In short, the concern of this innovative methodology is to bring the condition of marginalized people in South Asia to the attention of powers in the region and beyond. Obviously, the subaltern discourse came as a harsh indictment to the existing Euro-centric academic system that maintains, defends and even creates hierarchies of power. Because, "speaking truth to power"[35] is one of the basic tenets of the subaltern theory. In the words of Guha, it is a critique to "the distortions and imbalances generated by ... trend in academic work on South Asian questions."[36] The concern of the subaltern theory is not a new invention either by Guha or Said. In the 1960s, E. Zelliot had extensively studied the Dalit movement in India from what is now called "subaltern perspective."[37] She not only did break new grounds, but also laid the foundation for methodological breakthroughs that occurred nearly two decades after she began her work.[38] Various works of Scott have focused upon the marginalized people in South-east Asia. These scholars persistently analysed how marginalized people speak truth to power. While Guha and Said dealt with the intellectuals as speaking truth to power for the subalterns, Zelliot made considerable efforts to "let the subaltern speak" for themselves. At this juncture in 1988, we have G. C. Spivak asking a seminal question, "Can the Subaltern Speak?"[39] Scott's *Domination and the Arts of Resistance* (1990) denotes that the subaltern can speak. Yet, their voice is a "voice under domination" in terms of political disguise and anonymity.

1.3.2. The Relevance of Subaltern Perspective in Jewish Context

When we analyse the subaltern perspective in approaching the Biblical texts, we are aware of the complexities of the ancient Jewish society. The Jewish society—inclusive of former Israelites—was at that time very complex and highly stratified. The composition of the society includes priestly aristocrats, scribes and Pharisees, social class, peasant masses and marginalized ones.

34 E. Said, *Representations of the Intellectual: The Reith Lectures* (New York: Pantheon Books, 1994).

35 "Speaking truth to power" holds a prominent place in Quaker history. It is often associated with a meeting between G. Fox and O. Cromwell in 1653.

36 R. Guha, *Subaltern Studies I* (New Delhi: Oxford University Press, 1994 [1982]), viii.

37 She extensively writes on Dalit issues and these are her works that were published during the 1960s: "Buddhism and Politics in Maharastra," in *South Asian Politics and Religion*, ed. D. E. Smith (Princeton: Princeton University Press, 1966); "Background of the Mahar Buddhist Conversion," in *Studies on Asia*, edited by R. Sakai (Lincoln: University of Nebraska, 1966).

38 M. Bhagavan and A. Feldhaus, "Introduction" in *Speaking Truth to Power: Religion, Caste, and the Subaltern Question in India*, edited by them (New Delhi: Oxford University Press, 2008), 2.

39 G. C. Spivak, "Can the Subaltern Speak?" in *Marxism and the Interpretation of Culture*, ed. C. Nelson and L. Grossberg (Urbana: University of Illinois Press, 1988), 271-313.

Horsley divides the Jewish society of Jesus' time into three main groups: the dominant priestly aristocracy, the educated middle strata and the rural peasants.[40] The three distinctive groups that have been mentioned cannot in any sense be expected to have a similar degree of resistance or even acceptance to the domination. Each social movement has a location in the social structure and the revolutionary potential of certain classes must be examined historically. Any research on resistance must identify the sociopolitical location of the actions under discussion. The rural peasants, who were at the bottom of the societal structure, can surely be identified as the subalterns.[41] Guha, in the preface of this volume, defines:

> ... word 'subaltern' in the title stands for the meaning as given in the *Concise Oxford Dictionary*, that is, 'of inferior rank.' it will be used ... as a name for the general attribute of subornation in South Asian society whether this is expressed in terms of class, caste, age, gender, and office or in any other way ... There will be much ...which should relate to the history, politics, economics and sociology of subalternity as well as to the studies, ideologies and belief systems – in short, the culture informing that condition.[42]

Modern biblical scholarship has focused mainly upon the structure and policies of the imperialists and the role played by the dominant priestly aristocracy and the educated middle class in resisting or restoring the imperial domination. Hence, the initiatives on the part of the rural peasantry in resisting the Hellenistic and Roman powers as well as their local allies have been noticed by very few scholars. Peasants of various space and time, as D. K. Singha Roy observes, have always "borne the brunt of extreme forms of subordination and oppression in society first by being members of the lower strata of the social and economic hierarchy."[43] Peasants have always been portrayed as occupying a lower position in the political structure of the society. In the Jewish context, as the Gospels denote, peasantry represents a vast body of the socially deprived people, such as: landless agriculture labourers, sharecroppers, tenants, poor artisans and small and marginal cultivators (*e.g.* Mat 20: 1-16; 21: 28-32; Mk1-12; Lk 19: 11-27, *etc.*). In spite of the fact that the peasant societies in Judea and Galilee had undergone rapid transformation under Hellenistic and Roman rule, their social and economic oppression and domination by the powers assumingly continued unabated in one form or the other.

---

40 Horsley, *Jesus and the Spiral of Violence,* 16.

41 S. Clark, "Viewing the Bible through the Eyes and Ears of the Subalterns in India," *Biblical Interpretation* 10/3 (2002): 245-248.

42 Guha, *Subaltern Studies I*, vii.

43 Debal K. Singha Roy, *Peasant Movements in Post-colonial: Dynamics of Mobilization and Identity* (New Delhi/Thousand Oaks/London, 2004), 1.

Moreover, modern Biblical historiography has confused the agrarian resistance as a mere by-product of the initiative of the dominant social groups, such as: Pharisees, Sadducees, Essenes, in their course of the anti-imperialist struggles. Notably, the struggles of the Jewish peasantry of Hellenistic-Roman period had a history prior to the advent of the initiatives of the dominant social groups. Ostensibly, they had continued to move in a parallel direction throughout the Hellenistic and Roman regime and at times as a part of that stream of national movement which occurred under the leadership of Hasmonean priests. It is their movements that provided the Jewish peasantries a social and political identity.

The agrarian movements in the Jewish history were, however, not episodic. They underwent a process of transformation along with the broad social, economic and political transformations of the whole society. As already discussed in chapter 3 of this work, during and after the Modein Revolt, the resistance movement gave birth to a network of religious organizations. The religious outfits, such as: Essences, Pharisees, Sadducees, along with various religious crowds, emerged actively while participating in resistance movements of various forms while using God as the major factor in terms of resistance. Moreover, these religious groups facilitated the movements through the writing of literature. In turn, their faith in God served as a primary factor in the negotiation of the movements' collective identity. It is vital that we pay attention to how far their faith in God had provided the activists in the dissent movements with expressive symbols, icons, and rituals which served to rally and to embody their grievances publicly in powerful ways. An analysis of resistance movements in the Jewish context demands that we focus more on the historical resources that denote that the God factor had often contributed to resistance or protest movements. For the core motivation and sustaining nurturance of many, if not the majority, of Jewish activists was their religiosity. However, there has been a tendency to negate God's factor in the people's struggle among the ancient and modern scholars. We must examine the notion of God in relation to the subalterns in the parables of Jesus in Mark in order to ascertain whether the dynamics of God's reign are set in favour of the marginalised subalterns.

1.3.3. Some Christological Issues

The history of modern parable study is an integral part of the quest for the historical Jesus. There have been a lot of suggestions concerning who Jesus was and who narrated the parables. However, the exclusion of subaltern politics generates Christological confusion. Herzog highlights,

> Jeremias envisions Jesus as cross between a rabbi and a Christian theologian; Kenneth Bailey believes him to have been a poet and peasant;

> John Dominic Crossan, a master of metaphor and poet of the interior apocalypse; Dan Via, a purveyor of existential philosophy through comic and tragic stories; Robert funk, poetic philosopher who inaugurated a new language tradition that undermined its ossified predecessor. By turns, Jesus is a poet, philosopher, ethics, theologian, storyteller in the tradition of Franz Kafka or Jorge Luis Borges, "Christian rabbi, Jewish rabbi, Lutheran theologian, preacher, and Christian minister in disguise.[44]

This quotation conveys to us a differing portrayal of Jesus by the western methodological individualism. While a group of scholars portrayed Jesus as an individual teacher, preacher and even poet; other scholars depict him as an individual eschatological or apocalyptic prophet. We must relate Jesus with a movement and not as an individual actor. The formation of Jesus' movement is not *ex nihilo*. It is inherently better not to consider Jesus and his disciples as the founder of the movement. Against the Jesus backdrop, there were agrarian movements that resisted the domination. It is assumed that Jesus spearheaded the movement out of its sequestered sites and brought it out from its micro to macro level. Moreover, the modern historical critics largely failed to situate Jesus and his activities within power relations including the recent ones. Borg's *Conflict, Holiness & Politics* is an attempt to reconstruct the figure of the historical Jesus in the context of Rome's domination. Borg depicts Jesus as a holy man and a prophet as well as a sage who tried to bring about the renewal of Israel for the establishment of a holy nation.[45] Another major contribution to the reconstruction of the historical Jesus is Crossan's *The Historical Jesus: The Life of a Mediterranean Jewish Peasant*. In his attempt to interpret the historical Jesus against the backdrop of the agrarian-resistance in the first-century in Galilee and Judea, Crossan attempts to understand Jesus as a "peasant cynic" who announced the brokerless kingdom of God.[46] Crossan's portrayal of Jesus as a peasant and cynic and it captures well the elements of Scott's "resistance below the line" in Jesus' campaign. However, Cynic sages in the Hellenistic world were said to be active in the urban marketplace and there were more or less individualistic in nature. Thus, we need to go back to the Markan references to the identity of Jesus.

According to Mark, Jesus was a carpenter in the small village of Nazareth in Galilee (Mk 6: 3).[47] Jesus neither belonged to the priestly aristocracy nor the scribal middle class. The carpenter, according to C. U. Wolf, was "a craftsman who built yokes, plows, threshing boards, benches, beds, boxes, coffins, boats,

---

44 Herzog, *Parables as Subversive Speech*, 14-15.

45 Borg, *Conflict, Holiness & Politics*, 249-250.

46 Crossan, *The Historical Jesus*, 421-422.

47 For more details on Jesus' occupation and social status, see Oakman, *Jesus and the Economic Questions of His Day*, 176-182.

and houses."[48] Jesus' mission statement—"for that is what I came out to do" (1: 38)—takes us back to the days when Jesus was the carpenter for the agrarian villagers.[49] We must ask what determined Jesus to have the conviction to come out to resist the powers. This is a vital question in the context of subaltern politics. Scott's resistant theory suggests that the subalterns speak words of anger, revenge, and self-assertion in relatively safety places.[50] Supposedly, the house of Jesus in Nazareth was not only the place where the villagers met regularly for the repairing and maintenance of their agricultural tools, but it also provided a dissident space where they could freely express and share words of anger, revenge and dignity against the dominant ruling class. This could be the most likely socio-economic and political factor that convicted him to come out and depict the truth to the powers.[51] From the agrarian and subaltern standpoint, Mark's presentation of Jesus is best understood as a movement out of subaltern political struggles. Jesus witnessed the critique of power spoken behind the back of the dominant, not only in Galilee but also in Jerusalem. The challenge ahead of us is to seek the theological meaning of the agrarian-resistance within the context of Jesus-in-movement who declared the hidden transcript of the subalterns.

1.4. Summary

On the whole, the Protestant liberalism and the parable scholars, in one way or the other, have presented the kingdom of God as a supernatural gift from above, not a product of sociopolitical experiences of the subalterns, but purely a religious blessing. They emphasized upon the inner link with the living God. For them it seemed clear that the kingdom of God was the most important experience that a person could have that on which everything else depended–it permeated and dominated the entire human existence. The earliest modern parable scholars had to work within the theological parameter of the kingdom of God that had been established by the protestant liberal scholars and their adherents. Therefore, many parable scholars have dealt extensively with the kingdom of God in relation to Jesus' message. Nonetheless, seldom does this central message of Jesus receive the treatment it deserves in the parables, as it depicts God's activity in the history of the subalterns.

---

48 C. U. Wolf, "Carpenter," *IDB* Vol. 1, (New York/Nashville: Abingdon, 1962), 539. See also Joy, "Mark 10: 17-27 in the Light of the Issues of Poor and their Representation," 162.

49 This view deviates from Liew's explanation that the mission statement of Jesus refers to the events before Jesus came to Galilee. See, Liew, "The Gospel of Mark," 124.

50 Scott, *Domination and the Arts of Resistance*, 18.

51 Joy, "Mark 10: 17-27 in the Light of the Issues of Poor and their Representation," 162.

2. God's Kingdom and the Empire: Decoding Ideology, Disguise and Resistance in Subaltern Politics

One of the ways in which to approach the above topic is to situate Jesus' campaign within the understanding of powers. Power being comprised of the relational interplay of dominance and subordination. This section tries to understand the meaning or meanings of resistance that were embedded in Jesus' campaign which was set against Roman domination. Even though it would be wrong to state that Mark denotes the nature of domination in a systematic way, it is clear, at least in analytical terms, that in many ways, Mark reveals the Roman domination in the spheres of the ideological; both status and material. In the space opened by the domination, Jesus' campaign seemingly was on the rise. First of all, we shall attempt to understand God's kingdom as a counter-ideology to Rome's ideology and claim, and then we shall analyze the ideological negation in the spheres of status and material domination separately, to denote both covert and overt forms of resistance. The reference to God's kingdom in the Gospel of Mark will be the point of departure and we will analyse how Jesus used the parables as vehicles for resistance to the Roman domination.

2.1. God's Kingdom and Ideological Domination

2.1.1. The Roman Ideology

The empire hardly exercises it power by military might alone. In the case of Rome, it was paired with and driven by ideology in terms of mission. Rome claimed election by the gods to rule the 'empire without end' and to manifest god's will and blessing. Rome and its elite allies in the imperial provinces evidently promoted these ideas to justify their power. These expressions of and sanctions for Rome's rule had been circulated widely throughout the empire by using coins, handheld billboards, and images of imperial figures, statues of emperors, gods, and goddess. At various celebrations, such as: the emperor's birthday and military victory, they announced the imperial claims and beliefs. Imperial and military personnel were the face of this divinely sanctioned empire and the agents of god's will. While the Roman army coerced compliance, speeches at civic occasions and various forms of writings persuaded subalterns to be complaint and cooperative. Numerous writers, usually writing for literate elite audiences, repeated these aspects. For instance, Cicero articulated the conviction that "it was by our scrupulous attention to religion and by our grasp … that all things are ruled and directed by the gods that we have overcome all peoples and nations" (*Har resp*118-21). Seneca has denoted Nero's words: "Have I of all mortals found favour with Heaven and been chosen to serve on earth as vicar of the gods? I am the arbiter of life and death for the nations" (*Clem* 1.1.2). A Roman governor, as reported by Tactitus, reminded the leader of a German tribe that "all men had to bow to the commands of their betters; it had been decreed by those gods whom they implored that with the Roman people should rest decisions what to give and what to take away" (*Ann* 13.51).

Josephus—a priestly historian of the aristocrat—was one of the most prominent authors who believed that it was God's will that Rome would rule the world. "God who went the round of the nations, bringing to each in turn the rod of empire, now rested over Italy (*War* 5: 367). It appears from Josephus' report that God raised the new Flavian rule "to establish the empire which God had recently committed to their hands" (*War* 5: 2). Revolt against imperial power, for Josephus is "warring against the Romans only, but also against God ... The Deity has fled from the holy places and taken His [sic] stand on the side of those with whom you are now at war" (*War* 5: 378, 412). We must be critical in our analysis regarding whether Josephus represents the entire spectrum of Jewish society as his view on God-Empire relations is totally foreign to the subaltern masses of Jesus' time. This Roman imperial ideology claimed that the gods through Rome's elite-controlled empire were sovereign over the world. Thus, they had the right to direct it and to determine aspects that were related to human society, interactions and behaviour. Carter comments, "To submit to the will of the gods, and the means of participating in their blessing."[52] It is not clear if all the emperors were the appointed agents of the gods, but emperors like Augustus, Vespatian and Domitian were said to have been appointed by the gods. Compliance with Rome's rule was encouraged by presenting the empire's order as divinely sanctioned.[53] However, this set of ideological ideas is nothing but the public transcript of the empire to justify its "hierarchical society, the elite's self-enriching rule and its privileged existence."[54]

2.1.2. God's Kingdom as the main theme of Mark's Gospel

The frequency of occurrence and the central place it occupies in Jesus' campaign compels Mark to suggest that God's kingdom is the central message of Jesus. Even though there is nothing to doubt the centrality of God's kingdom in Mark's Gospel especially as this theme permeates the whole Gospel, yet interpreters differ in their understanding of the theological orientation of God's kingdom.[55] We must be skeptical about the traditional interpretation that God's kingdom in Mark's Gospel is apocalyptic and eschatological. When situated and analysed within the scale of Jesus-in-movement's campaign, we can

52 Carter, *The Empire and the New Testament*, 83.

53 Carter, *The Empire and the New Testament*, 85.

54 Carter, *The Empire and the New Testament*, 83.

55 For Borg, the kingdom of God is Jesus' call for "a national reorientation" for Israel. See, *Conflict, Holiness & Politics*, 236.

draw three insights which are perhaps decisive in determining the theological interests of Jesus.

First of all, we notice that Mark repeatedly asserts that the world does not belong to Rome, but to God. Jesus began his public ministry with a proclamation of "the good news of God" (1: 1). Jesus announced God's sovereignty with the words, "the kingdom of God has come near" (1: 15). This announcement must be considered as counter-assertion to the established ideology.[56] Mark denotes that the proclamation of God's kingdom originated from the villages of Galilee. He tells us that Jesus began his ministry in Galilee with the proclamation of "the good news of God" in which God's kingdom is the message (1: 14-15). Although Mark does not specify who the audiences were, he makes it clear that it happened in Galilee after the arrest of John the Baptist.[57] Mark seems to envisage the political chaotic situation in Judea when he referred to the political arrest of John the Baptist, the people's prophet.[58] Galilee seems to provide a sequestered site for the proclamation of God's kingdom. For Mark, the fact that Jesus began his campaign in Galilee is politically significant.

Second, we have Jesus moving out of the sequestered site to the larger Galilee and beyond and this continues to proclaim the same message. One may expect more references to God's kingdom in the second political discourse of Mark (3: 7–8: 30), which narrates Jesus' campaign in the wider Galilee and beyond. Ironically, Mark makes only four references to "kingdom" and "kingdom of God" which are also in the form of parable. That is to say, Jesus did not continue to proclaim God's kingdom in a direct and explicit reference as that of "The time is fulfilled, the kingdom of God has come near" (v.15) in the other part of the Gospel. In Jesus' response to the Scribes from Jerusalem, we have the reference: "If a kingdom is divided against itself, that kingdom cannot stand" (3: 24). The next reference to God's kingdom is from the Parable Discourse. To the surprise of his readers, Mark has "the secret of kingdom of God" being concealed from public view (4: 11). Then, he records a pair of parables of God's kingdom (4: 26, 30). These references to God's kingdom in this part of the Gospel seem to involve a politics of disguise and anonymity. Why does this occur?

---

56 Borg reads this passage as a call for a "departure from the existing structure," but in an ideological sense, it seems more of a counter-assertion against Rome's ideological claims. See, *Conflict, Holiness & Politics,* 236.

57 Mark's intention seems not to draw a demarcation between the forerunner and the protagonist of the story as assumed by Iersel. See, *Mark: A Reader-Response*, 104. From the subaltern point of view, the political situation "state of terrorism" due to the arrest of John is central. M. Gorretti, M. Daniel, A. M. A. Raja, *The Gospel According to Mark*, DBC, New Testament Vol. 2 (New Delhi: Centre for Dalit/Subaltern Studies, 2009), 37.

58 Dalit Bible Commentary has read this passage as good news amidst crisis. See, Gorretti, Daniel, Raja, *The Gospel According to Mark*, 37.

Third, one-third of the total references, are found in the third political discourse of Mark (8: 31–16: 20) which narrates Jesus' direct campaign against the powers in Jerusalem. Mark places four sayings regarding God's kingdom such as: coming of God's kingdom in power (9: 1), enter into God's kingdom (9: 47), belong to or receive God's kingdom (10: 14-15) and enter into God's kingdom (10: 23, 24, 25) in the context of Jesus on his way to Jerusalem. These sayings are always studied and interpreted as Jesus' directions concerning Christian discipleship. We must read these sayings in the context of Jesus' campaign which was moving closer to Jerusalem for a direct confrontation to the powers. Mark's presentation proposes that the kingdom sayings on the road to Jerusalem are the private discourse of Jesus. If it is so, it is very apt to assume that Jesus revealed the secret of God's kingdom which was hidden from the public view. Interestingly enough, Mark's final four references to God's kingdom were delivered in Jerusalem. Mark denotes that the crowd at the time of Jesus' entry into Jerusalem had shouted: "Blessed is the coming of kingdom of our ancestor David" (11: 10). This implies that the crowd rejected Caesar's kingdom and they wished their native kingdom to be re-established. Mark 12: 34 talks about Jesus as addressing a scribe, "You are not far from the kingdom of God." This is the only kingdom saying directly that addresses the elites. Mark 14: 24 denotes aspects about drinking a cup of renewed covenant in God's kingdom. This is a very solemn occurrence in terms of the private teaching of Jesus. Finally, we have Mark's description of Joseph of Arimathea as "waiting expectantly for the kingdom of God" and boldly approaching the Roman governor Pilate for the body of Jesus (15: 43).

Our brief survey on Markan kingdom references has revealed that nowhere in the Gospel does the Evangelist express the kingdom passages as belonging to or in favour of Rome or their client rulers such as Herods, High Priest, Sadducees, Pharisees and Scribes excepting in Mark 3: 24 which is, however, simply a "kingdom" without "of God." Perhaps the saying refers to the breaking of Herod's at his death. If this is true, then Jesus, in the words of Crossan, reminds the Jerusalem jurists of Rome's fate: "A kingdom divided is a kingdom defeated."[59] Mark has a reference to "kingdom of God" together with Pilate's name when he narrates the instance of Joseph of Arimathea who was seen approaching the Roman governor for the body of Jesus (15: 43). Mark situates the majority of Jesus' saying of God's kingdom to originate from his private discourse (4: 11; 9:1; 9:47; 10: 14-15, 23-25; 14: 25). When they are pointed to a public discourse (4: 3-8; 26, 30), they are in parables hiding the secret of it, or even if they are individuals, they are to mock them (3: 24; 10: 23-25; 12: 34). The most prominent one, "the kingdom of God has come near"

59 J. D. Crossan, *The Essential Jesus: What Jesus Really Taught* (New York: Harper SanFrancisco, 1994), 65.

was spoken in a village of Galilee. Mark's presentation of God's kingdom, to a great extent, possibly depicts that God's kingdom could reflect the religio-political belief held by the agrarian community in Galilee that influenced their values, mindset, and behaviour. This insight prompts us to note that God's kingdom was something that was related to the hopes and experiences of the agrarian populace which negates the apocalyptic or eschatological hope that had been cultivated in the urban elites.

2.1.3. God's Kingdom as Counter-Ideology Negating of the Ruling Ideology

Recent scholars have voiced serious concern about the other worldly interpretations of the word "kingdom" and the idea of "kingdom of God" and this excludes subaltern politics. In his 1975's analysis of the Parable of Unjust Judge (Lk 18: 2-5), Via concludes, "…the kingdom of God is not a cosmic apocalypse, or the eternal world beyond … but human existence as a realistic narrative in which the everyday is transected by the unexpected [God]…."[60] Via's views deserves careful attention as it incorporates a new way of viewing God's kingdom. We need to understand God's kingdom as something "accessible to all" as Borg envisages.[61] The ambiguity of the Greek term βασιλεία also invites scholarly attention. Some scholars do not approve the usual rendering of the term "kingdom" as it appears andocentric and bias to them. For example, Crossan opts for "state" in place of "kingdom" as it conveys the idea of rule and power. He defines, "State as a means way of life or mode of being, not nation or empire."[62] His insistence on state for the meaning βασιλεία leads Crossan to conclude, thus: "The kingdom of God is people under divine rule, and that, as ideal, transcends and judges all human rule."[63] Crossan offers us the insight to read the kingdom sayings in the context of the peasants. At this point, Crossan partly affirms Borg's ideology because he has asserted that God's kingdom is a community that embraces the mercy of

60 D. O. Via, "The Parable of the Unjust Judge: A Metaphor of the Unrealized Self" in *Semiology and Parables: Exploration of the Possibilities Offered by Structuralism for Exegesis*, ed. D. Patte (Pittsburgh: The Pickwwick Press, 1976), 27. More recently, Crossan also points out that the idea of eschatology and apocalypticism is most subject to mystification and misreading. He warns us to be critical in order to discern "end of what" in terms of what the Biblical eschatology is talking about. Crossan, *God and Empire*, 77. D. J. Neville argues that passages in Mark's Gospel like 8: 38, 13: 26, and 14: 62 should not be understood simply as references to imminent parousia, but should be considered in the light of Jesus moral vision. See, "Moral Vision and Eschatology in Mark's Gospel: Coherence or Conflict" *JBL* 127/2 (2008): 373.

61 Borg, *Conflict, Holiness & Politics,* 256.

62 Crossan, *The Historical Jesus*, 266.

63 Crossan, *The Historical Jesus*, 266.

God in a concrete situation.[64] However, Crossan goes further by establishing a direct relationship between God and the subalterns without any human brokers in between. His understanding of βασιλεία as a way of life implies that God's kingdom proclaimed by Jesus-in-movement must have contained a potential aspect of resistance. At the same time, we must be conscious on his observation of place or space in considering how it clashes with the Markan presentation of God's kingdom in some of the parables.

We must sincerely question as to what could be the expectation of the people who had in their history enjoyed life under theocratic form of governance in a just and egalitarian social order. It is important to delineate this aspect as to whether it becomes a reference point for the generation in Jesus' time who struggled under Roman-Herodian regime. Did the Jews of the Roman period find their existing situation contrary to the will of God? Did they receive the message of Jesus especially as God remains concerned to keep them free from subjugation? Perhaps, Mark could have been interested in God's kingdom as a counter-ideology of the imperial Roman ideology that propagated God ordained Rome to rule over others including Galilee. Our analysis of various kingdom passages in Mark's Gospel has depicted that Jesus basically spoke of the marginalized people's hopes and expectations. Modern New Testament scholars usually labelled it as apocalypse, in relation to the end of the world. For the agrarian communities in the rural Galilee of Jesus' time who were at the same time subaltern class, their hope for the end must possibly be the end of the tyrant rule of Rome.

Scott's exposition of the deeper dimensions of the politics of domination and resistance has some serious implication for parable studies. Many of Jesus' teaching including God's kingdom could have been part and parcel rendered as hidden transcripts of subaltern popular indignation and dignity that was cultivated in the villages of Galilee.[65] Their regular experience of degradation and exploitation generated a hidden transcript among the peasants to preserve their own dignity and to resist domination and insist upon justice. Horsley makes a significant comment in this regard, thus: "Beside and behind many hidden and disguised forms of resistance stands a popular ideology that comprises an alternative to the values and views articulated in the official public transcript controlled by the dominant."[66] In this way, God's kingdom as proclaimed by Jesus could be best considered as a popular ideology among the Galilean villagers. If this is the case, then the notion of God's kingdom has the intrinsic values opposing the standards and ideals of the elites in Jerusalem.

---

64 Borg, *Conflict, Holiness & Politics,* 256.

65 We have noted Scott's discussion on "hidden transcript as practice" here. See, *Domination and the Arts of Resistance*, 187-192.

66 Horsley, *Jesus in Context,*

Unfortunately, this has never been the primary focus of the New Testament scholar, especially in terms of the parable interpreters. Our task is to see if Mark reflects upon how the proclamation of the popular ideology comprises an alternative to the values and viewpoints that were articulated by the Jerusalem temple-state.

2.2. God's Kingdom and Status Domination

Having argued that God's kingdom is not merely an apocalyptic teaching, but a counter-ideology that negates the ideology of the ruling elites, we shall go on to discuss how this ideological negation influenced Jesus' campaign. Mark, in many ways, reveals how Jesus' message of God's kingdom negated the status domination. The Galileans always consistently suffered political domination from the imperial rulers and well as economic exploitation from the priestly aristocrats in Jerusalem. They regularly suffered humiliation, disprivilege, insults and assaults upon their dignity. Jesus' family and other villagers in Nazareth could have been the victim of one such aspect. Nazareth was a tiny village about four miles away from Sepphoris. As Sepphoris had been the target of the bandits (*War* 2: 56; 68), the people of Nazareth could be portrayed as vulnerable. Joseph, the father of Jesus, could have been one among many victims in such encounter. Crossan speculates, thus:

> In Nazareth around the time Jesus was born, men, women, and children who did not hide successfully would have been, respectively, killed, raped, and enslaved. Those who survived would have lost everything. I speculate, therefore, that the major stories Jesus would have heard while growing up in Nazareth would have been about "the year Roman came." I push the speculation a little further: At some chosen moment in Jesus' youth, did Mary bring him up to the top of the Nazareth ridge, point out Sepphoris, and talk about "the Year of the Romans"? From all such talk, what did the young Jesus decide about God, Rome, resistance, and violence?[67]

In such a circumstance, the people in Galilee, especially Nazareth and the nearby villages certainly took the sovereignty of God as their defense. The complete sovereignty of God, *i.e.*, God's kingdom, must have been more than their eschatological hope to be revealed, rather their present ideology that gave them a sense of identity and as well as existence in terms of God's covenantal people. We have discussed Jesus' campaign within Capernaum and nearby villages, as hidden transcript of anger, aggression and disguised dignity. We must note the entire rural scenario of Jesus' campaign as an autonomous social space for the assertion of dignity. What is equally important is to understand Jesus' campaign in Galilee and beyond as the public assertion of the worth.

---

67 Crossan, *God and the Empire*, 110.

2.2.1. *The Elitist's Attitude towards Jesus-in-movement*

The words and deeds of Jesus-in-movement had spread, through his preaching tours as well as possibly through rumor, throughout Galilee and beyond, Jesus not only invited the crowd, but there was also strict surveillances and criticism from the Pharisees and the Scribes. For most part, those challenges and questions entailed elements of status domination. This study sees those criticisms that were leveled against Jesus and his disciples as humiliation and insult to the people of rural Galilee. The Pharisees and the Scribes were mainly rivals who were hostile to Jesus. Right from the beginning till the end of Jesus' campaign, they appeared on the scene to question Jesus words and actions. Mark denotes that "some of the scribes" were indignant regarding Jesus' healing of a paralytic (2: 1-12). They considered Jesus' forgiving of the lepers as blasphemy (2: 6). The Scribes' question concerning the table fellowship with tax-collectors and sinners clearly shows their attitudes towards Galileans at least in certain sections of the society (Mk 2: 16).[68] Another question asking: "Why do John's disciples and the disciples of the Pharisees fast, but your disciples do not fast?" (Mk 2: 18) is also concerning status. Given that both the movements of John and Pharisees originated outside Galilee, this question might involve a hegemonic tone that puts down the movement rising from Galilee.

The more striking insults are found in the accusations that have been leveled against him by his family who would often hear people saying: "He has gone out of his mind" (3: 21) and the Scribes from Jerusalem who said: "He has Beelzebul and by the rulers of the demons he casts out demons" (3: 22). The context resonates Scott's elementary forms of disguise and anonymity. Scott devices that gossip, rumor and spirit possession are very common among the subalterns. The purpose of both aspects of criticisms is to ruin the reputation of Jesus. The accusation by the Scribes from Jerusalem especially has the element of domination to put down the religious experiences (*i.e.* exorcism) to the level of the worshipped Beelzebul. Mark 7: 1-14 depicts a conflict between Jesus and "the Pharisees and some of the scribes who had come from Jerusalem" over the disciples of Jesus as "eating with defiled hands." In the context of defining and defending the Torah, or to be more specific, protest and profanation of the "tradition of the elders," it may be possible to understand a glimpse of what this conflict would have looked like in the context of first-century Judea and Galilee.[69] The Pharisees and the scribes were the groups who aspired to wash their hands before a meal. According to Wilson, this ceremonial practice was

68 Borg considers the table fellowship as revolutionary action and protest to the dominant norms. See, *Conflict, Holiness & Politics*, 82.

69 On the new purity system of Jesus, see Neyrey, "Idea of Purity in Mark's Gospel," 115-117.

"a ritual act, intended to remove the defilement incurred by contact with the Gentiles, such as was inevitable in a district like Galilee."[70] Mark states that the Pharisees and the scribes from Jerusalem gathered around Jesus. Their attempt to negate the status of Jesus-in-movement continued as they kept all the activities of Jesus and his disciples under strict surveillance. They observed that some of the disciples were eating with defiled hands and asked Jesus, "Why do your disciples not live according to the tradition of the elders?" (v. 7). This is an assault upon the dignity of Jesus' disciples. This scene provides us a picture that conveys that the urban elitists who were in action also dominated the disciples as most of them were peasants in Galilee.

2.2.2. Jesus' Response to the Status Domination

Jesus-in-movement seems to fight the status domination at two levels. Mark's portrayal of anger and aggression especially at the time of cleansing a leper (1: 40-45) and the healing of the man with a withered hand (3: 5) Aggression healings and exorcisms of Jesus are symbolic actions against the domination. His forming of a band of disciples and meeting with them from time to time (3: 13-19; 4: 10-12; 13: 3-37) can be viewed as the creation of an autonomous social space for assertion of dignity.

2.2.2.1. Public Assertion of Worth by Parabolic Sayings

Jesus creatively employed proverbial sayings to respond to certain queries. Mark reveals that Jesus' response, "I have come to call not the righteous but sinners," (2: 17b) is not just a statement, but an open desecration of status symbols of the Scribes by representing them as "Those who are well have no need of a physician" (v. 17a). Even the people who were considered to be the lowest in terms of status were declared worthy. In the same vein, Jesus used a series of parables. The first one, the Parable of Wedding Guests declared the disciples—who were accused of not fasting, thus, kept under lower rank to John's disciples and of the Pharisees—to be the best friends of the bridegroom. Another saying: "No one sews a piece of unshrunk cloth on an old cloth…" (2: 21) and "No one puts new wine into old wineskins …" (2: 22) projected that Jesus' movement was above the status of others as new movement. Thus, these parables also serve as public assertion of worth by speech on behalf of the disciples. In fact, being a movement from the agrarian villages, Jesus' movement has distinctive features in many respects when compared to the other two. The idea of "unshrunk cloth" and "new wine" evoked the idea that newness in Christ in incompatible with that of the other moments.[71]

70 Wilson, "Mark," 807.

71 Gorretti, Daniel, and Raja, *The Gospel According to Mark*, 47.

Mark presents Jesus' response in a series of parabolic sayings, one of which states: "If a kingdom is divided against itself, that kingdom cannot stand" (3: 24). Mark's reference here is not God's kingdom, but simply a kingdom. There is a possibility that Jesus referred to the division of Herod's kingdom among his sons. If this assumption is correct, the other parables can be seen as Satan's empire (3: 23, 26) and the client kings as the strong man to be bound (3: 27). These parables can be considered as the vehicle to ruin the status symbols of the dominant.

2.2.2.2. The Parables: Disguise Discourse of the Subalterns

Mark, through the Parable of Sowing on Various Landscapes, conveys to us that the proclamation of God's kingdom, being the counter-ideology of the dominant had struggled through many hardships for its survival (4: 3-9; 14-20). Out of four aspects of different soil or land, one is fertile enough to nurture God's kingdom to producing successful harvest. Being an ideology that was developed and cultivated among the people who were considered to be of lower status, the seed of God's kingdom could not survive in hostile lands. According to Mark, the Parable of the Sower (4: 3-9) is Jesus' public discourse of "the secret of the kingdom of God" (4: 11), whereas Jesus' interpretation of his own parable (4: 14-20) is the private discourse of the same. The latter denotes that "the sower sowed the word" (4: 14). The "word" signifies Jesus' preaching tour in Galilee while preaching the ideal of God's reign that comprises an alternative to the values and views of the articulate in the official public transcript which was controlled either by the authorities in Sepphoris or Jerusalem. Since it was to negate the ruling values, it encountered obstructions of various kinds. Those who heard the ideology and accepted it were the ones that were sown on the good soil. It must be asked as to what association would have been most possible for Jesus' campaign in Capernaum and its surroundings. The sower went out to sow the seed on various landscapes in readiness for both failures as well as a highly successful result. In this, Schottroff's designation "a failed hearing and a successful hearing," for the parable discourse (4: 1-34) gives us light to probe into the parables for a deeper meaning.[72] The understanding of this parable basically depends on the question as to whether the parable is intended to function as an encouragement about the kingdom or as a reflection on how the crowd responded to the teachings of Jesus.[73]

Various interpretations have been proposed for this parable. It is probable that Jesus intended that the basic meaning was in connection with his proclamation of God's kingdom. However and surprisingly, this parable neither contains the phrase "kingdom of God" nor reveals "the secret of the kingdom

72 Schottroff, *The Parables of Jesus*, 67.

73 Naickanparampil, 117.

of God" to the crowd (v. 11). Moreover, the parable neither implies the notion of God's kingdom as eschatological realities. It represents the ideal—God's reign—as an ideology. What we want to establish here is the assumption that the ideal of the parable (*i.e.* God's kingdom) has been concerned with more ideology rather than eschatology. Myers' concept of "agrarian eschatology" must also be appreciated as it proposes subversive function.[74] For Horsley the kingdom of God is a "political metaphor and symbol."[75] Mark divulges that God's kingdom is not along the lines of Rome and its elite allies; rather it requires a farmer sowing the seeds on land.[76] There are two more parables explicitly dealing with God's kingdom. One is the Parable of the Growing Seed (4: 26-29). Unlike the Parable of Sower, the seeds were not sown by the sower. It was by the act of "someone"—anonymous—"scatter the seed on the ground" (4: 26). Mark assumes that the notion of the "kingdom of God" was spread through rumors. Secretly and in anonymity, the ideal of God's reign "sprout and grow" (v. 27). Jesus' emphasis on the powerful role of earth in this parable involves anonymity. The Parable of the Mustard Seed (4: 30-32) reveals that the kingdom of God as an alternative ideology was cultivated in an invisible manner beside and behind the hidden and disguise from of resistance in the villages of Galilee. But it grows and becomes worldwide. This perspective gives us to a better and deeper understanding of the parables of the kingdom in Mark.

Both the parables of Seed Growing Secretly and Mustard Seed have God's kingdom as their ultimate referent. Element of disguise and anonymity that are enshrined in this pair of parables cannot be overlooked. The Parable of Growing the Seed Secretly underlines the anonymity of the process of sowing God's kingdom while emphasizing the power of the land (4: 26-29). The Parable of the Mustard Seed signifies the small beginning of God's kingdom while emphasizing the quality of God's kingdom. When reading these parables in the context status domination, we can learn that the parables of God's kingdom are the disguised discourses of dignity of the subaltern masses living in Galilean villages. This is an encouragement for the Galilean peasants that their little efforts to resist injustice have the potential to yield good results in the future.[77] Mark's insertion of the private discourse of Jesus assumes that Jesus still created an autonomous social space for the assertion of dignity.

74 Myers, *Binding the Strong Man*, 177.

75 Horsley, *Jesus and the Spiral of Violence*, 170.

76 Gorretti, Daniel, Raja, The *Gospel According to Mark*, 55-56. Waetjen beautifully puts, "God's rule is like the activity of peasant." See, *A Reordering of Power*, 107.

77 Cf. Gorretti, Daniel, Raja, The *Gospel According to Mark*, 57-58.

2.2.2.3. The Defilement Saying as Desecration of Status Symbol of Jerusalem Jurists

Jesus' parabolic saying—"there is nothing outside a person that by going in can defile, but the things that come out are what defile"—is not only uttered in defence of the disciples, but it was conveyed to attach the Jerusalem jurists. Jesus' explanation of this parable in private reveals that this was given to desecrate the status symbol of the religious elites. The interpretation of the Torah had guardians who controlled its parameters and determined its interpretation. The office of the high priest was no doubt the guardian where the Pharisees and the scribes played the vital role in the propagation of the interpretation.[78] This interpretation, however, is referred to as τὴν παβάδοσιν τνῶ πρεσβυτέρων ("tradition of the elders"). The tradition is no other than what Scott devises as "public transcripts" of the Jerusalem aristocrats which is at the same time a "self-portrait of dominant elites as they would have themselves seen."[79] Some aspects of the "tradition of the elders" listed down by Mark include: washing of hands before a meal (v. 3), washing after coming back from market place (v. 4a), washing of cups, pots and bronze kettles (v. 4b). Mark's understanding of the "tradition of the elders" assumes that it focuses primarily on matters of purity.[80] This tradition of washing of various kinds, basically meant for public performance, is designed to impress the cleanliness of the guardians; thus, affirms and naturalizes the power of dominant elites, while concealing or euphemizing their oppressive regime.[81] However, insistence of the "tradition of the elders" upon the masses could maximize the social distance between the ruling elites and the rural peasants. Phrases like "they noticed that some of the disciples were eating with defiled hands" (v. 2) and "all the Jews do not eat unless they thoroughly wash their hands" (v. 3b) served as good evidence to convey that Mark denotes that the Pharisees and the scribes strictly insisted the masses follow the tradition. Jesus pronounced the public assertion of worth in the presence of the crowd and in the parables (vv. 14-15).

Jesus strongly defended his disciples against the attempt to push them down into that level of unclean status. Jesus' viewpoint comes alive as a discourse of dignity that resonates deeply with Israelite popular little tradition, over and against the behaviour of the religious elites and their exploitative great traditions.[82] First of all, Jesus set up a mocking dispute with the Pharisees and the scribes from Jerusalem by negating their Temple-based purity codes.[83]

78 Kingsbury, *Conflict in Mark*, 65.

79 Scott, *Domination and Arts of Resistance*, 18,

80 Herzog, "Onstage and Offstage with Jesus of Nazareth," 43.

81 Scott, *Domination and the Arts of Resistance*, 18.

82 Horsley, *Jesus in Context*, 192.

83 Horsley, *Jesus in Context*, 192.

Jesus condemned them as hypocrites and accused them of holding "human tradition" at the expense of God's commandment (vv. 6-8). Second, Jesus declared that the demand for peasant support of the Temple apparatus (*i.e. Korban*[84]) was a violation of the basic Mosaic "commandment of God" to honour father and mother. That is, against the temple-state's retainers attempt to secure support for the Temple, and Jesus insisted that the people rejected the efforts of the Pharisees and retain locally, their own households, and the scarce economic recourses which they needed to support their families (vv. 9-13).[85] Any failure to comply with the "tradition of the elders" could disprivilege them with the status of unclean. The attempt to force the subaltern agrarian communities in Galilee who lived with the Gentiles in proximity to adopt the tradition cultivated by the urban elites would actually serve to intensify their marginalization. Jesus-in-movement had taken severe note regarding this urban aggression in the villages of Galilee. The parables become an useful effective instrument for Jesus in the process. As they were the public performance of subjugated peasants acted out of coercion by the forces of domination arrayed against them, the parables of Jesus bore marks of concealment in some cases. In the case of the Galilean rural peasantry, the concept of kingdom of God and in terms of the values that it carries this aspect can be seen as counter-values to the dominant. Jesus-in-movement progressed with miracles and became stronger and larger in terms of its operation and fame. Evidently, apart from material domination, Jesus-in-movement suffered domination at the spheres of ideological and status. The regular experience of degradation and insult that it has suffered from the Pharisees and the Scribes generated a hidden transcript of indignation amongst the Galileans who were determined to preserve their own dignity, resist the worst effects of domination and also insist upon justice.

2.3. God's Kingdom and Material Domination

Under the dominance of Rome, the urban few elites exercised material domination over the subaltern masses living in villages by appropriating grain, taxes, labour and others. Cheap labour, whether slaves, day laborers, artisans, or peasant farmers, produced goods largely for elite consumption. For Waetjen, the ruling elites, such as: Herod Antipas, Pilate, and the high priest were the three individuals who were responsible for the ownership of the land and distribution of the agricultural produce by the peasants.[86] Taxes, tributes, and rents which were usually paid in the form of goods literally transferred

84 Schweizer argues that "Korban" is "what one denotes when he wants to dedicate object to God, i.e., to withdraw it from ordinary use, but without handing it over to the temple treasury." See, *The Good News According to Mark*, 148.

85 Horsley, *Jesus in Context*, 192; Liew, "The Gospel of Mark," 108.

86 Waetjen, *A Reordering of Power*, 5-8.

wealth from the subalterns to the ruling elites. The hard manual work of the subalterns and the coerced extractions of production sustained the ruling way of life. It exacted not only agricultural production but an enormous personal tool of anger, resentment and learned inferiority. Moreover, elites legitimated and expressed their domination with an ideology or set of convictions. They asserted that it was the will of God. They claimed that social hierarchy and exploitation were simply the manner in which things were. Our reading of God's kingdom as encountering the dominant ideology encourages us to read verses in Mark, especially concerning those in the third political discourse of Mark (8: 31–16: 20), if there is any attempt to resist the domination in the sphere of the material.

2.3.1. Resistance to Material Domination

How did the subalterns negotiate this world? The kingdom discourse in Mark's Gospel, when read from a perspective of public-private dichotomy, reveals that Jesus negated the material domination in two ways. First, by creating autonomous space, Jesus revealed the secret of God's kingdom to the trusted disciples. This is not only found in Mark 4:10-12, 9-20, but throughout the Gospel. Second, there are incidents that suggest that Jesus addressed this material domination either in parables or any other disguise forms.

2.3.1.1. The Undisclosed Resistance

Mark's Gospel disputes the claim that Rome and the ruling elites manifest the presence of the gods. Rather, it proposes an alternative way of ruling and organizing society. Jesus established a trusted community with whom he conveyed "the secret of God's kingdom" (4: 10). Mark locates some of the important kingdom sayings of Jesus in the context of his private discourse. Thus, the sayings which were delivered on his way to Jerusalem must comprise aspects that were related to the norms for the alternate kingdom.

First, Jesus' saying: "there are some standing here who will not taste death until they see that the kingdom of God has come with power" (9: 1) has never been read within the context of Rome practicing material appropriation from its subjects and the response to the practice. This saying relates "death" and the coming of God's kingdom with power. Mark seems not to refer to natural death as he indicates that some of the disciples would survive it. Since appropriate was largely the purpose of domination, incompliance might have invited severe punishment. It could be that Jesus hinted at the cost of resistance to material appropriation. Moreover, Rome's legal system exercised bias toward the elite and against the others. It protected elite wealth and status and employed punishments that were appropriate not to the crime but to the social status of the accused. Mark conveys to us the impression that Jesus' teachings on entering God's kingdom with some physical parts missing (9: 42-48) is for the protection of "one of these little ones" (*i.e.*, subaltern class) in the society.[87] On the other hand, Mark exhibits that Roman imperialism caused the "little ones" caused to stumble materially. Under their legal system and its practices, the "little ones" are always the victims. So, they deserved capital punishment (9: 42). Jesus set up better kingdom values by declaring, "It is better for you to enter the kingdom of God with one eye than to have two eyes and to be thrown into hell" (9: 47b).[88] Jesus' saying implies that in God's kingdom, people should remove from their life which contributes to the enslavement of the subaltern class.[89] Mark renders this saying in the defense of the right of "little ones" (9: 42). Mark records two more contrasting incidents: the inclusion of the little children in God's kingdom (10: 13-16) and the exclusion of the rich man from God's kingdom (10: 17-27).[90] Children were the most vulnerable group under the tyrant Roman regime. The massacre of the infants at the birth of Jesus (Mat 2: 16-18), to a great extent, reveals the Roman attitude towards the dignity of children. In the world of material domination, only a few elites possessed most of the empire's wealth. They not only controlled the production and distribution of wealth, but also the consumption of its production. The wealthy and powerful families including their children enjoyed an abundance of food supply. Given the prominence of sickness in the Gospels, malnutrition is widespread among the Jews; presumably, the children were the most affected ones. Mark does specify the social status of the children who were brought to Jesus. "People were bringing little children" (v. 13) implies that the children were from the social class. Jesus not only declared that God's kingdom belongs to the children (v. 14), but also he used "as a little children" (v. 15) the criteria for entrance into it. The co-relationship between kingdom and children has been the subject of discussion. When analysed in the context of excessive material appropriation, incidents of infanticide and children who were abandoned at birth by peasant parents in the first-century C. E. assumes that children's worth was of no value. In this context, Crossan draws our attention: "to be a child was to be a nobody."[91] He also beautifully coined the phrase "a Kingdom of Nobodies" to explain the relationship between the child and the kingdom.[92] This negates Rome's ideology that the emperor and

87 We take this expression as indicative of the subaltern masses in the Jewish society.

88 This statement is a clear evidence that the idea of God's kingdom is not eschatological in a sense of being imminent, but as ideological. See Waetjen, *A Reordering of Power*, 162.

89 Gorretti, Daniel, Raja, *The Gospel According to Mark*, 93.

90 Crossan observes that this child of Mark portrayed in 9: 36 and of 10: 15 have been deliberately connected images that are embracing each other. See, *The Historical Jesus*, 268.

91 Crossan, *The Historical Jesus*, 269.

92 Crossan, *The Historical Jesus*, 266.

the elites were God' ordained. Waetjen comments, "God's representatives are precisely those who have no status at all, who like children, are lowly weak and defenseless."[93] Mark seems to record this incident as a discourse of dignity and the indignation of the children.

The story of the rich man is another significant text in Mark that narrates aspects related to the material appropriation and resistance (10: 17-27). Mark remarks that he was a man of "many possessions" (v. 22). Mark uses the reference to the "kingdom of God" in relation to the denial of entry for "those who have wealth" (v. 23) and also as "someone who is rich" (v. 25). By using the analogy of the Camel and the Eye of the Needle, Jesus said, "It is easier for a camel to go through the eye of needle than for someone who is rich to enter the kingdom of God" (v. 25). Borg, who depicts Jesus as a prophet sage, finds a mystical aspect in that reversal of the kingdom that was expected by his contemporaries.[94] But, the core issue must be spelled out in terms of the material and not necessarily in spiritual or mystic terms. Mark makes it clear and denotes the parabolic saying as the man who was grieving (v. 22). Crossan is right in commenting that it may be regarded as "dark humor."[95] This rich man had been barred from the kingdom of God not merely because he was rich, but because he wanted to keep his status, privilege and power.[96] At the same time, Jesus mentioned that God's kingdom was opened wide for those who believe in God (v. 27).[97] Material domination deprives people of dignity. Mark convinces us that God's kingdom has the remedial measures for the degrading and humiliating.

2.3.1.2. Parables of God's Kingdom: Direct-Masked Resistance

The urban elites controlled all political office, including civic and military positions for their own benefit and not for the common good. They also controlled large estates of land. Land was basic for wealth. They also participated in trade by sea and land. V. G. Shillington discusses aspects related to the rural subaltern classes whose livelihood was completely based on land and the urban landlords who perceived differently the value of land. Shillington argues that land, for the agrarian Jews, was God's gift to Israel; whereas the elite landlords used it as commodity to generate surplus for their luxurious lives at the expense of the landless villagers.[98] Mark exhibits two

93 Waetjen, *A Reordering of Power*, 159.

94 Borg, *Conflict, Holiness & Politics,* 257.

95 Crossan, *The Historical Jesus*, 275.

96 Gorretti, Daniel, Raja, *The Gospel According to Mark*, 98.

97 Waetjen, *A Reordering of Power*, 171.

98 V. G. Shillington, "Engaging with the Parables," in *Jesus and His Parables: Interpreting the Parables of Jesus Today*, ed. V. G. Shillington (Edinburg: T&T Clark, 1997), 9-10.

ways in which Jesus: (a) by the transforming power of land to the crowd, (b) by narrating the account of people's revolt to powers, made an attempt to render an alternate account ideology or ideologies that were related to the dominant rulers.

2.3.1.2.1. Land Values

In all three major parables in the Parable Discourse (4:3-34), Mark relates God's kingdom with land. Even though scholars like Crossan have tried to argue regarding the aspect of place or space, God's kingdom as proclaimed by Jesus cannot be dissociated with the idea of place or land.[99] This is a clear indication that land, for the agrarian community, is a divine and significant aspect in their aspiration of liberation. A reader of the Parables of Sowing on Various Landscapes (vv. 3-8) may be resentful at the sowing of seeds on soils including those unlikely to produce harvest. Any expert sower must know where and where not to sow seeds. From a resistance point of view, can we not read sowing on the soil other than the fertile one as squatting or land invasion? Scott (2013) says, "Squatting, both urban and rural, has probably, as a matter of de facto control over property, 'won' more land than land invasions."[100] At least we can note that the sower does equal justice to all types of lands. For the agrarian community in Galilee, land was precious property that they had inherited as the promise of God. Another significant aspect that must be pointed is the phrase αὐτομάτη ἡ γῆ καρποφορεῖ ("the earth produces of itself," v. 28). Jesus rendered an emphasis of the power of transforming land over the sower. Land is not presented as mere property that generates material wealth. It is life giving power that nurtures the seeds. Jesus seems to pick up the quality and power of the land to explain God's kingdom. The Parable of the Mustard Seed affirms the transforming power of land where the smallest seed transforms into a tree. It is highly appropriate to read and understand the notion of God's kingdom as explicated with coherent reference to γῆν τὴν καλὴν (4: 8, 11), αὐτομάτη ἡ γῆ καρποφορεῖ (4: 26, 28) and ἐπὶ τῆς γῆς (4: 30) as popular ideology of the agrarian communities. This also envisages as to how God's kingdom will grow worldwide. Jesus used land values that were cherished by the agrarian communities in order to counter the ideology of the powerful elites.

2.3.1.2.2. The Story of Battle for Land

The Parable of Tenants in the Vineyard (12: 1-9) conveys the evidence that Jesus addressed the land issue in earnest. Jerusalem, along with other urban cites, displayed Rome elite power, wealth, and status and also extended control

99 Crossan, *The Historical Jesus*, 266.

100 Scott, *Decoding Subaltern Politics*, 65.

over the surrounding territory. Mark must have had immense theological interest to locate this particular parable in Jerusalem. The previous scholars who considered God's kingdom in a merely eschatological category have attempted to situate this parable in the relation to the coming of God's kingdom in one way or the other. Our primary interest is not to find out the meaning of God's kingdom within the image of the land, but to discern how land is portrayed in this parable.

This parable is a story of revolt of the tenants against the landlord. It is a difficult task to determine as to whose side Jesus was on from the present form of the parable. However, when one situates the story within the scale of Jesus' campaign, we can note that Jesus used this story to speak truth to powers in Jerusalem on behalf of the subalterns whose land had been taken away by the powerful elites. From the parable story, we can ascertain that it was common in Judea and Galilee of Jesus' time that urban elites also controlled large areas of land. It is natural to assume that the landlords employed the peasant farmers and produce largely for elite consumption. However, the case of tenants who fought against their landlords to regain ownership of land was not common under the Roman regime, for Rome was very sensitive towards any form of protest or resistance. Whenever there was uprising against the administration, they would deploy military troop to crush the uprising. Peasant revolts were few and not far from the sight of the ruling elites. Therefore, what is interesting and at the same time confusing in this parable is the revolt of the tenants to regain the ownership of the land. Jesus ended the story with the revolt of the tenants and asked the question: "What then will the owner of the vineyard do?" (v. 9). The crux of the parable lies in the fact as to what the reaction of the landlord would be. This was enough for Jesus to provoke the powers in Jerusalem and be punished (v. 12).

This parable also assumes that the rights of public open protest, public demonstration as well as open revolt were dangerous and commonly lethal. Just as a mention of the land values and story of revolt depicted in the Gospel is loud enough to speak against material domination.[101] The parables of Jesus effectively serve as modes of dissimulation as well.

2.4. God and the Subalterns

We now arrive at the crux of the thesis. The purpose of this section is not to switch over to a new area which we have not yet dealt with, but to highlight the God-factor in the subaltern movement, in the light of what has already been discussed. The prominence of God becomes an indispensable part of Mark's Gospel. The notion of God permeates the whole of Mark's Gospel, right from

101 Mark conveys to us that in an incident following this that Jesus had been confronted by the Pharisees and the Herodians on the most sensitive issue concerning material domination.

the beginning (1: 1) till the end (16: 19), we have Mark making references to "God." However, what makes the Gospel interesting is that Mark never refers to "God" without relating to something else.[102] Perhaps, Mark conveys fact that God is an infinite being; the finite human beings can only perceive God in relation to something of God's own revelation. Mark's presentation of the notion of God intertwines Christology and God's kingdom. Our purpose here is to delineate Mark's presentation of the dynamics of God's reign and the manner in which it was set in favour of the marginalised subalterns within these two.

The Galileans to whom Jesus declared the arrival God's kingdom first were peasantries, and were once free of the overload and kings, independent of foreign domination. They had enjoyed life under a theocratic form of governance in a just and egalitarian social order. This aspect seems to become a reference point for the subsequent generations who were not citizens, but subjects of Rome, who had struggled under the domination of various forms under the Roman imperial powers. Virtually, everything found in the Mark's Gospel about the Galileans, their livelihood, social organizations, ideologies, oral cultures, even their devotion to prophetic and messianic movements can be read as strategic positioning that were designed to keep away the powers.

Mark indicates that the declaration of the arrival of God's kingdom originated from the villages of Galilee. For the Galileans, God's kingdom refers back to the time when they enjoyed life under a theocratic form of governance. God's rule must be understood *vis-à-vis* Caesar's empire. Our analysis of "kingdom of God" in Mark suggests that it is best understood as counter-ideology of the Roman empire ideology. Jesus never tells the message of God's kingdom to the Jerusalem aristocrats, which he publicly declared to the Galilean peasant masses. On his way to Jerusalem to have directed campaign against the power, Mark places God's kingdom in terms of – to whom the kingdom belongs (10: 14-15) and who will enter into the kingdom (10: 23, 24-25). While declaring the children, who were nobodies under Roman power, as full member of God's kingdom; Jesus barred the rich man from entering into God's kingdom. This is a clear indication that the subalterns are privileged by God's power. Mark denotes that the crowd at the time of Jesus' entry into Jerusalem had shouted: "Blessed is the coming of our ancestor David" (11: 10). As argued earlier, this implies that the crowd rejected Caesar's kingdom and they wished for a native kingdom to be reestablished.

The Jews of the Roman period found their existing situation as contrary to the will of God. They looked forward someone to come for their rescue.

102 To illustrate: "the Son of God" (1: 1; 15: 39b), "the good news of God" (1: 14), "the kingdom of God" (1: 15; 4: 4: 11, 26, 30; 9: 1; 47; 10: 14; 25b; 12: 34; 14:24; 15: 43), "the Holy One of God" (1: 24b), and "right hand of God" (16: 19), *etc.*

Their devotion to prophetic and messianic movements is illustrative to this point. The Galileans received Jesus who had fled from Judea to escape from Archelaus as their messiah of God. Mark called him "Son of God." Their devotion to Jesus was largely because God remained concerned to keep them free from subjugation. They wanted to keep Rome and the temple-state at distance. The various religious crowds emerged actively participating in Jesus' campaign which used the God-factor as the major means of resistance. Moreover, this religious group facilitated the movement's growth through the writing of literature that became the Gospel. In turn, their religious faith served as a primary factor in the negotiation of the movements' collective identity.

It is vital that we pay attention to how far their faith in God had provided the activists in the dissent movements with expressive symbols, icons, and rituals which served to rally and to embody their grievances publicly in powerful ways. Analysis of resistance movements in the Jewish context demands us to focus more on the historical resources that God-factor had often contributed to resistance and protest movements, for the core motivation and sustaining nurturance of many (if not the majority), of Jewish activists was their religiosity. However, recent scholars have largely neglected the importance which religious faith could play a crucial role in the social and political movements. Perhaps because of theoretical limitations, personal proclivity, or anything else, resistance and protest movement analysts have inadequately accounted for the empirical reality that religion has served as a rich resource for a host of important movements. The case of ancient Judea and Galilee makes clear the decisive impact that religious faith and organization can make in generating, sustaining, and legitimating disruptive protest.

3. Conclusion

In this chapter, we have attempted to unlock the theological meaning and resistance leitmotifs that are embedded in the parables of Jesus. The study has revealed that Jesus' campaign was largely shaped by the ideal of God's kingdom as well as by imperial domination. The Roman domination in the form of ideological, status and material was the context within which the resistance movements grew and the condition to which Jesus-in-movement responded. Jesus' campaign which emerged from the villages of Galilee was one of conflicts that was created by the great gulf between the politics of urban elites which had been controlled and determined by Rome. The politics of the farmers in rural areas were also overwhelmed by the ideology God's kingdom. It has also been revealed as observed from the Gospel materials that resistance originates not simply from material appropriation but from the pattern of the personality that characterizes that exploitation. Our analysis has reflected that the parables are the effective tools for resistance to the dominant powers. Contrary to the theological stance that was drawn by western scholarship and generally accepted till recently, this study leads us to conclude that God's kingdom was not entirely an eschatological category, rather, it was the ideology of the subalterns that rendered an alternate to the accepted values and beliefs of the urban powerful elites.

Chapter 6

Sociopolitical and Theological Implications of "God and the Subalterns" for the Tribal Hermeneutics in North-east India

As part of our concluding chapter, we will render some theological comments on the significance of "God and the subalterns" that has been explored in relation to the agrarian-resistance motifs embedded in the parables of Jesus for the formulation of a tribal hermeneutics in the context of North-east India. The tribal theology that has emerged from the context North-east India since the last four decades has proposed new reading methods of the Bible for the tribals. There are areas where the tribal liberationist hermeneutics has yielded good results and attained great achievements within certain aspects. Moreover, as an indigenous theology, the tribal theology also seeks the experiences of faith of the tribal people as well as their worldviews, values, and ideologies that are embedded in their oral traditions in order to construct meaningful hermeneutics within a tribal context.

North-east India represents novelty in terms of research for at least two reasons. First, the tribals in North-east India live in a world of peripheries. Since this area is at the periphery of five international states, *viz*. Bhutan, China, Myanmar, Bangladesh and India, and at the centre of none, it becomes an interesting site for research. We assume that the region is the remaining part of India whose peoples have not yet been fully incorporated nation-states. The hill peoples may be best understood as "state-evading" and "state-preventing native peoples" considering their unique geopolitical situation.[1] Any academic studies on the tribals in North-east India based on sound and profound methodology, must investigate how these self-governing peoples

1 J. C. Scott, *The Art of Not Being Governed: An Anarchist History of Uplands Southeast Asia* (New Heaven & London: Yale University Press, 2009), ix.

reacted to forces that have attempted to incorporate them into statehood. This would most probably help to decipher the nature and characteristic of tribal resistance.

Second, the region is the meeting point of South Asia and Asia-east Asia, which possesses not only sociopolitical behaviour of South Asian (*i.e.* the Indian Sub-Continent) and South-east Asian politics, but also a distinguishing feature of its own.[2] Hence, it would further get a deeper understanding of Indian politics and South-east politics to make a study of the political culture of this area. A. W. Longchar says, "…because of the geographical, racial, and socio-political differences, the people of North East also feel excluded from the rest of India."[3] The tribal hermeneutics must privilege the indigenous history, experiences, and struggles for political justice as an authentic site for theology; it could not and should never overlook such great geo-political heritages of the peoples.

Tribal scholars have over the last four decades made sincere efforts based on an in-depth analysis of historical sources in order to explain the identity of the tribals and their organizing dynamics in facing westernisation, modernity, and Christianity. However, several issues are involved in the process of such endeavours. One of the major problems with those previous studies lies on the fact that most of them have overlooked the political discourses among the tribals and have failed to take the complexities of the tribal communities into consideration. The tribal society, inclusive of former state of Assam province, was very complex and highly stratified.

North-east India is an expanse of five thousand kilometres of international boundary containing about four hundred minority peoples of truly bewildering ethnic and linguistic variety.[4] Presently, the region is divided into different states (barring Sikkim), such as: Assam, Nagaland, Mizoram, Manipur, Meghalaya, Arunachal Pradesh, and Tripura.[5] Their nationalities are numerous, but according to a division of languages and ethnic

---

2 Z. Changli, "A Study of the Ethnic Origin and Customs of the Nationalities in North-Eastern Area in India: A Comparison between them and Some of the Nationalities in Yunnan and Xizang, China and Northern Burma" in *History and Ethnic Identity Formation in North-East India*, ed. J. V. Hluna (New Delhi: Concept Publishing Company, 2013), 39-40.

3 A. W. Longchar, *An Emerging Asian Theology: Tribal Theology, Issue, Method and Perspective* (Jorhat: Tribal Study Centre, 2000), 16.

4 According to Longchar, there are about four hundred tribes in north east India speaking hundreds of languages and dialects. See, *An Emerging Asian Theology*, 14.

5 Before Independence of India in 1947, almost all the units that now constitute North-east India were parts of the British administrative unit designated by the blanket nomenclature–"Assam." After independence, the administrative divisions of the North-east region have changed several times.

groups, there are roughly three categories. First, the Assamese who have the largest population and are mainly of Aryan origin and simultaneously mixed together with other native tribes belonging to the Mongoloid groups. Second, the Nagas, the Mizos, the Mikirs and the Garos belong to the Mongolian and the Tibeto-Burman branch of the Sino-Tibetan language family. Third, the Khasis belong to the South Asian branch of the Austro-Asiatic language family.

These three distinctive groups cannot in any sense be expected to have a similar degree of resistance or even acceptance to the domination. Given the complexity of the region and intricacy of their responses to powers, we cannot do justice to cover the whole area. This research has been limited to the context of Nagas and Mizo, the second group in the above given categories for they are illustratively self-governing peoples who have a common history of tirelessly resisting forces that have attempted to incorporate them into statehood. Due to limitation of space, our reflection upon the tribes will be in a nutshell with the purpose of revealing the resistance motifs, not in isolation but in relation to the other two linguistic groups.

1. Methodological Issues Involved in the Tribal Hermeneutics

In a postcolonial phase of Biblical interpretations, a perspectival reading—shaped and determined by experiences of a particular group of people—is highly preferable. J. Samuel, in his attempt to re-contextualize Dalit hermeneutics, urges us that we must read the Bible "from and through" the historical context of the people who are at the margin.[6] It further challenges us to further re-look into who are the hill peoples "through and from" whom the texts must be read. In the case of tribal hermeneutics too, the reading must be done "from and through" the tribal experiences of domination and resistance. At present, theological reflections on the history, nationalities, sociopolitical context of this area are very few. The tribal theology that has emerged from North-east India—with its greater concern being liberation and interaction between tribal culture and western culture—makes little no or less effort to the sociopolitical issues.

There has been a tendency among the tribal interpreters in North-east India to emphasize the lowly dimension of the tribals. Almost all of the theological literature that have come out in recent times have emphasized that the tribals are subjugated, alienated, defeated, and oppressed people. For instance, Longchar writes, "Today the tribals are people who are culturally alienated and uprooted and dehumanised, economically exploited and dominated, politically

---

6 J. Samuel, Re-contextualizing Dalit Hermeneutics: Exploring Hermeneutical Parameters for a Changing Community," in *Liberation Hermeneutics in the Indian Interpretation of the Bible*, ed. K. Jesurathnam, A. Saggu, and H. Chhungi (Tiruvalla: CSS, 2012), 93-123. Correction of the name "Chhungi" is mine.

powerless and divided, and theologically unheard and voiceless."[7] From an agrarian-resistance point of view, this kind of a dazzling display of tribal situation simply portrayed the hill peoples as apolitical, largely over-shows the resistive traits of the tribals. Paradoxically, the same thinkers are engaged in the liberation process by way of reclaiming, rediscovering, retrieving, and inculturating the culture, traditions, worldviews, and beliefs of whom they depicted as defeated community.

Longchar's depiction of the tribals as "defeated community" must be questioned in the light of tribals as it ostensibly represents the tribals as lacking resistance to powers. Recent tribal scholarship emerging from secular studies have stressed on the persistency of the tribals in their resistance and the importance of right to self-determination for their political struggles. Aosenba—a Research Consultant in Council of Social Science Research in New Delhi—in his exhaustive study on the Naga resistance movement reveals the persistence of the tribals in their resistance, writes:

> Interestingly, during the British colonial rule in India, they hardly attempted to conquer and control over the Naga Hills. From 1879 to 1945 they could not make any agreement with Naga Hills as their subject. They occupied only some parts for their administrative convenience, loosely, administered and treated separately the Nagas as a different ethnic stock with the plain people.[8]

Another exhaustive and holistic work on Naga movement by R. Vashum, *Naga's Right to Self-Determination: An Anthological-historical Perspective* (2000) alone contains enough evidences to state that their self-determination provides a conceptual framework understanding their struggles for dignity and justice.[9] As for the tribals in North-east India, their status cannot be graded as apolitical to fight for their justice and freedom, their strong desire for right to self-determination remains sources for their survival in the midst of various forms of domination.

Another significant issue concerning the inadequacy of the tribal theology, in its present form to address the deeper dynamics of tribal politics within a larger historical framework, lies on the fact that it is confined narrowly within the interaction of the tribal culture with Christianity, westernization, and modernity. Thus, the histories of tribal resistance movements that have occurred much earlier than those of the British colonial period and independent India have always been silenced. In this regard, F. S. Downs,

---

7 Longchar, "The Need for Doing Tribal Theology," 2.

8 Aosenba, *The Naga Resistance Movement: Prospects of Peace and Armed Conflict* (New Delhi: Regency Publications, 2001), 104.

9 R. Vashum, *Naga's Right to Self-Determination: An Anthological-Historical Perspective* (New Delhi: Mittal Publications, 2000), 37-56.

a noted historian who made enormous contributions towards Christianity in North-east India, must be given a credit for his works. Downs maintains that Christianity in general helped the peoples to adjust to the tremendous changes made by the British imperial power among the tribals. He advocates the new cultural synthesis that has developed out of the interaction of the tribal culture with the western culture. As result of the interaction, as observed by Downs, there are rejection, transformation and adoption of the tribal cultures.[10] His remarkable contributions offer a theoretical framework for reading the history of tribal Christianity in the light of their interaction with modernity towards the pioneers and also to an earlier generation of tribal theologians.

The imprints of Downs' thesis are clearly visible in the works of who those have championed tribal theology. In his article, "Tribal theological Trends in North East India" published in 2003, R. Keitzar tries to understand tribal theology as an outcome of the interaction of tribal culture with the western culture. Keitzar proposes "inculturation" and "transformation"—the basic components in Downs' method of reading—as the major theological tasks, if the theology is to remain relevant among the tribal Christians in North-east India.[11] Keitzar denotes that "the absence of tribal worldview and traditional values from our theological education" as the major setback in theological discourse of the tribal in North-east India.[12] Keitzar is, one among few scholars, who renders efforts to bring a tribal understanding of God, nature, human, and spirits as a single entity into the theological discourse in the tribal context. While advocating his great contributions in the construction of tribal theology, we must also discern that he did not touch upon the resistance motifs embedded in the tribal practices.

In his extensive works on tribal theology, A. W. Longchar—who has made massive contribution in the field of tribal theology—exhibits in many ways that his point of departure is from the interaction of tribal culture with modernity. Longchar blames modernity for creating restlessness and identity crisis among the tribals. He writes, "With the onset of modernization, the tribal society is experiencing a 'sudden break' between tradition and modernity, the disastrous consequence of which is manifested in corruption, drug culture,

10 Among his writings, these are the notable ones: *The Might Works of God: Brief History of the Council of Baptist Churches in North East India* (Guwahati: Christian Literature Centre, 1971); *Christianity in North East India* (Madras: CLS, 1976); *Christianity in North East India: Historical Perspectives* (Delhi: ISPCK, 1983); *History of Christianity in India: North East India in the Nineteenth and Twentieth Centuries* (Bangalore: Church History Association of India, 1992).

11 R. Keitzar, "Tribal Theological Trends in North East India," in *Tribal Theology: A Reader*, ed. S. Shimray (Jorhat: Tribal Study Centre, 2003), 40-51.

12 Keitzar, "Tribal Theological Trends in North East India," 45.

drunkenness, killing immortality, and dishonesty in work."[13] For Longchar, modernity makes the hill peoples to consider their traditional values and practices like songs and dances as primitive and uncultured way of life.[14] He portrays that acceptance of Christian faith as "rejection of the traditional festivals, songs, dances, sacrifices, observances and ethics."[15] In Longchar's theological stance, the tribal worldview, myths, concept of land, understanding of God, perception of humanity that relates other creation find central place. Longchar claims "creation/land" or "space" as the basic hermeneutical principle in tribal theology.[16] His attempt to theologize the tribal heritage for the construction of theology in tribal context, perhaps subversive to the western pattern of Christianity, is an outstanding one. However, it is assumed that if reading of the creation-land and space is carried out, within the larger historical framework of the hill peoples, which is also as strategic positioning designed to resist state, the conceptualisation of "space" in its tribal usage could become a sharper analytical and critical tool.

K. Thanzauva, another profound tribal thinker is also found operating within the framework of the tribal-western dialogue. His theological discussion is largely limited within the last hundred years during which the interaction between Christianity and tribal culture has occurred. Thanzauva tries his best to read and understand tribal Christianity in North-east India in terms of what he refers to as "Synthetic-Praxis"—"a synthesis of gospel and culture."[17] The scholar' concerned seems to address well cultural issues in the face of westernisation. However, when his methodology is analysed within a power differential, a "synthesis of gospel and culture" simply he proposes a peaceful existence of dominant and subject. M. Foucault's dictum, "Where there is power, there is resistance" denies such a peaceful existence.[18] Like Downs, Thanzauva also has a great concern for rejection, adoption, and transformation in his evaluation of the interaction of the two traditions. Thanzauva's significant contribution to the tribal theology is his discernment of alienation as tribal

---

13 A. W. Longchar, "The Need for Doing Tribal Theology," in *Tribal Theology: A Reader*, Tribal Study Series 12, ed. S. Shimray (Jorhat: Tribal Study Centre, 2003), 4.

14 Longchar, "The Need for Doing Tribal Theology," 4.

15 Longchar, "The Need for Doing Tribal Theology," 7.

16 Longchar, *An Emerging Asian Theology*, 25-27.

17 K. Thanzauva, *Theology of Community: Tribal Theology in the Making* (Aizawl: Mizo Theological Conference, 1997), 83-84; "Issues in Tribal Theology," in *Tribal Theology: A Reader*, Tribal Study Series 12, ed. S. Shimray (Jorhat: Tribal Study Centre, 2003), 19-20..

18 M. Foucault, "Method," in *The Global Resistance Reader*, ed. L. Amoore (London/New York: Routledge, 2005), 87.

hermeneutical paradigm. He writes, "For Tribal Theology I suggest alienation as the hermeneutical paradigm for the reasons given below."[19]

In this respect, Thanzauva, to a great extent, supports the hermeneutical stance developed by Downs whom he cited as saying that tribals must strive for liberation from any form of alienation for the safeguarding of their identity.[20] When placed in a larger historical context of the hill people in Northeast India, "alienation" can also be seen, in many respects, as a political deliberate choice of the hill peoples to distance themselves from state-control, rather than coerced from outside to their disadvantage. In doing tribal hermeneutics in the context of North-east India, one must seriously ponder upon how they make their existence in rugged terrain, why they developed such a socio-political organization that makes them feel excluded from the rest of the sub-continent. If their racial and socio-cultural identities become the factor that prevents them from incorporating the tribals, one would have to trace the history and ethnic identity formation in North-east India.

2. Towards a Hermeneutics of Resistance in Tribal Context

Having been sorted out the bankruptcy of the existing tribal theology to address the resistance motifs, we must engage with some hermeneutical questions of how to interpret the Bible as well as the history of the hill peoples. The tribals must read the Bible in the context of resistance to domination of various forms. Thanzauva rightly asserts, "Their context requires a reinterpretation of the Bible to address the problems that the[y] encounter in their lives."[21] Tribal reading of the Bible must be shaped and determined by their historical and political realities.

Historically, tribal theology along with other Asian theologies, such as: Minjung theology, Dalit theology, and feminist theology all belonged to the tradition of liberation theology that has emerged from Latin American. Being an offspring of Latin American liberation theology, tribal theology attempts to read the Scriptures from the liberation perspective. As Y. Vashum, a noted theological teacher in North-east India observes, tribal theology seriously searches for liberative messages in the Bible such as: Exodus, the prophetic messages, and the Nazareth Manifesto, and others.[22] In other words, tribal theology is a reduplication of the Latin American liberation theology. It is safe to state that the dominant presence of liberation theology in tribal theology

19 K. Thanzauva, "Issues in Tribal Theology," 27.

20 Thanzauva, *Theology of Community*, 95-96.

21 K. Thanzauva, "Issues in Tribal Theology," 25.

22 Y. Vashum, "Emerging Vision of Indigenous/Tribal Theology," in *Dalit-Tribal Theological Interface: Current Trends in Subaltern Theologies* (New Delhi: Centre for Dalit/Subaltern Studies, 2007), 37.

has tended to overshadow and conceal context sensitive tribal history and has also silenced the resistive aspect of the tribals. Thus, it has not deeply rooted in South-east Asian realities.

In their search for an authentic understanding of the Bible as well as their own history and present realities, the tribal peoples in North-east India must seriously take the following concerns posited by Scott into consideration:

a) The indigenous peoples' livelihoods, social organization, ideologies, oral cultures must be read and interpreted as strategic positioning designed to keep the state powers away.
b) Their dispersion in rugged terrain, their mobility, their agrarian practices including shifting cultivation and choice of crops, their kinship structure, their pliable ethnic identities must be taken as the vantage point for a critical understanding of how they serve to avoid incorporation into states.[23]

The relevance of our research for doing tribal hermeneutics in Northeast-east India lies on the fact that it reads Jesus' campaign in and beyond Galilee in which we found three significant political discourses of the subalterns political discourses—*viz*. the hidden transcript, the politics of disguise and anonymity, and the public declaration of the hidden transcript in the face of power.

2.1. Hidden Transcript of the Tribals in North-east India

First of all, the study tries to understand the geopolitical situation of North-east India as the "hidden Transcript" of popular dignity and indignation. Like the Galileans whom Jesus-in-movement represented, the tribal people in the region have been exploited, alienated and subjugated by the dominants.[24] There is no reason why we should not think that their regular experience of status domination would generate a hidden transcript.

2.1.1. Rugged Terrain as Social Space for a Dissident Sub-culture

One must look the hills in North-east India as the sequestered sites for the tribals where they have developed a hidden transcript of indignation and dignity. Their physical dispersion to the hilly areas is the most interesting aspect in tribal history as it directs us to the history of ethnic identity formation. In fact, the ethnic origin of the tribal in the North-east is an issue of an endless debate over a long period of time. It is intricate as to how these hill peoples have settled in this part of the region, for historical data in writing are very few. However, all of the tribal groups in the regions have a host of legends that have survived to this day and most of these incorporate their ethnic origins. It is remarkable that

23 Scott, *The Art of Not Being Governed*, x.

24 Longchar, "The Need for Doing Tribal Theology," 2.

every tribe has various legends concerning their ethnic origin from which we can out a common ground that their nationality came from the east.[25]

Many of the tribals in North-east India are hill dwellers. They must be understood as hill societies. Land—the most celebrated concept in tribal theological discourse in its real sense for the hill peoples in North-east India—is no other than the rugged terrain upon which they make their existence. If land, as articulated by the tribal theologians, is – life, source of origin, nourishment, support and identity for the tribals,[26] then to what extent can the concept of the hills can still hold on such qualities of life attributed to land? In this matter, one must raise a diagnostic question as to whether the hilly rugged terrain provides space for refuge or it becomes a mode of alienation that excludes the tribals from the rest of India, as argued by some theologians included the notable ones. When read from the encounter between states and self-governing peoples, the rugged terrain becomes a place of refuge for the latter ones. The tribal peoples live in "the shadow of the state, in the shadow of the hills."[27]

The legends of various tribes have inspired and instructed us to re-examine how the tribal people came to be out of the way in the first place. It is utmost importance to know why almost all the hill tribes in North-east India have such legends that denote that their origins are from the east, and what pushed them out to settle in these rugged terrains. Z. Changli, a professor in the Institute for Southeast Asian Studies in China, has conducted an in-depth study on the ethnic origin and customs of the tribals in North-east India. After comparing them with some of the nationalities in Yunnan and Xixang in China and Northern Burma, he concludes that they have the same origin of the nationalities, and then later they dispersed into the different geographical and social environments.[28] He also argues that in the Han Dynasty, the south

25 For instances, an ancient legend current among the Tangkhul Naga depicted that the Naga nationality came from "the East of the world." The Meiteis in Manipur have a similar version that they too belonged to the Sino-Tibetan language family in China. A legend circulated amongst the Mizos, also denote that their ancestors emerged from *chhinlung*, which was in China. An ancient folk song now still sung among the Kuki people also bears witness to the same. Some ethnographers are convinced that the tribal peoples in India's North-east have their ethnic origins in the south western part of China. The legends of the Garo tribe have mentioned that their initial place was Xizang. When they were out of Xizang, according to the legend, "they got into flatlands by the foot of the Himalayas, then went on moving eastward in search of pasture to the Brahmaputra Valley, and then returned along the original to the flatlands situated in between the Valley and hills where they live now." See, Changli, "A Study of the Ethnic Origin and Customs of the Nationalities," 40-50.

26 As for example, see, Longchar, "The Need for Doing Tribal Theology," 9-10.

27 Scott, *The Art of Not Being Governed*, 216.

28 Changli, "A Study of the Ethnic Origin and Customs of the Nationalities," 57.

western region of China belonged to the ancient Qiang language branch which later developed into Tibeto-Burman language branch.[29]

In his most recent work published in 2009, *The Art of Not Being Governed: An Anarchist History of Upland Southeast Asia*, Scott argues that the hill peoples in Southeast Asia are best understood as "runway, fugitive, maroon community who have, over the course of two millennia, been fleeing the oppressions of the state-making projects in the valley – slavery, conscription, taxes, corvée labor, epidemics, and warfare."[30] Scott further adds, "Most of the areas in which they reside may aptly called shatter zones or zones of refuge."[31] According to Scott's argument, the history of the hill peoples in South-east Asia, which includes the hill peoples in North-east India, have been largely destined and determined by their resistance to "being governed" by the Han-Chinese state.

In the light of the above recent research, the ethnic genesis of the tribal needs to be radically reconstructed based on their history. The entire history must be read and understood between Han-Chinese state and the British imperial state. As they escaped from the Han-Chinese rule, sovereignty and taxes stopped, and there precisely, ethnicity and tribes began, and the term 'tribal' remains a word which is used to describe any self-governing, non-subject people. Quite often such tribal identities have never been the focus of academic research.

2.1.2. Off-stage Performance of the Tribals

One of the most important potential gains in recognizing the reality of the hidden transcript for the tribal studies is the tribal scholars' enlargement to include various forms of domination and the resistance. It is true that recent tribal scholarship have realized various forms of domination, such as: alienation, suppression, exploitation, *etc*. We can categorize them as emotional-cultural dimension of the tribal realities. This dimension has an intrinsic quality that shapes the culture of the tribals. Some characteristics basic to the tribals in North-east India, such as: their physical mobility, their agricultural practices, and their egalitarianism, can be read as strategic positioning strategies to avoid incorporation into states and to prevent states from being formed.

First of all, the physical mobility of the hill tribes must also be seen as their strategic positioning to avoid state formation. The tribals are commonly described as having an autonomous and loosely structured society. This reality is a political construct, of their choice. The autonomy of hill peoples from

29 Changli, "A Study of the Ethnic Origin and Customs of the Nationalities," 47.

30 Scott, *The Art of Not Being Governed*, ix.

31 Scott, *The Art of Not Being Governed*, x.

permanent hierarchy and from state formation has depended absolutely on physical mobility. The practice of the tribal peoples to move for the cause of their worth and on the slightest pretext caused problems for both the colonial regimes and the independent states. Flight, not rebellion, has been the basis of freedom in the hills. For example, if a Mizo does not like his/her chief, he/she can migrate to someone else village.

Second, the tribals often value independence more highly than economic advantage. Their practice of shifting cultivation and crop choice are illustrative to this supposition. The peoples in the hilly region have been practising shifting cultivation for centuries. When compared to permanent cultivation in the plain areas, shifting cultivation is economically less advantages. This technique of farming is seen by non-tribals, including those in charge of development programmes in the hills, as both primitive and environmentally destructive. Moreover, the tribals who practice this are also adjudicated as backward or primitive.

Conceptualisation of land is only half way, if the resistive element of the use of land is not employed as the key component in the process of the construction of tribal hermeneutics. Longchar's attempt to understand the shifting cultivation as "reciprocal use of natural resources" by the tribal must be appreciated.[32] The tribal theology must be articulated to facilitate the commitment, because to opt for shifting cultivation is to opt for a sociopolitical life outside the framework of the state. Scott argues, "Shifting cultivation was a fiscally sterile form of agriculture: diverse, dispersed, and hard to monitor, hard to collect for corvée labor or conscription."[33] Thus, Scott offers us the insight that shifting cultivation is the most common agro-political strategy against raiding, state-making, and state appropriation.

That shifting cultivation was the strategy against raiding and state-making finds support in the selection of crops. A remarkable feature of shifting cultivation is that almost all varieties of cereals and vegetables are grown in one *Jhum* field.[34] In the fields of tribals, especially in Mizoram and Nagaland, rice, maize, cucumber, chilly, bean of various kinds, yams, mustard, water-melon, cotton, etc are grown together. These are crops that are sown within half a year or one year. More importantly, they are almost "appropriation proof."[35] This practice of shifting cultivation as well as the choice of the perennial crops is always understood within a framework of economic subsistence. In fact,

32 Longchar, "The Need for Doing Tribal Theology," 13-14.

33 Scott, *The Art of Not Being Governed*, 195.

34 P. S. Datta, *India's North-East: A Study in Transition* (New Delhi: Vikas Publishing House, 1992), 38.

35 Scott, *The Art of Not Being Governed*, 191.

both the practices are surely for economic subsistence, yet the political factor beneath the practices need to be unearthed.

Finally, the tribals in North-east India are best known for their communitarian lifestyle. It is important to understand egalitarianism as core to the tribal politics for the prevention of states. A comparison of egalitarian and hierarchical social formations points to some of the cultural practices that work to hinder the development of permanent hierarchies of state and power. The more they cultivate the spirit of egalitarianism, the more chances of survival they have. This insight encourages us to probe into the tribal values to see if they contain resistance values. Tribal altruism, *sobaliba* and *tlawmgaihna* have become the famous moral code adhered to by the Aos of Nagaland and the Mizo respectively.[36] From a resistance perspective, it is much more than a code of morals, but—like God's kingdom in Mark—it is a popular ideology that comprises an alternative to the values and views articulated in the official transcript controlled by the dominant. Their community centres like youth dormitory, popularly known as *zawlbuk* in Mizoram and *morung* in Nagaland becomes strategic social spaces as long as they promote, uphold the egalitarian ethos of the tribals.[37] Even, to a great extent, the youth dormitory of the tribals serves as the sequestered sites beyond the effective reach of the eyes and ears of power in. Thus, *pum* (blacksmith inn), *tuikhur* (water point), *zu hmun* (tavern) in the Mizo Hills and the Naga Hills remain the potential places where the resentful and anger of the villagers were articulated in their various languages and they acquired disciplined forms to become sophisticated and stable cultural forms.

2.2. Oral Culture of the Tribals as the Politics of Disguise and Anonymity

The tribals are evidently rich in oral culture. Their myths, legends, folklores, folktales, dances, *etc.* are anonymous for a simple reason–they have no individual authors. In fact, they resonate what Scott has devised as "politics of disguise and anonymity." More importantly, many of the things listed above fit well within the genre of the Biblical parable.

The orality of the tribal history has always been taken against their disadvantages by others. The tribals are typically stigmatized by neighboring cultures as peoples without history, as lacking the fundamental characteristics of civilization, namely historicity. Absence of writing and texts provides freedom of maneuver in history, genealogy, and legibility that frustrates state

36 For details, see, Longchar, "The Need for Doing Tribal Theology," 11; M. Kipgen, "Tlawmngaihna and Christianity," in *Tribal Theology: A Reader*, ed. S. Shimray (Jorhat: Tribal Study Centre, 2003), 79-104.

37 Vashum, Naga's *Right to Self Determination*, 15.

routines. Knowing the stigma which is historically attached to their non-literacy by lowland states and colonizers, most tribal peoples have oral legends that account for why they do not write.[38] The Mizo legend states that says their literature had been eaten up by a dog contains a grain of truth, though it does not explain why the knowledge was not passed on. Such legends are like ethnic identity itself, a strategic positioning *vis-à-vis* other groups.[39] Perhaps, these legends, myths, and folklores are attributable more to the common strategic location of most stateless hill peoples in relation to the large valley kingdoms than to any other cultural inactivity.

North-east India presents a picture of bewildering cultural diversity, particularly in regard to its tribal population. Apart from the fact that the largest number of different tribal communities live in hills and plains of the region, what is striking is that we have here the tribal and non-tribal, the acculturated and the assimilated, the Sanskritised and the non-Sanskritised, the highly refined and the obviously primitive, all coexisting in a remarkable state of conflict and resistance. Interestingly and challengingly, the tribal groups, hill tribes or plains, tribals or non-tribals, acculturated or assimilated, Sanskritised or non-Sanskritised, have their own stories, reflective of the various dimensions of contact (*viz*., physical, biological, cultural) are found in rich folkloristic materials of North-east India. In some cases, the folklores present situations of intertribal or tribal–non-tribal conflict, tension, conflict, or even open hostility.

A good number of tribal myths and legends from different parts of the region are concerned not only with the ethno-genesis of their respective communities but of those neighbouring communities as well, including the non-tribals in the plains. These folk culture and practices understood within the right perspective can become an invaluable source for hermeneutics in the context of the tribal people.

The oral culture of the tribals in North-east India has received academic interest in recent times. Broadly speaking, the academic interpretations can be divided into two: the theological and the secular. First, it seems clear that the tribal theologians have special interest in tribal myths, legends, and folktales. They are hopeful that these oral cultural heritages are useful resources for the formulation of a tribal theology in the North-east Indian context. In his 1995's book, *In Search of a Relevant Gospel Message*, Keitzar has made a seminal statement for the formulation of tribal hermeneutics. Keitzar identifies the oral tradition of the tribal people as the unwritten "Prime Bible," when he writes,

> These may be called as the written 'Prime Bible' of the tribal/indigenous people. One can find in these oral traditions, their beliefs, norms, and

38 Scott, *The Art of Not Being Governed*, 221-222.

39 Scott, *The Art of Not Being Governed*, 220.

> practices; hence a great and rich treasure of theological value is hidden with this 'Prime Bible' of the people."[40]

Keitzar offers a religio-culture context for the study of tribal oral cultural heritage. The tribal scholars after him have evidently accepted his view. For instance, Longchar and Y. Vashum, in their articles written separately, but published in a book entitled, *Tribal Theology: A Reader* (2003) have read the tribal myths as vehicle for conveying theological truth and meaning for a particular group of people.[41] They seem to be impressive that the tribals who had never relied on any written scripture have used their legends, myths, folklores and folktales as their scriptures. Longchar affirms, "Thus, myth is our sacred scripture and creed."[42]

In spite of the fact that the earlier studies have made significant contribution, yet a deeper dimension can still be expected if they are situated within the framework of tribal and non-tribal power relations. Thus, the hermeneutics of resistance proposes that the tribal oral cultures must be read as a strategic positioning designed to keep away the non-tribal state, that is to say: to avoid incorporation into a non-tribal state and to prevent the state from springing up among the tribals.

Second, we also have seen a good number of literatures coming up in recent times from secular studies. The scholarly work of B. Datta, a folklorist from Assam, *Cultural Contours of North-east India* (2012) is a good example in this area. Datta's assumption is that the tribal folklores in many ways reflect the relationship between tribal and non-tribal populations in North-east India.[43] The significance of this Assamese folklorist's contribution lies on the fact that he reads the tribal folklores from the perspective of togetherness and commonness. Batta finds evidences from tribal folklores to say that "all men were once brothers and they somewhat got separated later" and this has been reflected in some of the tribal folklores.[44] However, one must be conscious as to whether, if what Longchar once terms as "ethnocide and genocide policy towards the tribals"[45] is turning its face towards tribal folklores. We must read such recent interpretations with certain reservations since they are written from the perspective of the centre. Hence, the resistive aspect of tribal oral culture can be overshadowed by the idea of national integration. A diachronic

40 R. Keitzar, *In Search of a Relevant Gospel Message* (Guwahati: CLC, 1995), 85.

41 Y. Vashum, "Sources for Studying Tribal Theology," in *Tribal Theology: A Reader*, Tribal Study Series 12, ed. S. Shimray (Jorhat: Tribal Study Centre, 2003), 69.

42 Vashum, "Sources for Studying Tribal Theology," 69.

43 D. Datta, *Cultural Contours of North-east India* (New Delhi: Oxford University Press, 2012), 21-35.

44 Datta, *Cultural Contours of North-east India*, 23-31.

45 Longchar, "The Need for Doing Tribal Theology," 2.

interpretation of historical texts like the tribal legends, myths, and folklores can further lead to assimilation of tribal movements into a non-tribal complex, which is seemingly just the opposite of the original intention of the tribal folklores. Therefore, a different reading, and a more synchronic approach, is needed.

The tribal folklores clearly indeed reflect contacts among various communities, tribal and non-tribal which take place in the history of North-east India. However, the hermeneutics of resistance would assume the tribal folklores as the politics of disguise and anonymity. We shall cite some selected folkloric items, mostly verbal of the Nagas and the Mizo which bear witness to, or are suggestive of, the politics of disguise and anonymity of the tribals, particularly highlighting items that avoid the non-tribals and prevent states from springing up among them.

Some Naga myths and legends reflect the avoidance of state and the prevention of states from springing up among them. When the tribals—nonstate people—faced pressures for political and social incorporation into a state system, a variety of reasons are responsible. The Angami tale, popularly known as "The Tower of Babel" may be read and interpreted within this frame of thought. J.H. records the tale, thus:

> Ukepenopfii was the first being. Her descendants are very many. Instead of dying she was translated into Heaven. Later on her descendants thought to communicate with her by building a tower upto Heaven, up[on] which they would go and talk to her. She, however, knowing their thoughts, said to herself, 'They will all expect presents and I have no presents for so many men. The tower must be stopped before it gets higher.' So she made all the men working at the tower talk different languages, so that they could not understand one another.[46]

This Angami tale of Nagaland traces back the time when the Nagas, or at least a section of them (*i.e.* the Angami) were incorporated loosely or tightly perhaps as a tributary society with a designated head under the leadership of Ukepenopfii. After her death, they may have had to fight in order to defend their autonomy by forming a state with a socio-political structure. The fact that,"They will all expect presents" from power above by building a tower is suggestive that they made a grave attempt to establish a centrally sponsored state. However, Ukepenopfii, a symbol of power at the centre, stopped them from such a political project. So, they moved out of the way. Finally, they, by fissioning, became different people with different dialects and were scattered to different parts of the region. They changed their livelihood strategies and made themselves invisible or unattractive as objects of appropriation. This

46 J. H. Hutton, *The Angami Naga* (London: Oxford University Press, 1969), 165.

Angami tale tells of us how the slogan "Divide that you be not ruled" worked effectively among the tribals.

Ao's version of ethno-genesis comes from two different sub-tribes of the Mongsen and the Chongli.[47] Both the versions must be read as strategies of the Ao Nagas for resistance and evasion. At the superficial level, the narrative encompasses a close brotherly connection between the Nagas and the Assamese. This tale anchors upon two divergent livelihoods: shifting cultivation and dao making factory. The tale reminds us that the tribals had faced social and political pressures of choosing trades for their destination. We can sense the elder brother who became the ancestor of the Nagas holding the edges. We see the elder brother suppressing the steel making industrial works and preferring a shifting cultivation in the hills as his trade. This Mongsen tale tells of the Ao's strategy of prevention of "industrial state"—as "making daos" suggests so—from being established among them. In the same way, the Chongli's version of the tale looks back upon the social disintegration of a household into minimal units, accompanied by the hill people's adoption of subsistence strategies that favour small, scattered bands. Both the tales denote that to live in the hills and advocating shifting cultivation as their livelihood were the political choices of the hill tribals, whatever may be the cost.

The Mizo do not have such developed folklores depicting a biological link with the plain people. Even the famous *chhinlung* tradition which talks about the origins of various sub-tribes under the umbrella of Mizo contains

---

47 J. P. Mills captures both the folklores, thus: "There once lived, they say two brothers. The elder used to go down to the fields and work, but the younger used to at his home. Unknown to his brother spent his time making "daos." A pig's food-trough held the water for tempering, and his tool was a wooden hammer. Every evening before the elder brother came home the younger used to turn the trough upside down and hide under it the results of his day's work. But one day the elder brother turned the pig's trough up and saw what's underneath. Then he abused the younger brother for wasting his time instead of joining in work in the fields. After this quarrel they decided to part. The younger, who chose the plains as his inheritance, was the ancestor of the Assamese, and the elder, who went to the hills, the founder of the Naga race. Before they parted they agreed that whichever, as they went their ways, should turn round and look at the other should pay tribute to him. The younger went off singing with a cloth wound round his head like a pugaree, and the elder turned and shouted to him: 'A good journey to you, younger brother.' That is why the Aos paid tribute to the Assam Raja. The Chongli version is different. According to them there were once three brothers. Of these the eldest was the ancestor of the Aos, the middle of the Konyaks and other tribes now living to the East of the Dikhu, and the youngest of the Assamese. One night, when the two younger brothers were sleeping under one cloth and the elder alone under his cloth, the youngest got up and ran away with the cloth he was sharing. That is why Assamese have so many clothes and Konyaks none. The Aos have what they have always had, a man's proper costume. The two Naga-ancestor brothers eventually parted somewhere East of the Dikkhu." See, *The Ao Nagas* (Bombay: Oxford University Press, 1973), 310-311.

no single line referring, either openly or tacitly to the fact that they were once brothers with the plains tribes and that they had been separated from them. The reason may that the Mizo have least physical contact with the non-tribals, apart from economic transactions. Nonetheless, they have a good number of tales that express their relationship towards the animal kingdom. With regard to the Mizo animal tales, of all animals, money takes the prominent place in the Mizo animal tales in terms of frequency of appearances. Tales like *The Monkey and the Tortoise*,[48] *The Monkey and his Flute*[49] are worth mentioning here. It is interesting to observe the characterization of the monkey as mischievous in character, master in deceiving others, destructive to others; however, at the end story, the animal becomes the victim of his/her own deeds. The Mizo animal tales reveal how they discarded vile, mischievous, cunning behaviour and unfaithfulness. While situating their animal tales in the context of the interaction between the tribals–non-tribals, especially at the economic level, there are more insights to be revealed.

Physical contact between tribals and non-tribals is also depicted in terms of the biological aspect. Datta denotes, "Chiefs or warriors take wives from outside the community or when love affairs between individuals of different communities result in unions, with or without social approval."[50] A tale of the Angami in Nagaland about the Nagas and the plain people may be cited here. The story is about a family where inter cultural marriage took place. The wife, by name Ukepenopfii, was the ancestress of all humans. And her husband, whose name was unrevealed, had a big moustache and long beard that touched his feet. He was also depicted as very wise man. Since, men with long beards are rare among the tribals; the husband could be a non-tribal who originally hailed from the plain areas. Hence, it is a tale of inter-cultural marriage between a tribal woman and a man from the plain areas.

As far as the parents are concerned, the tale goes well. But, problem arose when it comes to their children and their relationship with their parents. The father had to live a hidden in a vessel lest his two sons should get scared by his appearance and failed to get his wisdom. However, at their insistence, the two sons were allowed to have a look at their father, whereupon the elder, who became the ancestor of the Nagas, was frightened and ran away. The young son, who was to later beget the plainsmen, welcomed the father. Ukepenopfii's husband advised her to take care of the elder son and he left for the plains with the younger one, teaching him all his wisdom.[51]

48 Margaret L. Pachuau, *Hand-Picked Tales from Mizoram* (Kolkata: Writers Workshop Books, 2008), 21-22.

49 Pachuau, *Hand-Picked Tales from Mizoram*, 37-38.

50 Datta, *Cultural Contours of North-east India,* 22-23.

51 J. H. Hutton, *The Angamis Naga* (London: Oxford University Press, 1969), 260-261.

Again, this tales has "fissioning" and "scattering" as its main thrust. The two brothers were divided into two tribes: the elder one to remain in the hills and the younger one to depart into the plains. This tale can be taken as a symbolism of the tribal and non-tribal interaction. If so, it symbolizes well that the tribals rendered preference to their political autonomy and the right to self-determination, other than values such as wisdom.

Within this framework, we fit in appropriately the famous Mizo romantic tale of *Tualvungi and Zawlpala*, a parable of resistance. Tualvungi was a beautiful and courteous tribal lady, married to a gentleman of her own tribe. While living a happily married life with her husband Zawlpala, Phunṭiha, a "*vai lal*"—a rich and powerful king of the valley empire—appeared on the scene. The non-tribal ruler took away Tualvungi to be his wife after giving her husband a huge, irresistible, extraordinary amount of treasures as a bridal price.[52] As the story goes on, the life of the lonely lover Zawlpala was terminated with contaminated food by the cruel plain ruler. Tualvungi later escaped from Phunṭiha and returned only to be laid next to Zawlpala in his grave. They happily rejoined in the next phase of life by becoming a couple of eye-catching butterflies. When that man heard that she left him, he went out in search of her, but at last he took his life. He too became a butterfly, but he was a big one and flew awkwardly, enviously chasing the couple flying up and down joyfully. This romantic tale, when read as positional strategies in its historical context of tribal–non-tribals relations, is a tale of great resistance story for the hill tribals. The particular group of butteries remains a flying parable of resistance for the hill people.

When examined with fresh eyes, the tribal people's socio-cultural systems, beliefs, values and attitudes exhibit all the features that Scott discusses as a hidden transcript. The core idea—"state evasion, state prevention"—finds expression in their parables, *i.e.,* legends, myths, and folklores. The tribals were determined to preserve their own dignity, and to resist the worst effects of domination, and insist upon justice. Indeed, the oral cultural heritages have been accumulated since many generations. We must consider these elements as the basic elements of their political disguise and anonymity.

2.3. Public Declaration of the Hidden Transcript: The Tribals in the Face of Power

From the disguise and anonymous forms of resistance, we shall shift to more public and direct form of resistance. The beginning of the 19th century marked

52 The bridal price of Tualvungi includes jewellery that could break an entire pole; guns when displayed covered the middle wall of their house; yaks, when herded filled the whole enclosure of a house; a brass bell as high as the roof of the house; and clothes that filled a hundred trunks. This is a huge bridal price when compare to today's bride price, four hundred and twenty rupees!

the struggle for supremacy between the South-East Asia, Burmese rule and the South Asia, by the British over Assam and north-east frontier which ended up with the First Anglo-Burmese War on 24th February 1824. In the war, the British defeated the Burmese and drove them out from Assam, and by the Treaty of Yandaboo in 1826, Assam was brought under British power.[53] There is no doubt that British interest to hold power over Assam was to exploit the vast economic potential of the Brahmaputra Valley. The British occupation of the Valley marked the beginning of punitive expeditions against the hill peoples in the frontier from the early part of the 19th century to safeguard the plain fertile areas from the war like the Nagas and the Mizo.

2.3.1. Preventing and Defending of the Hidden Transcript on the Hill

The Europeans, both secular and religious authorities, understood the danger of autonomous sites of dissident folk culture could pose. The British authorities made strenuous efforts to abolish or control such dissident sites by the hill peoples by sending military expeditions several times to punish and subdue the tribals and their chiefs. In order to check the tribals from further outrages, the British government created the Naga Hills and Lushai Hills (later Mizoram) during the nineteenth century. The Naga Hills suffered as many as ten British expeditions from 1839 to 1850. The main objective sought to be achieved, according to A. Mackenzie, was "to subdue all the Angamis north of the Water-Pent," especially the villages of "Mozemah and Konemah," whose chiefs were the "principal leaders of raids" on the British subjects.[54] After they were subdued, the Angamis had to give some tribute to the British as an acknowledgment of their supremacy. Despite this intended aim, there was no such "tangible result than the burning of many villages, destruction of much grain, and the loss of many lives and the confirmed hostility of the whole Angami Naga."[55] The expedition was followed by colonial control from 1866-1947. During the late 1860s and early 1870s, the British administration had expanded tea plantation in the frontier Mizo Hills which had aroused great resentment of the Mizo against the British and caused a lot of disturbance to the tea planters. In order to control the problem, the Inner Line Regulation was enforced in the Naga Hills and Mizo Hills. The Regulation was enforced prohibiting British subjects from entering the Naga Hills and Mizo Hills without prior permission.

---

53 Aosenba, *The Naga Resistance Movement: Prospect of Peace and Armed Conflict* (New Delhi: Regency Publications, 2001), 12.

54 A. Mackenzie, The North-East Frontier of Assam (Delhi: Mittal Publications, 1979), 106.

55 T. Ao, *British Occupation of Naga Country* (Mokokchung: Naga Literature Society, 1993), 12.

The occupation of hills by the British was initially to protect the plain peoples from tribal raids. But, later on, they started to penetrate the areas for their administrative as well as political convenience. The colonial power spilled over to the sequestered confines of the hidden transcript of the tribals to pose a direct threat to them. In this way, the British administration took great pain to prevent the creation of sites where hidden transcript could be created and shared. They were aided the plain people who were mainly Aryan origin. The British took pains to subdue the dissident sub-culture by bringing a labour force of the greatest linguistic and ethnic diversity, the native peoples were required to converse at work only in a form of English the colonial power could understand.

On the other hand, we have efforts put by the tribals to defend the hidden transcript as well. S. N. Lamare, a historian from Meghalaya, denotes that a peasant movement had broken out in Assam (1861), which was caused mainly by the ever increasing revenue extraction of the British government. Lamare states that there were taxes on almost everything and whatever that was earlier procured by the Assamese peasants free of coast like timber and fish. Reeds for constructing of houses and fodder for cattle were no longer free.[56] In fact, his book is an extensive study of the resistance by the Jaintia people in Meghalaya during 1860-1863 against the British Indian Government which had imposed a house tax imposed on them and the restrictions on their local customs.[57]

The most significant development had taken place when the tribals in North-east India who had been avoiding states for many centuries became states under the Indian Union. The founders of the states in North-east India had to assemble peoples of various backgrounds from among hitherto stateless populations. So often happened, a state disintegrated, subsequent state-makers had to re-assemble subjects or incorporate stateless hill peoples. The tribals in hilly areas were incorporated into the Assam valley polity. The process of state-making, of turning hill people into valley people, could, it seems clear, just as easily be reversed. Many of the tribes were vulnerable to the state.

Between 1872 and 1890, the Mizo *pasalṭha* (heroes, warriors) conducted raids against the Britishers. The latter had encroached upon the land by establishing tea estates within their territory in the northern part and threatened to encroach still more.[58] The British sent their troops and subjugated them in 1890. Ethnic identities in the hills are politically crafted and designed to position a group *vis-à-vis* others in competition for power and resources. This

56 S. N. Lamare, *Resistance Movements in North-East India: The Jaintias of Meghalaya 1860-1893* New Delhi: Regency Publications, 2001), 13.

57 Lamare, *Resistance Movements in North-East India,* 41-55.

58 J. M. Lloyd, *History of the Church in Mizoram: Harvest in the Hills* (Aizawl: Synod Publication Board, 1991), 5-9; see also, Pachuau, *Ethnic Identity and Christianity*, 68-69.

resistance war against the British was really agrarian as it involved protection of their land.

2.3.2. Open Declaration of the Hidden Transcript of the Tribals

The post independent India is marked by the beginning of tribal national movements. The tribals in North-east India are also known for their overt resistance movements.[59] Not only for this region, but for the whole world, the 1960s were "the high tide of what one might term as the romance with peasant wars of national liberation."[60] Almost all of the major tribal groups in the region have their own militant group, carrying "national" in their name (*e.g.* Kuki National Army, Naga National Socialist Council of Nagaland, Mizo National Front), while standing up for their identity and national liberation. Takatemjen is right when he observes, "No other region in the world has been the existence of so many ethnic based insurgent outfits as Northeast India does."[61] A major phenomena which generated regarding the tribal movements was regarding aspects related to "their inability to adjust themselves to the emerging socio-political situations on the eve of the Indian independence" and "the impending withdrawal of British administration, which they thought gave them a measure of special protection and some privileges," as told by some historians.[62] However, these overt tribal resistance movements in North-east India must be understood as the continuation of political process of the various non-state peoples of this region preventing them from the process incorporating into Indian statehood.

The Naga and Mizo insurgencies had their origin in the colonial period and were a part of an all India political process. According to T. Thou, "The imminence of India's independence was characterized by two opposite trends – one, a pan-Indian sentiment seeking to integrate and be a part of a single Indian nation-state; two, another perspective was that it could be separate from the Indian nation-state and seek its national destiny independently."[63] Most areas and peoples wanted to merge with the Indian identity, some group and princely states opted for separation from India. The princely states, namely

59 M. Ao, "Impact of the Context: Tribal Perspective," in *Dalit-Tribal Theological Interface: Current Trends in Subaltern Theologies* (New Delhi: Centre for Dalit/Subaltern Studies, 2007), 153, 158.

60 Scott, *Decoding Subaltern Politics*, 1.

61 Takatemjen, "Conflicts and Peacebuilding in Northeast India: Challenges and Prospects," in *Conflicts and Peacebuilding in Northeast India: Challenges and Prospects*, ed. Takatemjen (Mokokchung: Clark Centre for Peace Research and Action, 2013), ix.

62 N. K. Das, "The Naga Movement," in *Tribal Movements in India*, Vol. 1, ed. K. S. Singh (Delhi: Manohar, 1982), 40.

63 T. Thou, "A Comparative Analysis of Naga, Mizo, and Meitei Insurgencies," *Encyclopedia of Mizoram*, vol. 2 (New Delhi: Anmol Publications, 2009), 446.

Naga and Mizo movements were also restorative to their own systems. This was, according to Thou, "an attempt to put the clock back, which was resisted by the new social group – the representative middle classes which had emerged in the hills as the advent of modernity."[64]

In Mizoram, the popular masses, which later turned into a political party called the *Mizo Commoners*[65] voiced their concern against restoration of the oppressive rule of the chiefs. The new and first political party organised a political movement for integration with India to foster the abolishment of the institution of the chieftainship, which was a political agenda of the Indian National Congress. This popular resistance movement was very strong and hence eventually successful. On the other hand, the traditional ruling elite of the chiefs formed the *United Freedom Organisation* (UMFO) and propagated a concern against merging with India, so that their power will be restored.[66] The New political party gained popular support and the chiefs were defeated.

In the Naga Hills too, there were two predicaments. Aosenba writes: "Whether the Naga Hills would be able to constitute an Independent Sovereign State after the British left India; whether the Nagas would be able to attain independence and run a Sovereign state."[67] As the predicaments suggest, there were two political trends: one was seeking to merge with India at least for some time, and the other seeking to restore the old order of chiefs. The former was led by enlightened leaders like Aliba Inti and T. Sakhrie, while the latter was led by Naga chiefs turned interpreters of the colonial period. In this respect, the situation in Nagaland and Mizoram was different. The traditional leadership won the support of the masses, because of the Indian state's tackling of the whole crisis. The initial resistance of the new people's movement against the traditional leadership's insistence on outright sovereignty was so strong, but the Indian state's dealing with the Naga issue isolated these new people's movement. When the traditional leaders emphasized more on the restoration of their power, Phizo left the party and formed a separate group called the *People's Independence League*. However, the new group faded into oblivion and Phizo returned as the messiah of the Nagas after the NMC-Akbar Hydari Nine-Point Agreement fiasco.[68]

---

64 Thou, "A Comparative Analysis of Naga, Mizo, and Meitei Insurgencies," 446-447.

65 Subsequently, this name was changed into Mizo Union.

66 For B. B. Goswami and D. P. Mukherjee, the aim was "to merge the Mizo (Lushai Hills) area with the Union of Burma." See, "The Mizo Political Movement," in *Tribal Movements in India*, Vol. 1, ed. K. S. Singh (Delhi: Manohar, 1982), 135.

67 Aosenba, *The Naga Resistance Movement*, 36. Arrangement is mine.

68 The Nine Point Agreement was signed in 1947 between Sir Akbar Hydari then Governor of Assam and the leader of the leader of the NNC that dealt with the future relationship of the Nagas.

In Mizoram, after a successful struggle against the dispensation of the chiefs, the Mizo leadership settled down to peace and order within India. However, the Indian state failed to meet the aspirations of this new political party. Constituted as a district within Assam, the Assam leadership ignored the developmental needs of the tribals. Despite its promise, the Indian state delayed abolishing the institution of chieftainship. While the Indian state threatened to impose Hindi, the province tried to force Assamese; the District Council was a glorified debating society without any financial empowerment. When the periodic *mautam* (bamboo famine) stalked the Mizo hills in 1959-1960 resulting in starvation deaths, the Assam government appeared unconcerned.[69] Since the famine is periodic and occurs after a cycle of fifty years, and especially as the famine was also predicted, the Mizo were disappointed with the scanty measures taken by the Assam Government. All these developments prompted the traditional leadership to re-emerge and vigorously propagate the idea that their apprehension that the marginal tribes like the Mizo would always be treated unevenly by the Indian state had proven to be true. During the famine, the *Mizo National Famine Front* (MNFF) became a leading voluntary organization in the relief work.[70] And after the famine, the organization renamed itself *Mizo National Front* (MNF) and this led to an armed resistance during 1966-1986 which opened a new chapter in Mizo history.[71]

As mentioned above, the tribal resistance movements in North-east India had a distinctive character. Both in Mizoram and Nagaland, the movements were spearheaded by the old autocracy – the chiefs and his rank members, as they feared that, under a promised republican government, they would lose their power, prestige and status. The same pan-Indian feeling turned antipathy due to the failure of the leadership, as also the indifference on the Indian state.

3. God and the Tribals

Finally, it must be reiterated that this research has reflected upon "how the notion of God is set in favour of the marginalised subalterns" as the fundamental research question. Our findings concerning this theological question bear much significance to enhance hermeneutics of resistance in the contexts of tribals. Here, we shall critically assess the God-factor in the ongoing tribal theological discourse, and try to re-emphasize the tribal notion of God in the context of domination and resistance.

First of all, the primary task of hermeneutics in the context of the tribal context is to interpret this political aspect found in the tribal notion of God. The tribal theologians in recent times have brought forth the idea of

69 Pachuau, *Ethnic Identity and Christianity*, 85.

70 For detailed information, Goswami and Mukhejee, "The Mizo Political Movement," 138.

71 Pachuau, *Ethnic Identity and Christianity*, 86-87.

Supreme Being in the tribal religious beliefs and practices into the theological discourse. We must re-read the concept of the Supreme Being in the context of tribals defending their political autonomy. The tribal religious beliefs and practices are basically characterized by an underlining idea of a supreme being. Thanzauva has interestingly pointed out that this Supreme Being is known by different names to different tribes, such as: *Ukpenuaffu* (Angami), *Lijaba* (Ao), *U Blei* (Khasi), *Tartara Robunga* (Garo), *Pathian* (Mizo, Kuki, Chin), and so on.[72] It is evident that the tribals believed and worshiped the Supreme Being par excellence.[73] In an age when the tribals had their own power to govern, presumably the notion of God bore a strong political sense. Each tribe[74] worshipped the Supreme Being, the creator, the protector and the sustainer of the tribes. For sure, the Supreme Being was the source of power for each tribe in their struggles for the sustenance of their political autonomy. Thus, the notion of God as a supreme being is possibly a political construct. R. Chhuanliana Kawlni, in his pursuit for centrality of God to the Mizo Christianity, spells out clearly that the God as the "dispenser of justice."[75] We

72 Thanzauva, *Theology of Community*, 152.

73 Apart from the "Supreme Being," most of the tribals in the region also believed in the existence of both benevolent and malevolent spirits who were more active in human affairs. Since they believed that malevolent spirits caused misfortunes and sufferings, the tribals used to offer sacrifices to the spirits to principally appease them. As the tribals had undergone a lot of sufferings, they had to offer sacrifices more to the evil spirits. In the case of Mizo belief, which was also shared by most of the tribal groups in the region, disease, distress, and death were caused by the evil spirits. Therefore, in every village of ancient Mizoram, there were priests supporting the distressed people in offering the sacrifice. See, K. P. Nath, "Mizo Value, Beliefs and Practices vis-à-vis Christianity," in *History and Ethnic Identity Formation in North-East India*, ed. J. V. Hluna (New Delhi: Concept Publishing Company, 2013), 143. Zairema, one of the most trusted leaders of the Mizo Christians, says, "To placate these evil spirits, they had to offer endless sacrifices." See, Zairema, "The Mizo Church," in *Ground Works for Tribal Theology in the Mizo Context*, ed. R. Tochhawng, K. Lalrinmawia, L. H. Rawsea (Delhi: ISPCK, 2007), 23. Commenting upon the Nagas, Keitzar says they "spent more time in their possession to appease malevolent spirits than worshipping the good High God." See, Keitzar, "Tribal Theological Trends in North East India," 46. When the British colonizers and the missionaries came and saw the tribals offering sacrifices to the evil spirits, they thought that the tribals were worshippers of evil spirits, thus animists. Because of this misunderstanding, the early missionaries were hesitant to adopt the tribal concept of God for theological articulation. See, Keitzar, "Tribal Theological Trends in North East India," 47.

74 It is also possible that every family worshipped God who was specific to their family or clan. See, Zairema, "The Mizo Church," in *Ground Works for Tribal Theology in the Mizo Context*, ed. R. Tochhawng, K. Lalrinmawia, L. H. Rawsea (Delhi: ISPCK, 2007), 23.

75 R. Chhuanliana Kawlni, *Lord God Most High My Saviour: Theocentricity in Lukan Theology: An Exploration into the Portrayals of God in Luke-Acts* (Delhi: ISPCK, 2009), 248-249.

must assume that the tribal notion of God became the source of power for all the tribals to stand against their foes.

The tribals' notion of sovereignty is closely related to the concept of God's kingdom as proclaimed by Jesus. Time and again, we mention that the hill peoples, especially the Nagas and the Mizo, were self-governing who have persistently rejected incorporation into states. Every village in the hills in their pre-colonial era, had governed itself as politically independent, ruled over by the village chiefs.[76] The hill tribes have claimed that they had sovereign authority; nobody would interfere in matters relating to their political, social, and economic life. For them the notion of God is concrete, experienced within a political framework. Thus, their Mizo chiefs were said to have boldly claimed "*ni leh thla inkara leng kan ni*" (lit. "We are between the Sun and the Moon"), which expressed the sovereignty of the tribal chiefs, there are no intermediaries, except the celestial bodies. Their idea of political sovereignty is an integral part of their notion of God as Supreme Being, they are inseparable entities. This is a good example of "brokerless kingdom" which Crossan found in the teachings of Jesus.

Second, the hermeneutics of resistance must also seek to understand the notion of God as reflected in the oral literature. One prominent feature of the tribal understanding of God—upon which the tribal thinkers seriously focus upon—is the idea of God-world-human relationship embedded in their oral literature. It is evident that there is a consensus among the tribal theologians that God has never been understood in isolation from the creation. Many of them acknowledge the relevance of the tribal concept "God-world-human relationship" for the construction of relevant Christian theology.[77] The interest in re-discovering and re-emphasizing of this tribal unique notion of God is essentially tribal contribution to the Christian theology.

While it is true that the tribals understand the Supreme Being in relation to "world-human," yet, even at a cursory reading we can make out larger focus has always been given to the role and significance to "world-human" while neglecting the God aspect. That is to say, the tribal theologians have dwelt mostly upon the tribal cosmology in their discussion of the notion of God. As a result, we have come out with a profound result of the interrelatedness and independentness of creation and humans. The status and role of creations

76 The traditional notion of sovereignty has become an interesting topic for discourse on peace in the hills. A. Lanunungsang has creatively proposed "share sovereignty" as one of the options for peace process in the region. See, "A Critical Observation on the Current Indo-Naga Peace Process," in *Conflicts and Peacebuilding in Northeast India: Challenges and Prospects*, ed. Takatemjen (Mokokchung: Clark Centre for Peace Research and Action, 2013), 17-19.

77 Keitzar, "Tribal Theological Trends in North East India," 45-48; Longchar, "The Need for Doing Tribal Theology," 10-11; Thanzauva, *Theology of Community*, 149-172.

have received almost more attention than the creator. The tribal myths and tales of animals, like the cock persuading the sun to rise, the bird showing the water, the rat giving rice to humans, *etc*. have most often been quoted as proof-texts for the symbiotic relationship between humans and other creations. In our attempt to construct hermeneutics of resistance, these same stories of the tribals can be used while giving a larger space for the God-factor. In this way, many of the oral literature of the tribals can be seen as resistance stories for the defenseless peoples who have told and preserved those oral stories for many generations.

As we have shown in this research, much of the materials contained in Mark's Gospel, which has now become a part of our Christian scripture, are the products of Jesus' conflict with the ruling elites in the context of Galilee-Judea conflict. The parables, for examples, were powerful weapons for Jesus to silence his opponents. This insight inspires us to situate the tribal myths and legends within the intertribal or tribal–non-tribal power relations. In this regard, our research can have a greater impact upon the ongoing tribal theological discussions. This dimension of the tribal theology seems to be a fertile site for theological discussions in the postcolonial context of tribals.

The third task of hermeneutics of resistance is to explicate its relevance to the tribals in their present context. Here, we propose three areas in which we must fit the understanding of God relevant to the present context.

First, the hermeneutics of resistance must understand God in the context of status domination. Evidently, all the tribes in North-east India have suffered status domination from the non-tribal peoples who considered themselves "superior" in terms of religion, race, economy and culture, and they have consistently maintained an exclusive and negative attitude towards traditional religions and cultures. Besides, there are evidences that denote that the colonial rulers considered the tribals to be primitive, uncultured, uncivilized and even as vicious marauders.[78] From their point of view, their traditional religion was derided as demonic, superstitious and evil.

The western form of civilization that was introduced together with Christianity had destroyed their values. The westerners designated the tribal culture and religion as a religion without any system of thought, devoid of morality and spirituality. This kind of treatment renders a sense of inferiority to the tribals. The underlying assumption of research that regular dominations of various forms generated "hidden transcript" encourages us to read the tribal culture and tradition as hidden transcript of the tribals determined to preserve their dignity, resist the worst effect of domination and insist upon justice. The tribal people have a strong sense of justice, equality of persons, honesty in thought, word, and deed and the courage to stand for what one has promised.

78 Lloyd, *History of the Church in Mizoram*, 1.

Their customs and traditions guarantee that the poor and destitute among them be served with a sense of dignity and justice. They usually maintain high esteem and self-respect for them. Dignity of a person is upheld scrupulously. There is basic respect for every person irrespective of his/her gender or economic status. It is outside forces, including imperialism, which brought humiliation, disprivilege, insults and assaults upon their dignity.

The next task of hermeneutics of resistance is to appreciate the resistance motifs, expressions of anger, and frustration of the tribals. Some scholars have assumed that the parables have embraced the agrarian and rural elements because the parables are meant for the village communities. Our examination of the parables has denied this assumption. As Mark indicates, more than half of Jesus' parables have addressed the powerful urban elites. Almost all the parables in Mark—except the last two parables (Mk 13: 1, 28-29; 34-36)—are set over and against the opponents of Jesus. If the targets of the parables were not exclusively rural communities, what is the point of using the agrarian or rural images? It is hard to believe that Jesus—a rural carpenter in Nazareth—taught the Pharisees and Scribes, the teachers of the Law. We are also debating as to whether it is really possible for a person belonging to the subjugated rural community to teach the powerful elites about theology and ethics in story forms. In spite of the fact that Mark's portrayal of Jesus may render him to be like a person "having authority" in his teaching (Mk 1: 22) to the powerless peasantry, Jesus did not belong to the powerful elites. Jesus speaks truth to powers with the images drawn from subaltern culture. This suggests that Jesus affirms the culture and tradition of the lowly tribals.

Anger, humiliation and fantasies are always experienced within a cultural framework, thus they find expression in cultural arena. We must direct attention to the manifold strategies by which the tribals insinuated their resistance. Folk dances, folksongs, festivals of the tribals in North-east India can be seen explained in this way. In many tribal dances, men participated with any one of their weapons, while women danced with their best dresses. This can be taken as public assertion of worth by gestures and dresses. Thus, folk dance could serve as a vehicle for resisting status domination. Many of the tribal folktales and folklores are tales of revenge. During their festivals, the tribals, who worked for the entire year, lived in their fantasy world by enjoying plenty of food and rice beer. Their cultural festivals gave them space for assertion of dignity.

Finally, the hermeneutics of resistance acknowledges that God protects the tribal from material domination. Material domination finds its place everywhere though it may take different forms from one context to another. Since tribal societies are basically agrarian societies, they would all have land not merely as the basis of the economic resource. The land is not mere space; it is a place and a symbol of unity which renders identity to the community.

The land owns the people and not *vice versa.* Land gave them value, and their spirituality is rooted in the land. That is why people sing about land, dance about land, and also narrate aspects about land till today. To deny or uproot the people from the land is not only a serious violation of human rights; but also a denial of their identity. Not surprisingly, the many tribal groups in the north-east region believe that the earth is the mother of all; some tribes even believe that their ancestors emerged out of the bowel of the earth. Many tribal communities did not have private land ownership. The land, river, forest, mountains were everybody's property and nobody's monopoly. The land was cultivated collectively and the produce was fairly distributed among its members. They had an egalitarian form of social organization. With Christianity also came capitalism with excessive competitiveness, individualism and unbridled accumulation of individual wealth. This disrupted their close-knit communities.

Appropriation of land and labour was very rare in the pre-colonial period. All the tribes were economically self-sufficient, and they paid taxes out of their agricultural surplus. There were some crooked chiefs who would appropriate domestic animals for their own consumption. In the tribal context, there are clues to indicate that some chiefs might have appropriated material goods such as, ornaments or domestic animals from their citizens. Women from lower classes would wear ornaments of inferior quality to avoid the material appropriation. The tribals protect land by keeping a legitimate boundary, and they did not want to shift the boundary so as to encroach into other's property. A Mizo proverb that states: "Never shift divine or ordained boundary," prohibits shifting of boundaries. This saying attests that the tribals respect natural boundary as the handiworks of their God. Jesus' parable of sowing seeds on various landscapes also affirms the significance of land with its boundary. Despite the infertility of the land, the Sower still sowed the seed on the path, on the rock, and among the thorns (Mk 4: 3-9). J. M. Lloyd, a missionary from Wales to North-east India, called the Mizo Christians "'as a root out of dry ground,' in a remote and mountainous part of south-east Asia."[79] The tribal readings of the Parables of God's Kingdom (Mk 4: 3-9; 26-29; 30-32) cannot and should not overlook the land values inscribed in the parables of Jesus. Our study has denoted how Jesus has depicted that land was transforming power. Despite the sower's ignorance, the seeds produced abundant harvest, and even the smallest of seeds can transform a small seed into a tree, for such is the power of land. According to the parables of Jesus, land has the quality of God's kingdom values. As long as the parables in Mark 12: 1-12 are read in the Church, the tribal Christians will be reminded of what their chiefs and the village warriors rendered in the late nineteen-

79 Lloyd, *History of the Church in Mizoram,* 1.

century to protect their land from British encroachment. This was one of the most important incidents that occurred in history. As we read the Parable of Peasants in the Vineyard and the following verses (Mk 12: 1-12), from the tribals' experience of sacrificing their history of political sovereignty into the hands of the British imperial power, we are reminded of the sacrificial act of Jesus who boldly declared the hidden transcript of the subaltern powerless in the face of the powers (v. 12). Telling truth before the powers may be costly, but it is not the end. A time will come when the agrarian hill peoples would be reminded of the coming of the new kingdom by the budding of the fig tree in their farms (Mk 13: 28), if they are watchful (Mk 13: 34-36).

4. Summary

We have rendered some creative suggestions to enhance tribal hermeneutics with the insights that we have gained from our research. We have attempted to understand the tribals as a "self-governed" people. Their physical dispersion to and settlement in the rugged terrain, their socio-economic practices are read as their strategies to avoid attempts to incorporate them into states, or prevent states from springing up among them. It is evident that the rich oral cultural heritages of the tribals are powerful weapons that were effectively employed in their interaction with other tribal groups as well as the non-tribals. It is felt that their armed resistance movements are best understood as the tribals' open declaration of hidden transcript in the face of powers. The contribution of this chapter lies on its finding that the tribal notion of the Supreme Being remains their source of strength and motivating factor, and it is this that enables them to persist in their struggle against being governed by any outside powers, other than the Supreme Being.

Conclusion

The conclusion of this study provides a coherent perspective towards this research on the agrarian-resistance embedded in the parables of Jesus. Since we have already dealt with the sociopolitical and theological significance of the research for the tribal hermeneutics separately in the preceding chapter, we shall not repeat the implication part here apart of from a few references. The findings of this research can be summarized in the following manner along with some major theological and methodological issues that have arisen from our discussions in this research work.

Chapter 1, *Problems of Method in the Study of Parables,* as an introductory part has presented the basic problems that have prompted us to explain as to why we have undertaken this study and we have assumed that Jesus had used the parables as vehicles for resistance to the Roman imperialism. The intricate elements of Markan parables—such as: the wide range usage of the word παραβολή in Mark, public-private dichotomy beneath the parables, conflict and confrontation, rurality or rural colour in the parables, and the prominence of God in Mark's presentation of the parables—convinced us to explore the agrarian-resistance motifs that were embedded in the parables of Jesus. In response to this postulation, we read the parables in Mark's Gospel and its related areas to identify and comprehend as to who resisted and as to what they resisted. With regard to the methodological assumption, there are four basic contentions upon which the research was carried out. First, Jesus lived and taught his parables in Galilee and Judea in an age when the Jews carried out several protests and resistance movements towards the Roman imperial rule. Second, there was a great gulf between the politics of the rural subaltern masses and that of the urban powerful elites. For the most part, the historical sources concerning the protest, resistance, and revolt came from the urban centres that were written from the perspective of powerful literate elites. The study has insisted that historical data must be re-read from the perspective of the subalterns living in rural Galilee. Third, not only in Galilee and Judea but throughout the Mediterranean world, any form of public protests and overt movements of political opposition to powers were dangerous and lethal. The modes of dissimulation must be sought within the context of rural subaltern politics. This research has considered the Gospel as the story of Jesus-in-movement who spearheaded the agrarian-resistance movement of the subaltern masses in Galilee. Therefore, Mark's Gospel is capable of a potential historical source for the study of the modes of resistance by the subaltern classes in Galilee. It is assumed that the agrarian-resistance is not socially or politically organised but that it has found fragmented expression in the folk songs, proverbs, humor, and folk-tales of peasant culture, which are at the same time vital genre of the parables in Mark. Finally, in the ancient Jewish context, we have perceived that religion and politics were joined in an utopian vision of God's reign. Hence, our investigation, by linking with the theological theme – God's kingdom, examined the agrarian-resistance motifs that were embedded in the parables of Jesus in Mark's Gospel, in the context of subaltern struggles to analyse how the dynamics of God's kingdom were set in favour of the marginalised subalterns.

Chapter 2, *The Protest and Resistance in Judea and Galilee during the Roman-Herodian Period (63 B.C.E.–C.E. 70)*, has paved the way for creative discussion on the domination and resistance in Mark's Gospel for the rest of the research that is to follow in this dissertation. In this chapter, the Jewish political struggles during the Roman period were not considered as independent, apart for those struggles during the Hellenic regimes. Rather, they were considered to be an extension and continuation of the struggles under the previous regimes. We have moved the boundary of focus in terms of reading the history of Jewish protests and resistance movements from previous works that rendered basic preference to cultural and religious dimension from those documented by Tcherikover, Schürer, Hengel and Koester to the acts of resistance and defiance against policies and activities of the Hellenistic and Roman imperial rulers by linking the agrarian community in the context of religio-political domination. Given the centrality of the agrarian factor and the role of the subaltern masses in the Modein Resistance, we have envisaged the possibility of protests and resistance movements by the rural populace in the post Modein Jewish history. We also came across the emergence of various parties, such as: the Essene, the Pharisees and the "fourth philosophy" as strong resistance movements to the powers.

With this insight, we have examined various protests and resistance movements in Judea and Galilee during the Roman-Herodian Period (63 B.C.E.–C.E. 70) as recorded in the writings of Josephus. Following Scott's instruction, we have denoted that the resistance measures into two: public declared resistance and undisclosed resistance, *i.e.*, disguised and low profile. As for the domination in the sphere of status, we have also brought out an extensive analysis of both open desecration of the Roman status symbols (*e.g.* insurrection of populace on Roman golden eagle and Caligula's statue in the temple) and the public assertion of sanctity of the temple and authority of the Torah (*e.g*. the Roman soldier's indecency in the temple and the Roman soldier's disrespect for the Torah Scroll). It is clear from our discussion that the Jews remained under unbearable aspects in terms of humiliation, disprivilege, insults, and assaults on their dignity which they had suffered under the Romans. As the Jews continued to struggle in terms of the status domination, it is evident that their struggles transcended the border but it was in the form of masked appropriation or even anonymously. It has been further revealed that Rome's imperial regime heavily involved ideological domination. The public encounters by certain individuals (*viz*. Simon of Perea, a former royal servant, Athronges, the shepherd, Judea, and Jesus ben Ananias, an uneducated villager) and the social banditry in Judea and Galilee are regarded in this study as political actions to negate the Roman ideology. Among other empires that ruled over Galilee and Judea, Rome was known for the appropriation of agriculture surpluses, taxes, labour, amongst others. Actions taken by the Jews, such as: petition for a reduction of taxes, refusal to pay tribute to the Romans by Judas of Sepphoris in Galilee and Galilean cave bandits were understood and interpreted as resistance measures to the material domination that took place in public. The movement of Sicarii, however, was considered as direct resistance but it was in disguise to the material domination. On the whole, we have established that the struggles of the Jewish peasantry of Roman period had a history prior to the advent of the initiatives of the dominant social groups. This insight led us to deny the general presumption that popular resistance was a mere by-product of the initiative of the dominant social groups. However, our historical information and data were evidently written from urban centres and from the perspective of literate elites, and thus agrarian-resistance never emerges as it ought to be in the history. Therefore, this insight has led us to probe further into Mark's Gospel and the parables of Jesus in the Gospel for agrarian-resistance in the next two chapters.

Chapter 3, *The Domination and Resistance in the Gospel of Mark* consists of two major parts. The first part has dealt with a rereading of Mark's Gospel in the context of resistance movements. Given the confinement of literacy among few aristocrats and scribes in the ancient Greco-Roman world, it is assumed that the agrarian masses in Galilee to whom Jesus ministered were illiterates, *i.e*., they could not read and write. Thus, this study has favoured the idea and practices of oral performance rather than the written Gospel which is traditionally linked with Rome. This implies that the Gospel (*i.e*. the story of Jesus) was performed in public by the agrarian community in Galilee and others. The second part has dealt with the domination and resistance in the Gospel of Mark. Jesus' campaign as recorded in Mark has been viewed and analysed in terms of Scott's theory regarding the political discourses of the subalterns, such as: hidden transcript, politics of disguise and anonymity, and declaration of the hidden transcript in the face of powers. Accordingly, we have structured Mark's Gospel into three political discourses. We have attempted to understand the first part of Jesus' campaign (Mk 1: 14–3: 6) in Capernaum and the neighbourhoods as the hidden transcript of popular indignation and dignity. In agrarian-resistance terms, this was the critique of powers behind the back of the dominant. In this sense, Jesus' proclamation of God's kingdom (Mk 1: 14-15), his exorcism and healing (1: 21-39) are read and interpreted as expressions of anger and dignity. Jesus' campaign was soon under surveillance from above. All the activities of Jesus and the disciples recorded by Mark: the healing of a paralytic (2: 1-13), eating with sinners and tax-collectors (2: 13-16), failure to practice fasting (Mk 2: 18-19), plucking heads of grain on Sabbath (Mk 2: 23-28), healing on Sabbath (Mk 3: 1-6) were under strict surveillance by the Pharisees and the Scribes.

Chapter 4, *The Agrarian-Resistance Motifs in the Parables of Jesus in the Gospel of Mark* is the most essential part of the research as it dealt with the exploration of the agrarian-resistance hid in the parables. We have found out as much as twenty one passages consisting of parable story, simile, proverb, riddles, and sayings that can be termed as parables in its Hebraic sense. We approached all these parables and parabolic sayings by locating within the three political discourses of Mark.

First of all, three parabolic sayings about physician and the sick (2: 17), the wedding guests (2: 19-20), and the other two parabolic sayings of unshrunk cloth (2: 21) and new wine (2: 22) were located within the first political discourse that is assumed to represent the hidden transcript of the dignity and indignation of the Galilean villagers (Mk1: 14–3: 6). The context in which Mark presented these sayings assumed that status domination. Thus, these parabolic sayings are seen as the means of defending the hidden transcript. Defence, however, is not to hide truth about the hidden transcript, but to fairly reveal the truth. From this study, the parabolic and proverbial sayings in this discourse are deemed to be the property of the subaltern class in Galilee. Jesus used them as a riposte to the status domination imposed by the powerful elites. In this sense, parables are not merely "pedagogy of the oppressed" as portrayed by Herzog, but modes affirming worth of the status of the lowly ones in Galilee against those who looked them down.

We found that Mark locates the series of sayings in the Beelzebul controversy (3: 17-22), the Parable Discourse (4: 1-34), the defilement saying (7: 15) and the yeast of the Pharisees and Herod (8: 15) within the second political discourse of Mark (3: 7–8:30), focuses on Jesus' campaign in wider Galilee and beyond. At this stage we found Jesus continued to struggle beyond the sequestered site, and we observed Jesus' campaign entering into the politics of disguise and anonymity. The study has revealed that Jesus' campaign is no longer a critique of power beyond their effective reach, but public performance. Jesus used a series of riddles to respond to the accusation of "the scribes who came down from Jerusalem" that Jesus casted demons with the power of prince of demon (3: 22). Rumor and parables were found intertwined in this passage and could be best identified as the infra-political equivalent of open gestures of contempt and desecration. Since the question concerns about Jesus' status, these sayings are considered as public assertion of worth. At the same time, they can also be interpreted as open desecration of the symbol of the Rome's kingdom and the temple-state.

We have attempted to understand the Parable Discourse (4: 4: 1-34) as the politics of disguise and anonymity. Contrary to the previous interpretations, we proposed that Jesus uttered this parable in order to clarify his concept of God's kingdom as well as how it spread by means of rumor to the breadth and length of the Jewish inhabited world. As rumor about God's kingdom travelled, it was perhaps altered in a fashion with the political situation of those who heard and retold it. Three Parables of God's kingdom: the Parable of Various Landscapes (vv. 3-9), the Parable of Seed Growing Secretly (vv. 26-29), the Parable of Smallest Seeds Sown on Land (vv. 30-32) are analysed in this perspective.

The study has shown the possibilities that the image of various landscapes in vv. 3-9 mainly represents various reaction those who heard it; and the idea of seed growing secretly perhaps hides the identity; the picture of the mustard seed growing into worldwide disguises the message. According to this research, the central concern of these parables of God's kingdom is unlikely about the time its arrival—be it *consequente Eschatologie* (Schweitzer) or realised eschatology (Dodd)—but from where to where (*i.e.* space) of the in-breaking of God's kingdom. We discovered how Mark skilfully insinuates the concept of God's kingdom as more of ideology that negates the values of the power. We suggested that God's kingdom as presented in Mark's Gospel is an ideology that opposes the ruling ideology developed out of the subaltern experiences of political subjugation. The remaining parabolic sayings, *viz*., the Image of Lamp, Bushel Basket and Bed (v. 21), the Image of Measurement (v. 24b), the saying concerning have and have not (v. 25) that are assumed to be the private discourse of Jesus support this assertion.

Another parable found in this part of Mark's story of Jesus directly condemned the tradition of the elders by affirming "there is nothing outside a person that by going in can defile, but the things that come out are what defile" (7: 15). It is evident from the disciples' ignorance the meaning of the parables (4: 10; 7: 17) that there is politics of disguise and anonymity involved in this section. The Parable of Defilement (7:15) is another saying that negates the ruling ideology. This study read the ritual of hand washing before meals as the public transcript of the priestly aristocracy in Jerusalem that was possibly intended to hide their dirty linen of corruption. After which, we found the disciples were warned "beware of the yeast" of the corrupted leaders (Mk 8:

15). This study recognised that opened resistance but disguised from public view and undisclosed resistance but revealed in private within the Parable Discourse, most possibly for negating the ideology of the ruling elites.

From the parables found in the third political discourse of Mark (8: 31–16: 20), we may expect more direct and open attack on the powers. Ironically, this part of the Gospel contents only four parables, the first two parables are public discourse of Jesus and the other two are private discourse given to the selected disciples. The Parable of Camel and Needle Eye (Mk 10: 25) and the Parable of Tenants in the Vineyard (Mk 12: 1-9) are given in the context of material domination. This study assumed that the Parable of Needle Eye (10: 25) is surely resistance to material appropriation. If God's kingdom is ideology that was developed out of the hidden transcript of the subalterns as counter-ideology of the ruling powerful elites, entering into the kingdom of God for the rich is not possible. The Parable of the Tenants in the Vineyard really strikes hard the power in Jerusalem. From our analysis, it is likely that Jesus told this parable to resist land appropriation in which the priestly aristocrats took the leading part and the rural famers were the victims. In the parables of Jesus were "meant to be discussion-starters" as assumed by Herzog, then the Jewish leaders would have find time to discuss the matter with Jesus, but they left Jesus to find time for his fate (v. 12).

After Jesus boldly declared the hidden transcript of the subalterns, he retreated back to his disciples in private space. The final two parables are told in Jerusalem are significant because they depicted the new time to come. We have two parables in this context: the Budding Fig Free (13: 28-32) and the Watchman (13: 34-36). What makes these parables interesting is that they were given in a sequestered site, yet still even in Jerusalem (Mk 13: 28-36). These parables are given as a part of conclusion of the Apocalyptic Discourse, in which Jesus used millennial imagery and the symbolic reversal of in defining his new religion. The study discerned that they are the infra-political sayings equivalents of public counter-ideologies, both aimed at negating the public symbolism of ideological domination.

Chapter 5, *The Theology of the Agrarian-Resistance as Reflected in the Parables of Jesus: God and the Subalterns* has attempted to bring out the theological meaning of the agrarian-resistance motifs that have been explored in the previous chapters. This was carried out by linking the resistance motifs with God's kingdom as proclaimed by Jesus and to see how God's kingdom has been set in favour of the subalterns in their struggle. The study has discussed some theological thoughts that shaped and determined the present status of parable scholarship. We have noticed that the Protestant liberal school has brought the notion of God and God's kingdom to the forefront of modern theological discourse. While the nineteenth-century New Testament scholarship has shown interest in the ethical and moral aspects of God's kingdom, Weiss and Schweitzer have envisaged the apocalyptic kingdom of God that portrayed Jesus as an apocalyptic preacher at the end time. The modern parable scholarship has emerged as an integral to the eschatological reaction in the understanding of God and God's kingdom. Therefore, the conceptualization of God's kingdom in a concrete political sense has been replaced by the modern conceptualization of the apocalyptic eschatology that focuses merely upon the end of the present *aeon* instead of the end of the imperial oppressive regime. This study has attempted to establish that the ideal of God' sovereign power is part and parcel of the hidden transcript of dignity and indignation as cultivated by the subaltern powerless who were living in villages of Galilee.

In our endeavour to move away from the anachronizing context and to reconstruct a new context for analysing the parables, we have recommended that parables must be read in the context of subaltern politics of the first-century agrarian context. Scholars including Schweitzer, Cadoux, Dodd, Jeremias have tried hard to situate parables in the *Sitz-im-Leben* of Jesus. However, as they were preoccupied with what they called eschatology it did not allow them to decode the subaltern politics in the parables of Jesus. There are problems and challenges confronting us. First, we proposed that the notion of God's kingdom must be understood as the ideology of the subalterns in this aspect and not necessarily as eschatology. Second, we also proposed that 'space' and not 'time' must be given a priority in order to ascertain Jesus' meaning of God's Kingdom. Third, another concern is towards the meaning of resistance in the context of subaltern politics. Finally, we are challenged by certain Christological questions even as we asked who Christ is and whether Christ is an individual moral teacher or eschatological preacher of new age? All this without denying the fact that Christ is the Messiah of God or the Son of Man who came down from heaven to teach ignorant humanity about the heavenly aspects. This study has also acknowledged that the historical Jesus as Mark portrays is a village carpenter who helped the agrarian people in making their agrarian tools.

It is unlikely that Jesus is, as Herzog suggests, "Pedagogy of the oppressed," rather Jesus came out (Mk 1: 38) to carry out the hidden transcript, and to boldly declare it in the face of powers. More specifically, in Mark 1: 38b Jesus says, "I have come out to do." That Jesus came out from the smaller village set up to bigger towns and cities is a significant mission paradigm that must be employed as a hermeneutical tool for the interpretation of Mark's Gospel. Jesus used the parables as the vehicle of defending, disguising, and declaring the hidden transcript of the subalterns. This assumption helps us to escape from unnecessary debate on the theological theme of the parables, whether it is a theological theme (Dodd) or multiple themes (Jeremias).

On the whole, we have argued that the parables of Jesus are effective instruments of resistance to domination. We have advocated that the parables must be spotted in the life situation of Jesus-in-movement to ascertain the meaning of his parables. So, we have re-imagined Jesus, not simply as an individual preacher or teacher, but as the one who was in a movement. A reading of the parables from this perspective brings to surface that Jesus' voice—was rendered not only in his teachings but the movement as a whole—is "a voice under domination." We have found no evidence to support Bornkamm's view that Jesus summoned the Jewish leaders at the eleventh hour to make the decision. Rather, we questioned as to whether Jesus of Galilee convinced the powerful elites to make the decision. Even though it was considered as "a new teaching–with authority" by his co-villagers (Mk 1: 27), he was still under domination. Jesus-in-movement was a representation of the hidden transcript cultivated among the Galilean rural community comprising powerless people such as: fishermen, people who were sick with various diseases, demon possessed, and the like and their vulnerability had not permitted them the overt form of confrontation. As the movement had spread out of the sequestered sites by means of Jesus and his disciples crossing the borders and staying in what we labelled as the second scale, nothing about the Jesus-in-movement was entirely straightforward here. The basic means of Jesus' communication here was, no doubt, parables. We have indicated that most of the parables of Jesus are confined here.

Many of Jesus' parables—whether they addressed individual persons, or crowd or the disciples—thus require interpretation, precisely because they were intended to be cryptic and opaque. This is seemingly the realities of power for the powerless Jesus-in-movement. We are convinced that Jesus used the parables as the ideal vehicles for resistance. Unlike many of the previous historical critics (*e.g.*, Dodd, Jeremias, Stein, Herzog, *etc*) who have discerned Jesus employing the parables as a sort of teaching aid to explain to his audience about heavenly things with earthly words that were discernible to them, we assume the parables to be the effective instrument for Jesus to speak truth to powers. We also deviated from the claim of existentialist interpreters (Bultmann, Bornkamm) that the parables confront us to make decision. This insight opens our eyes to read the parables in a different manner as compared to what has been perceived by previous scholars.

It is discerned from the study that Mark gives us clues to perceive that God is active in the history of the subaltern politics. When we turn to the theological purpose of parables, it is visibly related to the themes of defence, disguise and declaration of the hidden transcript of the powerless in the face of power. The historical-critical analyses of the parables of the early part of the twentieth-century—Schweitzer, Dodd, Jeremias, Bultmann and others—tended to understand the God's kingdom as being primarily the theme of the parables. They generally understood God's kingdom as a religious experience of God's sovereignty in the hearts of humans while neglecting its political aspect. Given the excessive eschatological or apocalyptic component involved in their arguments, the early modern interpretation of parables (*viz*. Schweitzer, Dodd, etc.) can be observed as an eschatological reaction to Ritschlian School (also the Social Gospel Movement) that construed the kingdom as the ideal society on earth. This study has reclaimed—what has been rejected by Bultmann, Bornkamm, and some of the literary critics—the position held by the Protestant liberalism that God's sovereign rule is the highest value of humans.

We have further denoted that God's kingdom means ideological resistance upon which subaltern politics evolved, which was shielded from direct surveillance of the dominant powerful elites. In this way, Bultmann's view that Jesus called all people to make a decision finds little or no relevance in our endeavour to understand the agrarian-resistance motifs in the parables of Jesus. In the same way, this study has deviated from Herzog's thesis that argues that the parables focus upon the gory details of how oppression served the interests of the ruling class. This research has also posed a serious and vital question which demands appropriate answer: whose experiences and hopes are reflected in Jesus' proclamation of the kingdom of God– people who dominated or people who were dominated? This research has argued in favour of the latter. It is likely that Jesus proclaimed the new brand of βασιλεία that is different from that of Rome as it has been brought about by the divine-genitive, *i.e.* τοῦ θεοῦ. Jesus used the elaborate forms of disguise which are called the parables to convey the meaning of God's kingdom, suitably veiled, onto the public stage. Those various forms of parables displayed in Mark's Gospel are supposedly the property of a social class rather than the powerful elites. The reason why Jesus used folk-sayings as ways of expressing dissonant views also probably involved a demeaning of powerful folks.

Contrary to what we have so often learnt from the previous interpreters of the parables, things are always not clear, simple and straightforward in the world of Gospel parables. This study has perceived a wide range of what is designated as parable that is intertwined with certain elements of infra-politics, such as: conflict, gossip, rumour of spirit possession, amongst others. More surprisingly, most of the parables of Jesus required private interpretation precisely because the disciples could not understand. The motif of concealment from the crowd and powerful individuals in public and revelation to a few in private also seems to be very vital in Mark as it is intended to be cryptic and opaque in public. This has led us to conclude that Mark portrays Jesus as catalyzing the movement of resistance in the agrarian communities in Galilee and beyond. We, therefore, agree with Crossan who asserts, "Jesus' message must not have been as 'talky, preachy, speechy' as much of the western scholars has presented it."[1] The Parables of Jesus are perhaps best interpreted if one takes it as the means to speak truth to power.

The final Chapter, *Sociopolitical and Theological Implications of "God and the Subalterns" for the Tribal Hermeneutics in North-east India*, has rendered some creative comments and suggestions to enhance tribal hermeneutics with the constructive insights that we have gained from our analysis of how the notion of God is set in favour of the subalterns in the parables of Jesus as found in Mark's Gospel. The first part of the chapter attempted to identify methodological issues involved in the construction of a tribal theology in the context of tribals in North-east India by reviewing basic tribal theological literature. Two major methodological issues pertaining to the tribal theology were identified.

Our critical reading has revealed that the tribal theology, as an offshoot of liberation theology of the Latin American, largely portrays the lowly side of the tribals as though they are a defeated community, extremely alienated and the most exploited people, with the goal to liberate them from that such a lowly situation. This chapter took the other way round, and tried to understand the tribals, especially the hill peoples like the Nagas and the Mizo, as "self-governed" people. We have figured out how they avoided various attempts to incorporate them into states, or prevented states from springing up among them. With a lot of appreciations to the tribals' self-understanding, their history of being self-governed, and their persistency in maintaining their political autonomy, we then approached the tribals afresh.

Another deficiency of the tribal theology, at least in its initial stage according to our study, is that the tribal theological discourse was cradled and nurtured narrowly within a framework of the interaction between tribal culture and modernity. While recognizing the interaction as of one of the most basic factor that framed and destined the present state of the tribals in North-east India, we have also maintained that the interaction between the tribals and modernity is only a part of tribal history which covers barely a hundred years or so. So, we proposed that better insight can be denoted if the tribal theological discussion is situated within the larger part of their history. Here, as it is in the previous chapters as well, Scott's idea of the political discourses of the subalterns, *viz.* the hidden transcripts, the politics disguise and anonymity, and the direct confrontation, provides us a critical tool for the exploration of the agrarian-resistance motifs embedded in the tribal history. Their physical dispersion to and settlement in the rugged terrain, their socio-economic practices, such as: shifting cultivation, cropping system, and communitarian life-style are read as the hidden transcript of the tribals. So, also the rich oral cultural heritages of the tribals are seen as powerful weapons that were active

1 As cited by Borg, *Jesus in Contemporary Scholarship*, 34-35.

in their interaction with other tribal groups as well as the non-tribals. The overt protests, rebellions, armed resistance, which are rare in their earlier history, but now widespread in the region, are read and interpreted as the tribals' open declaration of hidden transcript in the face of powers. On the whole, the contribution of this final chapter lies on its finding that the tribal notion of the Supreme Being remains their source of strength and motivating factor for the tribals to be persistent in their struggle to not be governed by outside powers, except by the Supreme Being.

In the whole of our discussion, the most significant part is perhaps Mark's fascinating display of the notion of God in relation to the subalterns. By assuming that Mark gives us clues by which one can trace and see God as active in the history of the subaltern politics, we have delved into the parables by spotting them in the context of Jesus' campaign in Galilee and beyond. The study felt that the agrarian-resistance movements in the Jewish context should not be confused as a mere by-product of the initiative of the dominant groups, such as – the Pharisees, the Sadducees, the Essenes alike, for the agrarian-resistance had a history prior to the advent of the initiatives of those dominant groups. Being a nation that had originated as free peasantry in covenant with God, the Jews longed to regain their freedom. It is felt that this became a reference point for the subsequent generations who struggled under the Hellenistic-Roman imperial rulers. Their ultimate desire seems to be a re-establishment of their nation under the sovereign rule of God. Besides, we have also maintained that the agrarian-resistance movements in the Jewish history were not episodic; rather they underwent a process of transformation along with the broad social, economic and political transformations of the entire society. During the Roman imperial rule, the peasants in Galilee and Judea were found in a very pathetic situation. Most of the Jews of Jesus' time, including Jesus of Nazareth himself, were not regarded by Rome as its full-citizens, but as subjects. Many passages of Mark show that they had struggled domination of various forms under the Roman imperial powers.

We also noticed that Mark made visible the pathetic situation of the agrarian Jewish communities under the Roman imperial rule in terms of their devotion to the prophetic and millenarian leaders. Given the existence of various movements led by the Bandits, the messiahs, the popular prophets with crowds around them and their subversive activities towards the dominants powers, we assumed that the Jews of Jesus' time had longed and strived for a better world. Obviously, they received the messages of the prophets, the messiahs, and the bandits as God remains concerned to keep them free from subjugation. Fertility of soil for such resistance movements is clearly depicted in the emotion of the people displayed in the wake of Jesus' campaign. Even though Jesus started off his campaign individually in the wilderness (Mk 1: 12-13), but he was very speedily building himself into a movement, with huge crowds around him. His central message, the "good news of God" that was touched off by the power of God's reign as manifested in exorcisms and healings had rapidly spread throughout the length and breadth of the Jewish inhabited world. The context helps us to re-image historical Jesus not merely as an individual teacher, but as Jesus who was in the agrarian-resistance movement of the subaltern masses. The Galilean people's experiences and hopes have been represented and reflected in Jesus' proclamation of the kingdom of God in Mark's Gospel. Thus, God remains at the centre of their struggle for freedom and justice.

We have been sensitive in our study towards the question: what, if Mark's notion of God's kingdom carries not the hope, aspiration, and experiences of the urban powerful elites, but of the rural subaltern masses. It is noticed that the idea of God's kingdom has always been spelled out from the viewpoint of those have power to promote and preserve their views in literature. Our attempt to understand the meaning of God's kingdom from the perspective of the rural peasants in Galilee, suggests that God's kingdom must be understood as the counter-ideology negating of the established oppressive imperial ideology of Rome.

The research has given utmost importance to the scale of Jesus' campaign while determining the theological meaning of Mark's fascinating display of the notion of God in the life of the subalterns. Our reading of Jesus' campaign in Mark's Gospel has revealed that Jesus' campaign took two different directions: while moving gradually but definitely from the interior villages of Galilee to the larger Galilee, and to Jerusalem, the centre of powers, Jesus had constantly moved back and forth between public and private. The corporal movements of Jesus have received scholarly attention by and large for the construction of the Gospel's literary structures, sub-structures, and plots with least political interest. Our study has stressed upon the scale of Jesus' campaign as having had significance to decode resistance motifs in the subaltern politics. Jesus' physical movement towards Jerusalem as his final destiny has a great hermeneutical implication for both the subaltern masses in Galilee and the tribals in North-east India. Jesus' mission was not a "mission to" but a "mission from" rural Galilee to the cities with the purpose of speaking truth on behalf of the Galilean subalterns to the powers. This offers us with a helpful hermeneutical tool to re-discover Jesus' paradigm.

In the same way, we also tried to unpack the political discourses of the subalterns through Mark's portrayal of Jesus as swinging back and forth between the public and the private throughout the Gospel. Mark's carefully structuring of Jesus' campaign upon the private-public dichotomy helps us to appreciate the difference between the off-stage performance and on-stage performance of Jesus-in-movement. This aspect also assumes politically essential aspects for the subalterns in terms of insights it can offer to the contemporary parable studies and to the enrichment of tribal hermeneutics. It throws light to state that Mark considered various genres of the parables as basic elementary forms of political disguise and anonymity. A solid understanding of the meaning "parable" that embraces the essential part of political politics of the subalterns moves us towards a deeper understanding of the parable of Jesus form a viewpoint of the subalterns. It helps scholars to come out with a better solution towards understanding the purpose of Jesus' parables when it is read in the context of subaltern politics.

From Mark's presentation of Jesus' on-stage performance, it seems clear that Jesus interacted with the crowd and powerful individuals and used parables in the manner of obscuring his message. Mark also evidently tried to impress upon his readers that a generation of the empowerment of the disciples came from the private space where Jesus rendered an articulated and disciplined form to the ideas and emotions in terms of his interaction with the people. With regard to the significance of the private space in the campaign of Jesus, our research clearly reveals that the private, is a social space beyond the reach of the powerful elites. Our exploration of subaltern political discourses in Mark's Gospel convinces that the subalterns in the villages of Galilee created, out of their ordeal, a "hidden transcript" that represents a critique of power spoken behind the back of the dominant. What convinces us more is the role which Jesus played in making the hidden transcript known to the powers.

Finally, we are led to the conviction of the importance of God factor in the subaltern movement. However, recent scholars have largely neglected the importance of religious faith that could play a crucial role in the social and political movements. Perhaps because of theoretical limitations, resistance and protest movement analysts have inadequately accounted for the empirical reality that religion has served as a rich resource for a host of important movements. The case of ancient Judea and Galilee makes clear the decisive impact that religious faith and organisation can make in generating, sustaining, and legitimating disruptive protest. In turn, their religious faith has served as a primary factor in the negotiation of the movements' collective identity. It is vital that we pay attention to how their faith in God had provided the activists in the dissent movements with expressive parables which served to rally and to embody their grievances publicly in powerful ways.

Bibliography

A. Reference Works

Bartlett, J. R. *The First and Second Books of the Maccabees*. Cambridge: Cambridge University Press, 1973.

Bauer, W, W. F. Arndt, F.W. Gringrich, and F. W. Danker. *A Greek-English Lexicon of the New Testament and Other Early Christian Literature.* 2nd Edition. Chicago: University of Chicago Press, 1979.

Buttrick, G. A., *et al*., eds. *The Interpreter's Dictionary of the Bible*. 4 vols. New York/Nashville: Abingdon, 1962.

Charles, R. H., ed. *The Apocrypha and Pseudepigrapha of the Old Testament in English: With Introductions and Critical and Explanatory Notes to the Several Books*. Vol. I. Oxford: Clarendon Press, 1971.

Danby, H., trans. *The Mishnah*. London: Oxford University Press, 1933.

Feldman, L. H. and M. Reinhold, eds. *Jewish Life and Thought Among the Greeks and Romans*. Minneapolis: Fortress Press, 1996.

Friberg, B and T. Friberg. *Analytic Greek New Testament.* Grand Rapids, Michigan: 1981.

Green, J. B. and S. McKnight, eds. *Dictionary of Jesus and the Gospels.* Downers Grove, Illinois: InterVarsity Press, 1992.

Kittel, G., ed. *Theological Dictionary of the New Testament* 10 Vols. Trans. G. W. Bromiley. Grand Rapids, Michigan: Eerdmans, 1964-76.

Louw, J. P. and E.A. Nida. *Greek-English Lexicon of the New Testament*. New York: UBS, 1989.

Metzger, B. M. *A Textual Commentary of the Greek New Testament*. 2nd edition. Stuttgart: Deutche Bibelgegesellschaft, 1994.

Moulton, J. L. and G. Miligan. *The Vocabulary of the Greek Testament: Illustrated from the Papyri and Other Non-literary Sources*. Grand Rapids, Michigan: Eerdmans, 1930.

Schneemelcher, W. *New Testament Apocrypha Vol.1, Gospels and Related Writings.* Ed. E. Hennecke. London: Lutterworth, 1963.

B. Ancient Writers and Primary Sources

Aristotle. *Politics*. Trans. Rackham. LCL. Cambridge: Harvard University Press.

Bock, D. L. and G. J. Herrick, eds. *Jesus in Context: Background Readings for Gospel Study*. Grand Rapids, Michigan: Baker Academic, 2005.

Brenton, L.C.L., trans. *The Septuagint with Apocrypha: Greek and English*. Peabody Mass.:

Charlesworth, J. H., ed. *The Old Testament Psedepigragha*. 2 Vols. Garden City, N.Y.: Doubleday, 1983.

Josephus, F. *Jewish Antiquities, IX-XI*. Trans. R. Marcus. LCL. Cambridge: Harvard University Press.

__________. *Jewish Antiquities, XII-XIV*. Trans. R. Marcus. LCL. Cambridge: Harvard University Press.

__________. *Jewish Antiquities, XV-XVII*. Trans. R. Marcus and A. Wikgren. LCL. Cambridge: Harvard University Press.

__________. *Jewish Antiquities, XVIII-XIX*. Trans. L. H. Feldman. LCL. Cambridge: Harvard University Press.

__________. *Jewish War I-III*. Trans. by St. J. Thackeray. LCL. Cambridge: Harvard University Press.

__________. *Jewish War IV-VII*. Trans. St. J. Thackeray. LCL. Cambridge: Harvard University Press.

Tcherikover, V. A. and A. Fuks, eds. *Corpus Papyrorum Judaicarum* Vol. I. Cambridge, Massachusetts: Harvard University Press, 1957.

Whiston, W., trans. *The Complete Works of Josephus*. Rev. ed. Peabody, Mass.: Hendrickson, 1987.

C. Works Developing Theoretical Framework

Achteimeier, P. *An Introduction to the New Hermeneutic*. Philadelphia: Westminster Press, 1969.

Alavi, H. "Peasant Classes and Primordial Loyalties." *JPS*1 (1973): 23-62.

Allport, G. W. and L. Postman. *The Psychology of Rumor*. New York: Henry Holt and Company, 1947.

Amoore, L., ed. *The Global Resistance Reader*. London and New York: Routledge, 2005.

Asad, T. *Genealogies of Religion: Discipline and Reasons of Power in Christianity and Islam*. Baltimore: Johns Hopkins University Press, 1993.

Ashcroff, B., G. Griffiths, and H. Tiffin, eds. *The Post-Colonial Studies Reader*. 2nd and Special Indian Edition. London and New York: Routlegde, 1995.

Bakhtin, M. *Rebelais and His World*, Trans. H. Iswolaky. Bloomington: Indiana University Press, 1984.

Bernstein, H. and T. J. Byers. "From Peasant Studies to Agrarian Change." *JAC* 1 (2001): 1-56.

Bhagavan, M and A. Feldhaus, eds. *Speaking Truth to Power: Religion, Caste, and the Subaltern Question in India*. New Delhi: Oxford University Press, 2008.

Buttell F. H. and P. McMichael. "Sociology and Rural History: Summary and Critique." *SSH* 12 (1988): 93-120.

Caouette, D. and S. Turner, eds. *Agrarian Angst and Rural Resistance in Contemporary Southeast Asia*. London and New York: Routledge, 2009.

Chyanov, A.V. *The Theory of Peasants Economy*, Trans. D. Thornton, R.E.F. Smith and B. Kerblay. Clencoa: Irwin, 1966.

Clark, S. "Viewing the Bible through the Eyes and Ears of the Subalterns in India." *Biblical Interpretation* 10/3 (2002): 245-266.

Cobb J. and J. Robinson, eds. *The New Hermeneutic*. New York: Harper & Row, 1964.

Davidson, B. *Africa in Modern History: The Search for a New Society*. London: Allen Lane, 1978.

Dhanagare, D. N. *Peasant Movements in India 1920-1950*. Delhi: Oxford University Press, 1983.

Field, D. "James C. Scott. Domination and the Arts of Resistance: Hidden Transcripts." *AHR* 99/1 (1994): 195-196.

Gonsalves, F. *God of Our Soil: Towards Subaltern Trinitarian Theology*. New Delhi: ISPCK/VIEWS, 2010.

Gramsci, A. *Selections from the Prison Notebooks of Antonio Gramsci,* trans. & ed. Q. Hoare and G. N. Smith. New Delhi: Orient Black Swan, 2009.

Guha, R. *Subaltern Studies I.* 2nd edition. New Delhi: Oxford University Press, 1982.

Hadas, M. and M. Smith. *Heroes and Gods; Spiritual Biographies in Antiquity*. New York: Harper & Row, 1965.

Hanson, K C. "Jesus and the Social Bandits." In *Setting of Jesus and the Gospels.* Minneapolis: Fortress, 2002. *ATLA Religion Database with ATLASerials*, EBSCO*host* (February 6, 2013).

Heen, E. M. "Satunalicius Princeps: The Enthronement of Jesus in Early Christian Discourse." Ph.D. Dissertation, Columbia University, 1997.

Herzog, W. R. II. "The Work of James C Scott and Q." *Oral Performance, Popular Tradition, and Hidden Transcript in Q*, 211-216. Atlanta: SBL, 2006. *ATLA Religion Database with ATLASerials*, EBSCO*host* (February 7, 2013).

Hobsbawm, E. J. *Primitive Rebels*. New York: Norton, 1965.

Horsley, R. A., ed. *Hidden Transcripts and the Arts of Resistance: Applying the work of James C. Scott to Jesus and Paul*. Atlanta: SBL, 2004.

_________. "Moral Economy, Little Tradition, and Hidden Transcript: Applying the Work of James C. Scott to Q." *SBL Seminar Papers* 40 (January 1, 2001): 240-259. *ATLA Religion Database with ATLASerials*, EBSCO*host* (February 7, 2013).

_________. "Jesus and the Politics of Roman Palestine." *Journal for the Study of the Historical Jesus* 8/2 (July 2010): 99-145. *Religion and Philosophy Collection*, EBSCO*host* (February 7, 2013).

Johnson-DeBaufre, M. "Communities Resisting Fragmentation: Q and the Work of James C Scott." *Oral performance, Popular Tradition, and Hidden Transcript in Q*, 193-207. Atlanta: SBL, 2006. *ATLA Religion Database with ATLASerials*, EBSCO*host* (February 7, 2013).

Juergensmeyer, M. *Terror in the Mind of God*. Berkeley: University of California Press, 2000.

Karna, M. N. *Peasant and Peasant Protests in India*. New Delhi: Intellectual Publishing House, 1989.

Lefebvre, G. *The Great Fear of 1789: Rural Panic in Revolutionary France*. London: Vintage Books, 1973.

Lenski, G. E. *Power and Privilege: A Theory of Social Stratification*. New York: McGraw Hill, 1966.

Lloyd, J. M. *History of the Church in Mizoram: Harvest in the Hills*. Aizawl: Synod Publication Board, 1991.

Massey, J. and S. Shimray, eds. *Dalit-Tribal Theological Interface: Current Trends in Subaltern Theologies*. New Delhi: Centre for Dalit/Subaltern Studies, 2007.

Masson and D. Caouette. Vancouver: University of British Columbia Press, 2010.

Muthuraj, J. G. "New Testament and Methodology – An Overview." *AJT* 10/2 (October 1996): 253-277.

Nadkarni, M. V. *Farmers' Movements in India*. Ahmadabad: Allied Publishers, 1987.

Oakes, P. "Hidden Transcripts and the Arts of Resistance: Applying the Work of James C Scott to Jesus and Paul." *JSNT* 28/5 (January 1, 2006): 14-318. *ATLA Religion Database with ATLASerials*, EBSCO*host* (February 7, 2013).

Ong, W. J. *Orality and Literacy: The Technologizing of the Word*. London: Methuen, 2000.

Polanyi, K. *The Great Transformation*. Boston: Beacon Press, 1957.

Radhakrishnan, P. *Peasant Struggles, Land Reforms and Social Change: Malabar, 1836-1986*. New Delhi: Sage Publications, 1989.

Rajak, T. *The Historian and His Society*. Philadelphia: Fortress Press, 1983.

Redfield, R. *Peasant Society and Culture*. Chicago: University of Chicago Press, 1956.

Reiger, J. "Friedrich Schleiermacher." In *Empire and the Tradition: New Readings of Classical Theologians*. Ed. K. Pui-lan, D. H. Compier and J. Reiger. Minneapolis: Fortress Press, 2007.

Roy, D. K. S. *Peasant Movements in Post-colonial India: Dynamics of Mobilization and Identity*. New Delhi: Saga Publication, 2004.

Rudé, G. *The Crowd in History*. New York: Wiley, 1964.

Said, E. W. *Culture and Imperialism*. Chatto & Windus: London, 1993.

__________. *Representations of the Intellectual: The Reith Lectures*. New York: Pantheon Books, 1994.

Schein, R. H. "The Place of Landscape: A Conceptual Framework for Interpreting an American Scene." *AAAG* 87/4 (1997): 660-680.

Scott. J. C. *The Moral Economy of the Peasant*. New Heaven: Yale University Press, 1976.

__________. "Protest and Profanation: Agrarian Revolt and the Little Tradition." *Society and Theory* 4 (1977): 3-32.

__________. *Weapons of the Weak: Everyday forms of Peasant Resistance*. London: Yale University Press, 1985.

__________. "Prestige as the Public Discourse of Domination." *Cultural Critique* 12 (1989): 145-166.

__________. *Domination and the Arts of Resistance: Hidden Transcripts*. New Heaven and London: Yale University, 1990.

__________. *The Art of Not Being Governed: An Anarchist History of Upland Southeast Asia*. New Heaven & London: Yale University, 2009.

__________. *Decoding Subaltern Politics: Ideology, Disguise, and Resistance in Agrarian Politics*. London/New York: Routledge, 2013.

Segovia, F. F. and R. S. Sugirtharajah. *A Postcolonial Commentary on the New Testament Writings*. London: T&T Clark, 2007.

Shibutani, T. *Improvised News: A Sociological Study of Rumor*. Indianapolis and New York: The Bobbs-Merill Company, Inc., 1966.

Singha Roy, D. K. *Peasant Movements in Post-colonial India: Dynamics of Mobilization and Identity*. New Delhi: Saga Publication, 2004.

Spivak, G. C. "Can Subaltern Speak?" *Marxism and the Interpretation of Culture*. Ed. C. Nelson and L. Grossberg. Urbana: University of Illinois Press, 1988.

Sugirtharajah, R. S. *Bible and Postcolonialism*. Sheffield: Sheffield Academic Press, 1998.

_________. *Asian Biblical Hermeneutics and Postcolonialism: Contesting the Interpretations*. Sheffield: Sheffield Academic Press, 1999.

_________, ed. *The Postcolonial Bible.* Louisville, KY: Westminster, 2001. Top of Form

_________. *The Postcolonial Biblical Reader*. Malden, MA: Blackwell Pub, 2006.

Sunseri, A. R. "Roots of Resistance (Book Review)." *American Historical Review* 86/4 (October 1981): 926. *Religion and Philosophy Collection*, EBSCO*host* (February 6, 2013).

Tentz, M. *Orality and Literacy in Hellenic Greece*. Carbondale: Southern Illinois University Press, 1989.

Thomas, R. *Literacy and Orality in Ancient Greece*. Cambridge: Cambridge University Press, 1992.

Torrow, S. *Power in Movement*. Cambridge: Cambridge University Press, 1994.

Watson, J. *Speaking Volumes: Orality and Literacy in the Greek and Roman World*. Boston: Brill, 2001.

West, G. O. "Explicating Domination and Resistance: A Dialogue between James C. Scott and Biblical Scholars." *Hidden transcripts and the Arts of Resistance*, 173-194. Atlanta: SBL, 2004. *ATLA Religion Database with ATLASerials*, EBSCO*host* (February 7, 2013).

Wimbush, V. L. "Introduction: Interpreting Resistance, Resisting Interpretations." *Rhetorics of Resistance: A Colloquy on Early Christianity As Rhetorical Formation*. Semeia 79. Atlanta, Ga: Scholars Press, 1997.

Wink, W. *Engaging the Power: Discernment and Resistance in a World of Domination*. Minneapolis: Fortress Press, 1992.

Wolf, E. R. *Peasant Wars of the Twentieth Century*. New York: Harper & Row, 1969.

Zelliot, E. "Buddhism and Politics in Maharastra." *South Asian Politics and Religion*. Ed. D. E. Smith. Princeton: Princeton University Press, 1966.

D. Judea, Galilee, and Jesus

Top of Form Applebaum, S. *Judaea in Hellenistic and Roman Times: Historical and Archaeological Essays*. Leiden: Brill, 1989. Bottom of Form

Bammel, E. and C. F. D. Moule, eds. *Jesus and the Politics of His Day.* Cambridge: Cambridge University Press, 1984.

Barnett, P. W. "The Jewish Sign Prophets – A.D. 40-70: Their Intentions and Origins." *NTS* 27 (1980-81): 679-697.

__________. *Jesus and Zealots*. New York: Scribner's, 1967.

Berlin, A & J. A. Overman. *The First Jewish Revolt: Archaeology, History, and Ideology*. London: Routledge, 2002.

Betsworth, S. *Reign of God Is Such As These: A Socio-literary Analysis of Daughters in the Gospel of Mark.* London & New York: T&T Clark International, 2010.

Bevan, E. R. *The House of Seleucus*, Vol. 2. New York: Barnes & Noble, 1966.

Bickerman, E. *From Ezra to the Last of the Maccabees*. New York: 1975.

Blenkinsopp, J. "Temple and Society in Achaemenid Judah." *Second Temple Studies: 1. Persian Period.* Ed. by P. R. Davies. JSOTSup 117. Sheffield: JSOT Press, 1991.

Blok, A. "The Peasant and the Brigand: Social Banditry Reconsidered." *Comparative Studies in Society and History* 14 (1972): 494-503.

Bloom, J. J. *The Jewish Revolts Against Rome, A.D. 66-135: A Military Analysis*. Jefferson, N.C.: McFarland & Co, 2010.

Boren, H. C. *Roman Society: A Social, Economic, and Cultural History*. Lexington, Massachusetts and Toronto: D.C. Heath and Company, 1977.

Bornkamm, G. *Jesus of Nazareth*. Trans. by I. McLuskey, F. McLuskey with J. M. Robinson. New York: Harper & Row, [1956], 1960.

Bowker, J. *Jesus and the Pharisees.* Cambridge: University Press, 1973.

Brandon, S. G. F. *The Fall of Jerusalem and the Christian Church.* London: SCM Press, 1951.

Broshi, M. "The Cities of Eretz-Israel in the Herodian Period." *Qadmonioi* 14 (1981): 70-79.

Bull, R. "Caesarea Maritima: The Search for Herod's City." *BAR* 8/1 (1982): 25-40.

Bultmann, R. *Jesus and the Word.* Trans. by L. P. Smith & E. H. Lantero: New York: Charles Scribner's Sons, [1926], 1958.

Carter, C. *The Emergence of Yehud in the Persian Period: A Social and Demographic Study.* JSOTSup 294. Sheffield: JSOT Press, 1999.

__________. *The Roman Empire and the New Testament: An Essential Guide*. Nashville: Abingdon Press, 2006.

Cataldo, J. "Persian Policy and the Yehud Community during Nehemiah." *JSOT 28/2* (2003): 240-252.

Chancey, M. A. *The Myth of A Gentile Galilee*. Society for New Testament Studies Monograph Series 118. Cambridge: Cambridge University Press, 2002.

Collins, J. J. *The Apocalyptic Vision of the Book of Daniel*. Missoula: Scholars, 1977.

__________, ed. *The Origins of Apocalypticism in Judaism and Christianity*. The Encyclopaedia of Apocalypticism. Series 1. New York: Continuum, 1999.

Crossan, J. D. *The Historical Jesus: The Life of a Mediterranean Jewish Peasants*. New York: HarperCollins, 1991.

__________. "Jesus the Peasants." *Dialogue* 26 (1993): 156-168.

__________. *God and Empire: Jesus Against Rome, Then and Now*. New York: HarperSanFrancisco, 2007.

__________. *The Power of Parable: How Fiction by Jesus Became Fiction About Jesus*. New York: Harper One, 2012.

Deissmann, A. *Light from the Ancient East: The New Testament Illustrated by Recently Discovered Texts of the Graeco-Roman World*. Trans. Lionel R. M. Strachan. London: Hodder and Stoughton, 1908.

Echegaray, H. *The Practice of Jesus*. New York: Orbis, 1984.

Edwards, G. R. *Jesus and the Politics of Violence*. New York: Harper & Row, 1972.

Evans, C. A. *Jesus and His Contemporaries: Comparative Studies*. Boston & Leiden: Brill Academic Publishers, 2001.

Fenn, R. *The Death of Herod: An Essay in the Sociology of Religion*. Cambridge: Cambridge University Press, 1992.

Filmer, W. E. "The Chronology of the Reign of Herod the Great." *JTS* 17 (1966): 183-198.

Freyne, S. *Galilee from Alexander the Great to Hadrian 323 BCE to 135 CE: A Study of Second Temple Judaism*. Edinburgh: T&T Clark, 1980.

__________ . *Galilee, Jesus and the Gospels: Literary Approaches and Historical Investigation*. Philadelphia: Fortress Press, 1988.

Fuchs, E. *Studies of the Historical Jesus*. London: SCM Press, 1964.

Funk, R. W. *A Credible Jesus: Fragments of a Vision*. California: Polebridge Press, 2002.

Gera, D. "On the Credibility of the History of the Tobiads." *Greece and Rome in Eretz Israel*. Ed. A. Kasher, U. Rappaport and G. Fuks. Jerusalem: Israel Exploration Society, 1990.

Goldstein, J. A. *I Maccabees: A New Translation with Introduction and Commentary*. AB 41. New York: Doubleday, 1976.

__________. *II Maccabees: A New Translation with Introduction and Commentary*. AB 41A. New York: Doubleday, 1983.

Goodman, M. *The Ruling Class of Judaea: The Origins of the Jewish Revolt against Rome, A.D. 66-70*. Cambridge: Cambridge University Press, 1987.

Gowan, D. E. *Bridge between the Testaments: A Reappraisal of Judaism from the Exile to the Birth of Christianity*. Pittsburgh: The Pickwick Press, 1976.

Hanson, K. C. and D. E. Oakman. *Palestine in the Time of Jesus: Social Structures and Social Conflicts.* Minneapolis: Fortress Press, 1998.

Hengel, M. *Judaism and Hellenism: Studies in Their Encounter in Palestine during the Early Hellenistic Period,* 2 Vols. Philadelphia: Fortress Press, 1974.

__________. *Jews, Greeks, and Barbarians: Aspects of the Hellenization of Judaism in the Pre-Christian Period.* Philadelphia: Fortress Press, 1980.

Hoehner, H. W. *Herod Antipas*. Cambridge: Cambridge University, 1972.

Horowitz, G. "Town Planning of Hellenistic Marisa: A Reappraisal of the Excavations after Eighty Years." *PEQ* 112 (1980): 93-111.

__________. "Concerning the Conquest of John Hyrcanus in Moab and the Identity of Samaga." *Eretz-Israel* 15 (1981): 353-355.

Horsley, R. A. "Ancient Jewish Banditry and the Revolt Against Rome, A.D. 66-70." *CBQ* 43 (1981): 409-432.

__________. "The Zealots. Their Origin, Relationships and Importance in the Jewish Revolt." *NovT* 28/2 (1986): 159-192.

__________. *Galilee: History, Politics, People*. Valley Forge, Pa: Trinity Press International, 1995.

__________. *Jesus and Empire: The Kingdom of God and the New World Disorder*. Minneapolis, MN: Fortress Press, 2003.

__________. *Religion and Empire: People, Power, and the Life of the Spirit.* Minneapolis: Fortress Press, 2003.

__________, ed. *In the Shadow of Empire, Reclaiming the Bible as a History of Faithful Resistance*. Louisville/London: Westminster John Knox Press, 2008.

__________. *Jesus and the Powers: Conflict, Covenant, and the Hope of the Poor.* Minneapolis: Fortress Press, 2011.

Jagersma, H. *A History of Israel from Alexander the Great to Bar Kochba.* London: SCM Press, 1985.

Jeffers, J. S. *The Greco-Roman World of the New Testament Era: Exploring the Background of Early Christianity.* Downers Grove, Illinois: InterVarsity Press, 1999.

Jeremias, J. *Jerusalem in the Time of Jesus*. Philadelphia: Fortress, [1947], 1972.

Jesurathman, K. "Maccabean Revolt and Dalit Revolution: Can They Intersect." *BTF* 41/1 (June 2009): 135-158.

Joy, C. I. D. "Historical Jesus Research: A Postcolonial Cultural Reconstruction." *BTF* 4/2 (December, 2009): 132-142.

Kallet-Marx, R. M. *Hegemony to Empire: The Development of the Roman Imperium in the East from 148-62 B.C.* Berkeley: University of California Press, 1995.

Kippenberg, H. G. *Garizim und Synagogue*. Berlin/New York: W. de Gruyter, 1971.

Kloppenborg, J. S. *The Tenants in the Vineyard: Ideology, Economics, and Agrarian Conflict in Jewish Palestine.* Tübingen: Mohr Siebeck, 2006.

Kochavi, M. "The History and Archeology of Phek-Antipatris: A Biblical City in the Sharon Plain." *Biblical Archeologist* 44 (1981): 75-86.

Koester, H. *History, Culture, and Religion of the Hellenistic Age*. Philadelphia: Fortress Press, 1980.

Landau, Y. H. "A Greek Inscription Found Near Hefziba" *Israel Exploration Journal* 16 (1966): 54-70.

Leaney, A. R. C. and J. Neusner, "The Roman Era." *Israelite & Judaean History*. Ed. by J. H. Hayes and J. M. Miller. London: SCM Press, 1977.

Lightfoot, R. H. *Locality and Doctrine in the Gospel*. London: Hodder & Stoughton, 1938.

Lohmeyer, E. *Galiläa und Jerusalem*. Göttingen: Vandenhoeck & Ruprecht, 1936.

Lohse, E. *The New Testament Environments*. Rev. edition. Trans. J. E. Steely. Abingdon: Nashville, 1974.

Malbon, E. S. "Galilee and Jerusalem: History and Literature in Marcan Interpretation." *The Interpretation of Mark*. Ed. by William R. Telford. Second Edition. Edinburgh: T&T Clark, 2000.

Meier, J. P. "The Historical Jesus and the Historical Herodians." *JBL* 119/4 (2000): 740-746.

Meir Bar-Ilan, "Illiteracy in the Land of Israel in the First Centuries C.E." *Essays in the Social Scientific Study of Judaism and Jewish Society*, Ed. by S. Fishbane and S. Schoenfield. Hoboken, N.J.: KTAV, 1992.

Moxnes, H. *Putting Jesus in His Place: A Radical Vision of Household and Kingdom*. Louisville and London: Westminster John Knox Press, 2003.

Nickelsburg, G. W. E. "Social Aspects of Palestinian Jewish Apocalypticism." *Apocalypticism in the Mediterranean World and the Near East*. Ed. by D. Hellholm. Tubingen: Mohr, 1983.

Nolan, A. *Jesus Before Christianity.* New York: Orbis, 1978.

Noth, M. *History of Israel*, 2nd Edition. New York: Harper & Brothers, 1960.

Oakman, D. E. "The Countryside in Luke-Acts." *The Social World of Luke-Acts: Models for Interpretation*. Ed. by J. Neyrey. Peabody. Massachusetts: Hendrickson Publishers, 1991.

Pixley, G. *God's Kingdom: A Guide for Biblical Study*. New York: Orbis, 1981.

Riches, J. *The World of Jesus: First Century Judaism in Crisis*. Cambridge: University Press, 1990.

Rhoads, D. M. *Israel in Revolution, 6-74 C.E.* Philadelphia: Fortress Press, 1976.

Rostovtzeff, M. I. *The Social and Economic History of the Hellenistic World*. Oxford/New York, Clarendon Press, 1941.

__________. *The Social and Economic History of the Roman Empire*. Oxford: Clarendon Press, 1957.

Sanders, E. P. *Judaism: Practice and Belief 63 BCE-66CE*. London: SCM Press, 1992.

__________. *The Historical Figure of Jesus*. London: The Penguin Press, 1993.

Schäfer, P. "The Hellenistic and Maccabean Periods." *Israelite and Judaean History*. Ed. Hayes, J. H. and J. M. Miller. Philadelphia: Westminster Press, 1977.

Schürer, E. *The History of the Jewish People in the Age of Jesus Christ [175 B.C.-A.D. 135]*. Edinburgh: Clark, 1973.

Schwartz, D. "Josephus on the Jewish Constitution and Community." *Scripta Classica Israelica* 7 (1988): 30-42.

Schwartz, S. "John Hyrcanus I's Destruction of the Gerizim Temple and Judaean-Samaritan Relations." *Jewish History* 7/1 (1993): 9-25.

Schweitzer, A. *The Mystery of the Kingdom: The Secret of Jesus' Messiahship and Passion*. Trans. W. Lowrie. London: A. & C. Black, 1925.

__________. *The Quest of the Historical Jesus: A Critical Study of Its Progress from Reimarus to Wrede*. Trans. W. Montgomery and J. M. Robinson. New York: Macmillan, 1968.

Shaw, B. D. "Bandits in the Roman Empire." *Past and Present* 105 (1984): 5-52.

Smallwood, E. M. *The Jews under Roman Rule from Pompey to Dioclocian*. Leiden: Brill, 1981.

Sorek, S. *The Jews against Rome: War in Palestine AD 66-73*. London: Hambledon Continuum, 2008.

Stegemann, E. W. and W. Stegemann. *The Jesus Movement: A Social History of Its First Century*. Minneapolis: Fortress Press, 1999.

Storkey, A. *Jesus and Politics: Confronting the Powers*. Grand Rapids, Michigan: Baker Academic, 2005.

Streeter, B. H. *The Four Gospels*. London: Macmillan, 1951.

Tcherikover, V. A. *Hellenistic Civilization and the Jews.* Trans. S. Applebaum. New York: Atheneum, [1959], 1975.

__________. *Mizraim IV-V*. Ed. N. T. Reich. New York: G. E. Stechert, 1937.

Theissen, G. *Sociology of the Early Palestinian Christianity*. Trans. J. Bowden. Philadelphia: Fortress Press, 1978.

Weinberg, J. *The Citizen-Temple Community.* JSOTSup 151. Sheffield: JSOT Press, 1992.

Wrede, W. *The Messianic Secret*. Trans. J. C. C. Grieg. Greenwood, SC: Attic, [1901], 1971.

Yoder, J. H. *The Politics of Jesus*. Grand Rapids, Michigan: Eerdmans, 1972.

Zeitlin, S. *The First Book of Maccabees*. Trans. S. Tedesche. New York: Harper & Brothers, 1950.

__________. *The Second Book of Maccabees*. Trans. S. Tedesche. New York: Harper & Brothers, 1954.

E. Gospels and Other Literature

Achtemeier, P. J. "Toward the Isolation of Pre-Markan Miracle Catenae." *JBL* 89 (1970): 265-291.

__________. *Mark*. Proclamation Commentaries. Philadelphia: Fortress Press, 1975.

__________. "The Origin and Function of the Pre-Markan Miracle Catenae." *JBL* 91 (1972): 182-221.

Arnel, W. E. *Jesus and the Village Scribes: Galilean Conflicts and the Setting of Q*. Minneapolis: Fortress Press, 2001.

Aune, D. A. *The New Testament in Its Literary Environment*. Philadelphia: Westminster, 1987.

Bailey, K. E. "Informal Controlled Oral Tradition and the Synoptic Gospels." *AJT* 5 (1991): 34-54.

__________."Middle Eastern Oral Tradition and the Synoptic Gospels." *ExpTim* 106 (1995): 563-567.

__________. *Jesus through Middle Eastern Eyes: Cultural Studies in the Gospels*. Downers Grove, Illinois: IVP Academic, 2008.

Barclay, C. *The First Three Gospels*. Philadelphia: Westminster Press, 1966.

Barlet, J. V. *St. Mark*. Century Bible. Oxford: The Clarendon Bible, 1926.

Beasley-Murray, G. R. *Jesus and the Future: An Examination of the Criticism of the Eschatological Discourse, Mark 13, with Special Reference to the Little Apocalypse Theory.* London: Macmillan, 1954.

Beavis, M. A. *Mark's Audience: The Literary and Social Setting of Mark 4:11-12*. Sheffield: JSOT, 1989.

Beck, R. R. *Nonviolent Story: Narrative Conflict Resolution in the Gospel of Mark*. New York: Orbis Books, 1996.

Belo, F. *A Materialistic Reading of the Gospel of Mark*. Trans. M. J. O'Connell. NY: Orbis, 1975.

Best, E. *Mark the Gospel as Story: Studies of the New Testament and Its World.* Edinburgh: T&T Clark, 1983.

__________. "Mark's Narrative Technique." *JSNT* 37 (1989): 43-58.

Betsworth, S. *Reign of God Is Such As These: A Socio-literary Analysis of Daughters in the Gospel of Mark*. London & New York: T&T Clark International, 2010.

Blomberg, C. "Jesus, Sinners, and Table Fellowship." *BBR* 19/1 (2009): 35-62.

Borg, M. J. *Conflict, Holiness & Politics in the Teachings of Jesus*. New York/ Toronto: Edwin Mellen, 1984.

__________. *Jesus in Contemporary Scholarship*. Valley Forge, PA.: Trinity Press International, 1994.

Bornkamm, G. *Jesus of Nazareth*. Trans. I. McLuskey, F. McLuskey with J. M. Robinson. New York: Harper & Row, [1956], 1960.

Botha, P. J. J. "Mark's Story of Jesus and the Search for Virtue." *The Rhetorical Analysis of Scripture: Essays from the 1995 London Conference*. Ed. S. E. Porter and T. H. Olbricht. JSNT Sup 146. Sheffield: Sheffield Academic Press, 1997.

Brandenburger, E. *Markus 13 und die Apokalyptik*. Gottingen: Vandenhoeck & Ruprecht, 1989.

Branscomb, B. H. *The Gospel of Mark*. The Moffat New Testament Commentary. London: Hodder and Stoughton, 1937.

Bultmann, R. *The History of the Synoptic Gospel*. Trans. by J. Marsh. Oxford: Blackwell, 1968.

Busch, A. "Questioning and Conviction: Double-voiced Discourse in Mark 3: 22-30." *JBL* 125/3 (2006): 477-505.

Caneday, A. B. "He Wrote in Parables and Riddles: Mark's Gospel as a Literary Reproduction of Jesus' Teaching Method." *Didaskalia* 10/2 (1999): 35-67. *ATLA Religion Database with ATLASerials*, EBSCO*host* (February 15, 2013).

Carter, W. *Matthew and the Margins: A Sociopolitical and Religious Reading*. Bangalore: Theological Publications in India, 2007.

Chapman, D. W. *The Orphan Gospel: Mark's Perspective on Jesus*. Sheffield: JSOT, 1993.

Collins, A.Y. "Mark's Interpretation of the Death of Jesus." *JBL* 128/3 (2009): 545-554.

Cook, M. J. *Mark's Treatment of the Jewish Leaders*. Leiden: Brill, 1978.

Cranfield, C. E. B. *The Gospel According to Mark.* Cambridge Greek Testament Commentary. Cambridge: Cambridge University, 1959.

Christopher, B. *A Preface to Mark*. Oxford: Oxford University Press, 1993.

Debelius, M. *From Tradition to Gospel*, Trans. B. L. Woolf. London: Ivor Nicholson and Watson, [Ger. 1919], 1934.

Derrett, J.D.M. *Law in the New Testament*. London: Darton, Longman & Todd, 1970.

Dewey, J. *Markan Public Debate: Literary Technique, Concentric Structure, and Theology in Mark 2:1-3:6.* Chico, Calif: Scholars Press, 1979.

Donahue, J. R. *Are You the Christ? The Trail Narrative in the Gospel of Mark.* SBLD Series 10. Missoula, MT: Scholars, 1973.

__________. *The Gospel of Mark.* Collegeville, MN: Liturgical Press, 2002.

__________. and D. J. Harrington. *The Gospel of Mark.* Sacra Pagina Series 2. Collegeville, MN: Liturgical Press, 2002.

Doran, R. "The Pharisee and the Tax Collector: An Agonistic Story." *CBQ* 69 (2007): 259-270.

Dormandy, R. "The Expulsion of Legion: A Political Reading of Mark 1: 1-15." *ExpTim* 111/10 (2000): 335-337.

Dowd, S. and E. S. Malbon. "The Significance of Jesus' Death in Mark: Narrative Context and Authorial Audience." *SBL* 125/2 (2006): 271-297.

Dunn, J. G. D. "Mark 2:1–3: 6: A Bridge Between Jesus and Paul on the Question of the Law." *NTS* 30 (1984): 395-415.

__________. *Jesus Remembered.* Grand Rapids, Michigan: Eerdmans, 2003.

__________. "Altering the Default Setting: Re-envisaging the Early Transmission of the Jesus Tradition." *NTS* 49/2 (2003): 139-175.

Durber, S. "Political Reading: Jesus and the Samaritans – Reading in Today's Context." *Political Theology* 4/1 (2002): 67-79.

Edwards, J. R. *The Gospel According to Mark.* Grand Rapids, Michigan/ Cambridge: Eerdmans, 2002.

Edwards, R. A. "The Sign of Jonah in the Theology of the Evangelists and Q." *SBL* 2/18 (1971): 557-558.

Evans, C. A. *Mark 8: 27-16: 20.* WBC Vol. 34B. Nashville: Thomas Nelson Publishers, 2001.

France, R. T. and C. H. Talbert. *What Is a Gospel? The Genre of the Canonical Gospels*. Philadelphia: Fortress Press, 1977.

Fowler, R. M. *Loves and the Fishes: The Function of the Feeding Stories in the Gospel of Mark* Chico: Scholars Press, 1981.

Fuchs, E. *Studies of the Historical Jesus*. SBT 42. London: SCM Press, 1964.

Gerhardsson, B. *The Origins of the Gospel Traditions*. Philadelphia: Fortress Press, 1979.

__________. "The Secret of the Transmission of the Unwritten Jesus Tradition." *NTS* 51/1 (2005): 1-18.

Guelich, R. A. *Mark 1-8: 26*. WBC 34A . Dallas, Texas: Word Books, 1989.

Gundry, R. H. *Mark: A Commentary on His Apology for the Cross.* Grand Rapids, Michigan: Eerdmans, 1993.

Hagerland, T. "Jesus and the Rites of Repentance." *NTS* 52/2 (2006): 166-187.

Harnack, A.V. *What is Christianity?* Trans. T. B. Saunders. New York: Harper & Row, 1957.

Heil, J. P. *The Gospel of Mark as a Model for Action: A Reader Response Commentary*. New York: Paulist Press, 1992.

Hendrickx, H. *The Parables of Jesus*. San Francisco: Harper & Row, 1983.

Hengel, M. *Studies in the Gospel of Mark*. Trans. J. Bowden. Philadelphia: Fortress Press, 1985.

Hiers, R. H. *The Kingdom of God in the Synoptic Tradition*. Gainesville: University of Florida Press, 1970.

Herrmann, W. "*The Communion of the Christian with God.*" Ed. R.T. Voelkel. Philadelphia: Fortress Press, 1971.

Herzog II, W. R. *Jesus, Justice and the Reign of God: A Ministry of Liberation*. Louisville: Westminster John Knox, 2000.

Horsley, R.A. *Hearing the Whole Story: The Politics of Plot in Mark's Gospel*. Louisville/ London: Westminster John Knox Press, 2001.

Iersel, B. M. F. V. *Mark: A Reader-Response Commentary*. Trans. W. H. Bisscheroux, JSNTSupp 164. Sheffield: Sheffield Academic Press, 1998.

Joy, C. I. D. "Markan Subalterns/The Crowd and Their Strategies of Resistance: A Postcolonial Critique." *Black Theology* 3/1 (2005): 55-74.

__________. "Mark 10: 17-27 in the Light of the Issues of Poor and their Representation." *BTF* 38/1 (June 2006): 157-171.

__________. *Mark and Its Subalterns: A Hermeneutical Paradigm for a Postcolonial Context*. London/Oakville: Equinox, 2008.

Kawlni, R. Chhuanliana. *Lord God Most High My Svaviour: Theocentricity in Lakan Theology: An Exploration into the Portrayals of God in Luke-Acts*. Delhi: ISPCK, 2009.

Keck, L. E. "Introduction to Mark's Gospel." *NTS* 12 (1965-1966): 352-370.

Kelber, W. H. "Mark and Oral Tradition." *Semeia* 16 (1979): 7-55.

__________. *The Kingdom in Mark: A New Place and a New Time*. Philadelphia: Fortress Press, 1974.

__________. *The Oral and Written Gospel*. Philadelphia: Fortress Press, 1983.

Kingsbury, J. D. *Conflict in Mark: Jesus, Authorities, Disciples*. Minneapolis: Fortress Press, 1989.

Kloppenborg, J. S. *Excavating Q: The History and Setting of the Sayings Gospel*. Minneapolis: Fortress, 2000.

__________. "*Evocatio Deorum* and the Date of Mark." *JBL* 124/3 (2005): 419-450.

Labahn, M. and A. Schmidt, eds. *Jesus, Mark and Q: The Teaching and its Earliest Records*. JSNTSup 214. Sheffield: Sheffield Academic Press, 2001.

Lightfoot, R. H. *Locality and Doctrine in the Gospels*. London: Hodder & Stoughton, 1936.

Mack, B. L. *A Myth of Innocence: Mark and Christian Origins*. Philadelphia: Fortress, 1988.

Mann, C. S. *Mark: A New Translation with Introduction and Commentary*. AB 27. New York: Doubleday & Company, Inc., 1986.

Manson, T. W. *The Teaching of Jesus*. Cambridge: Cambridge University Press, 1939.

Marcus, J. *Mark 1–8: A New Translation with Introduction and Commentary*. AB 27. New York: Doubleday, 2000.

__________. "Crucifixion as Parodic Exaltation." *JBL* 125/1 (2006): 73-87.

Marxsen, W. *Mark the Evangelist*. New York/Nashville: Abingdon, 1969.

Masauda, S. "The Good News of the Miracle of the Bread: The Tradition and its Markan Redaction." *NTS* (1982): 191-219.

Matera, F. J. *What Are They Saying About Mark*. New York/Mahwah: Paulist Press, 1987.

Mazar, B. "Herodian Jerusalem in the Light of the Excavations South and South-West of the Temple Mount." *IEJ* 28 (1978): 230-237.

Meagher, P. M. "The Liturgical Year: The Gospel of Mark." *Vidyajyothi* 64/6 (2000): 460-466.

Micklem, N. and K. A. Saunders. *Systematic Theology*. New York: Macmillan. 1927.

Morgan, T., *el al.*, "Performing the Gospel: Orality, Memory and Mark." *JTS* 58/ 2 (2007): 638-640.

Myers, C. *Binding the Strong Man: A Political Reading of Mark's Story of Jesus*. New York: Orbis, 1991.

Naickanparampil, M. *The Gospel of Mark: Themes Explored*. Bangalore: ATC, 2009.

Neville, D. J. "Moral Vision and Eschatology in Mark's Gospel: Coherence or Conflict." *JBL* 127/2 (2008): 359-384.

Neyrey, J. H. "The Idea of Purity in Mark's Gospel." *Social-Scientific Criticism of the New Testament and its Social World*. Semeia 35. Decatur, GA: SBL 1986.

Ninehan, D. E. *The Gospel of St. Mark*. Baltimore: Penguin Books, 1963.

Nolan, A. *Jesus Before Christianity*. New York: Orbis, 1978.

Oakman, D. E. "Rulers' house, Thieves, and Usurpers: The Beelzebul Pericope." *Forum* 4/3 (1988): 115.

Patterson, D. N. *The Origins of Mark: The Markan Community in Current Debate*. Leiden/Boston/Köln: Brill, 2000.

Paul, G. J. *The Gospel According to Saint Mark: Introduction and Commentary*. CLS No. 13. Mysore: CLS, 1957.

Perrin, N. *The New Testament: An Introduction*. New York, 1974.

Plummer, A. *The Gospel According to St. Mark*. Cambridge: Cambridge University Press, 1914.

Quesnell, Q. *The Mind of Mark: Interpretation and Method through the Exegesis of Mark 6: 52*. Analecta Biblica 38. Rome: Pontifical Biblical Institute, 1969.

Räisänen, H. *The "Messianic Secret" in Mark*. Edinburgh: T&T Clark, 1990.

Rawlinson, A. E. J. *The Gospel According to St. Mark*. Westminster Commentaries. 7th edition. London, 1949.

Rhoads, D. and D. Michie. *Mark As Story: An Introduction to the Narrative of a Gospel*. Philadelphia: Fortress Press, 1982.

Ritschl, A. *The Christian Doctrine of Justification and Reconciliation*, Vol.3. Ed. Mackintosh and A.B. Macaulay. Edinburgh: T&T Clark, 1902.

Robbins, V. K. *Jesus the Teacher: A Socio-Rhetorical Interpretation of Mark*. Philadelphia: Fortress Press, 1984.

Robinson, J. M. *The Problem of History in Mark and other Marcan Studies*. Philadelphia: Fortress Press, 1982.

Rohrbaugh, R. L. "The Social Location of Mark's Audience." *BTB* 13 (1993): 114-127.

Roskam, H. N., ed. *The Purpose of the Gospel of Mark in its Historical and Social Context*. Leiden/Boston: Brill, 2004.

Samuel, S. *A Postcolonial Reading of Mark's Story of Jesus*. Edinburgh: T&T Clark, 2007.

Sanders, E. P. *The Historical Figure of Jesus*. London: The Penguin Press, 1993.

Schmidt, D. D. *The Gospel of Mark with Introduction, Notes, and Original Text Featuring the NEW Scholars Version Translation*. California: Polebridge Press, 1990.

Schweizer, E. *The Good News According to Mark.* Trans. D. H. Madvig. Richmond, Virginia: John Knox Press, 1970.

Sellew, P. "Oral and Written Sources in Mark 4: 1-34." *NTS* 36 (1990): 234-267.

Simmonds, A. "Mark's and Matthew's *Sub Rosa* Message in the Scene of Pilate and the Crowd." *JBL* 131/4 (2012): 733-754.

Steele, G. "The theology of Hiddenness in the Gospel of Mark: An Exploration of the Messianic Secret and Corollaries." *ResQ* 54/3 (2012), 169-185. (*ATLA Religion Database with ATLASerials*, EBSCO*host* (February 15, 2013).

Stein, R. H. *Mark: Baker Exegetical Commentary on the New Testament*. Grand Rapids, Michigan: Baker Academic, 2008.

Stock, A. "Chiastic Awareness and Education in Antiquity." *BTB* 14 (1984): 23-27.

Suh, J. S. *Discipleship and Community: Mark's Gospel in Sociological Perspective*. California: Centre for Asia-American Ministries, 1991

Sweete, H. B. *The Gospel According to St. Mark*. 3rd edition. London, 1928.

Talbert, C. H. *What Is a Gospel? The Genre of the Canonical Gospels*. Philadelphia: Fortress Press, 1977.

Telford, W. R. *The Interpretation of Mark*. Edinburgh: T&T Clark, 1995.

Theissen, G. "Itinerant Radicalism: The Tradition of Jesus Sayings from the Perspective of the Sociology of Literature." *Radical Religion* 2 (1975): 84-93.

__________. *The Gospels in Context: Social and Political History in the Synoptic Tradition*. Trans. L. M. Maloney. Edinburg: T&T Clark, 1992.

Tolbert, M. A. *Sowing the Gospel: Mark's World in Literary-Historical Perspective*. Minneapolis: Fortress Press, 1989.

Savarimuthu, S. *A Community in Search of Its Identity: Mt. 21: 28-22: 14 in a Subaltern Perspective.* Delhi: ISPCK, 2007.

Svartvik, J. *Mark and Mission: Mk. 7: 1-23 in Its Narrative and Historical Contexts.* Stockholm: Almqvist & Wikell International, 2000.

Via, D. O. *Kerygma and Comedy in the New Testament: A Structuralist Approach to Hermeneutic*. Philadelphia: Fortress Press, 1975.

Votaw, C. W. "The Gospels and Contemporary Biographies." *AJT* 19 (1915): 45-73, 217-249.

Waetjen, H. C. *A Reordering of Power: A Socio-Political Reading of Mark's Gospel.* Minneapolis: Fortress Press, 1989.

Walker, W. O. "Jesus and the Tax Collectors." *JBL* 97/2 (1978): 221-238.

Wicke, H. E. *Mark*, The People's Bible Series. Milwaukee, Wisconsin: Northwestern Publishing House, 1988.

Wilson, R. M. *Mark.* Peake's Commentary on the Bible Series. London and Edinburgh: Thomas Nelson and Sons, 1962.

Witherington III, B. *The Gospel of Mark: A Socio-Rhetorical Commentary.* Grand Rapids, Michigan / Cambridge UK: Eerdman, 2001.

F. Studies on Parables and Related Topics

Bailey, K. E. *Through Peasant Eyes: More Lukan Parables: Their Culture and Style.* Grand Rapids: Eerdmans, 1980.

__________. *Poet & Peasant and Through Peasants Eyes: A Literary-Cultural Approach to the Parables in Luke.* Grand Rapids, Michigan: Eerdmans, 1984.

__________. *The Parables.* Wilmington, Delaware: Michael Glazeir, 1983.

Blomberg, C. L. *Interpreting the Parables.* Second Ed. Downers Grove, Illinois: IVP Academic, 2012.

Boobyer, G. H. "Galilee and Galileans in St. Mark's Gospel." *Bulletin* 35 (1953): 334-348.

__________. "The Redaction of Mark IV. 1-34." *NTS* 8 (1961-62): 59-70.

Boucher, M. *The Mysterious Parable: A Literary Study.* CBQ Monograph Series 6. Washington D.C.: The Catholic Biblical Association of America, 1977.

Bowker, J. W. "Mystery and Parable: Mark IV: 1-20." *JTS* 25 (1974): 300-317.

Brown, R. E. "Parable and Allegory Reconsidered." *New Testament Essays.* New York: Doubleday, 1968.

Bultmann, R. *Jesus and the Word*, trans. L. P. Smith & E. H. Lantero. New York: Charles Scribner's Sons, [1926], 1958.

Burkill, T. A. "The Cryptology of Parables in St. Mark's Gospel." *NovT* 1/4 (October 1956): 246-262.

Buttrik, G. A. *The Parables of Jesus.* New York/London: Harper & Brothers, 1928.

Cadoux, A. T. *The Parables of Jesus: Their Art and Use.* London: James Clarke, 1930.

Capon, R. F. *The Parables of the Kingdom.* Grand Rapids, Michigan: Eerdmans, 1985.

Cowan, D. *Economic Parables: The Monetary Teachings of Jesus Christ.* London/Hyderabad: Paternoster, 2006.

Crossan, J. D. "The Parable of the Wicked Husbandmen." *JBL* 90/4 (December 1971): 451-465.

__________. *In Parables: The Challenge of the Historical Jesus*. New York: Harper & Row, 1973.

__________. *Cliff of Fall*. New York: Seabury, 1980.

__________. *The Power of Parable: How Fiction by Jesus Became Fiction About Jesus*. New York: HarperCollins Publishers, 2012.

Dodd, C. H. *The Parables of the Kingdom*. Rev. ed. New York: Charles Scribner's Sons, 1961.

Donahue, J. R. "Jesus as the Parable of God in the Gospel of Mark." *Interpretation* 32/4 (1978): 369-386.

Echegaray, H. *The Practice of Jesus*. New York: Orbis, 1984.

Feldam, A. *The Parables and Similes of the Rabbis*. Cambridge: Cambridge University Press, 1924.

Fisher, N. F. *The Parables of Jesus: Glimpses of God's Reign*. New York: Crossroad, 1990.

Folarin, G. O. "The Parable of the Talents in the African Context: An Inculturation Hermeneutics Approach." *AJT* 22/1 (2008): 94-95.

Friedrichsen, T. A. "The Temple, a Pharisee, a Tax Collector, and the Kingdom of God: Rereading a Jesus Parables (Luke 18: 10-14a)" *JBL* 124/1 (2005): 89-119.

Funk, R. W., ed. *The Parables of Jesus: A Report of the Jesus Seminar.* Sonoma, Calif.: Polebridge, 1988.

Gould, E. P. *A Critical and Exegetical Commentary on the Gospel According to St. Mark*. ICC Series. Edinburgh: T&T Clark, 1901.

Gowler, D. B. *What Are They Saying About the Parables?* New York/Mahwah, N. J.: Paulist Press, 2000.

Herzog II, W. R. *Parables as Subversive Speech: Jesus as Pedagogue of the Oppressed*. Louisville, Kentucky: Westminster / John Knox Press, 1994.

Huffman, N. A. "Atypical Features in the Parables of Jesus." *JBL* 97/2 (1978): 207-220.

Jeremias, J. *The Parables of Jesus*. Rev. ed. London: SCM Press, 1963.

John, V. J. *The Ecological Vision of Jesus: Nature in the Parables of Mark*. Bangalore: CSS-BTTBPSA, 2002.

Jones, G. V. *Art and Truth of the Parables*. London: SPCK, 1964.

Joy, C. I. D. "Matthew 25: 14-30: A Subaltern-cultural Reading." *BTF* 40/2 (2008): 131-142.

Kähler, M. *The so-called Historical Jesus and the Historic: Biblical Christ*. Philadelphia: Fortress Press, 1964.

Kilpatrick, G. D. "Jesus, His Family and His Disciples." *JSNT* 15 (1982): 3-8.

Kingsbury, J. D. *The Parables of Jesus in Matthew 13*. London: SPCK, 1969.

Linnemann, E. *Jesus of the Parables*. New York: Harper & Row and London: SPCK, 1966.

Longenecker, R. N., ed. *The Challenges of Jesus' Parables*. Grand Rapids, Michigan: Eerdmans, 2000.

Marcus, J. *The Mystery of the Kingdom of God*. SBL Dissertation Series 90. Atlanta, Georgia: Scholars Press, 1986.

Martin, T. W. "Watch during the Watches (Mark 13:35)." *JBL* 120/4 (2001): 685-701.

Oesterley, W. O. E. *The Gospel Parables in the Light of Their Jewish Background*. New York: Macmillan, 1936.

Patte, D., ed. *Semiology and the Parables: Exploration of the Possibilities Offered by Structuralism for Exegesis*. Pittsburgh Theological Monograph Series No. 9. Pittsburgh: Pickwick Press, 1976.

Payne, P. B. "The Order of Sowing and Ploughing in the Parable of the Sower." *NTS* 25 (1978): 123-129.

Perkins, P. *Hearing the Parables of Jesus*. New York: Paulist Press, 1981.

Perrin, N. "Historical Criticism, Literary Criticism, and Hermeneutics: The Interpretation of the Parables of Jesus and the Gospel of Mark Today." *The Journal of Religion* 52/4 (1972): 364-365.

__________. *Jesus and the Language of the Kingdom: Symbol and Metaphor in New Testament Interpretation*. London: SCM, 1976.

Rao, V. V. *A Century of Tribal Politics in North East India 1874-1974*. New Delhi: S. Chand & Company Ltd., 1975.

Robinson, W. H. *The Parables of Jesus in Their Relation to His Ministry*. Chicago: University of Chicago Press, 1928.

Savarimuthu, S. *A Community in Search of Its Identity: Mt. 21: 28-22: 14 in a Subaltern Perspective.* Delhi: ISPCK, 2007.

Schottroff, L. *The Parables of Jesus*. Trans. L. M. Maloney. Minneapolis: Fortress Press, 2006.

Schweitzer, A. *The Mystery of the Kingdom: The Secret of Jesus' Messiahship and Passion*. Trans. by W. Lowrie. London: A. & C. Black, 1925.

Scott, B. B. *Hear Then the Parables: A Commentary on the Parables of Jesus*. Minneapolis: Fortress Press, 1989.

Shillington, V., ed. *Jesus and His Parables: Interpreting the Parables of Jesus Today*. Edinburgh: T&T Clark, 1997.

Snodgrass, K. *The Parable of the Wicked Tenants: An Inquiry into Parable Interpretation*. Tubingen: Mohr/Siebeck, 1983.

__________. "Parables and the Hebrew Scriptures." *To Hear and Obey: Essays in Honour of Fredrick Carlson Holmgren*. Ed. B. J. Bergfalk and P. E. Koptak. Chicago: Covenant Publication, 1997.

__________. *Stories with Intent: A Comprehensive Guide to the Parables of Jesus*. Grand Rapids, Michigan/Cambridge: William B. Eerdmans, 2008.

Scott, B. B. *Hear Then the Parables: A Commentary on the Parables of Jesus*. Minneapolis: Fortress Press, 1989.

Stein, R. H. *An Introduction to the Parables of Jesus*. Philadelphia: Westminster, 1981.

Stern, D. "Jesus' Parables from the Perspective of Rabbinic Literature." *Parable and Story in Judaism*. Ed. C. Thomas and M. Wyschogrod. New York: Paulist, 1989.

__________. *Parable in Midrash: Narrative and Exegesis in Rabbinic Literature*. Cambridge, MA: Harvard University Press, 1991.

Schottroff, L. *The Parables of Jesus*. Trans. by L. M. Maloney. Minneapolis: Fortress Press, 2006.

Takatemjen. *The Banquet Is Ready: Rich and Poor in the Parables of Luke*. Delhi: ISPCK, 2003.

Theissen, G. "Itinerant Radicalism: The Tradition of Jesus Sayings from the Perspective of the Sociology of Literature." *Radical Religion* 2 (1975): 84-93.

Thurén, L. *Parables Unplugged: Reading the Lukan Parables in Their Rhetorical Context*. Minneapolis: Fortress Press, 2014.

Via, D. O. *Parables: Their Literary and Existential Dimension*. Philadelphia: Fortress Press, 1967.

Weiss, J. *Jesus' Proclamation of the Kingdom of God*. Trans. by R. H. Hiers and D. Larrimore Holland. Philadelphia: Fortress Press, [1900], 1971.

Westermann, C. *The Parables of Jesus in the Light of the Old Testament*. Trans. and edited by W. Golka and A. H. B. Logan. Minneapolis: Fortress, 1990.

Wilder, A. N. *Early Christian Rhetoric: The Language of the Gospel*. Rev. ed.. Cambridge, Mass.: Harvard University Press, 1971.

G. Tribal Studies

Ao, M. "Impact of the Context: Tribal Perspective." In *Dalit-Tribal Theological Interface: Current Trends in Subaltern Theologies*. New Delhi: Centre for Dalit/Subaltern Studies, 2007.

Ao, T. *British Occupation of Naga Country*. Mokokchung: Naga Literature Society, 1993.

Aosenba. *The Naga Resistance Movement: Prospects of Peace and Armed Conflict*. New Delhi: Regency Publications, 2001.

Datta, D. *Cultural Contours of North-east India*. New Delhi: Oxford University Press, 2012.

Datta, P. S. *India's North-East: A Study in Transition*. New Delhi: Vikas Publishing House, 1992.

Downs, F. S. *Christianity in North East India*. Madras: Christian Literature Society, 1976.

__________. *Christianity in North East India: Historical Perspectives*. Delhi: ISPCK, 1983.

__________. *History of Christianity in India: North East India in the Nineteenth and Twentieth Centuries*. Bangalore: Church History Association of India, 1992.

Hluna, J. V. ed. *History and Ethnic Identity Formation in North-East India*. New Delhi: Concept Publishing Company, 2013.

Hutton, J. H. *The Angami Naga* (London: Oxford University Press, 1969.

Keitzar, R. *In Search of a Relevant Gospel Message*. Guwahati: CLC, 1995.

Lalthangliana, B. *Culture and Folklore of Mizoram*. Delhi: Ministry of Information & Broadcasting, Government of India, 2005.

Lalruanga. *An Exploration into Mizo Folktales*. Aizawl: Zomi Book Agency, 2000.

Lamare, S. N. *Resistance Movements in North-East India: The Jaintias of Meghalaya 1860-1893.* New Delhi: Regency Publications, 2001.

Longchar, A.W. *An Emerging Asian Theology: Tribal Theology, Issue, Method and Perspective.* Jorhat: Tribal Study Centre, 2000.

Mackenzie, A. T*he North-East Frontier of Assam*. Delhi: Mittal Publications, 1979.

Mills, J. P. *The Ao Nagas*. Bombay: Oxford University Press, 1973.

Pachuau, Lalsangkima. *Ethnic Identity and Christianity: A Socio-Historical and Missiological Study of Christianity in Northeast India with Special Reference to Mizoram*. Frankfurt: Peter Lang, 2002.

Pachuau, Margaret L. *Hand-Picked Tales from Mizoram*. Kolkata: Writers Workshop Books, 2008.

Ralte, Lalrinawmi "Crab: Theology: A Critique of Patriarchy – Cultural Degradation and Empowerment of Mizo Women." D. Min Dissertation, Episcopal Divinity School, 1993.

Samuel, Re-contextualizing Dalit Hermeneutics: Exploring Hermeneutical Parameters for a Changing Community." In *Liberation Hermeneutics in the Indian Interpretation of the Bible*. Ed. K. Jesurathnam, A. Saggu, and H. Chhungi. Tiruvalla: CSS, 2012. 93-123.

Singh, K. S. ed. *Tribal Movements in India*. Vol. 1. Delhi: Manohar, 1982.